# ROUTLEDGE LIBRARY EDITIONS: HEGEL

Volume 1

# HEGEL'S POLITICAL PHILOSOPHY

# HEGEL'S POLITICAL PHILOSOPHY
## The Test Case of Constitutional Monarchy

STEPHEN C. BOSWORTH

LONDON AND NEW YORK

First published in 1991 by Garland Publishing Inc.

This edition first published in 2020
by Routledge
2 Park Square, Milton Park, Abingdon, Oxon OX14 4RN

and by Routledge
52 Vanderbilt Avenue, New York, NY 10017

*Routledge is an imprint of the Taylor & Francis Group, an informa business*

© 1991 Stephen C. Bosworth

All rights reserved. No part of this book may be reprinted or reproduced or utilised in any form or by any electronic, mechanical, or other means, now known or hereafter invented, including photocopying and recording, or in any information storage or retrieval system, without permission in writing from the publishers.

*Trademark notice*: Product or corporate names may be trademarks or registered trademarks, and are used only for identification and explanation without intent to infringe.

*British Library Cataloguing in Publication Data*
A catalogue record for this book is available from the British Library

ISBN: 978-0-367-37331-3 (Set)
ISBN: 978-0-367-81731-2 (Set) (ebk)
ISBN: 978-0-367-41994-3 (Volume 1) (hbk)
ISBN: 978-0-367-42003-1 (Volume 1) (pbk)
ISBN: 978-0-367-81725-1 (Volume 1) (ebk)

**Publisher's Note**
The publisher has gone to great lengths to ensure the quality of this reprint but points out that some imperfections in the original copies may be apparent.

**Disclaimer**
The publisher has made every effort to trace copyright holders and would welcome correspondence from those they have been unable to trace.

# HEGEL'S POLITICAL PHILOSOPHY

*The Test Case of Constitutional Monarchy*

Stephen C. Bosworth

GARLAND PUBLISHING, INC.
New York ———— London
*1991*

Copyright © 1991 by Stephen C. Bosworth

**Library of Congress Cataloging-in-Publication Data**

Bosworth, Stephen C.
Hegel's political philosophy: the test case of constitutional monarchy/ Stephen C. Bosworth.
p. cm.—(Political theory and political philosophy)
Revision of the author's thesis (Ph. D.)—Harvard, 1984, entitled: Democratic monarchy, a critical reconstruction of Hegel's constitutional theory.
Includes bibliographical references.
ISBN 0-8153-0129-4 (alk. paper)
1. Hegel, Georg Wilhelm Friedrich, 1770–1831—Contributions in political science. I. Title. II. Series.
JC233.H46B65    1991
320'.01—dc20       91-8900

Printed on acid-free, 250-year-life paper.
MANUFACTURED IN THE UNITED STATES OF AMERICA

*To Marilyn*

# TABLE OF CONTENTS

| | | |
|---|---|---|
| Abbreviations | | 3 |
| List of Figures | | 4 |
| | PREFACE | 5 |
| | INTRODUCTION | 9 |
| Chapter One: | THE MODEL CONSTITUTION | 13 |
| Chapter Two : | COMMON REPUBLICAN ARGUMENTS | 21 |
| Chapter Three: | FROM PLATO'S REPUBLIC TO DEMOCRATIC MONARCHY | 29 |
| Chapter Four: | FROM KANT'S REPUBLICANISM TO DEMOCRATIC MONARCHY | 35 |
| Chapter Five: | FROM MARX'S COMMUNAL CONSTITUTION TO DEMOCRATIC MONARCHY | 47 |
| Chapter Six: | METHODOLOGY AND 'PHILOSOPHICAL NECESSITY' | 57 |
| Chapter Seven: | HEGEL'S SYSTEM | 69 |
| Chapter Eight: | HEGEL'S PRESCRIPTION | 79 |
| Chapter Nine: | HEGEL'S NECESSITY | 91 |
| Chapter Ten: | HEGEL'S SOCIAL THEORY | 99 |
| Chapter Eleven: | THE THREE MOMENT STRUCTURE OF HEGEL'S STATE AND SYSTEM | 111 |
| Chapter Twelve: | FROM HEGEL'S CONSTITUTIONAL MONARCHY TO THE PRESCRIPTIVE IDEAL | 121 |
| | SUMMARY | 139 |
| Selective Bibliography | | 141 |
| Appendix: | LITERAL TRANSLATIONS | 145 |
| | GLOSSARY | 171 |

# ABBREVIATIONS

| | |
|---|---|
| An. | *Anmerkung* refers to the "remarks" which Hegel himself added to his numbered paragraphs, e.g. *Rechts*, PP279An. |
| **Bold** | The **bold** words in the passages quoted from others have been emphasised by the original author. However, when they appear within my own free translations of Hegel, they mark where my translation is different from Knox's. |
| [square brackets] | Square brackets mark the editorial additions to quotations which seem to be justified by the immediate context. |
| *Eng.* | "About the English Reform Bill" (1831) by Hegel |
| *Enz.* I, II, III | Volumes I, II and III of Hegel's *Encyclopaedia of the Philosophical Science's* (Enzyklopadie). |
| *Domestic Affairs* | Hegel's "On the Recent Domestic Affairs of Wurtemberg". |
| *G. Cons.* | Hegel's *The Constitution of Germany*. |
| *Geschichte* | Hegel's *Philosophy of History* (Geschichte). |
| *Italics* | *Italics* mark the emphasis I give both to my own words and to those quoted from others. |
| *Logik* I, II | Volumes I and II of Hegel's larger *Science of Logic*. |
| p. | A page number in the relevant English translation or text. |
| page | A page number within this book. |
| *Philosophie* I, I, III | Volumes I, II and III of Hegel's *History of Philosophy* (Philosophie). |
| PP | The numbered paragraphs in Hegel's works, e.g. *Rechts*, PP273. |
| quotation marks | 'Single' inverted commas mark my own special terms and phrases, "Double" inverted commas mark the words of others. |
| *Rechts* | Hegel's *Philosophy of Right* (Rechts). |
| S. | A page number in the relevant German Text. |
| *Wurt.* | Hegel's *Evaluating the Proceedings within the Assembly of the Country's Representative Chamber of the Kingdom of Wurtemberg in the Year 1815-1816*. |
| Z. | *Zusatz*. Refers to the less reliable or authoritative "additions" which Hegel's editors made to his numbered paragraphs based both upon Hegel's and students' lecture notes. |

## LIST OF FIGURES

| | | |
|---|---|---|
| FIGURE 1. | Reason | 74 |
| FIGURE 2. | The conception of Reason | 74 |
| FIGURE 3. | Reason-as-the-conception of Reason | 75 |
| FIGURE 4. | Reason-as-the-monarchical-organ and the conception of the monarchical organ | 76 |
| FIGURE 5. | Reason-as-the-genuine-Infinity which by contrast defines the spurious infinity | 87 |
| FIGURE 6. | Reason as the categories and actualities which by contrast define inessential appearance | 88 |
| FIGURE 7. | External necessity | 93 |
| FIGURE 8. | Inner necessity with natural and historical necessity | 93 |
| FIGURE 9. | The chain of eight circles from Reason | 114 |
| FIGURE 10. | The three sets of moments, functions and organs of Reason-as-the-constitution | 116 |

# PREFACE

This work is based on the thesis accepted for the award of a Ph.D in March 1984: *Democratic Monarchy - A Critical Reconstruction of Hegel's Constitutional Theory.* It has been thoroughly revised in the light of the intervening publications. It examines Hegel's political philosophy through the window of his constitutional monarchy. While its analysis is more obviously relevant for and to the remaining hereditary monarchies, sultanates, and sheikhdoms around the world, its conclusions are also important for the understanding, formulation, or modification of modern republican constitutions. It challenges the two opposing assumptions about 'monarchy',
1) that it is only an archaic and irrational institution which should have no part in today's world, and
2) that it ought to have an enduring role purely because of its mystical power to unite tradition and human needs.

Thus, modern republican arguments are assessed together with those of Plato, Kant, and Marx in order most severely to test Hegel's model. It is discovered that these challenges as well as the inner logic of Hegel's own philosophical system require his constitutional monarchy to be transformed into 'democratic monarchy'. The argument is also based on fresh translations of key passages.

Since October 1983, when the thesis was submitted, four books, one Ph.D. thesis, one chapter, two reviews, and three articles have been published having some potential relevance to the argument:

1983   F.R. Cristi, "The Hegelsche Mitte and Hegel's Monarchy", *Political Theory,* 11:4, pp.601-622;

1984   Karl-Heinz Ilting, "Hegel's Concept of the State and Marx's Early critique", trans. by H. Tudor and J.M. Tudor, *The state and Civil Society: Studies in Hegel's Political Philosophy,* Z.A.Pelczynski, ed., Cambridge, Cambridge University Press;[1]

1987   Howard Williams and Michael Levin, "Inherited Power and Popular Representation: a Tension in Hegel's Political Theory", *Political Studies,* Vol.35, pp.105-115;

1987   William Maker, ed., *Hegel on Economics and Freedom,* Macon, Georgia, Mercer University Press;

1987   Taik-Ho Lee, *In Rehabilitation of Hegelianism,* Ph.D. thesis, The University of North Carolina at Chapel Hill.

1988   Richard Dien Winfield, *Reason and Justice,* Albany, State University of New York Press;

1988   Tom Nairn, *The Enchanted Glass: Britain and its Monarchy,* London, Radius;

1989   Anthony Arblaster, "Taking Monarchy Seriously", *New Left Review,* Issue 174, pp.97-110;

1989   Victor Kiernan, "Meditation on a Theme by Tom Nairn", *New Left Review,* Issue 174, pp.111-120;

1989   Steven B. Smith, "What is 'Right' in Hegel's Philosophy of Right", *American Political Science Review,* Vol.83, No.1;

1989   Edgar Wilson, *The Myth of British Monarchy,* London, Journeyman Press and Republic.

None of these works has forced any fundamental changes to the original case for 'democratic monarchy' but they have suggested some clarifications and additions. All of these will be detailed later, but several of their arguments can be usefully highlighted here.

---

(1) Karl-Heinz Ilting, *"Hegels Begriff des Staates und die Kritik des jungen Marx,"* Rivista di Filosofia N.7-8-9, 1977:119, pp.93-113.

Of course, most academics regard any concern with monarchy as "ineffably silly - like women's fashion magazines".[1] However, Tom Nairn, for one, has taken it seriously of late, if only because he sees it as providing a "Royal dummy in the British mouth"[2] tending to inhibit the development of socialism in general and a socialist Scotland in particular. Even more recently, Edgar Wilson, another republican, wrote a very readable attack upon the British monarchy. In fact, his implicit challenge to my original conclusions have led me to make certain adjustments. To use one of his more colourful expression, the type of hereditary head of state favoured here would probably be called, "bicycle-monarchy",[3] after one of the means of transport used by the former Queen of the Netherlands. This characterisation is apt because my model constitution does not require its monarch to display anything like the "extravagant grandeur"[4] currently exhibited by the British monarchs. In any event, the case for 'democratic monarchy' will be seen to refute Wilson's claim that,

> "Whatever utility monarchy may have, may be equally served by alternative institutions which are less objectionable."[5]

At the same time, it will be contended that this sort of monarchy would form the most rational complement to a wide variety of modern societies, whether their economies are largely organized by *laissez-faire*, social democratic, or socialist principles. As a result, Wilson would be unable to justify the following comment regarding this model constitution which he makes about the "British Monarchy":

> [It] is a substantial obstacle to more real freedom ... both because it exemplifies and sustains gross maldistribution of social status and economic power, and because it is the main instrument of coercive constraint by organized propaganda.[6]

Wilson accepts Rawls's criterion of "fairness": inequalities in the distribution of various social and material goods are permissible provided "that the inequalities result in compensating benefits for everyone ...".[7] 'Democratic monarchy' will also be seen to pass this test.

Accordingly, it will be argued here that,
1) an *hereditary head* of state is an essential part of the most rational constitution; and that this constitution also,
2) is *democratic*,
3) is *written*, and has,
4) a *"parliamentary* form",
5) an *independent judiciary*, headed by a supreme court,
6) a prime minister and council of ministers selected by arrangements similar to those provided by the fundamental law of Germany, namely, the *"constructive vote of no confidence"* procedure (Articles 63, 67 & 68), and
7) a parliament composed of two houses,
   A) the *elected chamber* is *sovereign* between general elections,
      a) directly with regard to legislative questions, and,
      b) indirectly with regard to executive and judicial questions,
   B) the *non-elected chamber* (composed of some hereditary and some life peers) has only an advisory role.
8) The elected house of parliament is chosen by *universal adult suffrage* by,
9) an electoral system called, *'associational proportional representation'*.

As 'democratic', this constitution provides for rule by the 'majority' and for each adult to have the effective legal right to participate equally in the making of sovereign state decisions,
   a) directly in referenda to decide on any proposed changes to the constitution, and
   b) indirectly with regard to legislative, executive, and judicial decisions (through the choice of representatives to the elected assembly).

In the ideal state, the legal right of all adults to vote would be made 'effective' by the legislation, policies, and programmes sufficient to remove any of the known obstacles to such political participation, e.g. poverty, intimidation, and ignorance.

---

(1) Kiernan, p.113.  (2) Ibid., p.120.  (3) Wilson, p.177.  (4) Ibid., p.151.
(5) Ibid., p.4.  (6) Ibid., p.146.  (7) Ibid., p.151.

One month after the original thesis was submitted, Cristi published his article. Through a survey of some of the literature and some of the key passages from Hegel's *Philosophy of Right*, Cristi correctly shows that it is possible to read Hegel as favouring "absolute monarchy". He says that this is because it would provide the best guarantee for the free market individualism ("atomistic particularity") [1] which was coming to dominate the modern world when Hegel was writing. He writes that this monarchy is "liberal" in the minimal sense that it is not a "despotic regime bent on tyrannizing civil society and its members".[2] Yet,
> "political power is monopolized by one center of decision, the monarch, who can alternatively decide to irradiate a large measure of his power to other subordinate authorities or retrieve it in its totality".[3]

Accordingly, Cristi gives the most authoritarian interpretation possible to PP275 of the *Philosophy of Right*:
> "The power of the monarch contains in itself the three moments of the totality [including] ... the moment of ultimate decision as the self-determination to which everything else reverts and from which everything else derives the beginning of its actuality. This absolute self-determination constitutes the distinctive principle of the power of the monarch ...".[4]

Thus, "*constitutional* monarchy" is interpreted merely to be a cover for *absolute* monarchy.

However, Cristi can be accused of distortion because he does not quote any of the strong textual evidence on the other side which suggests that a genuinely limited monarch was what Hegel had in mind. In such a constitutional monarchy, as in the 'democratic monarchy' to be defended here, the throne would not have more than symbolic and ceremonial functions unless and until the other organs of the state failed to secure the unity which is a condition for a rational state. Therefore, at best, Cristi's article is a useful corrective for anyone who might naively have assumed that Hegel can, without any difficulty, be counted as one of "the fathers of Western democracy".[5]

It is not possible to determine with certainty whether Hegel himself had something close to 'democratic monarchy' in mind. This will be verified by the analysis of the two sets of his conflicting passages relevant to this question. However, the determination of what is the most accurate reading of Hegel is not the primary concern here. Instead, it is the discovery of a model constitution which can withstand the most rigorous philosophical criticism available. To this end, Hegel's political theory and philosophical system are seen as offering the widest and deepest pool available of such arguments for our consideration.

Ilting's chapter, published in English a year after the thesis had been completed, can be read largely to confirm its conclusions. In sharp contrast to Cristi, he marshals plausible evidence from Hegel's works prior to the publication of the *Philosophy of Right* in October 1820 [6] to show that Hegel was a "republican" from 1795, and synthesised the principles of republicanism with those of monarchy in his lectures between 1818-1819.[7] Ilting then argues that Hegel, for temporal political calculations during the restoration period, not for philosophical reasons, dropped the republican element almost entirely from the *Philosophy of Right*.[8] In this light, the model of 'democratic monarchy' suggested here could be seen as having resulted from my having picked up the remaining echos[9] in the *Philosophy of Right* of Hegel's own republicanism.

Therefore, Ilting plausibly claims that Hegel only retreated from his long standing republicanism in between 1819 and 1820 as a prudential tactic to secure the publication of the *Philosophy of Right* after the Karlsbad Decrees which had extended prior censorship even to scientific works.[10] Ilting's argument is appealing even though he, like Cristi, also exaggerates the extent to which

---

(1) Cristi, p.611. (2) Ibid., p.618. (3) Ibid., p.613. (4) Cited by Cristi, p.614.
(5) Cited by Cristi, p.601, from Henning Ottmann, *Individuum und Gemeinschaft bei Hegel*, Vol.I, *Hegel Spiegel der Interpretation*, Berlin, de Gruyter, 1977, p.226.
(6) Ilting, p.94. (7) Ibid. (8) Ibid., pp.100, 101 and 112.
(9) Ilting, for example, discusses *Rechts* PP261 and An. in this regard, p.100.
(10) Ibid., p.98.

Hegel retreated into "authoritarianism".[1] Thus, it might be said that Hegel,[2] Ilting [3] and I are all democrats [4] in one sense or another. However, we would still seem to differ with respect to the question of monarchy. I, arguably with the support of Hegel himself, see it as essential to the fullest democracy. Ilting sees it largely or entirely to have been an expedient of accommodation to the restoration monarchies of the time, "a politically motivated decision".[5] Also, Ilting correctly criticises Hegel for not making it clear exactly how his assertion that the "'moments' of universality, particularity, and singularity must be represented by special institutions (*Rechts*, PP273) ... was related to the universal end of the state ('the individual's destiny is the living of universal life'" (PP258An.). In effect, the present work seeks to make good this "inadequacy" [6] by offering an elaboration of the relevance of this "practical syllogism" [7] both with regard to the fulfilment of individuals and to the three function and three organ structure of the model democracy.

In the context of the above, the article by Williams and Levin adds nothing new. Their summaries of the tensions between "inherited power and popular representation", both in the literature and in Hegel's own writings, are quite unobjectionable . However, because they did not attempt an improving reconstruction of Hegel's constitutional theory themselves in order to resolve these tensions, they did not engage in the philosophical debate offered here.

Finally, I would like to express my appreciation for the help that I have received in the writing of this book. I am especially indebted to Professor Raymond Plant of Southampton University for his prudent tutorial guidance. Dr. G. Sathaye, my colleague and friend, carefully read previous versions of the original thesis and offered many useful suggestions. My immediate colleagues at Portsmouth Polytechnic gave me the time to begin the required research by relieving me of many of my teaching duties for one year. Students read or listened to versions of some of the arguments presented here and their criticisms forced me to clarify them. My wife and two daughters both encouraged and tolerated my efforts. For the production of this revised version of the original thesis, two institutions provided material assistance. As a guest Associate Professor of Political Science at Eastern Mediterranean University, currently on leave from Portsmouth Polytechnic, E.M.U. arranged for the original thesis to be typed onto disc so that the editing job could be eased. Portsmouth Polytechnic provided both the hardware and software needed to produce a laser printed master copy.

Steve Bosworth
Eastern Mediterranean University,
Gazi Magosa,
The Turkish Republic of Northern Cyprus

October 1990

(1) Ibid., p.101.
(2) Ibid. pp.95, 96, & 97n.18: Consider Hegel's "explanatory notes to PP122 [of his winter 1818-1819 lecture course on *Natural Law and the Science of the State*]: 'Princely power consists of the empty final decision; there is as yet no question of objective decisions based on reason.' This is the business of the government. Cf.PP124An. 'The regent puts his name to it.' 'It is often not important which decision is made, only that some decision should be made.' (cf. Ilting, *Hegel diverso*, Bari, 1977, p.35ff.)".
(3) Ibid., p.95.
(4) The argument that Hegel is one sort of democrat would seem to be supported by Taik-Ho Lee, *In Rehabilitation of Hegelianism*, Ph.D. thesis, The University of North Carolina at Chapel Hill, 1987, Abstract: "popular sovereignty [is] ... retained and absorbed in Hegel's theory of the state".
(5) Ibid., p.112.
(6) Ibid., p.109.
(7) Ibid.

Introduction

The commonly assumed dichotomy between democracy and monarchy will be shown to be false in the light of the model constitution to be outlined. Hegel's own political philosophy goes along way toward synthesising the two but the conceptual completion of this task is attempted here. Hegel's constitutional monarchy is not perfect, but arguably it does offer the closest available approximation to the best framework for modern political life. Here it has stimulated its own critique from within his wider system and then its reconstruction as 'democratic monarchy'[1] in the face of strong republican arguments. To whatever limited extent institutional arrangements can help to shape events, it will be argued that *democratic monarchy* would be the most supportive of the sort of human life which is both free and rational.

The question of Hegel's monarchy has been almost entirely ignored[2] by philosophical analysis. When dealt with at all, it has usually been,
1) mentioned blandly without understanding or critical comment;[3]
2) drained of all philosophical significance either by portraying it simply,
   a) as *typical* for a man of his time and circumstances,
   b) as *expedient* if he wished to attain high status or influence within the Prussian state, or
   c) as a skilful political ploy to detach monarchy from its absolutist past (rooted in the doctrines of 'divine right' and 'legitimacy') in order to help open it to more liberal reforms;[4] or
3) or simply rejected.

Commentators in the last category display varying degrees of hostility to Hegel's monarchical theory but they have not shown any penetrating philosophical analysis in doing so. Instead, they seem to display only the republican prejudices with which I myself read Hegel's *Philosophy of Right*[5] for the first time. Of course, it must be admitted that Hegel's complex, unusual, and obscure exposition of his philosophical grounds for an hereditary head of state does not make the removal of such prejudices easy. Thus, different writers have simply asserted that an hereditary head is not necessary (Reyburn, Stace and Taylor), is "smuggled in" (Berki), is "obscure and implausible" (Pelczynski), is "irrational" (Marcuse), or is "nauseating" (Hook).[6]

In contrast, shortly after the first substantial draft of the original thesis was completed, the articles by Yack[7] and Brudner[8] were published. Each offered different justifications for Hegel's

(1) 'Single' inverted commas will be used to mark my own special terms while the words of others will be marked by "double" inverted commas.
(2) Given the nature of Richard Dien Winfield's book, it is surprising that he does not even mention Hegel's monarchy, *Reason and Justice*, Albany, State University of New York Press, 1988.
(3) For example, Richard A. Davis, "Property and Labour in Hegel's Concept of Freedom," William Maker, ed., *Hegel on Economics and Freedom*, Macon, Georgia, Mercer University Press, 1987, p.207.
(4) For example, Shlomo Avineri, *Hegel's Theory of the Modern State*, C.U.P., 1972, p.187.
(5) When I have consulted the German text, references to Hegel's works will use a key word in the German title. Thus, the *Philosophy of Right* will be footnoted as *"Rechts"* after the *Grundlinien der Philosophie der Philosophie des Rechts*.
(6) H.A. Reyburn, *The Ethical Theory of Hegel*, Oxford 1921, pp.241-252. W.T. Stace, *The Philosophy of Hegel*, New York 1955, paragraphs 619 and 620. Charles Taylor, *Hegel*, Cambridge 1975, p.440. R.N. Berki, in Z.A. Pelczynski (ed) *Hegel's Political Philosophy: Problems and Perspectives*, Cambridge 1971, pp. 202-3. Z.N. Pelczynski, ibid., p.25 and 231. H. Marcuse, *Reason and Revolution*, London 1941, p.218. S. Hook, in *Hegel's Political Philosophy*, W. Kaufmann (ed), New York 1970, p.90.
(7) Bernard Yack, "The Rationality of Hegel's Concept of Monarchy", *American Political Science Review*, Vol.74, 1980, pp.708-720.
(8) Brudner, "Constitutional Monarchy as the Divine Regime: Hegel's Theory of the Just State, "*History of Political Thought*, Vol.II, No. 1. Spring. January 1981, pp.119-140.

monarchy. While the argument developed here is prefigured in some respects by both, both fail to see that a fully rational constitution must also be democratic. Nevertheless, extracted from the rest of Yack's argument, I agree with the following points:
1) Hegel's "hereditary monarch is the necessary apex of the rational political order",[1] an "interdependent unity".[2]
2) "The rational state requires a depersonalized power of final decision, exercised by an actual person. The fundamental problem of politics cannot be wished away. Someone must have the final say in any human society".[3] "The most personal form of sovereignty makes impersonal, rational rule possible".[4]
3) "By depoliticizing (or depersonalizing) the regime at the top, the monarch creates the conditions in which freedom of political association and competition can continue without disturbing the general rational administration of the state".[5]
4) Also, for practical reasons, the actuality of a rational monarchy would depend on "public acceptance of a dynastic tradition".[6]
5) "Since [constitutional monarchy] requires a tradition of accepting a royal family, as well as the historical experience and political conditions of post-Napoleonic Europe, Hegel's rational constitution is not a universally applicable blueprint for the best regime. It would have been absurd for the authors of the American constitution to try to impose this form of government .... The sad fact is that the rational and free constitution is *not* possible everywhere.[7]

The last admission that the most rational constitution does not simply provide a "blueprint" for every time and place should not be taken necessarily to exclude the possibility that it might serve as a 'model' for all. In this sense, it will be argued that 'democratic monarchy' both provides a key for understanding all constitutions, including republics, and may suggest some modifications which would help any regime provide a better framework for free and rational human life.

Thus, it is argued later that constitutions ought to be assessed according to the extent to which they inherently foster 'the maximization of both the quality and quantity of free, rational human life'. The meaning of this phrase will be elaborated in due course and it will be shown, with 'philosophical necessity' (Chapter Six) to follow as a moral principle from Hegel's own concept of "Reason" (Chapter Seven). Similarly, it will be demonstrated that maximizing the *quantity* of 'free and rational ... life' entails the conclusion that the model must be 'democratic'.

Implicitly, Yack's article rejects this conclusion, but perhaps only because he is a victim of the common but false assumption to be corrected here that monarchy and democracy are inherently incompatible. This mistake encouraged by his tacit equation between "democracy" and the "ancient republics".[8] Paraphrasing Hegel (*Rechts*, PP279), he criticises these republics for their reliance on the principle of "election". This left "the content of their public decisions ... to chance". They "required leaders of great talent, but could not guarantee their continued presence".[9] The same cannot be said of democratic monarchy. Yack also exaggerates the difficulties with elected officials in the following two passages and naively assumes that these same dangers are not perhaps even more applicable to his more authoritarian monarch:
A) "Any particular individual or group of individuals, elected or self-appointed, is bound to be partial and not represent the universal will of the nation, ... if only because they must depend on their own limited insights";[10]
B) "It is much harder to identify the universal will of the nation with elected or appointed figures. They remind one that ... they bring personal ambitions and perspectives to government".[11]

His comments seem to add up to a denial of the assumption central to modern democracies that it is desirable for rival political parties to compete for the main public offices. This is confirmed by his criticism that republics only can generate "an artificial collective will"[12] and that such "popular will" does "not end the personal competition for the ultimate power of decision in the state".[13] It also seems to deny what is affirmed here, namely, that the rational life of a people is encouraged both qualitatively and quantitatively by "competition" within and between political parties. It denies that such political parties tend to be spurred both to articulate and to rule according to "the universal will".

These views make it clear that Yack and I understand quite differently, points 2) and 3) quoted above. He sees the "depersonalized power of final decision" as justifying authoritarian hereditary rule. I see it as grounding a constitution which provides for the "power of final decision" to be

---

(1) Yack, p.710. (2) Ibid., p.712. (3) Ibid., p.715. (4) Ibid., p.716.(5) Ibid., p.715.
(6) Ibid., p.710. (7) Ibid., p.718. (8) Yack, p.712. (9) Ibid., p.712.
(10) Yack, p.714. (11) Ibid., p.717. (12) Ibid., p.714. (13) Ibid., p.714.

*Introduction*

exercised in an effective manner,
  a) by the citizens themselves in referenda on any constitutional proposals, and, at general election times, with regard to their representatives, but between general elections,
  b) by the "collective will" of the elected assembly as long as it continues to generate its own working majority and thus constitutes a legal or "actual person",[1]
  c) by one of a list of elected officials (governor general, deputy governor general, or speaker of the elected chamber) if such a majority fails, or
  d) by the hereditary head of state, but only in the absence of b) and c).

It will be seen later why this absence is not as unlikely as republicans might be inclined to assume. In any case, the monarch in my model constitution indeed helps to create "the conditions in which freedom of political association can continue".[2]

The conflict between Yack and myself may stem from our different understandings of "depoliticized" and "depersonalized". My head of state is depoliticized only in the sense that if he has had only to perform the ceremonial jobs symbolizing the unity of the relevant society and state, he will *not* be seen as involved in *party* politics. However, if she or he has had to exercise 'effective', as well as 'symbolic', sovereignty for some time, he or she will most definitely be, and be seen to be, 'political' in the wider sense of the term. While Yack's monarch would always be political in this wider sense, mine would not be except in the above mentioned circumstance.

Yack and I agree that the monarch is depersonalized in the sense that primogeniture is no respecter of personal qualities other than times of birth. We also agree that the monarch is depersonalized in the other sense that she or he plays a role in a rational constitution which minimizes the chances that merely personal whims will capture "the regime at the top".[3] However, he mistakenly believes that the risk of this is minimized when an hereditary official permanently has the effective "power of final decision".[4] I argue that it is minimized when the monarch is given this power only if and when a leadership which is positively supported by a working majority in the elected assembly fails to materialize. I would add, but Yack would not, that elected representatives and officials in a rational constitutional order would also tend to be depersonalized, simply by the procedures giving them office and by the institutional framework within which they must operate.

Brudner's article offers some points of agreement with the argument to be developed in the following chapters but it conflicts at other points. We both attempt, "to elucidate Hegel's theory of constitutional monarchy and to show how a sensible person could take it seriously".[5] We agree that Hegel's constitution is "organic" in the sense of it having been derived from within his philosophical system. Therefore, he makes an advance beyond Yack by mentioning the relation between the three "moment" structure of Hegel's system and the three organs of Hegel's state: universality (legislature), particularity (executive - judiciary and bureaucracy), and individuality (the crown).[6] However, his brief account of these relations fails to clarify the inner connected triplicity of the relevant moments, functions, and organs. Here, *Chapters Two* and *Eleven* address this problem. Also, in spite of Brudner's imprecise formulations, he correctly reminds us that Hegel's concept of the rational state is not to be equated with any past or existing state merely because it has arrived at a "contingent compromise" between "monarchical and republican elements". At most, such states "obscurely"[7] illustrate Hegel's concept of the state. However, the argument offered here conflicts with Brudner,
  1) most definitely when he asserts, without explanation, something which all of the textual evidence denies. He writes that Hegel does not identify "the paradigm of modern constitutional monarchy ... with the constitution of fully developed Reason";[8]
  2) in his assumption, shared by Yack, that Hegel's constitutional conclusions were in no way democratic. Thus, he writes that, "under popular sovereignty, government cannot escape the appearance of being a faction .... popular sovereignty leads to political fragmentation";[9]
  3) in his suggestion that "constitutional monarchy begins *logically* from a dominant Crown".[10] He should have said that it is derived logically from the concept of 'Reason as a constitution'. Consequently, Hegel's constitution begins *historically*, not "logically", from a "dominant Crown"; and

(1) Ibid., p.715. (2) Ibid. (3) Ibid. (4) Yack, p.715. (5) Brudner, p.121.
(6) Ibid., pp.125-127. Note that these terms receive somewhat different translations in the following chapters.
(7) Ibid., pp.129 & 130. (8) Brudner, p.130. (9) Ibid., p.124. (10) Ibid., p.130n.37.

4) possibly when he implies that Hegel's "God" cannot, or ought not, be reduced to "Reason",[1] assumed here to be the ground of all being (including rational human life). He might reject a humanist interpretation here which does not exclude the possibility that "Reason" may itself become entirely known and understood by human reason (see *Chapters Six* and *Seven*).

Before turning to outline the broad structure of my argument, the fundamental purpose for which this whole enterprise has been erected should be made explicit. This is to say, that this thesis seeks to foster 'free, rational' political thought and activity. This goal, in turn, is required by the more general prescription which the rest of the work will clarify and elaborate: 'Act so as to maximize the quality and quantity of free, rational living in the world'.

Crudely speaking, *democratic monarchy* could be likened empirically to the existing Japanese, Scandinavian, Benelux, Spanish and British Constitutions.[2] This is to say that it could be characterized as 'a parliamentary democracy with cabinet government'. Its hereditary head of state formally appoints the prime minister but his cabinet is made fully accountable to an elected chamber. The elected chamber is elected by universal adult suffrage but with a *new* system of proportional representation to be discussed in *Chapter One*.

As already implied, in order to defend *democratic* monarchy, I am going to have to argue against Hegel at certain points. At other times, I will receive Hegel's assistance against various republican arguments. *Chapter Two* refutes both 'parliamentary' and 'congressional' republican attacks. *Chapters Three, Four,* and *Five* will specifically consider those republican theories which can be extracted from Plato, Kant and Marx. Therefore, the book might be said to be divided into *two parts* separated by *Chapter Six*. This chapter stops to define and examine the methodology used throughout. It explains how 'philosophical necessity' characterises the strongest conceivable case that could be made out for any conclusion. Thus, the *first part* presents the main features of democratic monarchy and attempts to defeat various opposing republican arguments. The *second part* explores the extent to which democratic monarchy is compatible with Hegel's philosophy and political theory.

In *Chapter Three*, Plato's *Republic* is used as a heuristic spring board to introduce the philosophical case for democratic monarchy. Some will say that I *twist* Plato's republican argument into a support for my model constitution. Similarly, they will say that in later chapters, I attempt to *stretch*, pull or *drive* Kant, Hegel and Marx to the same prescriptive ideal. To some extent, such charges would be fair, but no apology is necessary for two reasons. Firstly, my glosses and reconstructions are usually made possible by the elements of residual ambiguity that these philosophers have left within their own formulations. Secondly and more importantly, in all cases I have sought readings and modifications of these theories in order to discover the strongest possible arguments *against* democratic monarchy as well as the strongest ones *for* it. At no time have I knowingly 'violated' the texts. When I go further than the texts can be stretched, this is declared. I am also aware that I have frequently departed from the so-called 'standard interpretations' of these four philosophers. This would not bother me unless this meant either that I had missed their strongest arguments.

In Hegel's case especially, different commentators have frequently given baldly *contradictory yet equally plausible* interpretations. This is not surprising when we consider the enormity of his complex system and the notorious obscurity of many of his formulations, i.e. what Marx charitably called the "stylistic peculiarity of Hegel".[3] To a somewhat lesser degree, the same problems arise when examining most any theorist; certainly Plato, Kant and Marx are not exceptions. For this reason, I do not expect that all of my interpretations and reconstructions will be accepted by all as unchallengable. The incompleteness, obscurity, diffuseness, complexity, or prolixity of their words would make such an expectation naive.

I can only hope that my interpretations and modifications will be found both to be plausibly fair to the philosophers examined and as contributing to our common discovery of the most rational model constitution. At least I can hope that my suggestions may constitute a fruitful part of the agenda for any philosophical investigations in search of such a theory.

(1) Ibid., see pp.125 and 131.
(2) I say 'crudely' because I adopt the same attitude towards my model as did Hegel, namely, that the "rational state" is not to be simply equated with any historically existent, "particular state" (*Rechts*, PP258An., i.e. the "Remark" to paragraph 258).
(3) K. Marx, *Critique of Hegel's 'Philosophy of Right'*, translated by Joseph O'Malley and Annette Jolin, C.U.P., 1970, p.13.

# Chapter One:
# THE MODEL CONSTITUTION

Because my model constitution can be seen as derived from Hegel's philosophical system and yet also departs from his own constitutional theory at certain points, it provides the basis for an intimate test of Hegel's political philosophy. Thus, the wide ranging comparison offered here will cast a penetrating light into Hegel's theory of the state. This chapter will first outline the structure of 'democratic monarchy' and then consider some of its practical advantages. Later, it will be seen how these are rooted in the more philosophical groundings to be elaborated in the chapters concerned with Plato, Kant, Marx, and, of course, Hegel. Accordingly, in support of the 'model constitution', this chapter will largely confine itself to laying some of the descriptive foundations for arguing that,

1) an *hereditary head* of state is an essential part of the most rational constitution; and that this constitution also,
2) is *democratic,*
3) is *written,* and has,
4) a "*parliamentary* form",
5) an *independent judiciary,* headed by a supreme court,
6) a prime minister and council of ministers selected by arrangements similar to those provided by the fundamental law of Germany, namely, the "*constructive vote of no confidence*" procedure (Articles 63, 67 & 68), and
7) a parliament composed of two houses,
    A) the *elected chamber* is *sovereign* between general elections,
        a) directly with regard to legislative questions, and,
        b) indirectly with regard to executive and judicial questions,
    B) the *non-elected chamber* (composed of some hereditary and some life peers) has only an advisory role.
8) The elected house of parliament is chosen by *universal adult suffrage* by,
9) an electoral system called, '*associational proportional representation*'.

As 'democratic', this constitution provides for rule by the 'majority' and for each adult to have the effective legal right to participate equally in the making of sovereign state decisions,
   a) directly in referenda to decide on any proposed changes to the constitution, and
   b) indirectly with regard to legislative, executive, and judicial decisions (through the choice of representatives to the elected assembly).

In the ideal state, the legal right of all adults to vote would be made 'effective' by the legislation, policies, and programmes sufficient to remove any of the known obstacles to such political participation, e.g. poverty, intimidation, and ignorance.

While most of the above features do not need much further explanation, several do:
1) the hereditary head of state,
2) the non-elective chamber,
3) the sovereignty of the elected assembly,
4) the 'constructive vote of no confidence' procedure, and
5) 'associational proportional representation'.

Before these are addressed, however, the intended status of the 'model' constitution must be made clear. This is especially important in view of what many people might feel are grandiose claims that will be made for democratic monarchy, e.g. 'most rational', 'best workable ideal', 'philosophically necessary'. It claims to be established by the most rigorous argument as the best *'general,* prescriptive guide' for political action. Although it hopes to be conceptually precise in its formulation, of course, its prescriptive implications for every political problem in all the existing countries of the world will rarely be immediately obvious. Even if we were to assume for the moment that it had already been fully established philosophically, I do not expect that this, by itself, would usually tell us *exactly* how we should conduct ourselves within the problematic of every concrete context. Usually, many additional practical and theoretical difficulties would have to be faced first. Thus, the formulation of operationally precise prescriptions for any empirically concrete state is beyond the scope of this thesis. I do not deny the importance of finding suitable courses of action in these cases, especially for those people directly involved. However, a detailed philosophical consideration of the problems contained even in one such concrete reality would add volumes to this work.[1] More importantly, such an enterprise would draw us into the uncertainties which are unavoidably attached to any action in the world which is partly moved by forces which may not yet be scientifically understood and partly by human wills which are 'free' and thus must always remain to some extent unpredictable.[2]

In one sense, therefore, this book is taking an easy way out. Yet, it seeks to define a *model* which will address, rather than be undermined by, such uncertainties. A 'model' can enjoy this immunity because it is a more abstract entity. It only hopes to offer a *general* way of coping with these uncertainties. It hopes to be an enduring conception of the ideal constitution. Some such conception is a 'philosophically necessary' reference point for the unavoidably uncertain assessment of rival tactics to be applied to any concrete situation. It ought to be a part of every political calculation. While I would argue that such a conception has an intrinsic as well as a practical value, it cannot be denied that most people (even "philosophers" under pressure or in moments of weakness) may act not as a result of such refined considerations but from impulse, feeling, instinct or intuition. The model, therefore, attempts to prescribe the *rational goal* of political activity with respect to constitutional arrangements. It seeks to formulate a guide to action, not to prescribe operationally precise tactics. Thus 'democratic monarchy' hopes to be *general*, not in the sense of being vague but in the sense of being a clear model which *all* should add to their probabilistic calculations concerning how they *ought* to conduct themselves in any given political situation.

With regard to the question of the hereditary head of state, a number of clarifications must be made. The monarch's constitutional obligation to exercise effective sovereignty in certain circumstances must be explained. He or she may receive this constitutional duty only as a member of the 'state prerogative council'. One designated member of this council is charged by the model constitution to make the essential sovereign decisions when the elected assembly fails to produce a 'working majority'. It is this majority which would normally make these decisions. In such times of crisis, the state prerogative council, formally called and chaired by the monarch, would meet in order to *advise* one of its members on how to exercise one or a combination of four prerogatives:

1) to appoint the prime minister,
2) to appoint a chairperson for the elected assembly,
3) to prorogue or dissolve the elected assembly, or
4) to require that any proposed constitutional changes be first ratified by the electorate in referenda.

Only the last one could be exercised when a 'working majority' existed in the elected assembly. The 'state prerogative council' would be composed of the following, assuming that none of the relevant offices was vacant. They are listed is order of their priority with regard to the personal exercise of the prerogatives:

a) the 'governor general' and the deputy governor general(s),
b) the 'speaker' of the elected chamber and deputy speaker(s),
c) *the monarch,*
d) the 'leader' of the non-elected chamber and deputy leaders,
e) (in the absence of a 'speaker', the 'chairperson' and deputy chairperson(s) of the elected assembly - whether elected by a mere plurality or appointed by a previous exercise of the prerogative), and
f) (the next adult heir to the throne if invited by the monarch could also participate, but he or she could not personally exercise the prerogatives until he or she inherited the throne).

(1) See *Chapter Six.*
(2) Ibid.

The practice of consulting one another in the 'state prerogative council' would both help the current holder of the prerogatives to think through any proposed courses of action and help to prepare the other men or women who might later be called upon personally to exercise these same constitutional powers. All exercises of the prerogatives by one of the above officials would be formally proclaimed in the name of the state prerogative council, the monarch, and the people. Each of the elected officials on the state prerogative council would be selected, as far as is possible, to have the qualities which Wilson rightly believes they ought to have, namely, to be,

... demonstrably able, representative, accountable, impartial, and capable of legitimate action in the national interest when necessary.[1]

Thus, the monarch, personally would have this constitutional right only if the elected officials who would normally also be members of this council and who would have priority were not available for any of the reasons to be elaborated later. Thus, the model's monarch could have this substantive role as well as remaining the prime symbol of the basic unity of his or her society. Later chapters will argue that the intrinsic qualities of an hereditary head of state makes it the institution best suited to serve as the apex of a society's symbols of unity. For most every particular state, this unity is complex and incomplete. It is usually a unity of an existing society both with its past and its future, as well as being a unity of its individuals, families, groups, associations, and of its various state functions and organs. The monarch's many ceremonial functions are meant dramatically and symbolically to affirm this unity.

In any case, no member of the state prerogative council has the right to exercise any of the first three prerogatives unless, because of intense factionalism, the 'working majority' in the elected assembly has either evaporated or has failed to materialize in the first place. A 'working majority' is present when at least 50% + 1 of the members of the assembly elect the prime minister, continue to give his or her council of ministers votes of confidence when asked, and pass the legislative, self-dissolving, or referenda proposals requested by the council of ministers (i.e. the 'executive council'). The history of parliamentary systems in the world has clearly shown that such majority support for executive council cannot be taken for granted, even or especially under many of the existing electoral systems. With regard to this problem, it must be noted that the model sovereign assembly is elected by the system to be described shortly: 'associational proportional representation'. The inclusion of proportional representation may fuel the fear that the model would make majority support for any executive council less likely than it needs to be. Whether such scrupulously democratic representation of the people would, in fact, makes "majority government" more or less likely in the long run is difficult to say. It is a question which is not capable of being settled by philosophical investigation. However, rigorous argument can show that this electoral system is a necessary part of a rational democracy. At the same time, provision must be made for any such potentially destabilizing eventualities. The model constitution's arrangements for the exercise of the above prerogatives fully address this issue.

With regard to the prerogative to appoint the prime minister when no candidate has secured majority support, the model constitution says that the holder of the prerogative should then appoint the candidate who has the support of a *plurality*, unless this, in his or her judgment, would

---

(1) Edgar Wilson, *The Myth of British Monarchy*, London, Journeyman Press and Republic, 1989, p.178. Wilson's discussion of constitutional reforms (Chapter 34) has led me to add the largely elected 'state prerogative council' to the original argument. However, my retention of the monarch as an essential member of this council runs against the thrust of his book. Both Wilson and I are 'democrats' because we are 'rationalists'. However, while I argue that a particular sort of limited monarchy would institutionally strengthen democracy, he sees "democracy" and "monarchy" as "incompatible ... in principle" (p.1). His main concern is the more narrow one of entirely defeating the many arguments for the *British* monarchy while mine is to outline a general constitution to serve as a rational guide to any modern state. Nevertheless, his avowed aim "to examine the [British] monarchy at the level of principle" (p.2) or "broadly from a philosophical perspective [concerned, as it is, with arguments about] ... truth ... and rightness..." (p.2), provides us with another side to our common ground. Both of us are seeking the most "rational" constitution. Wilson would probably call the type of hereditary head of state favoured by me "bicycle-monarchy" (p.177), presumably after one of the means of transport sometimes favoured by the former Queen of the Netherlands. This characterisation is apt because my constitution does not require its 'monarch' to display anything like the "extravagant grandeur" (p.151) currently exhibited by British monarchs. My hereditary head of state would have, as Wilson put it, been forced or "persuaded to continue as hereditary ceremonial head of state at Equity rates, plus expenses ..." (p.162). Still, as has been made clear, my model constitution requires the monarch to retain some of the effective constitutional powers which the Swedish monarch lost in 1974 (p.175).

threaten the unity of the society more than the appointment of an alternative candidate. With the same consideration in mind, and in the same circumstances, the holder of the prerogative would also have to decide whether to appoint a 'caretaker' prime minister, instead, and thus to dissolve the assembly and trigger a new general election.  The current holder of the prerogatives ought to have the same consideration in mind if and when an existing prime minister suffers a plurality vote of no confidence, whether he or she had initially received majority support or not.  No question of prerogative arises when an existing prime minister is replaced by a different leader elected by a working majority, whether the existing prime minister was initially elected by a majority or merely appointed by prerogative.[1]

As we have seen, if the elected assembly were to fail to produce a working majority, it would normally be the 'governor general', who the model constitution would require personally to exercise the above prerogatives.  She or he must be elected by at least 2/3rds of the elected assembly (for a term of one year longer than the maximum time between general elections).  Similarly, a 'deputy governor general' would be elected to perform these same prerogatives in the governor general's absence, indisposition, or incapacity.  The deputy would also be charged automatically to assume the office itself, either upon the existing governor general's death or upon his constitutional removal from office.[2]  The governor general could be removed from office by the elected chamber for any reason by a 2/3rds 'vote of no confidence' or by being convicted in the supreme court of having committed unconstitutional or other acts previously specified by law.  In this event, the constitution would require that a new deputy governor general be elected.  In the absence of a deputy in such circumstances, the 'speaker' of the elected chamber would be next in line to perform these prerogatives, the 'speaker' having been elected by at least 50% + 1 of the members of the elected assembly.

Therefore, the hereditary head of state would be constitutionally required personally to exercise these prerogatives only in the unlikely event that no 'governor general', 'deputy', or 'speaker' currently existed.  Nevertheless, this  may occur when the elected assembly lacks a working majority and the previously elected governor general, speaker, and their deputies had since died, been killed, or fallen into incompetence.  In this case, the assembly would probably also be too divided even to elect a new speaker by a simple majority (50% + 1), let alone a new governor general by a 2/3rds majority.  Of course, in order to conduct its business at all, without having had to rely on the current holder of the prerogative to appoint its chairperson, the assembly would have had to elect its own chairperson.  When the chairperson has be chosen by a majority, he or she is called the 'speaker' here; if merely by a plurality, the 'chairperson'.

The reason for the above order of priority between the members of the 'state prerogative council' is supplied by the recollection that the exercise of these prerogatives has the sole purpose of fostering as much voluntary, and therefore 'democratic', unity in the society as is possible in spite of the current disunity displayed in the elected chamber.  Thus, the holder of these prerogatives is charged with the task of "holding the ring" until sufficient practical rationality has returned to the elected chamber so that it can form a working majority and thus resume its own sovereign constitutional powers.  The most important of these would be to replace the existing prime minster, if it wished, by electing its own man or woman.  The desired voluntary unity of a society would seem clearly to be better encouraged by a person exercising the above prerogatives who had himself received at least 2/3rds support, rather than by one who had received the support of only between 50% and 2/3rds as in the case of the 'speaker', less than 50% as in the case of the 'chairperson', or had never been voted upon at all as in the cases of the monarch and 'leader' of the non-elected house.  The adoption of the '2/3rds' majority for the election of the governor general is not entirely arbitrary.  It is probably the lowest percentage of support that an elected official could receive without being thought by a substantial section of the community as representing only a factional interest.  Another seeming psychological truth is relevant.  The minimal unity defined as 'the bare absence of violence' is likely to obtain in a society which can muster a 2/3rds majority for its governor general if only because the 1/3rd minority sees that it would face odds of 1 to 2 if it were to use force in an attempt to get its own way.

(1) This last feature indicates that the model adopts the "constructive vote of no confidence" and other provisions of the German constitution to be discussed shortly, i.e. (Articles 63, 67 & 68).
(2) A society could logically choose to provide itself with more than one 'deputy governor general' in order to increase its security, but the length of this list of deputies would have to be balanced against the corresponding extra expense.

The very presence of the monarch in the above order needs to be explained, especially to democratic republicans. Again, it must be emphasised that an hereditary official is charged here with the personal exercise of the prerogatives only when no other person elected by a majority is available. In this event, however, he or she is given this constitutional power so as dramatically to signal to the members of the elected chamber (as well as to the public at large) that, for the moment, it has failed, and the longer it continues its factional squabbling, the more likely it will be that an unconstitutional, non-rational, involuntary, and probably anti-democratic unity will be imposed upon them, either from within or from without. This alarm is rung most clearly by the monarch because he or she is the leading member of a family which previously had a history of itself ruling - possibly without reference to reason but certainly without reference to democracy. It is precisely because the monarch represents such an institution that his personal exercise of the prerogatives gives his society an additional chance and stimulus to recapture its capacity to rule itself democratically. The monarch's role here is the clearest, yet least lethal personification of two related practical truths:
 a) If there is a power vacuum, it will be filled by non-reason if not by reason.
 b) If the majority cannot rule itself, it will be ruled by 'the one' or by 'the few' (rationally or not).

An hereditary official's accession to the prerogatives, in itself, is the best non-verbal declaration of the near and present danger of rule by non-rational forces. In this way, monarchy as an institution reminds each generation of its lower possibility so that it may grasp its higher possibility.

At the same time, because a monarch achieves his position by hereditary succession, his ability to function as the head of state in this substantive role is likely to survive any prolonged electoral divisiveness which may plague a society or its representative assembly. The same cannot be said of any of the elected officials discussed above. However, this not only makes it probable that he will be in place to perform this service for his society when needed, it also makes him the most likely focus of any eventual reassertion of autocratic rule. However, this is exactly why his personal exercise of the prerogatives sends the alarms ringing more loudly irrespective of his own democratic or anti-democratic intentions. It is only when the full range of the more obviously democratic institutions have temporarily failed that the monarchical element in this model constitution is called upon to act in order to foster the effective return to democracy. It is this dialectic of apparently opposite principles which are synthesized in 'democratic monarchy' in order best to strengthen both rational and democratic life in modern societies.

In further justification of the above order, it would seems less likely that a monarch's initial exercise of any of the above prerogatives would be perceived as partisan when compared to similar decisions which might be taken by the 'leader' of the non-elected chamber. This is because this leader is associated with the chamber which is expected to take an unflinching part in the political debates of the day while the monarch is prohibited from doing so. The monarch's ceremonial functions are initially more likely to have associated him or her with the benevolent maintenance of society's unity. Nevertheless, the 'leader' would seem to be better placed than would the 'chairperson' of the elected assembly (whether elected or appointed). This is because the latter has already been a participant in the elected assembly's factionalism, either having been elected by a plurality in the chamber and therefore having been openly not supported by more than half of its members, or, by having been imposed on the assembly from outside by a previous exercise of the second prerogative. Thus, the monarch's initial exercise of any of the prerogatives is seen as less likely to be greeted with factional suspicion than would similar action taken either by the 'leader' or by the 'chairperson'.

This last point opens the way for a clarification of the place and role of the non-elected chamber in the model constitution. It will be recalled that the non-elected chamber has an advisory function only. Thus, its 'teeth' are small. In addition to being placed in a highly visible position, freely to speak its mind publicly and to offer its considered advice to the other organs of state, it can do no more than asking the elected chamber to think again by requiring it to vote once more before a contentious bill could become law. This 'house' is justified by its capacity to raise the level of public debate. Because its members attain their positions by processes different from those which select representatives to the elected chamber, they would be more likely to complement and augment, rather than simply duplicate the deliberations which occur in the 'lower house'. It is composed of a combination of hereditary and life peers but on a smaller scale than the British example. The fixed number of life peers would be elected by the elected chamber for life. Such arrangements should produce a debating chamber in which the hereditary members could speak freely because of the relative economic independent which their tied lands would give them. For the same reason, they could afford the time and the money that is frequently necessary to engage in the sort of independence research which might be of public service. Since the life peers should include members with long and proven records of distinguished public service, their speeches and reports should frequently be very instructive. Therefore, in their various ways, both sorts of members should be able to enhance the *quality* of the deliberations, both of the general public and the other organs of the state which have more substantive powers.

The outline on the first page of this chapter refers to 'the prime minister and the council of ministers' as being 'selected by arrangements similar' to the German "constructive vote of no confidence". The relevant sections of Germany's "Fundamental Law" are as follows:

Article 63
4) If no candidate [for Chancellor] has been elected [by a majority], ... a new ballot shall be held without delay, in which the person obtaining *the largest number of votes* [i.e. a 'plurality'] shall be elected. ... If the person elected did not obtain ... a majority, the Federal President must within seven days either appoint him or dissolve the Bundestag.

Article 67 (Vote of no confidence).
1) The Bundestag can express its lack of confidence in the Federal Chancellor only by electing a successor with the majority of its members and by requesting the Federal President to dismiss the Federal Chancellor. The Federal President must comply with the request and appoint the person elected.
2) Forty-eight hours must elapse between the motion and the election.

Article 68 (Vote of confidence - Dissolution of the Bundestag).
1) If a motion of the Federal Chancellor for a vote of confidence is not assented to by the majority of the members of the Bundestag, the Federal President may, upon the proposal of the Federal Chancellor, dissolve the Bundestag within twenty-one days. The right to dissolve shall lapse as soon as the Bundestag with the majority of its members elects another Federal Chancellor.
2) Forty-eight hours must elapse between the motion and the vote thereon." [1]

Thus, the model constitution's current holder of the prerogatives has no discretion with regard to the appointment of the prime minister as long as a working majority exists in the elected assembly. It also gives him or her the same discretion to appoint a prime minister, supported only by a plurality, in the absence of a working majority. However, democratic monarchy also gives even greater discretion in this absence: the current holder of the prerogative could instead decide to appoint, as prime minister, anyone he or she judges will be more conducive to the lawful unity of the state. For the same reason, the model's holder of the prerogative has the additional discretion to replace or to sustain an existing prime minister if he or she has since failed a constructive vote of no confidence by a plurality. In this way, the model provides for the establishment of a 'working plurality' in the absence of a 'working majority'. The former is dependent on the discretion of the current holder of the prerogative powers while the latter is not.

Finally, we must briefly describe the system of 'associational proportional representation' (A.P.R.) [2] by which the normally sovereign assembly is elected. This system has no close historical precedent, even though it will be seen to incorporate the better features of those that have been used.[3] Nor does any other political theorist suggest a close approximation to it. Rather, it could be characterised as a modification of J.S. Mill's plan [4] in the light of an imaginative reconstruction of Hegel's representation for "corporations".[5]

Firstly, associational proportional representation (A.P.R.) is based on universal adult suffrage. It organizes the general elections which must occur at least every five years. Under this system, individual adults have the annual right to register their preference to channel their general election votes through any one of a wide range of *voluntary* associations. These associations would themselves have had previously to registered their own desire to be represented directly in the elected chamber. Thus, a voluntary association would automatically become an

(1) S.E. Finer, ed., *Five Constitutions,* Brighton, The Harvester Press, 1979, pp.218-220.
(2) Wilson's characterisation of the current British single member electoral system as "iniquitous" (Ibid., p.191.6), might be taken as an indication that he would be favourably disposed toward A.P.R.
(3) E.g. the 'party list' system (Holland, Denmark, Ireland and Israel) and 'two vote' system (Germany) systems.
(4) Mill's scheme adopted Hare's plan which suggested the application of a variety of what we now call "the Single Transferable Vote" (STV) system to the whole of Britain. Electors living in one constituency were to be allowed to vote for candidates in other constituencies; "Representative Government", *Utilitarianism; Liberty; Representative Government,* Everyman's Library, London 1962, pp.261-8.
(5) See *Chapter Ten.*

'electoral association' and have the right to send at least one deputy to the elected house as long as a sufficient number of citizens, country wide, had also declared their preference to vote through that association. The minimum quota for such representation would be calculated by dividing the number of registered voters by the number of seats in the elected chamber.

Whether the society was dominated by what Marx called a "capitalistic mode of production" or by a "communistic mode of production",[1] it would still contain an extensive range of interests based on geographical proximity, of identities based on common occupational concerns, and of groups based on common political beliefs. Some of the voluntary associations which would tend to grow from these various common interests, identities and beliefs could thus become 'electoral associations'.

It is argued that both capitalist and communist societies would be strengthened by A.P.R.[2] Thus, the lists of electoral associations which might emerge in either sort of modern society could well include geographical constituencies (e.g. those organized as municipal or as county councils), trade unions, commercial associations, self-managing sectors of production, communes, and political parties. Proportionality would be provided in A.P.R. by giving to each elected deputy the voting power in the 'elected chamber' equal to the number of citizens who had actually cast their ballots within his or her association on election day. Thus, the total voting power present in the elected chamber would be *exactly* equal to the number of citizens who had in fact voted in the country. In order both to fix the total number of deputies and to avoid any one deputy having vastly more voting power than another member, associations which had 1½ or more of the minimum quota of registered voters would have the right to send more than one deputy to the lower house. Those with 2, 3, 4 or X times the quota would send 2, 3, 4 or X deputies. Each such deputy would have a voting power in the chamber equal to 1/2, 1/3, 1/4, or 1/X of the votes cast through his or her association.

This electoral system, more than others, would foster 'rational living' because it would encourage *more people* to register, vote, and to participate more widely in the collective decision-making processes of their society. A.P.R. would tend to do this firstly by allowing each citizen to *choose* to cast his or her one vote through the association which he or she feels, for whatever reason, best represents his or her interests or ideals. Secondly, it would combat apathy by giving every person a good reason both to make the effort of registering and of voting because every vote would count. No vote would ever need to be wasted and every vote continues to count in every vote taken inside the elected chamber. Each vote might not only help determine who is elected but would automatically increase the voting power of the deputy(s) from the association of the citizen's choice. It would assist the development of patriotism or general social responsibility in the citizenry, one condition for the growth of the widest possible political rationality. According to Hegel, these feelings will tend to emerge from the more limited but spontaneously existing group identities which already have organized themselves into voluntary associations.[3] It provides (like the existing 'first past the post' systems) for the most effective accounting of deputies to their electorates. This is facilitated by the fact that the lists of those registered to vote through each association would be a matter of public record. The principle of the secret ballot would be retained, however, by designing all ballot papers so that any voter could easily and secretly choose to add his or her vote to the weight in the assembly of an electoral association (and candidate) other than the one within which he or she is publicly registered.

The model adds to this high degree of accountability by providing a 'recall' system similar to those which already exist in some of the states of the U.S.A. Thus, voters within a given electoral association would themselves have the possibility of triggering off a new election for their own deputy(s). All that would be required is that a designated percentage (e.g. 10%) of voters sign the official petition to this effect. These provisions seek to complete the thoroughly *democratic* character of the model constitution. They help to extend as much as possible the institutional scope for all people effectively to participate in the collective decision-making processes of their society.

Democracy is one of the implications of the relevant formulation of the prime moral prescription already asserted in the *Introduction,* namely, 'the best constitution will tend to maximize the quality and quantity of free, rational living in the world'. The *quantity* of actualized rationality is increased as more people have the institutional opportunity effectively to become involved in the deliberative processes which have the constitutional authority either to impose or to remove binding obligations on all citizens. Shortly, it will be explained how the *quality* of that rationality is encouraged by the institutional structure of the model itself.

(1) See *Chapter Five.* (2) See *Chapter Ten.* (3) Ibid.

However, the *quantity* is fostered especially by *democratic* monarchy's A.P.R. and recall systems. They help to organize 'popular sovereignty' within a maximally failsafe constitutional framework. They help to guarantee that the model's preference for working majority rule will itself provide a ladder for the majority of the whole population effectively and rationally to rule themselves. In spite of these hopes, however, one cannot exclude the possibility that a full actualization of the model on paper might still only become the vehicle by which a rational minority rules the rest who have currently proven themselves incapable of self-rule. Still, rule by a rational minority would be best in either of the following two circumstances:
1) when the articulated mass of the people momentarily fails to achieve, or fails to renew, their potentiality for rational self-rule, or,
2) if, the majority of the population continuously proves itself either disinclined or unable rationally to rule itself, even when the ideal social and political conditions are present.

The model constitution offers the most favourable institutional framework for the materialization of rational rule, whether with the explicit support of a majority of the citizenry or by a benevolent minority in the face of popular indifference or antagonism. Either way, the model would offer the best framework for testing, with minimal risk, the extent to which humankind has or does not have the deep and consistent capacity for rational self-rule.

The way in which the shape of democratic monarchy's own institutions both reflects the structure of rational thinking and thus tends to enhance the rational *quality* of political participation will be fully elaborated in later chapters. Nevertheless, an early glimpse of this argument is offered,
1) firstly, by the suggestion that the model's institutions are arranged so the three fundamental 'functions' of state (law-giving, particularizing, and uniting) are jointly yet differentially performed by the the three main 'organs' of the state: assembly, government (the council of ministers supervising the bureaucracy, and the system of courts headed by the supreme court), and the monarch;
2) secondly, by asserting that 'rational' thinking and acting involves making one's *particular* choices conform to *general* principle so that they form a consistent or *unified* whole, and
3) thirdly, by noting that the above functions and organs embody these same conceptual *moments* as follows:

```
MOMENTS              FUNCTIONS             ORGANS
generality           law-giving            assembly
particularity        particularizing       government
unity                uniting               monarch
```

The greater representativeness and large numbers in the assembly help to make it better able than the other two organs to arrive at truly *general* conclusions (laws) which are also rational. However, these same numbers make it impossible for it to deal with all of the particular decisions which a state must make. These same numbers make it less likely always to achieve the unity which is a condition of a rational society. This is why the *particularizing* decisions are sensibly left to the bureaucratic and judicial hierarchies, supervised as they are, by relatively small groups: the (executive) council of ministers and the supreme court, respectively. The key difference between these two agencies of particularization is that,
a) a 'judge' requires someone else first to request him to decide some dispute according to existing law before he or she can act, while
b) an 'executive' can act entirely on his or her own initiative, both to apply existing laws or to solve perceived problems according to his or her interpretation of the 'spirit' of the law but not literally covered by existing laws.

Executive decisions are only under the general supervision of the assembly. For example, if it does not like the decisions being taken by the current council of ministers, it cannot make them itself but can only elect a new prime minister. Of course, both separately and together, the assembly and executive council will seek to establish or re-establish a *unity* to their own liking, but again, their numbers make these organs less able than the one designated member of the 'state prerogative council' to guarantee unity. It has already been explained how the monarch's unique qualities strengthen the uniting function of this council.

The remaining chapters will elaborate on the argument begun here. They will attempt to show how 20th Century Platonists, Kantians, Hegelians and Marxians might, by extending the logic of their own positions, be driven to endorse democratic monarchy as their own general, prescriptive guide. The next chapter will test the model against the the cases that can be made for two different types of republican constitution.

# Chapter Two:
## COMMON REPUBLICAN ARGUMENTS

While the previous chapter sought simply to present the model constitution, this chapter will defend it against various common republican arguments. Before reading Hegel, I naively supposed that such attacks would defeat every sort of monarchy but this chapter will show why every republican constitution is inherently inferior to democratic monarchy. The most obvious implication of the model is that the head of state should not be elected. While the previous chapter began the explanation of why the head of state should be hereditary, the second part of this chapter hopes to confirm this argument with a feature by feature comparison of the advantages and disadvantages of the two types of head.

Before turning to that comparison, however, it will be helpful to distinguish between two types of republican constitution: 'congressional' (after the example of the U.S.A.), and 'parliamentary' (after the examples of Germany and Italy).[1] The first part of this chapter assesses the faults and virtues of these two kinds of republican constitution and finds that the *parliamentary* form (even with an elected head of state) is inherently better than the *congressional* form. So, the second-best parliamentary constitution, one in which the head of state is elected, is still better than any congressional republic organized according to the American version of the famous doctrine of 'the separation of powers'.[2] This is referred to here as 'the separation of *branches*' in order sharply to distinguish it from 'the differentiation of organs' which is incorporated into the parliamentary model. This also underlines the conclusion that the model constitution must have a parliamentary form. It will be recalled that the ideal constitution provides for a division of labour between the three *distinct* organs which nevertheless are charged *jointly* to perform the three functions. The arrangement of this 'division' and of these 'distinct' organs and functions is taken to be the only valid teaching of the 'separation of powers' doctrine.

In contrast, the American interpretation requires that there be no overlap of personnel between the three branches (legislative, executive, and judicial). More importantly, it excludes any branch from acting on its own from selecting or replacing the people who hold offices in one of the other branches. In contrast, the parliamentary form gives the elected chamber the constitutional power to elect and replace the 'chief executive council'. The other key difference between the congressional and parliamentary forms is that the latter explicitly recognizes the 'uniting function'. The paliamentary system is more rational because it distinguishes yet unites the three functions and organs in such a way as to give a people a greater institutional support for the

---

(1) The 'model' could be called a 'parliamentary monarchy' (after the Dutch or British examples).
(2) It is, of course, Montesquieu who put forward the doctrine of the 'separation of powers' in its first substantial form. However, he did not use this exact phrase, (*The Spirit of the Laws*, Hafner Press, New York, Book XI, Chapter Six. See Franz Neumann's *Introduction*, p. Lii). Democratic monarchy departs from Montesquieu's formulation at several points. The former makes cabinet government explicit while it is perhaps only implicit in Montesquieu, p.158. Thus, Montesquieu's ambiguity might allow either the reading which became the the American view or the interpretation adopted here for the model. Another relevant difference is that the model as well as Hegel's own constitutional monarchy explicitly recognizes one constitutional function additional to the three listed by Montesquieu, Kant and the U.S. Constitution (legislative, executive and judicial), namely, 'the uniting function', for which the monarch has the formal responsibility.

consistent achievement of its collective unity. A parliamentary system assists a people more than does a congressional system both to formulate and to implement its own unity over time. It fosters a unity which is,

    A> more accountable,
    B> more deliberate,
    C> more flexible, and
    D> more clearly perceived by the public.

In these ways, it tends to maximize both the quantity and the quality of free, rational living.

A> Greater *accountability* is encouraged by the fact that a majority of the members of parliament can, in effect, elect and remove the cabinet. This makes them accountable to the electorate for the executive council of the day. They cannot hide behind a constitutional impotence as can a congressional majority, criticising on the side lines of particularizing power. Parliamentarians are accountable for the council of ministers and its acts because they have the constitutional power to replace the prime minister, whether he or she had previously been elected by them or simply appointed by the holder of the prerogatives acting in an earlier absence of a working majority. The congressional form gives a constitutional excuse for each branch to complain about the others without *doing* anything about it, i.e. without being put to the test of placing its own theoretical options into practice. Some conflicts between the branches thus tend to be left to fester, each branch tending to undermine the authority of the other, no branch having to take full responsibility for the results. Each can more easily deny responsibility for any unpopular decisions, for the ineffectual (because undermined) decisions, or for the vacillation.

B> Because accountability is less clear in the congressional system, this tends to make *deliberation* less rational, i.e. more compartmentalized and less complete. The elected representatives and officials as well as the electors tend to be less inclined to tie up their considerations of *general* principles and laws with particularizations into *one* package (i.e. into a totality). Each branch tends to devote itself only to one side of deliberations and no person or branch takes the responsibility for the complex unity or lack of it. This *'separation* of branches' violates the rational demand that the organs be distinguished but not separate: "what disorganizes the unity of logical rationalness, equally disorganizes actuality." [1] The divisions between the branches, in turn, make it more difficult for the public rationally to lay blame on, or give praise to, the various officials. Therefore, the public itself will tend to be less able independently to arrive at a sufficient consensus to elect only those candidates for the branches who will work together in the way it desires. In a congressional system, the electorate also tends to find itself less able to formulate and to put into practice at election time the complex *unity* which this system makes their elected representatives less likely to achieve between elections. By contrast, the parliamentary system tends to force the elected representatives both to formulate and to implement *one package* which the electorate can assess as a whole both in the light of the past working majority's performances and of the manifestos of the competing parties.

C> The parliamentary system is more *flexible* by assisting a dynamic unity to be achieved in no matter what changing circumstances may obtain at the time. To begin with, it allows both laws and their particularizations to be quickly changed by changing the council of ministers if required. Such may be necessary as a result of changed perceptions, problems or majorities. Like the congressional system, still the parliamentary system makes provision both for the execution of established laws or for new particularizations even when there is no majority in the elected chamber. However, the congressional form relies more heavily upon the virtue, strength and skill of one practically irremovable man, the president. The parliamentary system's flexibility is more comprehensive because, while a skilful head of state can equally appoint a strong prime minister, if the head of state happens to be weak in a parliamentary constitution, he or she still has the chance of appointing a strong prime minister. A weak president in a congressional constitution does not have the same scope for openly delegating the effective leadership of the executive organ to one other person. In this way, the parliamentary system provides one more chance than does the congressional system that a clear and firm governmental

---

(1) *Enz.* III, PP541An.

unity will be secured. Over all, therefore, the parliamentary system is more flexible in guaranteeing unity, a unity which is maintained by a firm executive, whether a working majority is absent or present, and if present, whether it has changed its mind or not.

The executive of the day within the parliamentary system tends to be more authoritative because it can only briefly be challenged by a majority in the elected chamber only for a shor time before it is either again openly supported (or repaced) by a majority (or supported or replaced by a plurality with the agreement of the current holder of the prerogatives). In contrast, a president's authority in the congressional form can be diminished over an extended period of time by the continued opposition of a congressional majority, a conflict which may not be removed until the next fixed election or even longer, or until the completion of a long court case, or until the completion of a long impeachment procedure. Such a paralysis may prevent a society from escaping serious or fatal injuries. Such a stalemate is structurally prevented by the parliamentary system. While a long period of opposition between the *branches* is not unusual within the congressional systems, it is impossible between the corresponding *organs* of a parliamentary constitution. Lengthy conflict may sufficiently diminish the authority of the branches concerned so that a people fails to select its own deliberative unity. Such conflict may make each branch vacillate within its own sphere, and if it acts, its authority may be undermined by the opposition of another branch so that its action is either ineffective or counter productive. Again, this may result in that people falling victim to events which no one intended and for which no branch can be held accountable. This catalogue of eventualities exposes the possibility that the congressional form may hinder rather than aid a people's deliberative political life. The parliamentary constitution reduces the chance that a people will suffer such a fate by providing an authoritative yet accountable executive in a much wider range of circumstances.

D> The lack of stalemate between the organs has the additional advantage that the *public* will more easily be able to *perceive* what has and what has not been the result of the working majority's and its executive's intentions. If they have no policy, this will not be as easily disguised as it can be in the congressional form where an opposing branch can be blamed by the president for his or her own failure to implement a policy which he or she only insincerely espouses. If the executive has a genuine policy, this and the degree to which it has succeeded in particularizing that policy, will be more easily seen in the parliamentary form. If this policy and particularization have established a unity rather than a self-contradictory multiplicity, this also will be more plainly seen by the public. This clarity should assist all concerned to apportion praise or blame accurately. If the existing executive has succeeded in particularizing a clear unity, then all citizens are able to decide more easily whether they wish to support it or replace it at election time. In this way, the parliamentary, more than the congressional constitution, assists a people consistently to achieve its own unity - knowingly, flexibly, deliberately, and accountably. Thus, the parliamentary form is more rational. It gives greater institutional support for the maximization of the quality and quantity of free, rational living.

While the parliamentary form encourages this, it does not depend as much as does the congressional form for its survival on rationality being the ever present quality of all those who have been elected, let alone of most of the electorate. If all judges, congressmen and the president had the ability and commitment to reconcile their differences with others by rational deliberation, it is assumed here that the congressional constitution would also function without any lengthy opposition between the branches. Given such consistent and widespread rationality, a people would find little difficulty in consistently choosing its own unity even through the less rational congressional form. However, to the extent that this rationality is not present, there will be conflict and the consequent degrees if irresponsibility, lack of deliberation, inflexibility and clouded public sight, perhaps leading to the very destruction of a state and its constitution. The parliamentary constitution is not as vulnerable to this because it is flexible enough to secure a more authoritative and accountable executive council even when initially or temporarily there is insufficient practical rationality among the elected representatives to allow them to form a working majority. Because its cabinet tends to particularize an accountable, deliberate and clearly known unity, the parliamentary form also encourages the more extensive participation of an expanding public rationality if and when it develops. The parliamentary form complements such participation in proportion to its real growth among its officials, representatives, associations, and electors.

If the case has now been made that a parliamentary republic is more rational than a congressional republic, next we can turn to the more obvious question posed by this work: 'Within a parliamentary constitution, is an hereditary head of state more rational than an elected head?' However, before comparing the flaws and virtues of these two, it will be useful to formulate what republicans commonly say about this issue:

> 'Royal inbreeding makes the birth of mentally handicapped heirs more likely than are such births in the population at large. In any case, an elective process eliminates imbeciles and, moreover, guarantees that the head of state will be one of the most seasoned and skilful politicians with a proven record of public service. Election guarantees both a head of state's competence and commitment to parliamentary democracy. Also, a republican constitution makes provision for the removal of senile or otherwise dangerously incompetent or dangerously anti-democratic heads of state.'

Some of the points raised by this criticism of monarchy will be discussed in the following sections, but now it can be made clear that the model's constitutional monarchy both does not restrict royals to the marriage of royals, and that it is equal to the best republic in its provision for replacing dangerous heads of state.

The model constitution provides for the impeachment and replacement of a monarch in a way similar to that for the removal of an existing governor general outlined in the previous chapter. Firstly, like every other state official, they can be removed from office by being convicted in court (in the supreme court in this case) for having violated his or her office as defined either by the model constitution or by laws which conform to that constitution. It will be recalled that the governor general can be removed for any reason by a 2/3rds majority of the elected assembly, a deputy having already been elected and ready to take over. The principle of the 'constructive vote of no confidence' also applies to the removal and replacement of the monarch. The procedure would begin by a 50%+1 majority vote in the assembly immediately to suspend and replace the monarch for no more than two months. However, suspension would be transformed into removal upon the agreement of a referendum held within this time. Both the assembly's vote and that of the public would have to be *constructive* in that the person who would assume the monarch's functions would have to be named at the same time. This person would take over temporarily during the period of the two months suspension but permanently if confirmed by the referendum.[1] In order maximally to retain the hereditary character of the head of state, the assembly should select a replacement judged by the assembly to be suitable and considered in the following order:

1) firstly, the next heir from the existing royal family,
2) secondly, a person from a different royal family, or
3) finally, anyone else.

If there appears to be a suitable heir from the same royal family but he or she is not yet old enough to assume the functions of the head of state, a suitable 'regent' should similarly be chosen,

a) firstly, from the existing royal family,
b) secondly, from the 'state prerogative council', each member being considered in the order of his or her priority in the council, or
c) finally, anyone else.

The previous chapter outlined the argument both for the figurehead and prerogative roles of the hereditary head of state. His succession was said best to alert a people to its own lower possibility by reminding them that if they do not rule themselves rationally, they risk being ruled by non-reason. This non-verbal reminder stems from his or her non-elective succession, resulting as it does from natural (or non-rational) processes which do not depend on self-consciously rational determinations. Thus, a monarch personifies the truth that if a people fails to attain its higher potentiality of deliberative self-rule, then one of its lower potentialities will be actualized. Non-rational or even anti-rational subjectivity will rule if rational subjectivity does not. An elected head of state could never as clearly signal this danger. On the contrary, his very election would tend to obscure a people's sight of this residual, if not present, threat to democracy. The monarch dramatises this danger at the same time as symbolising the aspiration for a *unity* of *general* and *particular* decisions which is so vital if a society is to thrive. These are the two sides of his figurehead role. Just as the deliberative subjectivity of a people is based upon their natural subjectivity, so, only a monarch who consistently submits to the deliberations of the working majority and its council of ministers most transparently personifies both the deliberative and the natural subjectivities which alone can repeatedly secure the developing unity of a society. A constitutionally limited and hereditary head of state most

---

(1) The model's procedure for the removal of a supreme court judge is exactly the same as for the monarch.

transparently represents the appropriate relation between *nature* and reason in the political world. This is why a monarch intrinsically makes a better figurehead than any elected official: president, governor general, speaker, or chairperson.

In the absence of a working majority, the 'caretaking' role of the monarch, in the context of the 'state prerogative council', helps to secure the institutions which provide both the opportunity for the citizenry to organize themselves into electoral associations and for their deputies to organize themselves into a new working majority. Both of these are required if the rational structure is to be filled with democratic life. As caretaker, the head of state's task is to foster the emergence or re-emergence of democratic self-rule. In order to give the minority factions time to re-think, to re-negotiate, and to re-form a working majority, he or she "holds the ring". Thus, a collective unity may be assisted to revive in spite of the divisiveness which is currently dominant. He or she is protecting the existing parliamentary institutions. In both roles, the model's monarch is claimed to be an integral part of the model constitution which would contain the best 'carrots' and 'sticks' to assist a people to maximize their rational living. The monarch's non-elective character would best alert all concerned that the state of affairs which had called his or her caretaking role into existence was a less rational actuality than would be rule by an executive elected by a working majority. Thus, his or her role would be more clearly seen as second-best, as a last resort, or as a failsafe, rather than as a satisfactory substitute for working majority rule. This awareness should help to spur a divided society to construct or reconstruct a democratic unity which would again confine the monarch to his or her figurehead role. In contrast, an elected head of state's caretaking role would less obviously be 'second-best'. His elective legitimacy is more likely to tempt a president to subvert the parliamentary institutions. He would be more encouraged to complete with, rather than submit to the wider deliberative unity which could be led later by a new working majority's prime minister. In similar circumstances, we are more assured that the model's governor general is less likely to be the sort of person who would want to subvert the democratic constitution. This greater confidence is suggested by the fact that at least 2/3rds of the representatives of his or her fellow citizens would have implicitly expressed their own confidence in this regard. While the 'speaker' may only have had the support of 50% + 1 of the elected house, he or she would initially have been elected and sustained in office because of his or her commitment to parliamentary sovereignty and known capacity to act impartially and fairly as between the parties in the house. Here, 'president' refers only to a head of state who is elected by a system which requires the victor to receive at least 50% + 1 of the votes on the first ballot (or, if this proves impossible, to receive either a majority or a plurality on a later ballot), either of the voting electorate as a whole or of the members of the elected chamber. It should be noted that any advantages their would be in having such a president who was elected on the first ballot exercise the prerogatives, have already been integrated into the model constitution by its giving priority over the monarch to the 'governor general' and the 'speaker' and their deputies in the 'state prerogative council'. By the same token, the argument of the previous chapter for giving priority to the monarch over the 'chairperson' would apply equally to the 'president' who had won only as a result of a later ballot.

Now that the inherent superiority of a monarch over a second or later ballot president in the performance of the caretaking role has been suggested, it remains to offer a more systematic comparison of the two kinds of head on this score. Thus, it will be contended that a monarch is better than a president on five counts, inferior on none. The caretaking role requires a head of state to have at least one key quality which the purely figurehead role does not demand. He must have the skill to select a good prime minister. In the figurehead role, he need only sign his name to what others have already decided. In the caretaker role, however, the holder of the prerogatives is most importantly charged to foster the return of majoritarian parliamentary rule. In order best to do this, he must provide a clear and firm executive council by appointing a prime minister who has a strong personality, who has great practical political skill, and who is committed to the earliest possible return of working majority rule. A council of ministers led by such a prime minister will tend to provide the clear lead which will not only tend to preserve the existing democratic institutions but will provide a focal point in support of which, or against which, a new working majority and loyal opposition can most easily form themselves.

The comparison of the monarch and the 'president' (who might only have been elected on a second or subsequent ballot) will be organized by the answers to five questions: *logically,* which head is more likely,

1> to exist at all, let alone have a strong power base in the face of the factional divisions?
2> to alert the citizenry and their representatives to the fact of their current failure to have achieved enduring. working majority rule?
3> to act in such a way as not to inflame the current minority factionalism?
4> to appoint a prime minister who is committed to parliamentary democracy? and
5> to appoint a prime minister with the requisite political skill?

1> An hereditary head is more likely to be available to perform the caretaking role. Even when a president is available, his currently suspected or demonstrated minority status would tend to make him 'a lame duck'. From what I have already said, it is clear that hereditary succession, being independent of the contingent achievement of majorities or pluralities, offers a greater guarantee that there will actually be a holder of the prerogatives in office to perform the caretaking role when this is required. In a parliamentary republic, this could be placed in serious doubt, especially if the majority party happened to collapse just before a presidential election. This danger would be partially removed, at least in theory, by the best republican constitution which would provide for the election of a plurality head when no candidate achieves an overall majority. However, in such a case, the new president would have been publicly shown to be opposed by a 'segmented majority' [1] and supported only by a defined faction or minority. This demonstration is hardly likely to help him to be received by the elements that composed the segmented majority as a 'caretaker', i.e. as an impartial arbiter, preserving the democratic constitution for the benefit of all. The effect would be similar even if he had been elected by a clear majority well before the collapse of the majority in the elected assembly. This very collapse could fuel the doubt that his majority had also dissolved. Whether the existing president had been shown to be opposed by a segmented majority or whether there was only good reason to doubt the current existence of his majority support, he would be weakened, hardly the best figure to perform the caretaking role.

2> An hereditary caretaker head is a more dramatic demonstration of a people's current failure to achieve parliamentary self-rule. This has already been explained.

3> An hereditary caretaker head is more likely to be perceived by each of the warring factions as impartial. His hereditary rise to the throne allows him more easily to be seen as independent of the factional struggle which destroyed the majority in the elected chamber. Therefore, he is less likely to be seen as unfairly favouring one faction over the others. Each party will be more inclined to look upon him as an impartial arbiter. They will tend to have more confidence that he or she will allow them an equal constitutional chance to achieve their aims, by making new party alliances or by gaining the necessary electoral support. Such perceptions would foster the attitude of a 'loyal opposition' which is so important if democratic self-rule is again to be enjoyed. In contrast to these implications of hereditary succession, the electoral succession of a president has forced him publicly to align himself throughout his career with one set of interests rather than with others. This may lead opposing parties to despair of a constitutional path for the achievement of their aims. A president is thus less likely to be able to 'hold the ring' peacefully because his past is more likely to spark off civic disorder.

4> They are equally likely or unlikely to appoint a prime minister who favours the earliest possible return to parliamentary rule. However, a monarch would inherently find it more difficult to disguise any attempt on his part to frustrate its return. The answers to questions four and five depend on our answer to the question, 'which head is himself more likely both to be committed to parliamentary democracy and to be politically skilful?' While both heads would seem equally likely (or unlikely) to be committed to the earliest possible return to parliamentary rule because both have lived within the same society, the non-election of a monarch would make it more difficult

---

(1) A majority composed of disparate factions which have not agreed on one candidate to represent them all.

for him than a president to disguise any attempt which he might nevertheless make to frustrate or subvert its return. His rule would be more readily seen by the public as being a 'last resort' while a president's rule, because he is elected, might appear to be a possible or fully adequate *substitute* for the elected rule by a parliamentary majority and its prime minister. This perception would tend to increase a president's temptation openly or covertly to replace the parliamentary institutions either with those of a congressional republic or those of a dictatorial 'plebiscitary democracy'.

5> They are equally likely or unlikely to appoint a prime minister with the requisite political skill because each head is equally likely or unlikely,
   a) to be without mental incapacity,
   b) to have a beneficially strong personality, and
   c) to have the requisite political education and experience.

5a> While either head of state is equally likely or unlikely to suffer from mental illness, it can be argued logically that royal heirs would be more likely to be feeble minded and presidents more likely to be senile. The risk of either disability occurring would seem to be extremely small but the most rational constitution must plan for every foreseeable contingency. It is possible for a feeble minded heir to succeed to the throne because an otherwise competent monarch might nevertheless not have the heart to take the requisite steps effectively to deny the throne to his or her loved but feeble-minded child. Of course, electors would be much more likely to ignore any feeble-minded candidate for the presidency. A sitting president, however, would be more likely to become senile because of the much higher average age of presidents. Older monarchs would tend equally to be subject to this disease. However, the probable existence of a wider royal family and of an eligible heir would seem to make it easier either for the senile monarch to be persuaded to abdicate or for the succession of the heir to be quietly engineered by others. This might be done by the royal family alone or in consultation with the other organs of state in spite of an incapacitated monarch's refusal to cooperate. It must be remembered that the formal removal and replacement procedure already outline could probably not be used assuming, as we are here, the absence of a working majority. While the best republican constitution would also designate a line of succession in cases of emergency, and while the president's own family and friends might similarly be able to persuade an incapacitated president to resign, a royal family would tend to provide a larger number of loving yet authoritative and disinterested persuaders who would tend also to have more scope for instituting the succession less controversially and divisively even when it is against the reigning head's will. Because of the lack of a family connection, those next in line for the presidency would be more subject to the charge of personal power seeking.

These points lead to the conclusion that a monarchy has a marginally better chance of removing a dangerously abnormal head of state in the absence of a working majority and thus has a better chance of having a better caretaker head. This follows not because it was found less likely that a monarch might be dangerously incapacitated but because a royal family's replacement of such a monarch, either with his heir or with another member of the family, would be both more likely to succeed and less likely to inflame the minority factionalism in the elected assembly and population. This second point is confirmed by the recollection that each official in line for the presidency (e.g. a vice-president) would tend, more than an heir, to be associated with one of the contending factions. Therefore, the elevation of any one of these officials to the presidency would be more likely to be interpreted by opposing factions as a key battle lost which would now require them to carry on their struggle either outside of, or in opposition to, the existing constitution. Of course, the other perception of the replacement of the president as being the result of someone's successful scheme to gain personal power would have a similar destabilizing effect. In contrast, the royal family's effectual making of a new monarch would tend to occur and would be more likely to be seen as occurring independently of the factional struggles. If so, all parties would be more likely to accept the authority of the new monarch as a caretaker head of state and would thus be more likely to accept the authority both of the prime minister and of the executive council which he or she would appoint.

5b> While both might have a beneficially strong personality, a monarch would be less able to disguise the perversion of his strength when acting to subvert the return of representative government. If the head has a strong personality himself and is committed to representative democracy in addition to having suitable formal education and experience, then he is likely to see the need for appointing a similar person to be the caretaker prime minister. An hereditary and an elected head would seem to have an equal chance of having or not having such a strong personality. However, if these skills were directed against, rather than to assist the re-emergence of working majority rule, as argued in answer to the first question posed above, the strong monarch inherently would be less able to disguise this than a strong president.

5c> Neither caretaker head is likely to be better on the basis of their somewhat different sorts of political education and experience. The very process which produces an elected head would tend to make him a master at *competitive* political practices. If these were the only skills required of a caretaker head, the president would easily be seen to be the best. In this case, the contrast would seem especially strong if we were to compare,
   1) the scant political knowledge and skill of a monarch who was twenty years old and who had just succeeded to the throne, to
   2) the richer knowledge and skill of an elected head of state who was sixty years old and had himself been a prime minister.

However, such a presidential advantage could be balanced by the possibly greater caretaking skill which a monarch might have in arbitrating, reconciling or mediating. These qualities would be cultivate by the monarch's greater average number of years of actually performing the functions of a head of state. This calculation follows from the probability that individual monarchs would tend to reign longer than individual presidents can hold office. A president, when elected, is not likely to be as young as an heir. For monarchy, this advantage might be increase by the fact that the future role of an heir would be quite well known from the time of his or her birth. Both this fore-knowledge itself, and the appropriate preparatory formal education which this fore-knowledge would recommend for an heir, may act better to prepare a monarch for the caretaking role than might the school of competitive politics necessarily attended by a president. It might even be argued, that the constant factional struggle which a president, as a successful party politician has had to engage in, might make it more difficult for him to delegate effective political power to another person: a prime minister.

Thus, the arguments for the greater political education and experience of either of the two sorts of head seem to me to be evenly balanced. I see no way of determining whether the life time of competitive political practice which the president may bring to his office is more or less use than the early specialized education and 'on the job experience' which a monarch may bring to the handling of crises. Therefore, if the whole argument between the elected and the hereditary heads hinged on this issue alone, a draw would have to be declare. However, the findings with regard to the first four questions which have already tipped the scales heavily in favour of democratic monarchy cannot be altered by the addition of equal weights to each side on this last account. Moreover, it should be recalled that the model constitution's 'state prerogative council' has already incorporated the advantages both of election and of heredity with regard to exercises of the caretaking role.

With this more detailed *comparative* [1] testing of parliamentary monarchy against various republican constitutions, we have completed the more descriptive and practical stage of the argument. The remaining chapters will develop and test the more philosophical foundations for the model constitution. These will be introduced in the next chapter through the eyes of Plato.

(1) *Chapter Six* will explain that 'comparative tests' are integral to the search for 'philosophical necessity'.

## Chapter Three:
## FROM PLATO'S REPUBLIC
## TO DEMOCRATIC MONARCHY

Plato's *Republic* provides us with a familiar vantage point from which to begin to consider the philosophical underpinnings of democratic monarchy. It will supply a heuristic spring board for appreciating these. As already implied, I will attempt to stretch or pull Plato's republican argument until any twentieth century Platonist sees how he might also be driven to support democratic monarchy by the inner logic of his own philosophy. Again, I do not assume that my interpretations and reconstructions of Plato, will be easily seen by all as unchallengable. Plato's words are too incomplete and ambiguous to allow such an expectation.

A philosophical debate is possible only on the assumption that we as rational beings may be able to find truth and wisdom. It is because this is the great enterprise to which Plato directs us [1] that an examination of his arguments will offer some preliminary clarifications of this work's central concerns and terms. I take Plato's "dialectic" to provide us with an approximate definition of human 'rationality' and thus the criterion of what 'rational living' means. Its nature will be discussed shortly but first its relation to our theme must be clarified. The suggestion that democratic monarchy is rational means that this constitution best supports both the search for wisdom by 'dialectical reasoning' and the lives which follow the moral precepts discovered by this process. Democratic monarchy plans best for the fostering of free, rational living in a society,

1) whether no people or *few* can be relied upon to be dialecticians (philosophers) in anything like Plato's sense and, therefore, trusted to rule; or
2) whether *most* if not all people can attain the political essentials of such philosophical wisdom and, thus, can be trusted to govern themselves democratically.[2]

Democratic monarchy would best foster rational living in the different conditions which might obtain: when no, few, many or all people have the innate potentiality to become philosophers in Plato's sense. This proposition will progressively be elaborated but I can say now that, if we assume, as a Platonist must, that the rational search for wisdom and truth is possible, we are at the same time unable to dismiss out of hand that one (at least the one making this assumption), few, many or all may be capable of ruling rationally.

In contrast to Hegel's "dialectic" which is primarily conceptual and Marx's which is primarily historical in execution, Plato's "dialectic" refers to a method of enquiry. Plato distinguishes this method from the deductive reasoning that is required in the mathematical studies and which his potential rulers must practice between the ages of 20 and 30 (arithmetic, plane and solid geometry, harmonics, and astronomy). With these disciplines, one must uncritically start with axioms and definitions and then proceed to deduce various theorems or conclusions. In contrast, dialectic is the process by which one can lay bare and examine the possible axioms and definitions of any such

---

(1) The Republic, 475 b + e, 485 b + c. All quotations are taken from the Desmond Lee translation of *The Republic,* Harmondsworth, Penguin, 1974. They have been checked against the other translations listed in the bibliography.
(2) It will be argued in *Chapter Five* that Marx believed that this democratic self-rule will be possible partly as a result of the vast majority of the population being educated by their struggle with the "capitalist mode of production" and then as positively fostered by their life within a "communist mode of production". It can also be argued that he derived this view partly on the basis of some implicit Platonic assumptions about the potential rationality of human nature.

theorems. It can go on to assess whether the axioms which might be discovered by this imaginative analysis are replaceable by different sets of axioms and definitions. Dialectic "climbs up the ladder" of abstraction to the "forms" and ultimately to "the form of the good".[1]

Plato's voice in *The Republic*, Socrates, surprisingly refrains from giving what he considers to be a philosophically adequate definition of "the good"[2] but he does point to it by analogies (especially the "sun" in the simile of the cave). In spite of this shortcoming, however, I will propose the following definition of the good in order to complete his argument. The "good" is 'Reason' or 'the rational'. As an adjective, "good" thus refers to all which directly or indirectly tends to maximize the quality and quantity of free, rational living [3] (i.e. the prime prescription here first announced in the *Introduction*). This interpretation of "good" as that which promotes 'rational living' might be seen as suggested both by "the good's" strong association with "justice" and by various other references such as the following:

> I call anything that harms or destroys a thing evil, and anything that preserves and benefits it good (608 e).
> ...what is good is not destructive, nor what is neutral (609 b).

Plato is satisfied that he has given a philosophically adequate definition of "justice" as "proper functioning". Proper functioning refers both to society and to the soul. Thus, justice is the best coordinate organization of the three social functions (producing, guarding and ruling), the three classes (producers, auxiliaries, and rulers), and the three natural types of individual. According to Plato, each individual has three motives or elements within their soul (appetitive, spiritive and rational), but only one of these dominates each type of person. Thus, in Plato's coordinate scheme, adult individuals who are dominated by the following elements are "justly" required to perform the related social function for which she or he is best suited. The soul of each type of person is represented by a different metal as follows:

| DOMINANT ELEMENT | SOCIAL FUNCTION | METAL |
|---|---|---|
| appetitive | producing | bronze & iron |
| spiritive | guarding | silver |
| rational | ruling | gold |

"Justice writ large" is thus achieved when each class is performing the function for which it is best suited. "Justice writ small" is present when each element of the soul is performing its appropriate function, i.e. when the rational element assigns to itself the task of both dialectically searching for wisdom and of limiting the other two elements to the measures of their gratification which will not disrupt the soul's harmony. The "gold souls" who become the philosopher rulers thus seek knowledge and to rule both themselves and the other two classes according to the moral precepts discovered by reason.

In line with the above suggested meaning of "good", as that which maximizes the quality and quantity of rational living, one can see how "justice" could be characterized as "the form of the good" as it applies both to individual and to collective human conduct. Thus, Plato's ideal state is seen as "ideal" because:

1) it best fosters *internal* rational life (i.e. dialectical thinking for all those whose gold natures make this possible given an appropriate education), and
2) it best encourages *outer* rational life, i.e. those behaviour patterns in the rest of the population (silver, bronze and iron) which approximate as nearly as is possible to those with philosophic natures.

In this connection, justice is the special case of "the good" which applies directly to human organization. Other applications of "the good" refer to the qualities and arrangements of nature, for example, those which provide either material or inspirational bases for the development, enjoyment and extension of human life in the light of the procedures and tentative conclusions of dialectical reasoning. Again, "the good" is that which directly or indirectly contributes to the maximization of the quality and quantity of free, rational living in the world.

---

(1) 534b.
(2) 506 d + e.
(3) This phrase will frequently be abbreviated simply to 'rational living'. This is on the understanding that 'reason', at least with freedom of the mind, is impossible.

This interpretation of Plato makes it clear that the prescription of rational living primarily seeks a world in which all potentially rational souls actualize this power by coming ultimately to organize their individual and collective lives by dialectical reasoning. Such deliberation,[1]

1) is nourished by (and therefore it must value) the varied delights of art, religion, play, and humour;
2) is dependent upon (and thus it must value) many automatic, spontaneous, habitual, and emotional qualities; and
3) is dependent upon (and therefore it must value) a vast array of elements, creatures, and structures in nature.

All these together constitute a complex network of what might be called the non-rational but spiritually and existentially necessary conditions for the actualization of rational human life. Of course, this is only to recognize the obvious point that rational living is both predated and simultaneously supported by many other natural and social realities and thus it must also involve much consideration of all those factors which are not capable of becoming self-consciously deliberative themselves and are thus not rational in a narrow or direct sense. 'Reasoning' must be concerned not only with *reasoning* but with its non-rational conditions. One of the tasks of dialectic is to identify and to re-shape, when necessary, these beings and structures so they come better to provide the ground upon which explicit rational living can flourish, e.g. agronomy.

Therefore, these non-rational beings and structures can, nevertheless, be said to be 'rational' in two *indirect* senses:

a) because they can be classified, and their laws understood by the reasoned disciplines of scientific investigation, and
b) because they serve or can be made to serve the interests of dialectical reasoning.

*Chapters Six* and *Seven* will suggest that the above indirect and direct senses of 'rational' are contained within Hegel's "Reason". He and I take Reason to be the essential core of the whole human and natural world. In Plato's proximate terms, this essential core of the world is "the good", i.e. that which alone makes order and preservation actual in the face of the "chaotic matter" (*Timaeus* and *Statesman*) of which he suggests the existent world is also composed.

The prescription that we should act so as to maximize rational living thus enjoins us to take steps to make the natural, social and political environments better if possible both to foster deliberation and activity in conformity to deliberation's tentative conclusions. It is the burden of this work to claim that democratic monarchy is the best specification of the constitutional part of such an environment, that it is the most rational constitution for modern conditions. It might seem that it is an exceptionally odd proposition even to associate Plato's philosophy with the model because of his well known dismissal of "democracy" in favour of his elitist republic (his "aristocracy"). However, in spite of these obvious differences between Plato's republic and democratic monarchy, both constitutions seek to foster and to reflect the dialectic. Nevertheless, we would be forced to agree with Plato's conclusion that philosophers *alone* should rule if the following chain of four of his implicit but doubtful empirical assumptions proved to be as unavoidable as is his prescription to serve "the good":

1) Only a *few* people both have the potential to acquire knowledge (by dialectical reasoning) and accordingly to subordinate their desires for physical gratification and social praise.
2) An *infallible* education and selection system can be devised both to discover those few and to lead them to knowledge.
3) When one has attained moral knowledge, one is not capable of acting contrary to its imperatives, i.e. an *evil* will is impossible.
4) Once one has moral knowledge, one will *consistently* display the self discipline which it enjoins and cannot unconsciously lose it either by illness or by old age.

A successful denial by us of any one of these would cast serious doubt on Plato's own political conclusions. In fact, not a single scientific or philosophical argument seems to require us to accept any one of these assumptions as they stand. Most empirical (and thus inconclusive) evidence would seem to encourage their rejection. In the face of the questionable status of these assumptions, therefore, the best constitution would plan both for those empirical circumstances which might conform to, and those which might contradict them. This is precisely the claim made for democratic monarchy. Democratic monarchy caters for the maximization of rational rule whether *all* or *no* citizens prove capable of being genuine *philosopher rulers* in Plato's sense; whether or

(1) A more complete analysis of the procedures and horizon of this 'deliberation', "dialectical reasoning", or of what 'rational' means here will be given in *Chapter Six*.

not *evil* willing is possible; and whether or not moral and political *virtue* can be *lost* once attained. While democratic monarchy encourages philosophic rule, it neither expects nor depends on it. Of course, if true philosopher rulers were to emerge for a time, at least in that respect, the community would be better off. However, it is argued here that the very structure of democratic monarchy would tend over time to foster a united package of legislative, executive and judicial decisions, even in a community without philosophers, which would approximate to those which would issue from philosopher legislators, executives and judges.

It is not sufficient simply to assert the sovereignty of "Reason" without also translating this into an operational definition of the exercise of political authority. This is what the model constitution begins to do. In particular, we have seen how it caters for our serious doubt that any ruler can be completely relied upon. In effect, it assumes that neither "philosophical" nor non-philosophical officials are wholly to be trusted - the non-philosophical ones for all the reasons which Plato gives himself. Officials who were previously found to be philosophers in Plato's sense could not be wholly relied upon because the educational and selection process might have made a *mistake* in their cases or because the official concerned might have an *evil* will, or because he might have *lost* the necessary knowledge or self-discipline. These truths argue for a constitution in which each organ of the state is constructively checkable either by another organ or by the citizens as voters. Democratic monarchy arranges for this.

Plato does not face this problem explicitly, but an imaginative and sympathetic reader [1] of *The Republic* might suggest that Plato would say that a falsely promoted or corrupted philosopher king could be demoted again by a majority vote of the other philosophers. On the other hand, a supporter of the model would argue that such judgements are better guaranteed when a different body, less dependent on the official in question, has the constitutional authority to appoint and remove him from office. In order to meet this argument, Plato would have had to suggest that his philosophers would form both the citizenry and the officials in a constitutional monarchy. Thus, a latter day Platonist would have to adopt a version of the model constitution allowing the vote only to "philosophers". However, it will be argued shortly that the our doubts about the four empirical assumptions mentioned above implies that Platonists ought to accept universal adult suffrage.

It will be recalled that the characters in *The Republic* too readily agreed to the suggestion that only a few have the potentiality to be philosophers. They agreed presumably because of their common and understandable prejudices. However, they did not explore the possible egalitarian implications of their plan agreed elsewhere for equal opportunity in education to be given to each new generation. This is even more remarkable because they also accepted that potential philosophers had been corrupted by unjust societies. They did not consider the possibility that most if not all souls might be born "gold". If so, after having benefited from the proposed scheme of education, most or all would prove themselves to be philosophers. This would suggest that philosophic and communal democracy rather than a society ruled by a small elite would logically have to be demanded by Plato's own definition of justice: each must perform the function in the circumstances for which she or he is best suited. In this event, the majority of the population (i.e. philosophers) would appreciate the necessity of their taking turns to perform the material production functions, as well as the guarding and ruling functions.

In a large enough state (which in principle could extend to the world), this philosophical majority would see that they would have to form the assembly either by a system of *election,* as in the model or by systems of rotation or lottery. However, a lottery would be defensible from a Platonic point of view only if all citizens could be guaranteed to be philosophers. However, this is one of the assumption already cast into doubt. If there is no *infallible* education and selection system, if there is the possibility of *evil* willing, and if there is the possibility that knowledge and virtue can be *lost* through illness or old age, this means that any designated philosopher may not currently be worthy of the title. If he was, he may still abuse his knowledge and rationality later or he may have lost both through illness. At the same time, some persons who did not received the title of philosopher may have deserved it and thus, intentionally or not, been denied "justice". Such doubts could not be minimized until a genuinely equal opportunity education system

---

(1) *Chapter Six* will distinguish between two types of *imaginative* readings of a text: *'lenient* interpretation' and *'improving* additions'.

for producing philosophers had existed for several generations. Human history seems not to have produced even one example of such a society, although some have been less remote from this ideal than others. In the face of such unremoved doubts, therefore, philosophers can only say that greater injustice (as defined by Plato) may be done by 'selecting' rather than automatically allowing all adults to be citizens.

The basic argument for universal adult citizenship, however, is that it registers philosophy's inherent respect for all human beings as *potentially* rational. Plato's philosopher must presume (until proven otherwise) that each person, either is, or may become a self-controlling dialectical reasoner. Each may be capable of 'rational living'. This assumption supports universal adult suffrage because such suffrage encourages rational living. Also, voting gives an additional practical point to reasoning and for enjoying the the general freedoms of speech, press and association.

If universal adult citizenship, when combined with the other arrangements of democratic monarchy, would maximally encourage rational living, it would help to fulfil Plato's own prime prescription to philosophers: to act so as to make the existent world more closely approximate to the ideal world which is ordered by "the form of the good", i.e. to go "on till he has made human nature as acceptable to God as may be".[1] This same Platonic prescription, however, has required me to criticise four of Plato's presumed empirical assumptions. Consequently, we have seen how the model constitution could be supported by the inner logic of Plato's philosophy. In addition, democratic monarchy would provide the best framework both for testing the validity of Plato's four assumptions and for coping with the reality whatever it might be. The model would encourage the maximization of rational living whether the social reality were discovered to accorded with his four empirical assumptions or not.

The next chapter will approach democratic monarchy through a consideration of Kant's philosophy.

---

(1) *Republic*, 501c.  (1) Ibid.,588 c - 589 c.

# Chapter Four:
## FROM KANT'S REPUBLICANISM TO DEMOCRATIC MONARCHY

Having already considered Plato's position as well as some of the common republican arguments against democratic monarchy, this chapter will seek especially to examine the republican theory which might be extracted from Kant. Nevertheless, it will be shown that his philosophy can be read to provide a broad support for the model. This demonstration should help any twentieth century Kantians to begin to appreciate how they might also be driven to endorse it as their own prescriptive ideal. As suggested earlier, I do not assume that all will find my interpretations and reconstructions of Kant to be obviously unchallengable. The incompleteness, complexity and prolixity of his words would make such an expectation unrealistic. While *Chapter Six* will footnote the largely compatible relation between my reading of Kant's *Critique of Pure Reason* and this work's methodological foundations, this chapter will examine how his moral and political philosophy can be seen both to provide alternative expressions of the most general prescription upon which democratic monarchy rests and of some of the specific arguments for many of the key features of that constitution.

First, the many formulations of Kant's "categorical imperative" can be read to have an implication which is the same as that of my own prime prescription: 'Act so as to promote free, rational living'. Kant's categorical imperative seeks to guide all "rational" and "autonomous" [1] beings as to how they "ought" to respond to their sense of "duty" [2] to all other rational beings. The following quotations illustrate this point:

> The concept of every rational being as one who must regard himself as legislating universal law by all his will's maxims, .... leads to another very fruitful concept...viz., that of *a kingdom of ends*.[3]
> The practical imperative will therefore be the following: Act in such a way that you treat humanity, whether in your own person or in the person of another, always at the same time as an end never simply as a means.[4]
> The achievement of the highest good in the world is the necessary object of a will determinable by the moral law.[5]
> ... therefore the supreme good (as the first condition of the highest good) is morality; and happiness, though it indeed constitutes the second element of the highest good, does so only as the morally conditioned ... consequence ....[6]
> ... metaphysics .... in dealing with reason ... treats of those elements and highest maxims which must form the basis of the very possibility of some sciences, and of the use of all. That, as mere speculation, it serves rather to prevent errors than to extend knowledge, does not detract from its value. On the contrary this gives it dignity and authority, through that censorship which secures general order and harmony, and indeed the well-being of *the scientific commonwealth*, preventing those who labour courageously and fruitfully on its behalf from losing sight of *the supreme end, the happiness of all mankind*.[7]

(1) I. Kant, *Grounding for the Metaphysics of Morals,* trans. by J.W. Ellington, Indianapolis, Hackett, 1081. p.39.
(2) I. Kant, *Critique of Practical Reason,* trans. by Lewis White Beck, Indianapolis, Bobbs-Merrill, 1956, p.130.
(3) Op. cit.,*Grounding*, p.39
(4) Ibid., p.36
(5) Op. cit., *Practical*, p.126.
(6) Ibid., p.123.
(7) I. Kant, *The Critique of Pure Reason,* translated by Norman Kemp Smith, St. Martin's Press, New York 1965, B879.

The above reference to the "world", the "kingdom of ends", "the scientific commonwealth" and "the happiness of all mankind" have some strong political implications. Also, in *The Critique of Pure Reason,* Kant explicitly writes of his ideal constitution in the sort of broad terms which could be read at least out of context, to support democratic monarchy:

> A constitution allowing **the greatest possible human freedom** in accordance with laws by which **the freedom of each is made to be consistent with that of all others** - I do not speak of the greatest happiness, for this will follow of itself - is at any rate a necessary idea, which must be taken as fundamental not only in first projecting a constitution but in all its laws.[1]

This quotation's reference to "human freedom" also suggests that my own prescription of 'maximizing rational living' can be alternatively restated as 'maximizing human freedom'. This is possible because it is the freedom of rational beings living in a community which is my concern. In this light, the most free (or rational) constitution will be made up of those standing arrangements which, more than any others, help to foster the sort of political context within which rational discourse, deliberation and behaviour can thrive and not encounter politically removable barriers.[2] Thus, by definition, 'rational living' is free and 'freedom' is living in accordance with the processes and conclusions of the 'dialectical reasoning' outlined in *Chapter Three* [3] and to be detailed in *Chapter Six*.

The above 'most free (or rational) .... standing arrangements' also define what Kant, Hegel and I mean by "right". Kant says that "justice", [4] or,

> Right is therefore the sum total of those conditions within which the will of one person can be reconciled with the will of another in accordance with a universal law of freedom
>
> ....
> Every action which by itself or by its maxim enables the freedom of each individual's will to co-exist with the freedom of everyone in accordance with universal law is right.[5]
> In its "strict" Sense, Right can also be envisaged as the Possibility of a general and reciprocal Coercion consonant with the Freedom of Everyone in accordance with Universal Laws.[6]

Kant can also be read to speak both for Hegel and for me when he stresses that we rational beings have the "unconditional" obligation to foster a rational constitution, right, or "the rights of man":

> ... both aspects, philanthropy and respect for the rights of man, are obligatory. And while the former is only a conditional duty, the latter is an **unconditional** and absolutely imperative one; anyone must first be completely sure that he has not infringed it if he wishes to enjoy the sweet sense of having acted justly.
> ... although politics in itself is a difficult art, no art is required to combine it with morality. For as soon as the two come into conflict, morality can cut through the knot which politics cannot untie.
> ... all politics must bend the knee before right ....[8]

Having suggested the place of Kant's political writings within his wider critical and moral philosophy, I can now turn to a more direct discussion of his political theory as it is presented piecemeal in a number of his separate essays. While there is no doubt that Kant is a "republican", it is not clear that this necessarily implies the rejection of all monarchies (especially not of democratic monarchy) as one might at first suppose. It is true that the more obvious implication of his words is opposed to monarchy. What he says certainly dismisses *absolute* monarchy but his words never explicitly reject what he calls a "limited monarchy" [9] (of which democratic monarchy is a variety). In fact, his phrases are ambiguous enough to allow us to construe them as support for any 'parliamentary' constitution whether it has an elected or an hereditary head of state. However, they do not allow us to read them in support of a 'congressional' constitution. We will see this in

(1) Ibid., A316, B373.
(2) By implication, *Chapter Six* will argue that the possibility of *free* evil willing by individuals or groups may constitute one sort of "political barrier" which could not be removed entirely.
(3) Kant, of course, usually uses "dialectical" in a pejorative sense.
(4) There are two translations of the parts of Kant's *Metaphysik der Sitten* (1797) which I will be quoting. H.B. Nisbet, in Hans Reiss, editor, *Kant's Political Writings*, C.U.P. 1971, uses the title of the whole work, "The Metaphysics of Morals". John Ladd, uses the title of Part I of the work, *The Metaphysical Elements of Justice* (Metaphysiche Anfangsgrunde der Rechtslehre), Bobbs-Merrill, Indianapolis 1965.
(5) Ibid., Nisbet, p.133; Ladd, p.35
(6) Ibid., Nisbet, p.134. This is the sub-title for Section E.
(7) Ibid., Nisbet, "Perpetual Peace", p.129.
(8) Ibid., p.125.
(9) Ibid., Nisbet, "The Contest of Faculties", p.187

the following two quotations. The first declares the "sovereignty" of the representative assembly (the "corps of deputies") [1] and the second, makes it clear that this appropriately includes the power to appoint and dismiss the executive or "ruler". We thus seem to have Kant, by implication at least, supporting the essentials of parliamentary government with cabinet responsibility to the representative assembly, the key difference between the 'parliamentary' and 'congressional' systems. Kant observes:

> Any true republic ... is and cannot be anything other than a representative system of the people whereby the people's rights are looked after on their behalf by deputies who represent the united will of the citizens ... [*The assembly of* these deputies, as] the united people then does not merely represent the sovereign, but actually *is the sovereign itself.*[2]
>
> The sovereign (Beherrscher) of the people (the legislator) cannot .... also be the ruler, for the ruler is subject to the law, through which he is consequently beholden to another party, i.e. the sovereign. *The sovereign may divest the ruler of his power, depose him, or reform his administration ....*[3]

That this parliamentary sovereignty must for Kant be exercised by a *majority* of the representatives in the "corps of deputies" is made clear in the passage shortly to be quoted. His justification for this also can be seen to provide a basis for *Chapter One* more specific formulation of 'working majority rule' which asserted the constitutional right of the 'working majority' in the elected chamber to prevail over any opposition that might arise from any combination of the non-elected chamber, the government (executive and judiciary), and the monarch. Kant does not fully spell out every step by which he derives majority rule from his *a priori* principles, but he presumably would argue as follows: at first sight, the principles that *all* have the potential to be rational, that the autonomy of each person must be respected, that each is to be treated as an end in himself, and that laws should be universal in form, together imply that in a republican "kingdom of ends" all decisions must be *unanimous*. Unanimity, however, would depend not just on the *potential* but on the consistent and *actual* rationality of *all*. Therefore, in the realization that not all may consistently actualize this potential, an actual rational being will consent to a constitution or "original contract" [4] which authorises majority rule to be "right" within the commonwealth. I take this to be Kant's argument behind the following:

> An entire people cannot .... be expected to reach unanimity, but only to show a majority of votes (and not even of direct votes, but simply of the votes of those delegated in a large nation to represent the people). Thus the actual principle of being content with majority decisions must be accepted unanimously and embodied in a contract; and this itself must be the ultimate basis on which a civil constitution is established.[5]

Such a majority will is the best empirical evidence that the citizenry are what Kant calls "a people of mature rational powers" [6] and have risen to something like the universal view which is required of us by Kant's first formulation of the "categorical imperative", "Act only according to that maxim whereby you can at the same time will that it should become a universal law".[7] Kant seems to be agreeing that the requirement of politics for majority rule is necessary and right as an empirical approximation of philosophy's demand for universality.

Before considering those additional details of Kant's constitutional proposals which are relevant to the question of democratic monarchy, I should recall that his constitutional arguments were only a part of his wider political thinking which also prominently included a passionate appeal for world peace. He was fully aware that this goal could not be secured in the near future and that there were many difficulties, but he hoped, nevertheless, for a "gradually expanding federation".[8] He says that this is the "one rational way in which states co-existing with other states can emerge from the lawless condition of pure warfare".[9] Kant is aware that many say that "human nature" makes such a world order impossible but in answer he writes:

> I ... cannot and will not see it as so deeply immersed in evil that practical moral reason will not triumph in the end, after many unsuccessful attempts, thereby showing that it is worthy of admiration after all. On the cosmopolitan level too, it thus remains true to say that whatever reason shows to be valid in theory, is valid in practice.[10]

(1) Ibid., "The Metaphysics of Morals", Nisbet, p.149, Ladd, p.92
(2) Ibid., Nisbet, p.163, Ladd, p.113.
(3) Ibid., Nisbet, pp.141-2; Ladd, p.82.
(4) Op. cit., Nisbet, "Theory and Practice", p.77.
(5) Ibid., p.79.
(6) Ibid., Nisbet, "The Contest of Faculties", p.187. (more fully quoted later).
(7) Op. cit., *Grounding,* p.30.
(8) Op. cit., Nisbet, "Perpetual Peace", p.105.
(9) Ibid.
(10) Op. cit., Nisbet, "Theory and Practice", p.92

Of course, Hegel ridiculed these Kantian views [1] but any detailed consideration of this controversy is beyond the scope of this thesis. Nevertheless, it may be useful both briefly to record that my sympathies are broadly on Kant's side of the argument (given that his hope is in the face of his recognition that world peace is most improbable for the foreseeable future). Also, I assert that if a world state were ever to prove achievable, democratic monarchy should provide its constitution.

These views of Kant's are exemplified in the following extract but it also makes clear that Kant sees peace as ultimately dependent on the evolution of republican constitutions. He says that "All forms of state" ought to be,

> ... based on the ideal of a constitution which is compatible with the natural rights of man, so that those who obey the law should also act as a *unified* body of legislators. And if we accordingly think of the commonwealth in terms of concepts of pure reason, it may be called a *Platonic ideal* (**respublican noumenon**), which is not an empty figment of the imagination, but the eternal norm for all civil constitutions whatsoever and a means of ending all wars. A civic society organised in conformity with it and governed by laws of freedom is an example representing it in the world of experience (**respublica phaenomenon**), and it can only be achieved by a laborious process, after innumerable wars and conflicts. But this constitution, once it has been attained as a whole, is the best qualified of all to keep out war, the destroyer of everything good. Thus it is our duty to enter into a constitution of this kind; and *in the meantime,* since it will be a considerable time before this takes place, it is the duty of *monarchs* to govern in a republican *(not a democratic)* manner, even although they may **rule autocratically.** In other words, they should treat the people in accordance with principles akin in spirit to the laws of freedom which a *people of mature rational* powers would prescribe for itself, even if the people is not literally asked for its consent.[2]

The above references to "monarchs" and "not a democratic ... manner" signal two possible implications which might seem to require us to hold that Kant could not see 'democratic monarchy' as the "ideal". First, "monarchs" are associated with "autocratic rule" which ought to "treat the people in accordance with principles akin in spirit to the laws of freedom.....even if the people is not literally asked for its consent". The more obvious implication of these phrases is that a monarch's governing "in a republican .... manner" is only a step towards the ideal. Yet this passage does not necessarily drive us to this conclusion because it does not explicitly consider the case where the monarch *must* ask the "corps of deputies" for its consent (i.e. democratic monarchy). I see no way that a Kantian could successfully resist this sort of monarchy. It would seem to conform entirely to the logic of his ideal. In fact, Kant could be read to be acknowledging just this point in a footnote starting on the previous page in which he distinguishes between an "absolute" and a "limited" monarch by saying that the latter "must first ask the people whether or not there is to be a war, and if the people say ... no ..., then there will be none".

Nevertheless, there are some other of Kant's arguments which also might very easily be read by extension to imply the rejection of any sort of monarchy even though they only explicitly criticise an hereditary nobility. These implications occur as part of his argument for the promotion of subjects and the appointment of state officials only according to individual merit. He says of the "prerogatives" of a nobility, that since, rationally,

> .... it is impossible for the universal will of the people to agree to so groundless a prerogative; the sovereign [the monarch] cannot make it valid either.
> It may be, however, that an anomaly of this sort has crept into .... government .... in past ages (as with the feudal system ...) In this case, the state can make good its mistake .... by a gradual process ... The state thus has a provisional right to allow such dignities to persist as titles until public opinion allow realises that the hierarchy of sovereign, nobility and people should give way to the more natural division of *sovereign* and *people.*[3]

While Kant uses the term "sovereign" quite unsystematically, sometimes to refer to an autocrat and at other times to refer to a ruling aristocracy, to the whole people in a democracy, or to the representative assembly in a republican constitution (as in the earlier quotation), in the above passage and in many other contexts, it seems to refer to a monarch. In fact, the last phrase in the quotation above can be plausibly read to confirm rather than to undermine the position of the monarch as the earlier part of the quotation might be read to imply. Such texts give us reason to

---

(1) See *Rechts*, PP259Z, PP324An. & Z, and PP333An.
(2) Op. cit., Nisbet, "The Contest of Faculties", p.187.
(3) "Metaphysics of Morals", Nisbet, p.153; Ladd, pp.97-98.

question whether Kant cared at all whether the head of state was hereditary or chosen according to merit. The above passage leaves us to wonder this in spite again of the seemingly strict meritocratic tone of the following words:

> ... every member of the commonwealth must be entitled to reach any degree of rank which a subject can earn through his talent, his industry and his good fortune.[1]

That Kant holds that there needs to be a "physical" or "moral" person to be the "head of state" is clear from the following quotation. However, it does not necessarily require the head of state to be one person, let alone hereditary, because Kant unfortunately used the phrase "head of state", as widely and as ambiguously as he does "sovereign":

> ... this head of state (the sovereign) is only an abstraction (representing the entire people) so long as there is no physical person to represent the highest power in the state ....[2]

The above passages confirms my conclusion that Kant's words on the question of monarchy are equivocal. While he never explicitly endorses constitutional monarchy, let alone 'democratic monarchy', neither does he ever explicitly reject constitutional monarchy as one formulation of his ideal.

While his arguments for meritocracy would seem more clearly to exclude the hereditary chamber within my 'democratic monarchy' and less clearly the institution of monarchy itself, he does not explicitly consider, and his arguments would not seem to be able to resist, the strong case for these elements of the model. At the same time, one might even argue that references like the one above to "limited monarchy" suggest that he would accept what might paradoxically be called 'republican monarchy' as one formulation of his "model"[3] constitution. This is to say, that a few of his words when added to his usual silence on these questions might be taken, if the reader is so disposed, to imply possible support for such a monarchy. At the same time, a combination of Kant's clear arguments, his ambiguity, his silences, and my conjectures about his unknowable intentions, has provided us as yet with no Kantian reasons to modify the contentions of previous chapters. In fact, it is my view that those arguments should lead a Kantian to favour a 'representative monarchy' over a 'representative republic'.

The question of whether such a 'republican monarchy' is the same as *democratic* monarchy is a second question raised by the first of the above three quoted extracts where Kant says, that "in the mean time .... it is the duty of monarchs to govern in a republican (not a democratic) manner". Kant defines "democracy" in the Rousseauian[4] sense as direct popular control, i.e. a state in which the "supreme authority" is exercised *directly* by "*all*" those who together constitute civil society".[5] However, since I use 'democracy' in the sense of a representative democracy, there seems to be only a semantic difference between a 'republican' and a 'democratic' monarchy.

Nevertheless, there is a clear difference between Kant's and my representative democracy when it comes to the definition of the electorate and the system for electing the "corps of deputies". Kant says nothing about the appropriate system of representation. He gives us no guidance on whether a 'first past the post' or some proportional representation system would be a part of his "morally superior state".[6] I take it that this silence gives us no reason to resist the strong case offered in *Chapter Two* arguing that 'associational proportional representation' (A.P.R.) would tend most to foster the maximization of both the quality and *quantity* of communal deliberations. On the question of the electorate, Kant, like Hegel[7] but unlike Plato, automatically excludes women[8] from "active citizenship".[9] Thus, Kant excludes women from the right to vote for "deputies". This thesis assumes that such a restriction of the electorate has only a cultural explanation rather than a philosophical justification and thus that no modern Kantian (or Hegelian) could sustain an opposition to women's suffrage. In addition to women, however, Kant relegates all "subjects" who are not their own "masters" to "passive citizenship". In one less than convincing explanation of what he means by 'not being one's own master', he writes about an economic dependence which forces one to allow "others to make use of him" and which supposedly results from one only having his

(1) Ibid., Nisbet, "Theory and Practice", p.75
(2) Op. cit., "The Metaphysics of Morals", Nisbet, p.161; Ladd, p.109.
(3) Ibid., "Perpetual Peace", Nisbet, p.118.
(4) *The Social Contract,* Book III, Chapter IV.
(5) Op. cit., "Perpetual Peace", Nisbet, p.100.
(6) Ibid., "Theory and Practice", p.91.
(7) See later chapters for references.
(8) Op. cit., Nisbet, "Theory and Practice", p. 78 quoted below.
(9) Ibid., "The Metaphysics of Morals", Nisbet, p.139; Ladd, p.79.

labour rather than owning a "commodity" to sell, i.e., being able only to guarantee "one's labour (prostatio)".[1] On this basis, Kant gives the following examples of those who should be denied "active citizenship": apprentices, servants, shop assistants, labourers, barbers, tithe-holders, domestic tutors, travelling blacksmiths and woodcutters. Examples of those judged to be worthy of full citizenship are the following: small and large landowners, artisans, tailors, artists, tradesmen, and wig-makers.[2]

In seeming contrast to the above lists which contain contentious and culturally bound examples, earlier, Kant had offered a less problematic formulation of his voting qualifications even though, as we have said, it excludes women:

> The only qualification required by a citizen (apart, of course, from being an adult male) is that he must be his own master (sui iuris), and must have some **property** (which can include any *skill, trade, fine art or science*) to support himself.[3]

If by "any skill" he had meant 'an ability to perform any useful service to the community' so as certainly to include those relegated in the above list to being mere "subjects", then Kant's definition of citizenship would have been much closer to that contained in democratic monarchy. However, it is because even this requirement may deny the presumption of rationality to some adults which Kant's own categorical imperative can be read to enshrine, that even this formulation may fall short also of the model's universal adult suffrage. In one respect, however, his view is perfect from the model's point of view. He does not weight the vote of each person in proportion to his "commodities", "property" or "skill" but argues for a one-citizen-one-vote system:

> ... artisans and large or small landowners are all equal, and each is entitled to one vote only. ...The number of those entitled to vote on matters of legislation must be calculated purely from the number of property owners, not from the size of their properties.[4]

It is worth recalling as well that, in line with our previous discussion of Kant's meritocratic argument, he does not, of course, see the above divisions as being hereditary and he insists that all must be allowed to earn the vote by their "ability, industry and good fortune".[5]

At the same time, Kant expressed some doubt about the possibility of administering his division between "active" and "passive" citizens justly. He admits in the footnote on the same page "that it is somewhat difficult to define the qualifications which entitle anyone to claim the status of being his own master". Indeed, it would seem so "difficult" that my model does not contain this division at all. This is not to deny, however, that Kant's words raise some valid principles. They could be taken more broadly to imply the importance of two which my political philosophy would also endorse: It is desirable both that each citizen,

1) have the power of 'rational self mastery' and that they
2) be 'economically independent' of the pressure which other individual citizens or minority groupings of citizens might attempt to exert upon them.

In line with the first principle, my own ideal, as well as presumably Kant's, would not only exclude children from voting but any 'adults' who by objective criteria could be proven to lack a required minimum of 'rational self mastery' (e.g. the feeble minded and the insane). At the same time, my own system of universal adult suffrage would accept the unavoidable probability that at least some individually unpredictable electors of whatever age may in fact vote destructively. However, I know of no reason to expect that this destructiveness would be any more than that which would tend to be perpetrated by any differently defined electorate including Kant's, made up as it was, of "landowners" and "wig-makers". What is quite certain is that in Kant's system, many actually or potentially rational "women", "apprentices" and "labourers" would correctly have a sense of injustice at being arbitrarily excluded from the community's deliberations, i.e. at being denied that they are "ends in themselves" and "co-legislators". Kant himself says that,

> ... a citizen must always be regarded as a co-legislative member of the state (i.e. not just as a means, but also as an end in himself), and he must [for example] therefore give his free consent through his representatives .... to every particular declaration of war.[6]

(1) Ibid., Nisbet, "Theory and Practice", p.78.
(2) These lists were compiled from ibid., and from op. cit., "The Metaphysics of Morals", Nisbet, p.139; Ladd, p.79.
(3) Op. cit., Nisbet, "Theory and Practice", p.78
(4) Ibid.
(5) Ibid.
(1) Op. cit., "The Metaphysics of Morals", Nisbet, p.166-7; Ladd, p.118.

In any case, we must remember that democratic monarchy (and perhaps Kant's own model constitution) does not leave a commonwealth's fate totally in the hands of voters who may be "self-seeking". Both Kant and I see our respective constitutions as ideal, partly because their structures help to channel human relations in such a way that the various destructive effects of human selfishness tend to cancel each other out. I agree with Kant's observation that,

> ... a good organisation of the state [because if] arranges .... that self-seeking energies are opposed to one another, each thereby neutralising or eliminating the destructive effects of the rest. And as far as reason is concerned, the result is the same as if man's selfish tendencies were non-existent, so that man, even if he is not morally good in himself, is nevertheless compelled to be a good citizen.[1]

The "good organisation" of democratic monarchy explicitly plans for the contingency that, for a time, the elected chamber may be dominated by merely sectional interests or the "self-seeking" which might make the formation of a working majority impossible. It does this by providing for the monarch to act in this case within the 'state prerogative council' to appoint his own prime ministers until a working majority has been re-formed.

At the same time, it should be recalled that one of the arguments for 'associational proportional representation' was that it recognizes a broad range of electoral associations within which citizens may more easily discover their wider identity. Their membership and participation in such associations and the representation which these have in the elected chamber were seen to provide a spiral staircase of broadening interests and relationships which will tend to foster the development of the alliances within and between the associations which would make majority and party government possible.[2] This is to say that democratic monarchy guards against most levels of destructive self-seeking which may come to exist in a society. Its voluntary associations and its representative system also are institutions which would tend to foster the development of sufficient levels of common interest and mature rationality so that working majority rule becomes a reality. The welfare provisions of democratic monarchy not only help to guarantee the material and educational conditions for all to become actual "rational beings", they help to secure the *one-citizen-one* vote feature. Without such a guarantee, the wealthy would tend to acquire much more political power than the poor.

It may be worth noting that some of Kant's own words might also be imaginatively construed to suggest a welfare role for his ideal state. Since Kant says that "active citizens" must not be "obliged to depend for their living (i.e. food and protection) on the offices of others (excluding the state)", he might, by implication, be at least allowing that "active citizens" could have an economic dependence *on the state*. Whether Kant had this in mind or not, my constitution would allow such a dependence. In my model, the social security and other welfare measures upon which some would find themselves having to rely, would of course, like everything else, ultimately stand or fall on the will of working majorities in the elected chamber. Nevertheless, as Kant might also desire, such arrangements would remove the occasion for individuals to become beholden to other individuals or to minority factions. Again, these provisions are part of my ideal because they would help to extend 'the *quantity* of rational living'.

Welfare measures are frequently already informally present within independent families and thus the following quotation might also be taken logically to suggest that Kant's model commonwealth could be some sort of welfare state. He says that his ideal would be characterised by a "patriotic" rather than by a "paternal" government:

> A patriotic government (regimen cititatis et patriae) means that although the state itself (civitas) treats its subjects as if they were members of *one family*, it also treats them as citizens of the state, i.e. in accordance with *laws guaranteeing their own independence*. Thus each is responsible for himself and does not depend upon the absolute will of *anyone* equal or superior to him.[3]

These possible intimations of welfare measures are quite unequivocally confirmed when Kant says that,

> ... the government is authorized to require the wealthy to provide the means of sustenance to those who are unable to provide the most necessary needs of nature for themselves.[4]

---

(1) Op. cit., Nisbet, "Perpetual Peace", p. 112.
(2) *Chapters Ten* and *Twelve* elaborate the same argument in relation to Hegel.
(3) Ibid., Nisbet, p. 141; Ladd, p. 82.
(4) Op. cit., Ladd, p. 93.

The prior suggestion that these provisions should foster "independence" is also confirmed when Kant recommended that one who is in need should be given "a certain sum of money" rather than be well taken care of by a "magnificent institution - such as a Greenwich Hospital - which is served by highly paid personnel, where his freedom is nevertheless extremely limited." [1]

So far in this chapter, I have considered,
1) the general relation between Kant's political and his wider philosophy,
2) his argument for the sovereignty of the representative assembly and for majority rule,
3) whether his republicanism necessarily rejects monarchy,
4) his definition of the electorate and the representative system, and
5) his welfare measures.

Now we can explicitly turn to the way Kant unites all these features within his "separation of powers" doctrine (legislative, executive and judicial). While Kant's doctrine can be seen as similar in some respects to that contained within democratic monarchy, even though it is much less elaborate, it is also significantly different. First, it is different by not explicitly recognizing the 'unifying function' and second, of course, in not being committed to an hereditary head of state. Kant sketches the three "powers" in the following extract. Like Hegel and most other writers as well, Kant uses "power" (Gewalt) ambiguously. On some occasions it refers to what *Chapter One* called a 'function', and at other times an 'organ'.

> Every state [ought to contain] .... three powers, i.e. the universally united will is made up of three separate persons (**trias politica**). These are the **ruling power** (or sovereignty) in the person of the legislator, the **executive power** in the person of the individual who governs in accordance with the law, and the **judicial power** (which allots to everyone what is his by law) **in the person of judge (potestas legislatoria, rectoria at iudiciaria).** They can be likened to the three propositions in a practical operation of reason: the major premise, which contains the law of the sovereign will, the minor premise which contains the command to act in accordance with the law (i.e. the principle of subsumption under the general will), and the conclusion, which contains the legal decision (the sentence) as to the rights and wrongs of each particular case.[2]

Before discussing this paragraph in some detail, I must say that while Kant does claim that this separation of powers is "necessary *a priori*" on the same page, he only hints in the above passage at how this might be so by drawing the various parallels with the propositions of a syllogism. Neither here nor elsewhere does he go on to expound its derivation from these roots systematically. However, by piecing together what he does say in support of the three powers at various places, his argument would seem to run as follows: as philosophers, we must assume *a priori* that we as humans *may* be capable of being rational and thus of seeking both to know and to abide by universal laws. On the other hand, however, we know both ourselves and probably others as frequently to be tempting to bend or to ignore such laws for personal or factional gain, especially if we think our illegality will not be detected, by others, or if detected not punished. Therefore, since all men and women must be assumed to be pulled in both of these directions, a constitution should be so constructed that the affairs of state are conducted under the public eye, leaving no state official or body (i.e. its "physical" or "moral" [1] persons) in the position of being his own or its own legislator, executor and judge. If each of these three *functions* of state is performed jointly yet primarily by each of the three *organs* (as outlined in *Chapter One*) then, not only all subjects but especially all state officials are put in the position of at least completing their activities under the scrutiny of others. Each should have a "master" as Kant puts it:

> ... if he lives among others of his own species, man is an animal who needs a master. For he certainly abuses his freedom in relation to others of his own kind. And even although, as a rational creature, he desires a law to impose limits on the freedom of all, he is still misled by his self-seeking ... into exempting himself from the law where he can. He thus requires a master to break his self-will and force him to obey a universally valid will under which everyone can be free.[4]

Appropriately, Kant extends his distrust of "man" even to philosophers. He remarks that it,

> ... is not to be expected that kings will philosophise or that philosophers will become kings; *nor is it to be desired* ..... since the possession of power inevitably corrupts the free judgement of reason. Kings ..... should not, however, force the class of philosophers to disappear or to remain silent, but should allow them to speak publicly.[3]

(1) Op. cit., Nisbet, "Perpetual Peace", p. 112.
(2) *Chapters Ten* and *Twelve* elaborate the same argument in relation to Hegel.
(3) Op. cit., "The Metaphysics of Morals", Nisbet, p. 141; ladd, p. 81.
(4) Op. cit., Nisbet, "Idea for a Universal History", p. 46.
(5) Op. cit., "Perpetual Peace", p.115. Perhaps Kant's exaggerated choice of words can be explained by his desire to deflect the censors from any thought that he might himself be seeking political power.

Quite plainly, this is an attack upon Plato's prescription which is that philosophers should be the sole legislators, executors and judges. At the same time it is a reinforcement of the above argument in favour of the separation of powers. In a constitution so ordered, even the sovereign representative *assembly* must depend on the executive and judicial organs to apply its law. A government *minister* is both constrained by the law and subject to the decisions which judges may make in disputes under the law which he may have with subjects. A *judge* is not only bound by the law but is confined only to respond to the legal initiatives which may be taken by others.

While this argument seems valid, the above extract's surprising reject the *desirability* of philosophers being kings. Nevertheless, this could perhaps make Kantian sense either,
   a) if it only expresses the truth that one would have an additional reason to mistrust the academic work of a philosopher if he had political power; or
   b) if Kant is here attempting to reassure the censors that he is just a harmless academic rather than a politician.

However, if Kant is saying what the words can more easily be taken to mean, namely, that self-consciously rational men should take no active part in performing the necessary state functions, this would contradict the whole thrust of his writing elsewhere which asserts the possibility that "pure practical reason" can and *ought* to have a shaping effect on human affairs. Equally problematic is his assertion that "the possession of power *inevitably* corrupts the free judgement of reason". He should have said that it *frequently* corrupts. This correction as well as my remark above would seem to be encouraged by his own acceptance of the possibility of a "moral politician".[1] This gloss would also be assisted by our seeing this *corruptibility* as largely removed by a system as in the model in which the organ's of state jointly yet differentially perform the three integral functions of the state. If this is so, that Kant may only have meant that the possession of absolute or constitutionally *unlimited* power, like that held by Plato's philosopher rulers, *almost certainly* corrupts. The model's differentiation of the organs would help both philosopher and non-philosopher legislators, executors and judges to resist the temptations of power.

In the passage quoted near the beginning of our discussion of the separation of powers and which outlined their character, Kant seems to be attempting to explain why he favours these three powers rather than another three. In effect, he seems to say that the structure of formal logic demands it. The legislative organ is associated with the *universal* form of the major premise in a syllogism, the executive organ is associated with the connecting of the *particular* with the general laws which characterises the minor premise, and the judicial organ is associated with the *singleness* of each conclusion it must render regarding individual disputes. In a different tract, Kant states the case for the separation of the legislative and executive organs in only somewhat different terms:

> **Republicanism** is that political principle whereby the executive power (the government) is separated from the legislative power. Despotism prevails in a state if the laws are made and arbitrarily executed by one and the same power [organ] ....
> ... any form of government which is not representative is essentially an *anomaly*, because one and the same person cannot at the same time be both the legislator and the executor of his own will, just as the general proposition in logical reasoning cannot at the same time be a secondary proposition subsuming the particular within the general.[2]

At first these explanations of Kant's three organs might seem abstract and perhaps not even relevant because, while it is true that the characters of the major premise, minor premise and conclusion can indeed be so distinguished, one person or group can in fact consider and relate all three. Syllogistic arguments do not literally require three different people to work together to complete them. If this were to be what Kant meant, therefore, it would not stand up but perhaps he meant instead to suggest that if three persons concentrate on each of these three elements of rational decision-making, this division of labour will both help to make each step be performed with greater precision and excellence and help to alert all members of the state, including its officials, to the logical structure which should characterize the collective deliberations of rational beings. This excellence and awareness, therefore, would increase 'the *quality* of rational living' in the republican community as well as establish the three publicly known and mutual "masters" with each necessarily having to observe the work of the other two in order to carry out its own prime function.

(1) Ibid., p.117.
(2) Ibid., p.101.

Kant briefly expounds the united yet articulated character of the operations of these three organs as follows:

> The three powers in the state are related to one another in the following ways. Firstly, as moral persons, they are coordinate (**potestates coordinatae**), i.e. each is complementary to the others in forming the complete constitution of the state (**complementum ad sufficientiam**). But secondly, they are also subordinate (**subordinatae**) to one another, so that the one cannot usurp any function of the others to which it ministers; for each has its own principle, so that although it issues orders in the quality of a distinct person, it does so under the condition of a superior person's will .....[1]

Shortly, I will consider how democratic monarchy reinterprets this "coordinate" and "complementary" character of these three powers, but first, I must attempt to answer the question which may arise from our remembering that Kant is claiming both that the representative organ is sovereign yet that each organ has two masters in the other two organs. How can the "sovereign" have a master other than itself? I have already quoted the passage in which the supremacy of the "corps of deputies" was asserted through its ability to remove the executive. The question remains, therefore, who is to remove the sovereign? If we look at this question more carefully, we can see that Kant need not be read to be advocating anything which departs from the arrangements in the model where the elected chamber only has the right to remove and replace, not the executive or judicial *organs,* but, their office holders. Kant does not make this entirely clear but if we are explicitly to add as democratic monarchy does, the provision that before any minister or judge could be removed, a named replacement would have to be designated to assume the office immediately upon the removal of the previous official, this would help solve the problem. Such an arrangement would insure that at all times, *directly* independent executors and judges would be in office. Named officials would always be in place with their full constitutional authority to speak out or to act in their own constitutional ways to restrain the representative assembly when they judged this to be warranted, e.g. when they judged the assembly to be usurping the primary executive or judicial functions, or to be violating its own legislative trust.

With such a provision, while the corps of deputies, as the sovereign republican voice, is *indirectly* also its own executor and judge because it can appoint and remove these office holders; *directly,* it is not its own executor and judge. This interpretation of Kant is perhaps strongly suggested by a few of his own words:

> ... the executive power .... alone possess the supreme authority to apply **coercion** in accordance with the law ....
> .... the executive power of the supreme ruler (summi rectoris) cannot be opposed (i.e. it is irresistible), and the verdict of the supreme judge (supremi iudicis) cannot be altered (i.e. it is without appeal).
> .... neither the sovereign [representative assembly] nor the ruler [executor] may pass judgement; they can only appoint judges as magistrates. The people judge themselves ... by juries ....[2]

In addition to these direct checks upon a possibly antirepublican representative assembly, I should also recall that at general election time, the citizenry would have the opportunity to *replace* any offending deputies with others who seemed to be more likely to defend the appropriate differentiation of functions and organs. In this sense, it is the electorate which is the "master" of the sovereign representative body.

So far, these interpretations of Kant agree with the corresponding provisions of democratic monarchy. At the same time, I must repeat that Kant's words are frequently equivocal and incomplete as they stand so that they could as easily be read in support of a 'parliamentary' constitution with an elected head of state. In order fully to complete this claim of rough correspondence, however, it remains to be explained both why the 'unifying function' should be added to Kant's list of three "powers" (legislative, executive and judicial) and why the judicial and executive functions are better seen as just two ways in which the 'particularizing function' is appropriately performed. The latter conclusion in democratic monarchy leads to the formation of two parallel hierarchies of executives and administrators, on the one hand, and of judges and juries on the other hand, which together constitute the 'governing organ'. I have already argued that while they both are primarily concerned to apply the law of the land to particular and single cases, the way the two appropriately do this is different. Executives are charged to take initiatives while judges are not. My argument in favour of arranging the two hierarchies within the one 'governing organ' is that this not only makes pragmatic sense but that it most clearly

---

(1) Op. cit., "The Metaphysics of Morals", Nisbet, p.141; Ladd, p.81.
(2) Ibid., Nisbet, pp.141-142; Ladd, pp.81-83.

demonstrates that this constitution is a structure of reason, i.e. both are more readily seen as applying the universal to the particular as can minor premises (when combined with universal premises) imply conclusions. In this way, a 'parliamentary constitution' both distinguishes and relates the two manners in which laws can and should be applied. However, Kant's intimations of the logical basis for the difference between the executive and judicial functions are somewhat mistaken. In associating the "minor premise" with the executive functions *only*, and the judicial function with the "conclusion" *only*, he loses sight of the fact that both executives and judges "subsume" single cases "under the general will". Equally, both arrive at "conclusions ... as to the rights or wrongs of each particular case".[1] This is to say that both must exercise the "judgement" which "distinguishes instances where the rule applies".[2]

In later chapters I will consider how democratic monarchy can more easily be seen to be rooted in Hegel's similar yet different explanation of how the functions are manifestations of the three logical "moments" of "generality, particularity and singularity" (Allgemeinheit, Besonderheit und Einzelheit). I can say now, however, that "generality" easily corresponds to Kant's *"universally united will"* of the "major premise" and that "particularity" corresponds to the "subsumption" of "each *particular* case" which relates both to the "minor premise" and the "conclusion". However, the way that "singularity" relates to the findings of this chapter is not so obvious and it is to this question that we will now turn.

The case will be argued more fully later but its thrust will be that the 'unifying function' discussed in *Chapters One* and *Two* correspond to the moment of "singularity". The unifying function, as will be recalled, fulfils the requirement that for a society to survive and especially to thrive rationally, there needs to be an overall consistency between the various statutes which constitute its laws, between the various executive and judicial decisions, and between these laws and these decisions. Kant *implicitly seems to recognize the importance of this unity* and although he does not explicitly translate this appreciation into an argument for a separate organ to be formally responsible for this vital function as Hegel and I do, a modern Kantian would seem to have no reason to resist this conclusion. Such a Kantian would seem to be put in this position, for example, by many of Kant's own phrases which seem clearly to recognize the need for this unity, e.g.,

> ... the universally *united* will ....[1]
> [Legislation] ... for a commonwealth ... requires freedom, equality and **unity** of the will of **all** members. And the pre-requisite of *unity*, since it necessitates a general vote (if freedom and equality are both present), is independence. This basic law, which can come only from the general, *united* will of the people, is called the **original contract**.[2]
> A republican constitution is founded upon three principles: firstly ... **freedom** for all ... men; secondly, the ... dependence of everyone upon a *single* common legislation (as subjects); and thirdly ... **equality** for everyone (as citizens).[3]
> It is perfectly true that the will of all individual men to live in accordance with the principles of freedom within a lawful constitution (i.e. the **distributive** unity of the will of all) is not sufficient for (the goal of eternal peace to be attained) .... Before so difficult a problem can be solved, all men together (i.e. the collective **unity** of the combined will) must desire to attain this goal; only then can civil society exist as a single whole.[4]

It is also worth noting that my separation of the monarch from the governing organ does not substantially conflict with Kant's words where he charges the chief "executive" [5] (i.e. the monarch where there is one) with the task of appointing "ministers" and the public officials who serve them:

> ... (rex, princeps) that moral or physical person who wields the executive power ... is the agent of the state who appoints the magistrates ... and their superiors (ministers) who are responsible for administering the state (gubernatio).[6]

---

(1) Ibid., Nisbet, p.138; Ladd, pp.77-78.
(2) Op. cit., Nisbet, "On the Common Saying: 'This May be True in Theory, but it does not Apply in Practice'", p.61.
(3) Op. cit., "The Metaphysics ....," Nisbet, p.138; Ladd, p.77.
(4) Op. cit., Nisbet, "Theory and Practice", p. 76.
(5) Op. cit., Nisbet, "Perpetual Peace", p.99.
(6) Ibid., p.117.
(7) In democratic monarchy, the monarch is *formally* not only the chief executive but the chief legislator and the chief judge as well. At the same time, the prime minister is the *primary* chief executive.
(8) Op. cit., "The Metaphysics of Morals", Nisbet, p.141; Ladd, p.81.

This would seem to be just another way of interpreting the view of the monarch which Kant applauds when he reports that Frederick the Great "said that he was merely the highest servant of the state".[1]  Of course, this accords with the model constitution. Also within it, the monarch is at least *formally* always the highest state official. This is his or her figurehead role. He or she should only be the *effective* head of the executive as well when the caretaking role is thrust upon her or him by the absence of a working majority in the elected chamber and when only a weak prime minister can be found for appointment.

This chapter has tried to show both that Kant offers no republican arguments which seriously threaten democratic monarchy and that most of his relatively few and unsystematic words can even be imaginatively construed to offer varying degrees of vague support for it. More surprisingly, perhaps, the next chapter will make similar claims about Marx's political theory. It will argue that democratic monarchy would be the best framework for Marx's "communal constitution".

---

(1) Op. cit., Nisbet, "Perpetual Peace", p.101.

## Chapter Five:
## FROM MARX'S COMMUNAL CONSTITUTION TO DEMOCRATIC MONARCHY

Up to a point, it could be said that the model constitution issues from a synthesis of Hegel and Marx's critique of him, that its monarchy comes from Hegel while its democracy comes from Marx. The remaining chapters will clarify the extent to which this simplification is true. Of course, this chapter concentrates on the Marxian element of this synthesis but it must be admitted that because Marx showed only scant interest in discussing either the constitutional details of existing states or of his own future communist society, very little can be said with certainty about what his view of 'democratic monarchy' might be. What is developed here as Marx's own ideal constitution has had largely to be constructed by me from the plausible implications of the relevant fragments which Marx scatters within several of his works.

The least controversial claim is that Marx's preferred constitution is "democratic". The further suggestion, however, that by extension he should logically support democratic monarchy will probably seem much more doubtful to most readers. At the same time, some *crude* Marxists might want to dismiss even the first claim as trivial. They might go so far as to claim that the very notion of a Marxian ideal constitution is made void by his materialist approach to the analysis of history and society. Such interpreters would say that every constitution is only a part of the "superstructure" and therefore could have no independent power to shape human life. They say that constitutional theories should be replaced by more fundamental economic analysis because political arrangements are ultimately determined by the dominant "mode of production" within any given "social formation". I refer to this as a 'crude' interpretation for several reasons. *First*, it ignores the inherent importance which Marx himself gives to thoughtful political activity as displayed by his own strategic and tactical involvements before, within, and after the First International. *Second,* it fails to take account of those passages, such as the following, which can be read to suggest that Marx did have a conception of something like a model constitution in mind:
> ... democracy is *the essence* of every political constitution ... It stands related to other constitutions as the genus to its species; only here *the genus* itself appears as an existent ... opposed to those existents which do not conform to the essence.[1]

*Third,* this overly deterministic interpretation of Marx relies on a simplistic understanding of Marx's occasional references to the "inevitable"[2] character of future events and upon narrow readings of such phrases as the following:
> It is not the consciousness of men that determines their existence, but their social existence that determines their consciousness.[3]
> ... laws ... working themselves out with iron necessity.[4]

---

(1) Karl Marx, *Critique of Hegel's 'Philosophy of Right'*, edited by J. O'Malley and translated with Annette Jolin, CUP, 1970, p.30.
(2) See for example, K. Marx and F. Engels, "The Manifesto of the Communist Party (1848", in *The Revolutions of 1848*, Harmondsworth, Penguin, 1973, pp.79 & 90; and *Capital,* Vol. I, Penguin, 1976, Postface, pp.102 & 103. Also see the following for Marx's expression of confidence in the future, but with a less deterministic tone: "The Civil War in France", p.232; "Speech on the Hague Congress", p.326; both in *The First International and After*, Penguin, 1974.
(3) Preface to "A Contribution to the Critique of Political Economy", Early Writings, Penguin, 1975, p.425, Also see K. Marx and F. Engels, *The German Ideology,* Collected Works, Vol. 5. Lawrence & Wishart, London, 1976. p.37.
(4) *Capital,* ibid., p.91.

It overlooks the mutual shaping powers of body and mind which arguably are contained even in the above phrase, "social existence", especially when such as the following voluntaristic passages are considered:
> Men make their own history, but not [completely] of their own free will; not under circumstances they themselves have chosen but under the given and inherited circumstances with which they are directly confronted.[1]
>
> ... circumstances make men just as much as *men make circumstances*. [2]
>
> Just as .... at an earlier period, a section of the nobility went over to the bourgeoisie, so now a portion of the bourgeoisie goes over to the proletariat, and in particular, a portion of the bourgeois ideologists, who have *raised themselves* to the level of comprehending theoretically the historical movement as a whole.[3]
>
> *Mankind* thus inevitably *sets itself* only such tasks as *it is able to solve*, since closer examination will always show that the problem itself arises only when the material conditions for its solution are already present or at least in the course of formation.[4]

The next to the last extract above could be Marx's own explanation of how he, a child of a middle class family, came consciously to align himself with the proletariat after his study of "the historical movement as a whole". *Fourth*, a deterministic [5] rendering of Marx must be rejected in the light of Marx's recognition of human fallibility, e.g. he praised the Paris Commune for,
> ... acting in bright daylight, with no pretensions to infallibility ... not ashamed to confess blunders by correcting them. [6]

He also criticised the Commune for making various tactical mistakes, e.g. just before 21 March 1871, he judged that the,
> ... Central Committee made itself .... guilty of a decisive mistake in not at once marching upon Versailles, then completely helpless ....[7]

Such recognition of a "mistake", as well as of any notions of skill, virtue and right would be irrelevant or impossible if all were completely determined by material processes and forces beyond human control. Therefore, the narrow materialist's attempt to dismiss our search for a general, prescriptive constitution in Marx will not detain us any longer.

Marx both openly and implicitly declared his support for "democracy" and its institutions in pamphlets written from the 1840s to 1870s. Marx's "Critique of Hegel's 'Philosophy of Right'" (c. 1843) gives us a striking example:
> The democratic element should be ... the actual element that acquires its rational form in the whole organism of the state.[8]

It is not until 1871, however, when Marx wrote about the Paris Commune in "The Civil War in France" that he offers us something like a comprehensive outline of "really democratic institutions".[9] He approvingly claimed that in its political practice and plan, the Commune had achieved "a government of the people by the people".[10] More fundamentally, Marx sees democracy as providing the essential means for achieving the change from the capitalistic to the communistic mode of production, i.e. he held that the Commune "at last discovered .... the political form .... under which to work out the economical emancipation of labour".[11]

Marx never systematically presented his theory of the state but an examination of "The Civil War in France" will help us to infer the outline of such a theory. Following Hegel, I usually use the term 'state' to denote 'that *organized unity* of a whole people which they recognize (at least tacitly) as sovereign'. In contrast, Marx uses the term more narrowly to refer only to such an authority in *class* societies. In this sense of the "state" as 'the agent of class rule', Marx

---

(1) "The Eighteenth Brumaire of Louis Bonaparte", *Surveys from Exile,* Penguin, 1973, p.146.
(2) *The German Ideology,* op. cit., p.54.
(3) "Manifesto", op. cit., p.77, See ibid., p.52, for a similar passage.
(4) Preface to "*A Contribution ....*", op. cit., p.426.
(5) The next chapter will offer a refutation of 'total, external determinism'.
(6) "First Draft of 'The Civil War in France", op. cit., p.252, Also see p.219.
(7) Ibid., p.204.
(8) Op. cit., p.116. Implied endorsements for the following can also be found: "universal suffrage" (e.g. "The Chartists" (1852), *Surveys from Exile,* op. cit., p.264; the freedoms of speech, press and association (e.g. "The Eighteenth Brumaire", op. cit., p.186: ".... to simplify the state administration, reduce the army of officials as much as possible, and finally let civil society and public opinion create their own organs independent of the power of government", (and "The Curtain Raised", *The First International and After,* op. cit., p.399); "popular sovereignty" (e.g. "The Eighteenth Brumaire", ibid., p.195) and "popular government" (e.g. "The Curtain Raised", ibid.).
(9) Op. cit., p.212.  (10) Ibid., p.217.  (11) Ibid., p. 212.

occasionally refers to "the dictatorship of the proletariat" [1] as a "workers' state" [2] as well as to "the modern state",[3] i.e. to what is more informatively, but rarely, called "the bourgeois state".[4] However, when Marx was writing about the Paris Commune, he seems to have adopted an even more restricted use. Here, "the state" referred exclusively to the *bourgeois* state, especially as it had evolved in mid-nineteenth century France, where "a centralized and organized governmental power" [5] had established itself so that it could coordinate and control the "great central state organs".[6] Thus, he referred to the "state parasites" [7] with "great independence from society".[8] He spoke of,

> The centralized state power, with its ubiquitous organs of standing army, police, bureaucracy, clergy, and judicature - organs wrought after the plan of a systematic and hierarchic division of labour ... serving ... middle class society as a mighty weapon in its struggles ...

It is this very restricted meaning of "the state" which I take him to intend when he wrote about what he took to be the Commune's correct view that, at least in France,

> .... the working class cannot simply lay hold of the readymade state machinery, and wield it for its own purposes.[10]

A month earlier, Marx had made the same point more dramatically in his famous letter to Kugelmann (12 April 1871) by saying that "the precondition for every real people's revolution on the continent" is not "to transfer the military-bureaucratic machine from one hand to another, but to *smash* it".[11] Thus, the Commune sought "the reabsorption of the [bourgeoisie's] state power by society,[12] by "the communal form of political organization".[13]

> This was, therefore, a revolution not against this or that Legitimate Constitutional Republican or Imperialist form of state power. It was a revolution against the [bourgeois] *state* itself, this supernaturalist abortion of society, a resumption by the people of its own social life. It was not a revolution to transfer it from one fraction of the ruling classes to the other, but a revolution to break down this horrid machinery of [bourgeois] class domination itself.[14]

Accordingly, during its brief survival,[15] the Commune began to "break down this horrid machinery". It did away with the police in Paris.[16] It transformed the standing army (i.e. the Paris National Guard) into a "militia" or an "armed people" [17] which in peace time would require from each citizen only an "extremely short term of service",[18] but in war, "every able man".[19] It sought to reduce the numbers of "functionaries" [20] as much as possible, transforming the remaining "officials of all branches of the administration [and judges] [21] ... into [elective] [22] responsible and revokable agents of the Commune ... at workmen's wages".[23]

The "Commune" was also the name given to the democratically elected assembly which was to retain full legislative and executive powers [24] and thus to which the above "officials" were made responsible. Members of this assembly were elected by "universal suffrage" [25] from the 20 wards or "arrondissements" [26] of Paris. Members were to be responsible to their electorate, their election to be "revocable at short term".[27] In any case, as implied almost 30 years earlier in his "Critique of 'Hegel's Philosophy of Right'", Marx wants the "electors" to have "the option of deliberating and deciding themselves about public affairs *or* of delegating definite individuals to discharge these things ...".[28] Thus, Marx would probably have favoured at least the 'recall' and 'referenda' provisions outlined in *Chapter One*.

(1) "The Class Struggles in France: 1848 to 1850" *Surveys from Exile,* op. cit., pp.61, 92 and 123; "Critique of the Gotha Programme" (1875), *The First International,* op. cit., p.355. Also see in "The Manifesto", op. cit., "The sway of the proletariat" (pp.78 and 85) and "to raise the proletariat to the position of ruling class to win the battle of democracy" (p.86).
(2) "The Class Struggles", op. cit.,p.84; "Conspectus of Bakunin's Statism and Anarchy", *The First International,* op. cit., p.337.
(3) "The Civil War", op. cit., pp.206 and 211. (4) "The Manifesto", op. cit., pp.74, 76 and 77.
(5) "Civil War", op. cit., p.250. (6) Op. cit., p.211. (7) Ibid., p.211 and 247. (8) Ibid., p.250.
(9) Ibid.,p.206.
(10) "The Civil War", ibid., p.206. Marx implied that much the same problem would face the proletariat almost everywhere but specifically mentions Prussia and Austria on p.250.
(11) K. Marx and F. Engels, *Selected Works,* Vol. II, Lawrence & Wishart, London, 1962, p. 463.
(12) "Civil War", op. cit., p.250. (13) Ibid., p.254. (14) Ibid., p.249.
(15) From January 28, March 3, 18 or 26, 1871 - depending on which event one judges to mark its beginning - to May 28, 1871.
(16) "Civil War", op. cit., pp.219, 251 and 268. (17) Ibid., pp.209 and 210. (18) Ibid., p.251.
(19) Ibid., p.238. (20) Ibid., pp.210 and 251. (21) Ibid., p.210. (22) Ibid. (23) Ibid., p.209.
(24) Ibid. (25) Ibid. (26) Ibid., p.246. (27) Ibid., p.209. (28) O'Malley, op. cit., p.123.

Marx goes on to report the Paris Commune's constitutional plans for the whole of France as follows:

> ... the commune was to be the political form of even the smallest country hamlet ... The rural communes of every district were to administer their common affairs by an assembly of delegates in the central town, and these district assemblies were again to send deputies to the national delegation in Paris, each delegate to be at any time revocable and bound by the *mandat imperatif* (formal instructions) of his constituents. The few but important functions which still would remain for the central government .... were to be discharged by Communal, and therefore strictly responsible agents. The unity of the nation was not to be broken, but, on the contrary, to be organized by *the Communal constitution* ...[1]

While asserting the democratic character of the Commune, Marx did not claim that it had achieved a change in the mode of production. Referring to the actual measures that it put into effect, he said that "there is nothing socialist in them except their tendency".[2] It did "intend to abolish class property ... to make individual property a truth by transforming the means of production ... into mere instruments of free and associated labour".[3] It did hope for the achievement of "communism ..., united cooperative societies ... to regulate national production upon a common plan".[4] Presumably, for these reasons, Marx occasionally called the Commune a "communal republic"[5] or a "social republic".[6] For its international character[7] and perhaps for its moral superiority, he called it "the Universal Republic".[8] Therefore, for Marx, the Commune is "the political form of social emancipation".[9] While it could "not do away with class struggles, through which the working classes strive to the abolition of all classes",[10] the "Commune is ... the organized means of action".[11] It "affords the *rational* medium in which that class struggle can run through its different phases in the most *rational* and humane way".[12] Marx repeats this claim and again undermines his crudely deterministic interpreters by saying that, "The working class know that they have to pass through different phases of class struggle".[13] They know that their *"spontaneous action"* in "the Communal form of *political* organization"[14] can make "great strides" in "the progressive work of time" toward "the superseding of the economical conditions of the slavery of labour", toward "a new organization of production".[15]

Therefore, with the help of "The Civil War in France", we have some idea of Marx's constitution for any future communist society: a democratic decision-taking system, with full legislative, executive and judicial powers held by a maximally devolved hierarchy of delegate assemblies. This "Communal constitution"[16] may not at first appear to be compatible with, let alone, as claimed here, to entail 'democratic monarchy' as its own prescriptive ideal. Before defending this view, however, the problem posed by two additional features of Marx's theory must be resolved.

The first might be supposed to arise from the anticipation that in communist society, "the state .... withers away", as Engels put it.[17] If "in true democracy the political state disappears",[18] as Marx put it 20 years earlier, then perhaps there is no need for a constitution. If so, the question of Marx's possible endorsement of the model constitution with its "hierarchic investiture"[19] need not arise. However, this problem only occurs because of the misunderstanding of what Marx means by "the state". It is clear that this future society will indeed need a constitution for its 'state' in my sense of the term: 'the sovereign organization of a society'. The problem is complicated somewhat by a second feature which was explicitly added to his suggestions for communist society in 1875 when Marx drew the distinction between "the first phase of communist society" and "a more advanced phase",[20] the first having a "workers' state" and the second having no "state" at all. Marx also saw the *first phase* as quickly making the communistic mode of production dominant, at least in one country. However, it would not as yet have grown sufficiently beyond the bourgeois attitudes and these would require it to organize work on the principle of each worker receiving only in proportion to his or her labour. By contrast, in a *more advanced phase*, in addition to

---

(1) Ibid., p.210. (2) Ibid., p 262. (3) Ibid., p.213. (4) Ibid., p.213. (5) Ibid., p.255.
(6) Ibid., p.259. (7) Ibid., pp.216 & 239. (8) Ibid., p.239. (9) Ibid., p.252. (10) Ibid., p.253.
(11) Ibid., p.253. (12) Ibid., p.253. (13) Ibid., p.253. (14) Ibid., p.254. (15) Ibid., p.253.
(16) Ibid., p.210.
(17) F. Engels, *Anti-Duhring* (1878), Lawrence & Wishart, London, 1969 (1st printing 1947) p.333; translated more literally as "goes to sleep of itself ... dies off" (schlaft von selbst ein ... stirbt ab.)
(18) "Critique of 'Hegel's Philosophy of Right'", op. cit., p.31.
(19) "Civil War", op. cit., p.211.
(20) Critique of the Gotha Programme", *The First International*, op, cit., p.347.

having developed on a world wide scale, anti-communistic attitudes would have had to diminish and productive capacity expand sufficiently to allow a much different principle to apply: "From each according to his abilities, to each according to his needs!" [1]

The "bourgeois state" and "the worker's state" are only special cases of the "state" as 'the agent of class rule', i.e. of "the state" or "political power" understood as "the organized power of one class for subordinating (Unterdruckung) another".[2] Accordingly, it is Marx's view that the *bourgeois* state should be transformed into the worker's state, into the first phase of communist society. In turn, the worker's state should eventually wither, "vanish",[3] "die off",[4] or be "superseded"[5] if a more advanced communist society is to be attained. In this latest society, "the public power (die öffenliche Gewalt) will lose (verliert) its political character".[6] Also, although Marx does not say so explicitly, we could quite plausibly suggest that he had it in mind for this "communal constitution" for France to be extended to the whole world, i.e. the advanced communist society. If so, the national assemblies would send delegates to a world assembly.[7] Of such a phase, it could be truly said that it had allowed the "re-absorption of the state power by society"[8] that the,

> ... few but important functions which still would remain for a central [world] government were to be discharged by Communal, and therefore strictly responsible agents .... unity to become a reality by the destruction of the state power ... the merely repressive organs of the old governmental power ... to be amputated.[9]

Again, this world "public power" operating according to a "communal constitution", could be seen as just another formulation of the organized "anarchy" which Marx claimed to be the appropriate goal for all socialists:

> To all socialists anarchy means this: the aim of the proletarian movement - that is the abolition of social classes - once achieved, the power of the state, which now serves only to keep the vast majority of producers under the yoke of a small minority of exploiters, will vanish, and the functions of government become purely administrative.[10]

I construe "*purely* administrative" only to mean that the government within the sovereign organization of society would cease to be the agent of class subordination.

Now that the two phased character of Marx's future society has been addressed, we can turn to the contentious claim that 'democratic monarchy' should be seen as the best model constitution for both phases, for the dictatorship of the proletariat and for classless society. This reconstruction of Marx's "Communal constitution" includes the plan that the 'elected chamber' would be at the head of the maximally devolved, yet hierarchically arranged, delegate assemblies of the world. Accordingly, this chamber of the world would proportionately represent all the national, city or regional "communes", as well as all of the other voluntary 'associations', according to the electoral system of associational proportional representation (A.P.R) outlined in *Chapter One*. Such a communal assembly would seem fully to meet Marx's requirements.

Still, on the face of it, the hereditary features of democratic monarchy would seem to conflict with almost everything Marx says both specifically in regard to the Prussian, French and British monarchies, and about monarchy in general. He refers, for example, to Hegel's constitutional

---

(1) Ibid.
(2) "Manifesto", op. cit., p.87.
(3) "The Alleged Splits in the International", *The First International*, op. cit., p.314.
(4) Engels, op. cit.
(5) *hebt ... auf*, "Manifesto", op. cit., p.87.
(6) Ibid.
(7) "The Commune was ... the truly national government" and yet "emphatically international", "The Civil War", op. cit., p.216, cf. p.239.
(8) Ibid., p.250.
(9) Ibid., p.210.
(10) "The Alleged Splits", *The First International*, op. cit., p.313.

monarchy as an "unhappy hybrid".[1] Nevertheless, these attacks on monarchy need not be read as a threat to the essence of monarchy. Instead, they may be seen merely as understandable responses to the dominantly anti-democratic character of the monarchies of the Europe he was analysing, and to Hegel's clearly anti-democratic phrases. Thus, it is argued that Marx's energetic rejections of absolute, feudal and bourgeois monarchy, as well as of what he takes to be Hegel's monarchy, do not weaken the case for democratic monarchy.[2] The need to defend the model from his particular attacks is obviated by the fact that it diverges from these monarchies just at those points which are vulnerable. It is a thoroughly democratic organization of popular sovereignty while they were not. Moreover, the distinctive ability of an hereditary head of state to provide both the best symbol of a society's unity and a unique institutional guarantee against the total breakdown of the rule of reason enables the model to accept one more of Marx's scathing jibes against Hegel as a compliment to itself. Marx wrote that hereditary institutions are based on "zoology".[3] Indeed, the monarch dramatically sounds the alarm that "zoology" always rules when 'rational humanity' fails. The model provides the best institutional guarantee for the achievement, maintenance or restoration of rational living even in 'the human zoo'. For the same reasons, Marx would have logically to praise rather than ridicule this sort of monarchy as "the last charm against anarchy".[4]

(1) "Critique of Hegel's 'Philosophy of Right'", op. cit., p.83. Taken out of context, some of Marx's phrases might, however, seem to mark his acceptance of monarchy as desirable, e.g. "a ... developed idea of democracy. Democracy is the truth of monarchy, monarchy is not the truth of democracy .... the *monarchical moment* is no contradiction within democracy" (Ibid., p.29). Presumably, Marx did not intended "monarchical moment" to mean 'an hereditary head of state' here but only the abstractly perceivable and complex 'unity' which "a ... developed idea of democracy" must have. The fact that these phrases are embedded within an unrelenting attack upon monarchy would seem to counsel this interpretation. However, even if these words probably do not constitute an obscure confirmation of the model, they may remind us of the argument that an hereditary head of state can best both symbolize and help guarantee the *complex unity* which a real democracy must achieve and repeatedly renew. Again, if taken out of context, the following passages suggesting that communism might emerge peacefully within the monarchies of Britain and Holland, might imply that he could agree with the model constitution: "The workers will have to seize political power one day in order to construct the new organization of labour; they will have to overthrow the old politics which bolster up the old institutions .... We know that heed must be paid to the institutions, customs and traditions of the various countries, and *we do not deny* that there are countries, such as America and England, and if I was familiar with its institutions, I might include Holland, where *the workers may attain their goal by peaceful means*. That being the case, we must recognize that in most continental countries the lever of the revolution will have to be force; a resort to force will be necessary one day in order to set up the rule of labour" ("Speech on the Hague Congress" (1872) *The First International*, op. cit., p.324.). Marx does not explicitly say that it is the democratic institutions of these three countries which might make a peaceful road to communism possible, but this implication, especially in the case of England, is strongly suggested by Marx words twenty years earlier in 1852 when he was discussing "universal suffrage", one of the Chartist's six points: "the carrying of universal suffrage in England would ... be a far more socialist measure than anything which has been honoured with that name on the continent. Its inevitable result, here [England], is the political supremacy of the working class" ("The Chartists", *Surveys from Exile*, op. cit., p.264.). Similarly, in the July of 1871, Marx is reported to have said in an interview, "In England ... the way to show political power lies open to the working class. Insurrection would be madness where peaceful agitation would more simply and surely do the work" ("The Curtain Raised", *The First International*, op. cit., p.395.). Later, Lenin recalled the relevant passages of Marx and Engels which this chapter has already quoted. He argued not only that "democracy" (V. I. Lenin, *The State and Revolution*, Foreign Languages Publishing House, Moscow, p.31) would also "wither away" with the "proletarian state", but that Marx's assertion of the need "to smash the bureaucratic military machine" (ibid., p.64) had also made it clear that violence would be necessary in all modern states since they had developed the sort of centralized state apparatuses which had characterized mid-nineteenth century France. While this Leninist gloss on Marx is plausible, Marx's own words are ambiguous enough to allow us to see him as continuing to accept that a peaceful path might be possible even in such states as long as they also contained strong democratic assemblies which, because they represented civil society, might be able to prevent the "bureaucratic-military machine" from acquiring such a great and dangerous independence. Having suggested that the above passage *might* indicate Marx's own willingness to accept a very limited monarchy for his communist societies, I must again emphasize that nowhere does he make this explicit, and the tone of almost everything he wrote would much more easily lead us to suppose the opposite. Therefore, perhaps the most that can be said is that his words never explicitly exclude 'democratic monarchy'.
(2) See *Chapter Twelve*.
(3) "Critique of 'Hegel's Philosophy of Right'", op.cit., p.106.
(4) "The Eighteenth Brumaire", op.cit., p.218.

These justifications remind us of the positive reasons why a follower of Marx should logically embrace democratic monarchy as his or her own model. A future communist society, like all societies will have to face the previously discussed possibility that 'working majorities' may evaporate or fail to materialize in the first place. Also, in the light of socialism's egalitarianism, it must be recalled that the model would allow a monarchy within a communist society to be significantly different, both in relative scale and in style, from most past and existing monarchies. Great reductions in the monarch's private wealth and in the size of the civil list would probably be seen as appropriate. 'Communist monarchy' certainly need not be like the mid-nineteenth century British monarchy about which Marx commented: "Royalty, with its 'barbarous splendours' its court, its civil list and its flunkeys ...".[1]

Marx's own implicit acceptance of the possible failure of 'working majorities' can be inferred both from what he does and does not say. For example, he does not deny that,

1) even in a classless society, *conflicts* may still arise from non-class differences, e.g. age, personal, psychological, pathological, opinion;
2) in order to minimize the chances that communist society will fall absent mindedly or be pushed unwittingly into becoming another class society, it is necessary for each new generation to be educated about the historical origins of advanced communist society, about the residual dangers which all societies must continue to face and about the reasons for seeing communism as the best imagined for humankind.

The *first* assumption is never voiced by Marx but it would save him from the charge of utopianism. It is also a possible implication of his praise of the Paris Commune for making delegates and officials both "responsible and revokable". Similarly, the following two implicit endorsements of the parliamentary form would seem to rest on the same assumption:

a) his criticism of "the National Assembly" of the Second French Republic, twenty years earlier, "when it lost control of the ministerial portfolios".[2]
b) his criticism of the same republic's "two heads at the top".[3]

Parliamentary control of the "portfolios" and the possession of a single "head" would not be necessary for an advanced communist society unless he thought disagreements and conflicts were thought to be possible.

The second assumption concerning the necessity of education would not seem to be at all controversial. Thus, we can turn immediately to the task of explaining how the continued need for the appropriate education of each new generation will tend to be directly and indirectly facilitated by the institutions of democratic monarchy better than by any other known constitution. It is contended here that as an institution, an hereditary head of state is an essential part of the communal constitution which would encourage better than any other the development in each new generation of a conscious appreciation of the real foundations, the inherent dangers, and the ethical superiority of the classless society in which it lives. First, the apparent contradiction in public life of having, on the one hand, a hereditary head and, on the other hand, a reflective and sophisticated working majority and its government which confine the crown to ceremonial functions provides an empirically real anomaly. This seeming contradiction could spur developing minds to question, and, perhaps by something like a Socratic dialogue, eventually to appreciate its dialectical explanation. It would seem to be the best paradox to stimulate the study and thought which has the prospect of finding a philosophically correct understanding of the complex foundations upon which enduring public life in a classless society could rest. It displays a patterned paradox which would help to lead the pre-rational mind to a rational conception of public life. Nature and human history provide the foundations for all societies and classless society would be no exception. The special educational advantage which having a communal monarchy would offer to a communist society is that such a constitution would be a relatively visible miniature of the complex natural and historical realities which had produced this constitution and society. By study and thought, the monarch's attainment of office by birth could be seen by a Marxist to recall the quite natural self-assertiveness which some humans were led to display over others in social formations prior to advanced communism. Because these societies were dominated by the "primitive communistic",[4]

---

(1) "The Chartists", op. cit., p.262.
(2) "The Eighteenth Brumaire", op. cit., p.160.
(3) Ibid., p.186.
(4) *The German Ideology*, op. cit., p.33; "Manifesto, op. cit. p.65 & p.67n.13 (Engels); *Grundrisse*, Harmondsworth, Penguin, 1973, p.107.

"ancient"[1] slave, "asiatic",[2] "feudal",[3] or "bourgeois"[4] modes of production, this required natural self-assertiveness to become the paternalistic, arbitrary, or egoistic rule of some over others. *Communal* monarchy would thus preeminently record in its own institutions the great extent to which this self-assertiveness had been tamed in classless society through a long historical process to become the rational *self*-determination of the whole species.

To the extent that the study and thought of each generation thus comes to appreciate its society's institutions as the forms by which the species has come to maximize the quality and quantity of rational living, it would see the ethical superiority of communist society over all previous social formations. This should help each person to develop the conscious resolve to sustain classless society against any residual or recurring threats. One of these was posed above: the possible loss of a voluntary working majority in the communal assembly. Such a loss, especially if prolonged, would both mark and encourage a degree of social disintegration which could lead to the reassertion of class society. If the communal constitution were also monarchical in the sense of the model, this loss would require the monarch, in the context of the 'state prerogative council', to appoint the prime minister at his or her own unconfined discretion. Therefore, in democratic monarchy, this loss is dramatically signalled by the public activity of its institutions. The monarch's caretaking role both marks and helps to limit the damage which might otherwise follow a collapse of a working majority and the relative loss of collective rationality which such a contingency embodies. The monarch's appointment of a prime minister in such circumstances would both broadcast the danger and give a people and its communal assembly some time to recreate a working majority before it is too late. It would both highlight the problem and give some additional time for a rational solution to be found. The monarch's *unconfined* appointment of a prime minister helps a people and its representatives consciously and constructively to respond to the natural and historical truth that unless they assert themselves rationally through majority self-rule, they will be ruled by some person's or by some minority's paternalistic, arbitrary or egoistic self-assertion. The power vacuum will be filled one way or another. Democracy is the 'carrot'; monarchy is the symbol of the 'stick'. Thus, if Marx is interpreted to have both assumed that,

1) majorities may not always be secured even in the advanced communist society, and that
2) each new generation in such a society must be educated about the foundations, dangers and superiority of classless society,

then a communal or democratic monarchy should also be his model constitution.

With regard to Hegel's part of the synthesis mention earlier, later chapters will also examine those passages, which were probably not available to Marx. Some of these will be seen perhaps to have a democratic implication. The most striking example is offered by the editor's addition to paragraph 290[5] where he says that "it is of the highest importance" that "the multitude ... become organized for only so is it ... powerful".[6] In spite of a few such hints, it is true that Hegel's words more usually discourage a democratic interpretation, even when they are ambiguous or suffer from what Marx calls Hegel's "stylistic peculiarity".[7] Therefore, Hegel's unadulterated words clearly make a thoroughly democratic construction impossible. A reconstruction is necessary. Thus, the model constitution could be said to arise, for example, from my agreement with Marx's criticism of Hegel's insistence that the monarch should have the right to appoint his ministers at his own "unconfined discretion".[8] As we have seen, democratic or communal monarchy would require the leader of the majority party in the elected chamber automatically to be appointed as prime minister. The second clearly anti-democratic paragraph is not discussed by Marx. It places the conduct of foreign affairs "directly and solely"[9] in the hands of the monarch instead of in those of the foreign minister and cabinet with the support of the working majority.[10]

(1) The German Ideology, op. cit., p.33; "Manifesto" op. cit., 85; Preface to "A Contribution", op. cit. p.426; *Grundrisse*, ibid. pp.105-7.
(2) Preface to "A Contribution", ibid., p.426; *Grundrisse*, ibid., p.106.
(3) "Manifesto", op. cit., p.68; Preface to "A Contribution", ibid., p.426; *Grundrisse*, ibid., pp.106 & 107.
(4) Manifesto", op. cit., e.g. pp.71 & 83.
(5) *Rechts*, PP29OZ.
(6) See *Chapter Twelve*.
(7) "Critique of Hegel's 'Philosophy of Right'", op. cit., p.13.
(8) *Rechts*, PP283.
(9) Ibid., PP329.
(10) See *Chapter Twelve*.

Let us conclude with the assertion which will be elaborated more fully in *Chapter Ten:* the model is not only the most rational constitution, it offers an ideologically neutral organization of society. Accordingly, it allows the maintenance of capitalism or the establishment of communism. It allows either to be lost or restored depending on the current will of the people.

This chapter has sought to show why a follower of Marx should logically endorse democratic monarchy as his or her own general prescriptive guide. Future chapters will consider why followers of Hegel should come to the same conclusion. The next chapter, however, both lays the methodological foundations which will guide these later chapters and which have implicitly provided the grounds upon which this and all previous chapters have rested.

# Chapter Six:
## METHODOLOGY AND 'PHILOSOPHICAL NECESSITY'

The first five chapters have sought both to introduce democratic monarchy and to test it against various republican arguments. Before I continue to assess it with regard to Hegel's philosophy in the last six chapters, however, this chapter will stand back from the specific constitutional arguments for a moment in order to pursue a higher level methodological question, 'How is it philosophically possible to resolve conflicts between competing theories of whatever sort'? The answer to this question will have a much wider import than the precise concerns of this book yet it will involve, by implication, the outlining of the general method by which democratic monarchy is shown to be the best model constitution. Thus, this method will be seen to order the investigations contained in the remaining chapters just as it has been the implicit guide for the arguments in the earlier chapters.

If the method proves to be valid for the examination of *all* competing theories, even those in conflict with each other about questions of method, this is partly made possible by its being 'reflexive' in the sense of being 'self-critical'. It includes the philosophical demand that the best methodological framework must contain a self-critical perspective. This framework can be describe with regard to its aim which is to search for a 'philosophical necessary' theory. Such a theory is an alternative expression for 'truth' and it will be define shortly. However, it will be helpful to recall *Chapter Three's* suggestion that our methodology has been largely suggested by Plato's "dialectic". Like Plato, I expect that conflicts between theories will be best resolved and truth found in the context of an extended Socratic dialogue. For this reason, I occasionally want to write in the first person plural. This is one way for me to register my understanding both of my methodology and of my constitutional arguments as being distillations of many real and imaginary discussions with others (with friends, colleagues, students, and with a number of political and philosophical works). It also serves to suggest the hope that this book may stimulate continuations of Plato's *intersubjective* process.[1] Previous chapters have repeatedly deployed the terms 'rational', 'reason' and 'rationality' in these Platonic ways. This chapter's specification of our methodology provides a more complete definition of these terms. It makes clear how the central claim, that democratic monarchy is the most rational constitution, amounts to the contention that its institutions would best foster the resolution of conflicts by deliberations which approximate to investigations in search of a philosophically necessary theory.

The methodological framework argued for here is such that it will not be easily rejected, whether one has positivist, empiricist, materialist, rationalist or idealist leanings. This is so because it is rooted in each of these approaches. At least, it may provide an item on the agenda for any philosophical search for the best methodology. Again, this approach requires the scrutiny of competing theories in search of a 'philosophically necessary' theory. Such a theory would have to be seen in our dialogue as *comprehensive* and to have flawlessly passed all known tests: *experiential*, *logical*, and *comparative*.

---

(1) Kant says that the "touchstone whereby we decide whether our holding a thing to be true is conviction or mere persuasion is ... external, namely, the possibility of communicating it and finding it to be valid for all human reason". *The Critique of Pure Reason*, op. cit., A820, B848.

## Comprehensiveness

The demand that a philosophically necessary theory be *comprehensive* requires that it be concerned with *all* the areas of sensuous and non-sensuous experience [1] of which we are aware to date. This is to say that it must address itself to all the empirical evidence of the world coming to us through our five senses as well as to every other awareness which may not be entirely reducible to such sensuous experience. A comprehensive theory would thus have to give an account, for example, of matter, light, plants, and historical events, as well as, of our emotions, dreams, reasoning processes and the abstract categories [2] of thought itself. Such demands make it clear that a comprehensive theory would have to integrate within itself not only a political theory but, for example, theories of nature (the physical sciences), of psychology, of society and of the whole of human history. This is to say that a political theory which could claim philosophical necessity would have to show how it is an integral part of a comprehensive theory. Of course, it must be admitted that most if not all known political theories fall far short of this requirement but this chapter is only concerned to outline the methodological conditions of our attaining what seems to be the highest possible aim of human enquiry: philosophical necessity. This is not to say that it has ever been achieved or that it can be easily secured by us.

## Not Absolute Necessity

Before going on to discuss the three remaining conditions for philosophical necessity (experimental, logical and comparative tests), it should also be made clear that even if we were ever to judge a theory to be philosophically necessary, we could *never* claim it to be 'absolute'. This is the case in spite of the other grand-sounding adjectives which have been used to describe it: 'all', 'comprehensive' and 'necessary'. Philosophical necessity is *not* 'absolute necessity'. Absolute necessity is humanly unachievable because it would give an account of all experience - past, present *and future*, i.e. an account which would leave us *no doubts* as to its truth. Philosophically speaking, while we must by definition eliminate all our *specific* doubts about a theory before we could authorize its being called philosophically necessary, we could not remove all our *vague* doubts. For example, the vague doubt seems irremovable that tomorrow *may* bring a new perspective which *may* require us to modify or reject the theory which we currently judge to be philosophically necessary. The difference between specific and vague doubts is that in a *specific* doubt we have a definite test or enquiry in mind which we have not yet conducted. Depending on the results, we see *exactly* how it may force us to reject or modify the theory under review. For the unavoidable, residual *vague* doubts we would have no such precise anticipation. Instead, they arise from our recognition that we have neither read all that has been written nor have we had dialogues with all living philosophers. Similarly, we are aware that new readings of works previously read may produce significantly new perspectives. Such doubts are said to be *vague* because with them we as yet have no specific reason to think that this or that new experiment, this or that new book, this or that re-reading, or this or that new discussion will provide us with a crucial test of the theory in question. We recognize that they *may* do, but we have no *specific anticipation* of how. As soon as we have such an anticipation, the theory under discussion cannot claim the title of philosophical necessity until it survives the new specific test. Just before this test, the theory could be called 'the best', or 'the unrefuted', but not the 'philosophically necessary' theory. We would have had to eliminate *all our* specific doubts about a theory before we could judge it to be philosophically necessary, i.e. all the specific doubts which any participant in our intersubjective search is able to sustain. If the dialogue is able to remove all such doubts for a time, for that time, the theory under review would appropriately be granted the status of philosophical necessity, never absolute necessity. This holds even if we recognize the remote

---

(1) I am using "experience" (Erfahrung) differently from Kant. For him, it is equivalent to "empirical knowledge" which issues from the arranging of "appearances" (Erscheinungen) and "sensations" (Emfindungen) under the "Categories" (Kategorie) of the "understanding" (Verstand) and its "laws" (Gesetzen). Instead, I use 'experience' as a blanket term also to include every other possible item of consciousness, e.g. also what Kant calls "thought-entities (Gedenkendinge, Gedankenwesen), "imagination" (Einbildung), "thinking" (Denken), "representations" (Vorstellungen), and "ideas" (Ideen). While Kant's use refers to the result of a mediating process, my use also includes those seemingly isolated or only vaguely related items which may only be immediately present in our consciousness at any given time. These items, so to speak, are awaiting mediation, i.e., awaiting analysis and synthesis into the consciously worked out, articulate and unified whole which is a 'theory'.

(2) Also in contrast to Kant's "categories" which only refer to those prime and pure "concepts" (Begriff) under which "appearances" are to be organised. I use it as an equivalent for the many concepts and "conceptions" which together compose Hegel's philosophical system.

possibility that a theory which one day attained this status might year after year maintain this position. As time passed, people would tend to view it with more and more confidence and it would justly retain this status perpetually if it happened to *coincide* with the humanly *unachievable* absolute theory mentioned above. This is to say that while we might some day formulate a theory which *is* absolute, we could never *know* that we had done so. This is to say that, with one exception, a philosophically necessary theory could coincide with the absolute theory. If this happened, we could not know that it had happened. The unavoidable exception would be our lack of the knowledge that we possessed the absolute theory. The inescapable presents of the vague doubts make it impossible for the absolute and the philosophically necessary to coincide in this respect. We could *never* exclude the sort of vague doubts discussed above.[1]

Another example of such irremovable doubts would seem to arise from the imaginable possibility that the world of our experience may contain an infinite number of *irreducible* potential experiences. Here, 'irreducible' means 'not capable of being seen as just another instance of a type of experience already noted by us'. If the world is composed of such an infinity (and we could never know with certainty one way or the other), we could be perpetually prevented from ever formulating a theory which we considered to be 'comprehensive', let alone 'philosophically necessary'. This prevention could be effected by our continually being exposed to at least one new seemingly irreducible experience before we had time to integrate the previous one into our currently leading theory. We must also emphasize the fact that it would seem that we could never exclude the possibility of this infinity even if we had achieved a theory which seemed to be philosophically necessary. We could not exclude it because our securing of such a theory may have been possible only because of our experience of but a segment of this infinity.[2] The next chapter argues that this denial of *absolute* necessity leads us to interpret Hegel's "conception of Reason" just as one of his names for his system. This system is read to aspire to the status of *philosophical* not *absolute* necessity. This is the case in spite of the fact that Hegel frequently

(1) These claims for 'philosophical necessity', like Hegel's many suggestions that we as "spirit" may come to know the "Infinite" (e.g. Enz. I, PP60Z) and see *Chapter Seven)*, might easily be seen as conflicting with Kant's many assertions that we can never "know" the "thing in itself" (die Sache an sich selbst) or "noumenon". However, to the reader who is so disposed, this conflict may not necessarily be interpreted to be present in Kant's words. For example, we might read Kant's denial of the knowability of noumenon as just another way of referring to the unavoidable 'vague doubts' discussed here. This interpretation would be facilitated first by seeing noumenon as just another name for "the ground of the order of the world" (op. cit., *Critique of Pure Reason* A696, B724). Thus, it seems that the search for 'philosophical necessity' would require such a concept as the 'absolute theory' or "the thing in itself" (called "Reason" in *Chapter Seven*) in order to think about and to interpret the "world of appearance" (A802, B830). The same concept seems to be a condition for reconciling this world with the "experience" of "practical freedom" (A802, B830 and A803, B831). In Kant's idiom, noumenon or "the ground of the order of the world" is a necessary "idea" which is not "experienced" or "known" but "thought". As a necessary thought, therefore, I see that it would have to have a defined place within a philosophically necessary theory, just as does the concept of an 'absolute theory'. Kant writes, and I agree, that "noumenon" is a condition for interpreting, rather than itself being, "an object of our sensible intuition" (B307). Accordingly, he says that he accepts the so-called "negative" (rather than the "positive") meaning of noumenon for which "it is still an open question whether the notion of noumenon be not a mere form of concept, and whether .... an object whatsoever is left" (A253). If noumenon or the thing-in-itself were thus taken to the "ground of the order" in this "negative" sense, Kant's position might also be seen as compatible with Hegel's claims in spite of Kant's repeated phrases which *suggest* the contrary. We might consider, as well, whether our inability to determine with complete certainty whether a given philosophically necessary theory wholly coincides with the 'absolute theory' might not be an instance of what Kant calls a "determinate knowledge of the ignorance which for us is unavoidable" (A767, B795).

(2) Kant seems to give expression to similar 'vague doubts' when he says, for example, that the "regulative idea" of God as "deistic" (ibid., A675, B703) is "*postulated* only *problematically* ... in order that we may view all connections of the things of the world of sense as if they had their ground in such a being" (A681, B709). He says that this being or this "something we cannot think otherwise than on the *analogy* of a real substance" (A675, B703), "we must think" it in "the pursuit of that complete systematic unity in our knowledge to which reason at least sets no limits". As such it is thought to be the ground of this unity of appearances but, as he says of the grounds of the soul, "simplicity and other properties of substance are intended to be only a schema ... not the actual ground of the soul [for] these may rest on altogether different grounds, of which we know nothing" (A683, B711). Thus Kant refers to such "regulative ideas" as "devices" (A676, B704) or as "heuristic fictions" (A771, B799) which must be assumed not in the "absolute" but in the "relative sense" (A676, B704).

refers to this conception as the crowning achievement of *"absolute* spirit" (Geist). This is read as equal to saying that it appears to be "comprehensive", 'complete', 'reflexive' or "in-and-for-itself".[1]

**More than Scientific Necessity**

Also, before turning to consider the experiential, logical and comparative tests for philosophical necessity, it will be convenient at this juncture to distinguish 'scientific' from 'philosophical' necessity. In order to attain 'scientific necessity', a theory need not intend to be comprehensive but need only relate to a segment of our experiences. Nevertheless, such a theory must flawlessly pass all the experiential tests for that segment as well as the relevant logical and comparative tests discussed more fully below. This distinction between 'philosophy' and 'science' follows one of Hegel's uses which has the ancient meaning (e.g. Aristotle's) referring to any systematic treatment of an area of experience, e.g. mathematics and ethics as well as physics. This use contrasts with the more modern empiricist and positivist meanings which prefer to reserve the term for those bodies of knowledge which can be decisively tested by our five senses. 'Science' can also refer to non-sensuous experiences as it does in Hegel's "science of logic". If the area of experience to be studied by a 'science' is defined philosophically, then a relevant theory in this field which became seen as scientifically necessary might also secure the status of philosophical necessity. This is because to define a science 'philosophically' is explicitly to place it within a comprehensive theory. On the other hand, if the area of the science in question is not defined philosophically but only tacitly or arbitrarily, then theories concerning it could attain no higher status than 'scientific necessity'.

**A Comprehensive Theory Must Both Be Descriptive and Evaluative**

Within our non-sensuous experience there seems to be only two sorts of motives for theorizing. We want to know both *what is* the case and *what ought* to be the case. We want a philosophically necessary theory which both *describes* and *evaluates*. Since both are concerns within our non-sensuous experience, both must be answered by a theory which claims to be comprehensive. To use Hegel's terms, both must be seen as "moments" of one "totality". While the questions of *is* and *ought* are distinguishable, they are not separable. Each logically depends upon the other. Even the physicist who simply enjoys the attempt to understand the laws of motion is at least implicitly affirming the human *value* of understanding 'the is' of the world. This example serves also to emphasizes that here, the term 'descriptive theory' is being used in a wider than usual sense. It includes *abstract* descriptions like those expounded through casual laws and Weberian "pure types" as well as the simple empirically concrete reports of past or present events and entitles. Thus, the following interrelated list of empirical science concerns are also called 'descriptive': casual, explanatory, predictive and probabilistic theories. In contrast, the term 'evaluative' refers to all arguments concerned to specify *what ought* to be the case in the world. It includes all those theories which are more commonly called moral, ethical, normative or prescriptive. It will be argued that, in some ways, the *evaluative* as well as the *descriptive* aspects of a theory are subject to the tests of experience, as well as to the tests of comprehensiveness, logic, and comparison.

**A Comprehensive Theory Must be Reflexive**

A truly comprehensive theory would have to be 'reflexive'. It must be 'self-critical' in the sense of including within itself a scrutiny of its own foundations: it would have to give an account of its own *history* and conceptual generation. It would have to include its own *epistemology* (i.e. a theory about the appropriate criteria for assessing the validity of competing methods for the discovery of knowledge.[2] Plato's theory in *The Republic* was not completely *reflexive* because he admittedly relied on similes and myths when such questions were raised, e.g. the simile of the cave. Kant's *Critique of Pure Reason* is a challenging example of this reflexive, philosophical pursuit and Hegel frequently addressed himself to these reflexive questions in his system and in his history of philosophy. Marx's brief discussions of the relations between material

---

(1) This meaning would appropriately not exclude the 'vague' doubts which must always remain and which ceaselessly invite us to discover new questions, arguments and tests.
(2) 'Knowledge' here is not restricted to Kant's use which usually refers only to a valid account of "appearances". My use designates valid accounts of any area of consciousness, including moral principles. Kant says rather that such principles are "indispensably necessary" (A328, B385) in relation to human activity while I say that they are 'philosophically necessary'. I take this only to be difference of words.

### Experiential Tests

It will be more convenient, first, to discuss the tests of experience which a theory would have to pass before it could achieve the status of 'scientific necessity'. The extra demands made by philosophical necessity will be added later. The tests of experience require that a theory be *compatible* with the relevant sensuous (i.e. empirical) or non-sensuous elements about which we are aware. 'Compatibility' requires a descriptive theory 1) accurately to *report* the concrete area of experience concerned and 2) to present a fully adequate abstract description of this area. An *abstract* description uses theorized concepts, categories and definitions. It will be seen as *adequate* if these seem to capture the essence of the relevant area. If so, the theory *explains* how each item is an example of the *logical linkage* discussed in the next section. For the empirical sciences, descriptions are correctly argued by Popper and others to be abstractly adequate if they constitute causal theories which are also predictive. This makes them empirically testable. In this case, compatability requires the predictions to square with the events predicted. If a predicted event does not occur, the theory is said to be "falsified",[2] i.e. demonstrated to be somewhat mistaken. The non-sensuous descriptions of others can be tested by our own introspective experiences. We can report them to each other and we can discuss them. An example of such a description has already been provided by the earlier assertion that, philosophically, we want both to describe and to evaluate. Each of us can check this and any other non-sensuous description both by introspection and by discussion.

The experiential testing of evaluative theories again requires compatibility. The evaluative theory must be *relevant* to the area of experience concerned, i.e. it must be able to specify the extent to which each factor within that area is or is not as it *ought to be*. If the knower of both 'the is' and 'the ought' of a given situation consequently believes that he or she has the power to change some factors in the direction of how they *should be*, then he or she is logically required by his or her evaluative theory to act accordingly. Such a *knower* ought logically to be such an *actor*. An evaluative theory in such circumstances is also a *prescriptive* theory. A given evaluative or prescriptive theory may prove to be inadequate when measured against this experiential test because it does not offer evaluations (or prescriptions) on each factor within a situation in question. The theory's formulation may be too vague or it may have been originally framed for a different age and so its implications for some contemporary question may not be obvious. For example, because Plato's definition of justice was formulated in relation to the ancient Greek world, the evaluative implications of this definition for the question of proportional representation in modern Britain are by no means obvious. Until someone has devoted the time and

---

(1) There are certain methodological and political similarities between the views here and those of Jürgen Habermas. His "critique" or "critical sociology" also includes an "intersubjective structure" *Theory and Practice*, Heinemann, London 1974, p.28) and a reflexive element (pp.3, 24, 37, 37, 79, 153, 211, 254 and 276). He also seeks *"a comprehensive concept of rationality ....* that does not hesitate to reflect on its own interrelationship with the historical stage of development attained by the knowing subjects ...(p.280). While he does not explicitly discuss specific constitutional arrangements, my democratic monarchy's capacity to help maximize rationality would seem to complement many of his phrases, e.g. "Critique... only finds its own rationality in its partisanship for rationality" (p.276); "moving forward in the direction of emancipation", "enlightened communication to be institutionalized in the political sphere", "dissolution of all substantial forms of domination", "noncompulsive consensus" (p.278); "social intercourse which ultimately is freed from the compulsion and domination of nature - and thereby achieves the political autonomy of adult maturity" (p.261); "the institutional preconditions for practical discourse among the general public" (p.3); a constitution which would both allow for "a decentralized and uninhibited discursive formation of the public will" (p.4), and a liberation from "systematically distorted communication ... by the process of critique" (p.9) and which would provide "an organized praxis adequate for the requirements of enlightenment on a mass scale" (p.16) which in turn, would require "the effective equality of opportunities" (p.23). Of course, I also agree with him that "a political struggle can only be legitimately conducted under the precondition that all decisions of consequence will depend on the practical discourse of the participants ..." (p.34). Habermas also reminds us of *Chapter One's* acceptance of the uncertainties attached to any political action when he writes that "No theory and no enlightenment can relieve us of the risk of taking a partisan position and of the unintended consequences involved in this" (p.36). Similarly, we are reminded of the suggestion that the empirical establishment of a democratic monarchy would provide the conditions for a significant 'experiment' when he observes that "Attempts at emancipation ... are also tests; they test the limits within which human nature can be changed and above all, the limits of the historically variable structure of motivation, limits about which we possess no theoretical knowledge ..." (p.37).

(2) Karl R. Popper, *Conjectures and Refutations*, Routledge and Kegan Paul, 1963, p.36.

imagination required to elaborate Plato's political theory into prescriptions for 20th Century conditions, his prescriptions will continue to seem irrelevant. To the extent that it is irrelevant, it will have failed this test of experience. However, because there would seem to be nothing to prevent someone from working up each vague or outdated evaluation into a relevant theory, a failure of the above sort would not permit us to reject any evaluative theory altogether. Nevertheless, even a clearly relevant prescriptive theory could still be shown to be experientially inadequate either because it proved to be so in practice or was found theoretically to be so as a result of our discovering that its expectations conflict with the implications of the predictive theory we currently accept. In either case, the prescribed actions would have been shown to be unworkable [1] or to be counter-productive.[2]

The possibility that a prescriptive theory may logically conflict with a predictive theory raises a further problem. If our leading descriptive theory were able to sustain the doctrine of 'determinism' (i.e. *total, external determinism*), then, every prescriptive theory would be disposed of as having no power to shape the empirical world. All political theories in the sense used here would suffer the same fate. In the light of this threat, I propose next to show why the threat of such determinism cannot be sustained. Two sorts of determinism have been proposed. Those like Hobbes' mechanistic conception imply that the determining process operates by humanly knowable [3] causal laws. This determinism also suggests the possibility of our achieving a totally accurate *predictive* knowledge of every future detail. The second type of determinism does not believe that the determining process can be known by humans, e.g. the Epicureans see the determining process as spontaneous and therefore not humanly knowable in advance while St. Augustine believed events to follow from the partially unknowable laws and will of God.[4] The threats posed by these two types of *unknowable* determinism can swiftly be removed by our noticing the self-contradictory character of both positions. Both claim to *know* something which they also say is *unknowable*.

It will take more time to refute knowable or totally predictive determinism.[5] Nevertheless, its threat can be removed by our considering the following thought experiment. Since such a predictive

(1) I take this to be one of the implications of Max Weber's argument, *The Methodology of the Social Sciences*, The Free Press, New York, 1949, pp. 52-55.
(2) This is the point made by Marx when criticizing Feurbach in his Thesis II as follows: "The question of whether objective truth can be attributed to human thinking is not [merely] a question of theory but is a practical question" (K. Marx, "Concerning Feuerbach", *Early Writings*, The Pelican Marx Library, 1975, p.422).
(3) Hobbes' position amounts to the claim that the laws of "body" and "motion" are in principle knowable. His determinism can be extracted from his *Leviathan*, Basil Blackwell Oxford, n.d., edited with an Introduction by Michael Oakeshott, pp. 5, 17, 27, 38, 243 & 440.
(4) Not only does this seem to be the flaw in St. Augustine's argument in the *City of God* (Everyman's Library, 1945, see especially the last sentence of Book V, Chapter X), but similarly seems to be present in Kant's assertion of human freedom and responsibility, on the one hand, and his argument, on the other hand, that God as postulated "must be omniscient, in order to be able to know my conduct *even to the most intimate parts of my intention in all* possible cases and in the *entire* future" and "He must be omnipotent, omnipresent, eternal, etc." (op. cit., *Critique of Practical Reason*, p. 145.
(5) Alvin Goldman, *A Theory of Human Action*, Princeton Univ. Press, 1980. His Chapter 6 outlines a special case in which such prediction could not be total. This case is like the one in the first part of my argument to follow shortly. He analyses the problem of the predictor having to disclose his true prediction about an agent's future action to the agent, an agent which the predictor has discovered is *determined* to do the opposite of any disclosed predictions. The "logical impossibility" of such a true prediction to be disclosed allows Goldman, at least momentarily, to distinguish "determinism" from "predictionism". However, Goldman's claim on this basis that "determinism" is "tenable" (though not proven) is, in effect, undermined by his own later claim, which I see as correct, that knowable determinism implies that a complete "book of life" could in principle be written for each one of us before we had fully lived our lives. If so, my argument is that once I read my book of life, I believe I could deviate from its predictions, at least on trivial matters. This is to say, using his own terms against him, such a belief is "logically incompossible" with "determinism". It is important to stress, however, that neither this way of putting it nor my own argument removes determinism 'absolutely'. Determinism is not removed at all for those people (if there are any) who may *believe* that they could never deviate from disclosed predictions concerning them. Even for those, like myself, who believe they could deviate, it does not exclude the imaginable doubt arising from the following logical possibility for which I can see no argument by which we could either affirm it or deny it: '*An unknowable* or only as yet unknown set of causes may have determined me both to feel that I am free and to argue that I am free' (as I am doing here). While for these reasons, determinism has not been entirely refuted, in this form, it is not a threat to prescriptive theories. Our inability to know that we are determined in this way, does not logically prevent us from believing that we are free and responsible for doing what is right.

theory claims to be *total,* it must accept the challenge to predict where I will be in exactly five minutes. Logically, I must either be entirely inside my house or at least partly outside my house. Also, as *total* determinism, it will accept the challenge to predict my location even if I were to be told the prediction before the five minutes had passed. That I had been so informed should be accepted merely as one more factor to be taken into account by the predictive calculation. Would not each one of us be as confident as I am that they could step outside of their house if the prediction were that they will be inside, or that they could step inside if the prediction were that they will be outside after the five minutes? Of course, in some cases a fire in the house or the door being locked might prevent us from falsifying some such predictions, but we would only need to disprove one prediction to show that the predictive determinism is not total. Neither could the total determinist escape this refutation by saying that he had not given us the true prediction and that we had in fact behaved in exactly the way that he had secretly predicted to himself. In response to this we would require him to teach us his predictive theory. With this theory, if it were for the moment presumed to be valid, each one of us could calculate a prediction for himself or herself. Each of us, I assume, could similarly prove the calculation to be false by doing the opposite of one of these predictions. Nor shall the total determinist escape by saying that the prediction failed because his information or his theory is as yet incomplete. While we fully accept that a knowledge of such a complete determinism would indeed be so demanding and difficult that none would seriously claim to have achieved it today, the thought experiment is deliberately constructed on the assumption that this level of presumed competence had now been attained.[1]

While the above thought experiment indeed seems to refute determinism, some may say that it has only demonstrated a trivial empirical effect which a knowing *free* human will can have. However, determinism would still be falsified by such a demonstration. If 'trivial' means 'small' bodily movements, it should be recalled that some such movements can have effects which evaluatively are surely not trivial in other senses, e.g. tipping over a lighted paraffin heater; refraining from maintaining the brakes on one's car; deciding to vote this way rather than that way in a marginal constituency. The above argument has removed the threat which determinism may have posed to the prescriptive potency of evaluative theorizing. Nevertheless, the potential and actual shaping effect of any given evaluative theory will vary depending on the theory and on the empirical circumstances concerned.

To summarize, experiential tests of evaluative (e.g. political) theories can show that a given theory is either *compatible* or incompatible with our experience of relevant area. If compatible, this means that it is seen as clearly capable of prescribing actions which have some prospect of success. If incompatible, it is shown a) not to be wholly relevant, b) to require counter productive actions or c) to require the impossible.

**Logical Tests**

Logical tests require a theory to be 1) clear, 2) coherent, and 3) simple. It has already been asserted that in some cases 'an evaluative theory also becomes a prescriptive theory', that 'a *knower*' must 'logically' become 'an *actor*' seeking 'to change some factors in a situation in the direction of how they should be'. The reason why this is 'logical' and why we accept the importance

---

(1) In spite of the differences, this refutation of determinism is essentially the same as that offered by Frederick Olafson, *Principles and Persons: An Ethical Interpretation of Existentialism,* the John Hopkins University Press, 1967 (in Paul W. Taylor, *Problems of Moral Philosophy,* Wadsworth 1978, p. 672). Plato does not address this question explicitly. While his political theory would seem to assume 'free will' at least for his philosopher rulers, a literal interpretation of "The Myth of Er" in *The Republic* (618b) would confine such freedom to the choices of future lives which all "souls" must make just before they pass through "the river of forgetfulness" and are reborn into this world. While most of what Kant says is compatible with the view here (e.g. op. cit., *Critique of Practical Reason,* p. 104) he seems to contradict both me and himself when he says that "if we could exhaustively investigate all of the appearances of men's wills, there would not be found a single human action which we could not predict with certainty ..." (op. cit., *Critique of Pure Reason,* A550, B578. Marx does not address this issue of 'free will' directly but his own political activity, his belief in the possibility of a future "advanced phase of communist society", discussed in the previous chapter, and his enthusiastic writing would make no sense if such a power were not at least tacitly assumed. In spite of this, we noted some of his phrases which seem to deny this autonomy to conscious human activity.

of testing both descriptive and evaluative theories by experience is because we non-sensuously experience the impossibility of thinking in any way other than according to the fundamental logical principle that 'the truth is one', i.e. 'the *axiom* of non-contradiction'.[1] It is logically impossible for us to accept that opposites can both be true at the same time and in the same sense, that 'A' and 'not A' can both be true. It is impossible both that an hereditary head of state is more appropriate to a given modern state than is an elected head AND that a president is more appropriate than is a monarch for the same state. Before we might become aware of this law as a principle, contradictions intuitively bother us. Experiential tests rest on the assumption that any contradictions that might appear between elements of our experience and our theory shows that the theory is mistaken. We cannot rest easily with the discovery that items of our sensuous or non-sensuous experience seemed to demonstrate that 'A is the case', while an element of our non-sensuous experience (i.e. our theory) says that 'A is *not* the case'. Our unease in such circumstances leads us to re-check our experience, and if required, to reject the theory. We seek to make our new theory compatible with all of our experiences to date. This is an example of the "dialectical"[2] relation between theory and experience. In a science we try to discover a theory which is compatible with a defined but limited area of experience while in philosophy we seek a theory which is compatible with *all* of our experience. Equally, since a theory is one complex element of our non-sensuous experience, we could say that philosophy attempts to discover a complex non-sensuous experience (i.e. a theory) which is compatible with all other non-sensuous and sensuous experiences. In addition to this requirement of comprehensiveness for a philosophically necessary theory, the logical tests discussed in this section check to see that this complex non-sensuous experience is consistent with itself, i.e. that it is, in fact, *one* theory. If a theory under review is discovered to be ambiguous or seems clearly to contain two opposing elements, it is not one but a mixture of at least two conflicting theories. Our logical scrutiny may enable us to reformulate and repair such a theory so that we are left only to test a *clear* and coherent theory against the experiential criteria already discussed and against the comparative criteria yet to be elaborated.

*Coherence* requires all the elements of a theory to be seen as parts of one system. Its elements are logically linked both to the whole and to each other.[3] To be *logically linked* means that one element of a theory is required by another, either by extension or in order that self-contradiction in the whole may be avoided. In our earlier example of an evaluative theory which might prescribe the knower to take specified actions, this was seen to be logically required because such actions, were seen as helping to remove the experienced contradictions between one's evaluations and one's sight of the existing world. To the extent that our values come to live within the practices of our world, our evaluative and descriptive theories of that world will not be in conflict and the axiom of non-contradiction will be satisfied.

So far, we have seen both how logical scrutiny requires a theory to be *clear* and *coherent*, i.e. logically linked and avoiding self-contradiction. The last requirement that a theory be as *simple* as possible means that it should be no more complicated than the varieties of experience demand. If over-elaborate theories are cut down to their simplest form, nothing important is lost which could not be recaptured merely with the aid of arithmetical multiplication. This point can be

(1) This axiom is usually but paradoxical referred to as "the law of contradiction". See Aristotle's *Metaphysics*, ed. and trans. by John Warrington, Introduction by Sir David Ross, London, Dent, 1966, pp.123-125.
(2) Here "dialectical" is being used not so much in the Platonic as in the Hegelian and Marxian senses which imply a mutual shaping power between thought and action. This is in contrast to Kant's usually pejorative use of "dialectical" to refer to "illusions" into which pure reason is prone to fall (e.g. op. cit., *Pure,* A406, B433 to A568, B596).
(3) Kant goes so far as to say that in the case of "transcendental assertions which lay claim to insight into what is beyond the field of all possible experience, ... they are so constituted that what is erroneous in them can never be detected by means of any experience. Transcendental reason consequently admits of no other test than the endeavour to harmonize its various assertions" (ibid., A425, B453).

illustrated by a version of the Old Testament's *Genesis* which prefaced the existing story of creation by saying that, in the very beginning, God 1 created god 2, and then god 2 created god 3, and then god 3 created god 4, and so on until god 100 created the world. If we were not to eliminate such superfluities, we would have no chance of approaching either a scientifically or a philosophically necessary theory. The one potential theory of this character which might exist would be progressively lost under a growing heap of endlessly multiplying versions both of itself and of other theories.[1] This sort of diverting and boring endlessness is one example of what Hegel called "the spurious infinity" (die schlechte Unendlichkeit) to be discussed in a later chapter. He distinguished this infinity from "the genuine Infinity", a version of which I see as one of the clear competitors for the status of philosophical necessity, given its logically linked character and seeming completeness.

A *complete* assessment of the systematic logic of Hegel's conception of monarchy will be seen to be beyond the scope of the argument here. Such an assessment would require many more volumes than Hegel himself took to expound his system in the first place. It would require a step by step examination of the relation between this conception and each of the many hundreds of other categories, distinctions, relations, arguments, and conclusions of which his system is composed. As such, the analysis contained in the later chapters will offer only a small contribution to such a completely methodical project. Nevertheless, they do seek to consider the most difficult, important and controversial issues related to the question of whether either Hegel's or the model's constitutional monarchy can be granted the status of philosophical necessity. It can helpfully be said now that they find no serious gaps between the thrust of his political argument and the rest of his system. More importantly, they see democratic monarchy as entirely complemented by an interpretation of the rest of Hegel's system. However, we will note some of the *superfluities* within Hegel's presentation which would have to be removed before it could be granted the status of philosophical necessity. For example, for simplicity's sake, the many equivalent terms for "Reason" should not be used, e.g. "the Idea", "the universal Spirit" (Geist) and "the world Spirit".

In this section we have seen how logical tests require a theory to be

1) *clear* (i.e. precise and unambiguous)
2) *coherent* (i.e. systematic, logically linked and consistent), and
3) *simple* (i.e. parsimonious [2] or not superfluous),

before it could be granted the status either of scientific of philosophical necessity.

**Comparative Tests**

The axiom of non-contradiction can also be seen to inspire the comparative testing of theories. As soon as we notice that another theory purports to deal with the same field(s) of concern as the one under review we are driven by this axiom to compare them. If there are two competing theories we know that they both cannot be true at the same time and in the same sense. If they prove to be irreconcilably different, at least one of them must be false. They may both be false but they cannot both be *true*. The axiom of non-contradiction tells us that we can approach either scientific or philosophical necessity only if the competitors can be reduced to one. There are four ways in which this might be achieved. The first two ways again seek to eliminate all but one by submitting the competitors to the above a) experiential and b) logical tests. If more than one theory survives these tests, we can still attempt to reduce them to one by c) checking more carefully to see whether in substance, they might not in fact only be optional formulations of the same theory. Such a reconciliation of any superficial differences between competitors might allow all of them to be seen as *absorbed* or assimilated into one theory. Two theories concerned with a limited section of experience and which had both survived these first three comparative tests might still be reduced to one if d) one of them were shown also to relate to a wider segment of experience and to have flawlessly passed all the relevant tests in these areas as well. The other theory would be subordinated to this one because of its silence or failure in the face these wider tests. In fact, if the wider theory were so broad as to prove to be *comprehensive,* it would appropriately be granted the status of philosophical necessity. However, if it proved not to be comprehensive but only wider than any other, it would appropriately be accorded the status of

---

(1) This is an elaboration of the principle of "Occam's razor".
(2) Kant also explicitly demands this in *Critique of Pure Reason,* op. cit., A623, B652; A623, B652, A649, B677; A652, B680.

scientific necessity. The bulk of the argument here has been and will continue to be concerned with the testing of democratic monarchy by *comparing* it with competing constitutional theories.

Summary

The proposed methodology for assessing the validity of competing political theories would equally allow us to examine all other types of theories. Therefore, it has been argued that all competing theories, including (evaluative) political theories, are best measured against the four criteria for philosophical necessity.

1) *Comprehensiveness:* philosophy must be concerned with all areas of *experience,* e.g. it must be *descriptive, evaluative* (e.g. *prescriptive* in relation to the present and future) and *reflexive* (e.g. contain its own epistemology and methodology). The area of a *science's* concern may be more limited. The status of 'absolute necessity' can *never* be granted to a theory.
2) *Experiential Tests:* a theory must be *compatible* with all of the experiences concerned, e.g. the prescriptive aspect of an evaluative theory must be seen to be *relevant* to the future which one has in mind.
3) *Logical Tests:* a theory must be *clear, coherent* and *simple.* These tests and the rest of the criteria are required by *the axiom of non-contradiction.*
4) *Comparative Tests* attempt to reduce the competing theories to *one* by eliminating as many as possible,
   (a) with experiential tests,
   (b) with logical tests,
   (c) by *absorbing* the remainder into one theory, or
   (d) by seeing which one has the widest experiential scope.

This chapter attempts to formulate the fundamentally *reflexive* aspect which would seem to be an essential element of any theory having the status of philosophical necessity. Its reflexive element itself seems to be philosophically necessary. It seems flawlessly to satisfy the four criteria associated with comprehensiveness, experiential tests, logical tests and comparative tests. Each of the four criteria can be seen as an articulation of any one of the other three. Thus, for example, the requirement that a theory be comprehensive,

a) is the demand that a theory pass *all* known experiential tests (sensuous and non-sensuous); or
b) is the demand that a theory conform to logic's axiom of non-contradiction and thus prove both to be self-consistent and consistent with *all* other sensuous and non-sensuous phenomena;[1] or
c) is the demand that a theory show by *comparison* how *all* other theories are either flawed by experiential or logical tests or are appropriately seen as having been absorbed into itself.

The four criteria offer *four* ways of expounding the *one* criterion for philosophical necessity, i.e. the one integrated system of criteria or the one critical perspective, each of whose articulated distinctions can be fully understood only with reference to the set of other distinctions which together constitute the methodological totality. The demonstration of this interrelatedness uses the sort of *dialectical reasoning* found in the works of Plato, Hegel and Marx.[2] The way the exposition of each part leads to the other parts, to the totality and back again to itself is the wider *reflexiveness* which characterizes every part of a dialectical totality. We have been concerned here with the *fundamental* reflexiveness which critically examines the epistemological and methodological bases for all sorts of scientific and philosophical theorizing. We have offered a theory about all theories and therefore a theory which must also be about itself.

Interpretations and Translations

Finally, it will be helpful to explain how I have sought both to read all of the philosophers discussed and to translate Hegel's texts. History has given us many philosophical and political texts which provide us with a rich source of competing theories. A selection of these has thus given me a demanding testing ground for the constitutional and methodological arguments considered

(1) This formulation recalls Kant's "ideal of pure reason" which requires "the scheme [to follow]....the regulative principle of the systematic unity of all knowledge of nature" (ibid., A674, B702).
(2) Marx rarely reflected on his "dialectic". However, at one point, he argued that the "syllogism" of "production" ("generality"), "distribution" ("particularity"), and "consumption" ("singularity") is not only a matter of balancing ... concepts" but also of "grasping real relations". *Grundrisse,* Pelican Marx Library, Harmondsworth, 1973, pp.89-90.

here.  Initially, I read these works with the intuitive aim and then with the conscious goal of discovering a political theory which could be called philosophically necessary.  As a result, these texts have been studied in a particular way.  At some points they are *clear* and at other points not.  When they are ambiguous, I have sought to record this.  In these cases, I have also tried either to think of an interpretation of the vague words or to replace the pregnant silences with words which would make the theory being considered less likely to fall foul of any of the four criteria of philosophical necessity.  The results of such attempts are here called *lenient* interpretations or lenient additions.  However, if a passage, whether ambiguous or not, seemed not to lend itself to a construction which would allow it to escape being judged deficient according to one of the four criteria, then I have tried to identify the precise *changes* in the words which would allow it to do so.  Such *improving* changes are also called here, *reconstructions* or *modifications*.  Accordingly, I have changed some of Hegel's words, e.g. my *improved* version of *The Philosophy of Right's* PP283 says that the monarch's "discretion" to appoint his prime minister is constitutionally *confined* by the will of a working majority in the elected chamber and by the rules of the 'state prerogative council' even though Hegel himself says that the monarch's discretion in this matter is "unconfined".  Such *improving* changes have required me to speak of defending the model which is a *reconstructed* version rather than of Hegel's own constitutional monarchy.

Of course, Hegel is not the only theorist who requires such treatment.  For example, Plato's brief references both to upward and downward mobility according to merit (415b&c and 423d) may lead us *leniently* [1] to add more of the practical details of just how the children from the economic class might be given an equal opportunity to become philosopher rulers.  Also, Plato's expressed hope that after several generations even the philosopher rulers will accept the foundation myth (414b&c and 415d) requires us to *improve* upon his words if a Plato-like theory is not easily to fall into the contradiction of first hoping that his philosophers will literally "believe" a myth and later arguing that they will have comprehensive philosophical "knowledge".

Thus, the aid which this work has received from Hegel has followed from some *clear* readings, from some *lenient* interpretations and from some *improving* alterations of his words.  Stage by stage, the following chapters make clear the ways in which democratic monarchy have issued from such a mixture of readings, interpretations, and alterations.  In addition to the few *improving* changes to Hegel's texts which will be discussed, I have consistently translated the many quoted passages in a *lenient* manner.  This approach has issued in many *free* translations.  When Hegel's German seemed ambiguous enough to lend itself to several possible translations, I selected the one which would accord most easily with what I argue Hegel *should* be saying.  Therefore, these *free* translations record my *lenient* interpretations of Hegel's German.  This plan has be followed in order to present these readings and arguments as simply as possible.  This is to say, that I have chosen not to complicate the substantive arguments within the body of the following chapters by the problems of translation.  Instead, these problems and my solutions to them are precisely recorded in the *Appendix* and in the *Glossary* of terms.

*Appendix B* includes an ordered list of my *literal* translations of the passages receiving a free and lenient translation in earlier chapters.  A comparison of these should make it clear which parts of the former resulted from lenient interpretations.

This chapter has outlined this work's methodological foundations.  At the same time, it has given, by implication, more exact specifications of the related meanings of the following key terms: reason, rationality, philosophy, and necessity.  The next chapter will begin to show how this approach and these terms can be interpreted to be similar to Hegel's own.

---

(1) This approach which tries to improve the faulty arguments of others before deciding whether or not they should be entirely rejected is, of course, frequently exemplified in the character of Plato's Socrates.  Also, Kant seems to follow a similar path by giving what I call lenient interpretations.  When Kant writes of Plato, for example, he says that, "If we set aside the exaggerations in Plato's methods of expression, the ... spiritual flight from the ectypal mode of reflecting upon the physical world-order to the architectonic ordering of it according to ends ... [It] is an enterprise which calls for respect and imitation" (ibid., A318, 375.)  Hegel and Marx rarely show such benevolence when treating the formulations of others.

# Chapter Seven:
# HEGEL'S SYSTEM

Previous chapters have both argued directly for the merits of democratic monarchy and have shown how republicans might be driven by the logic of their own value assumptions also to endorse the model constitution. This is the case to the extent that these accord with my own prescription: 'Act so as to maximize rational living'. Kant came closest to accepting this prescription explicitly but I find it to be implicit in the other republican arguments as well as in Hegel's philosophy. In fact, it can be argued itself to be 'philosophical necessity'. No participant in a philosophical dialogue could sustain his or her rejection of this principle without self-contradiction.

This chapter begins to trace the extent to which the model constitution is rooted within Hegel's own philosophy. The model claim to philosophical necessity will be seen to rest heavily both on Hegel's social and political theory and on his wider system. I say this in spite of the fact that several of Hegel's formulations in *The Philosophy of Right* are plainly incompatible with democratic monarchy. While later chapters will weigh the degrees of support and hostility to the ideal constitution which might be read into Hegel's social and political theories, this chapter is concerned with his wider philosophy. It begins to explain how his system can be read to provide a comprehensive theory within which democratic monarch fits even more neatly than does Hegel's own constitutional monarchy. Later chapters will show how democratic monarchy was fashioned by making some 'improving' changes to the political part of Hegel's philosophical system.

Given the great enormity of his system and the notorious obscurity of many of his formulations, it cannot be expected that all will see my interpretations as obviously correct. For example, perhaps not everyone will be happy with the equation that this chapter makes between "Reason", "the Idea" and "God".[1] Some will not readily agree that there is a prescriptive side to Hegel's analysis of "actuality" (*Chapter Eight*). Many may question the claimed parallel between Hegel's "necessity" and my concept of 'philosophical necessity' (*Chapter Nine*). Others may want to challenge the account of how each section of *The Philosophy of Right* builds to become an outline of the subjective and objective conditions for a rational state (*Chapters Ten to Twelve*). In some cases, the enforced brevity of this work may encourage such doubts. Nevertheless, it intends to deal with the most important issues. At least, it hopes to provide a clear and strong 'position paper' to be placed on the agenda of any later disputations. This chapter will not explicitly draw out many of the political implications of Hegel's wider philosophy, but its focus on "Reason" should implicitly help to clarify the main claim for democratic monarchy. This, using Hegel's[2] words, it is a "*rational* constitution",[3] it is a "hieroglyph of Reason".[4] A state so organized is an "architectonic of ... life's rationality".[5] It is a central feature of "the rational living of self-

---

(1) In the article mentioned in the *Introduction*, some of Brudner's formulations might be read to suggest that he would deny this reduction of "the divine" to "the rational", of "God" to "Reason" (e.g. pp.137-8). See also his insistence on the "divine-human distinction" (p.131).
(2) I would also say that in a model state, we "desire .... nothing except what is an expression of rationality" (Rechts PP272Z). 'Z' refers to the less reliable additions which Hegel's editors constructed by combining students' with Hegel's own lecture notes.
(3) See the *Glossary* for references to this and to many other of Hegel's special terms. There, the original German terms are noted and occasionally the problems of translation are discussed.
(4) *Rechts*, PP279Z.
(5) *Rechts*, Preface S.19 (p.6). 'S' numbers refer to the pages in the German text. These will also be added to the paragraph (PP) numbers when the paragraph is more than one page long.

conscious freedom".[1] This chapter will begin the argument for seeing democratic monarchy as a *logical* part of Hegel's comprehensive theory. While empirically existent constitutions are not analysed here in order more fully to pursue the countless number of possible *experiential* tests for the philosophical necessity of the model, the more important *comparative* tests are offered.

Reason [2]

Because "Reason" is taken to be the central concept in Hegel's system, only it and its equivalents among Hegel's special terms will be capitalized. Hegel argues that "philosophy" is possible only on the assumption [3] that we may be able to discover "the truth" about "the universe":

*Philosophie* I, S. 13-14 (p. xiii):
The courage to search for the truth or the belief [4] in the power of the human spirit is the first condition for the pursuit of philosophy. Humankind, because it is spirit, can and should respect itself as worthy of the highest. We humans cannot think too highly of the greatness and power of our spirit. With this conviction, nothing will be so coy or difficult that it will not reveal itself to us. The essence of the universe which at first is hidden and locked away has no strength to resist the courage of our struggle to know it. It must layout its wealth and depth before the eyes of the searcher for his enjoyment.[5]

(1) *Rechts,* PP270An., S.423 (p.170). 'An.' (Anmerkung) refers to the remarks to the paragraphs which Hegel added himself after the first edition.
(2) *Vernunft.*
(3) This "assumption" according to Kant would presumably be called a "transcendental idea" which is "necessary" in the "relative sense" for the "speculative employment" of reason and in the "absolute sense" *Critique of Pure Reason* (ibid., A676, B704) for the "practical employment of pure reason" (A841, B869). At the same time, he says that because this assumption does not offer an object of possible experience and cannot be given an "apodeictic" (A624, 652) proof but can only be shown to be "useful" (A826, B854) in the first case and "in the highest degree fruitful and ... indispensably necessary" (A328, B385) in the second case, this assumption is still "problematic" A256, B311). This is to admit that such an assumption *may* only be a "regulative" idea or a "heuristic fiction" (A771, B779). However, both because of, and in spite of, these same reasons, I take this assumption to be 'philosophically necessary'. In effect, this is to recognize that a philosophically necessary theory may also include what Kant calls "principles", "postulates", "hypotheses", "schema", "representations" and "intuitions".
(4) I have no reason to read Hegel's use of "belief" to be essentially different from Kant's exposition of it as distinct both from "opining" and from "knowing". Kant says that "belief" holds a judgement to be true on grounds which are both "subjectively sufficient and at the same time taken as being objectively sufficient". "*Opining* is such a holding of a judgement as is consciously insufficient, not only objectively, but also subjectively" (yet it is "more than arbitrary fiction"). When "the holding of a thing to be true is sufficient both subjectively and objectively, it is *knowledge*" (ibid., A822, B850). The difference between the "objective sufficiency" in believing and knowing is that, in the latter case, it "*is* sufficient where, in the former, it is only "*taken as being* sufficient". Kant illustrates this difference by proclaiming his "firm *belief*" (A825, B853 and A826, B854) in "the existence of God" in spite of the fact that he says, I can *cite* nothing which necessarily presupposes this thought as the condition of my explanations of the appearances exhibited by the world". On the other hand, he says that "nothing decisive can be cited against it". He also says that this "useful" postulate which sees the world as a "purposive unity" as if ordered by a "supreme intelligence" is one which experience "so frequently confirms". At the same time, "I know of no other condition under which this unity can supply me with guidance in the investigation of nature". This postulate is seen as analogous to "the highest of all genera ... which comprehends under itself all manifoldness ; genera, species, and subspecies" (A659, B687). In this thesis, for similar reasons, I proclaim my "firm belief" in the objective reality of "Reason" which Hegel also sometimes calls "God". I argue that this postulate is 'philosophically necessary' yet I choose not to call it God because "Reason" less misleadingly notes my agreement with Kant's comment that it is "a matter of indifference whether it be asserted that divine wisdom has disposed all things in accordance with its supreme ends, or that the idea of supreme wisdom is a regulative principle in the investigation of nature", i.e. "it must be a matter of complete indifference to us, when we perceive such unity, whether we say that God ... willed it ... or that nature has wisely arranged it thus" (A699, B727). This chapter uses "Reason" to name what Kant calls the articulated and "organized unity" (A676, B704) believed to be present in nature, human activity and thought. I prefer the term "Reason" to "God" also because it is less likely to imply my agreement with another of Kant's views which I deny, namely, that "moral sentiment" (A820 B857) requires us to go further by saying that "I am morally certain that" there is "a future life" (A828, B856) in which those "worthy of happiness" will be rewarded in exact proportion to their moral worthiness.
(5) At the following points, Hegel uses a similar tone to express his optimism concerning philosophical study: "thought is all truth" (*Philosophie* II, S.164(p.149); "Reason (Idee) as [the conception of Reason] is absolute and all truth ..." *(Enz.* I, PP236); and "absolute truth" *(Enz.* I, PP242 and PP244). As asserted in *Chapter Six,* I take Hegel's "absolute" not to mean 'absolute' but to mean 'philosophically necessary', i.e. not to mean so certain as not to allow any '*vague* doubts' to persist.

In the next passage, Hegel refers to the above "essence of the universe which at first is hidden and locked away" as "*Reason* which has being" but which may not be as yet discovered by us, i.e. not yet reconciled with "our self-conscious reason":
> *Enz. I*, PP6:
> ... it is equally important to understand that the content of philosophy is none other than the domain of Reason-as-the-living-human-spirit which originally brought itself forth into the world. This is to say that *actuality* is philosophy's subject matter. Our initial consciousness of this content we call *experience*. Even a sensuous study of the world distinguishes between what is only inessential appearance (i.e. transitory and insignificant experience) and what inherently and genuinely deserves the name, "actuality", i.e. distinguishes between external and inner definite existence within the wide realm of experience. In this respect, philosophy is to be distinguished *only in form* [1] from such empirical sciences (i.e. the other modes of becoming conscious). It shares with them the same experiential content. Philosophy must also be compatible with actuality and experience.[2] Indeed, this compatibility is at least one external test of the truth of a philosophy. Conversely, for science as well as for philosophy, it is seen to be the highest and ultimate aim to bring about a reconciliation of our *self-conscious reason* with the *Reason which has being*, i.e. with actuality. This is to say that, while we all experience both self-consciousness and being, both science and philosophy seek to know the rational correspondence or compatibility between consciousness and being. This reconciliation can be attained by the philosophical knowledge of Reason because ....
>
> *Enz.* I, PP6An.:
> .... Some of what is rational (vernünftig) is actual, and all of what is actual (or only part of what exists) is rational.[3]

Chapter Six defined the difference between 'science' and 'philosophy' as one of scope. Science may be concerned with a limited area of 'experience' while philosophy must attempt to make the connections between all areas. The above paragraph is taken to agree with this when it says that they are to be "distinguished only in form". In a similar vein, PP7 and An. go on to say that the content of "philosophy" is "taken from our own observing and considering of the external and inner world as presented within our experience of nature" and of both objective and subjective human living, i.e. "as presented in nature, in spirit and in the breast of humankind". He also says that we call some "sciences ... empirical only because of the sensuous starting point which they take. Like philosophy, however, their essential aim is to develop thoughts about experience or what is present-to-hand, i.e., laws, general propositions or a theory". Again, such a "theory" if achieved would constitute the above "reconciliation" between "the Reason which has being" and "self-conscious reason".

In the light of the above passages, we are now in a position to begin the interpretation of what Hegel means by "Reason". It is 'the sense which is there to be made of all our experiences'. It is that which must "reveal itself" to "the courage of our struggle to know it". It is the "rational" structure of all the "being" which we can "experience" whether or not we have yet done so. It is that which our "self-conscious reason" attempts to discover as a result of "considering" all its experience of both the "external and inner world", of "nature and ... humankind". As suggested

---

(1) As in this case, my free translations have taken the liberty of some time underlining words which Hegel did not.
(2) Hegel's clear acceptance here of the principle, that "Philosophy must also be compatible with actuality and experience", would help to provide him with a defence against Marx's polemic which implied that he was not interested in measuring his ideas by the world: "Hegel, however, is a philosopher of right, and develops the generic Idea of the state (die Staatsgattung). He is not allowed to measure the Idea by what exists; he must measure what exists by the Idea", *Critique of Hegel's 'Philosophy of Right'*, op. cit., p.55. Of course it is true that Hegel did not fully measure his philosophy by what Marx took to be the processes of the actual world. Marx seems to have ignored Hegel's distinction between "actuality" and "existence" (see *Glossary*) which will be discussed in the next chapter.
(3) This last sentence illustrates well the difference between my *free* and *literal* translations (see the Appendix). This famous epigram is more literally rendered, "What is rational that is actual; and what is actual, that is rational". My free translation is less obscure because it explicitly uses Hegel's distinction between "existence" (which included both essential and "inessential appearance") and "actuality" (which included only the essential or rational reality). He says that "the obvious is not always the essential", *Rechts* PP272Z). Marx seems not to have noticed that Hegel made this distinction and this may explain why he offered some unnecessary criticisms of Hegel, e.g., "Hegel is not to be blamed for depicting the nature of the modern state as it is, but rather for presenting what is as the essence of the state. The claim that the rational is actual is contradicted precisely by an irrational actuality, which everywhere is the contrary of what it asserts and asserts the contrary of what it is", *Critique of Hegel's 'Philosophy of Right'*, op. cit., p.64.

earlier, philosophy must assume that our experience may have a knowable-rational structure and "Reason" is Hegel's name for that "object". This is to say that it names that objective structure both at the stage in human development when a knowledge of it is not yet pursued, i.e. when it is only a possible "object" (objekt) of human consciousness, and at the stage when it has consciously become an "object" (Gegenstand) of human inquiry. When as a *Gegenstand,* it first comes into our view, it is "intuited or ... *unmediated* Reason" (*Enz.* PP244), i.e. it is 'all experience', 'simply that which includes everything else', the all embracing vague 'One' or 'the black box into which everything is thrown'.[1] Thus "Reason" is Hegel's name for the most *comprehensive* object which can come before our minds. It is similar to what other philosophers have called "the Good", "God", "the Absolute", "Substance", "Being", "the Ultimate" or "the Idea". The fact that Hegel sometimes varies his own exposition of "Reason" by using some of these alternative names is understandable, especially if we see Hegel's philosophy as a *dialectical* result of his own real and imaginary dialogues with previous philosophies. In fact, it would seem appropriate for us to see, Hegel's *Lectures on the History of Philosophy* as his report on this extended dialogue and to see his *Encyclopaedia* as an outline of the most important conclusions of that dialogue. That Hegel himself saw his philosophy as partially resulting from and thus surviving such *comparative tests* seems to be clear from the following:

> *Enz.* I, PP13:
> The most recent philosophy, provided that it *is* philosophy, is the result of all previous philosophies and must therefore contain the principles of all these philosophies. In consequence, the most recent philosophy is the most developed, the most rich and the most concrete.[2]

The *Appendix* and the *Glossary* record Hegel's own use of such equivalents for "Reason" as "the Idea" and "the Absolute". However, in order to minimize both ambiguity and superfluity, both within the free translations and within the expositions here, I will either replace or supplement the original equivalent terms by "Reason". When the original term remains, it also will be marked by an initial capital letter, e.g. "the in-and-for-itself Will".[3] When "reason appears without a capital, it refers to the subjective thought process (i.e. "self-conscious reason"[4] which consciously seeks to know "Reason". The object (Gegenstand) of reason is Reason. Both when reason is seen in its simplicity and grasped it in its complexity, its name will not change. This is because "Reason is its own result and as such, this result is as much unmediated as mediated".[5] Often, when Hegel is speaking of one aspect or stage of this "unmediated and mediated" Reason, he misleadingly refers simply to it as "Reason", i.e. he does not explicitly qualify it by the appropriate adjective. Thus, it is not always clear when he is only speaking of one such aspect rather than of the whole of Reason. In an attempt to avoid this ambiguity, when necessary, I will add what I take to be the appropriate qualifiers to "Reason". Most frequently, '*as* phrases' will be added but sometimes '*of* phrases' or 'adjectives', e.g. Reason-*as*-logic, *as*-nature or *as*-human-spirit (e.g. Reason-*as*-the-monarchical-organ of the constitution); the conception *of* Reason; and *unmediated* Reason.

Conception [6]

Because "philosophy is conceptual knowing"[7] when we have achieved a full grasp of Reason in all its dynamic complexity, we have attained what Hegel calls "the conception of Reason".[8] In the language of the above extract from *Enz.* I, PP6, it is this "conception" which reconciles "our self-conscious reason with the Reason which has being". In the words of *Chapter Six,* "the conception of Reason" is read to be Hegel's name for the comprehensive *theory* or system to which he is proposing that we grant the status of *philosophical necessity.* Thus "the conception of Reason" would provide

(1) I see Hegel's "Reason" or Kant's "God" as also characterized by Kant as the "transcendental principle" which is presupposed by "the unity of rules", "a systematic unity ... inherent in the objects" (op. cit., A650, B678 and A651, B679). Kant assumes this unity in spite of our also being "free to admit as likewise possible that all powers may be heterogeneous" (ibid.). Nevertheless, he says, and I agree, that "reason finds itself constrained to assume" (A811, B839) this unity "since without it we should have no reason at all, and without reason no coherent employment of the understanding, and in the absence of this no sufficient criterion of empirical truth" (A651, B679).
(2) For additional textual confirmations that Hegel accepts the importance of what I call *comparative tests,* see, e.g. *Philosophie* I, S.49 (p.30), *Logic* II, S.249 (p.580) and S.264 (p.591).
(3) *Rechts,* PP3-1An.
(4) *Enz.* I. PP6.
(5) *Enz.* I, PP213Z.
(6) *Begriff.*
(7) *Enz.* I, PP16OZ.
(8) *der Begriff der Idee, Enz.* I, PP236.

the best conscious foundation for the theoretical definition, assessment, generation, defence, and renewal of 'rational living'. Hegel uses many equivalent terms for "the conception of Reason" and these are recorded in the *Appendix* and in the *Glossary*. Again, in order to minimize ambiguity and superfluity, only this phrase will be used in the free translations except at the points were Hegel himself employs the equivalent terms which *Chapter Six* has already refined, i.e., 'knowledge', 'system', 'philosophy', and 'theory'. The human achievement of "the conception of Reason" in modern times is said by Hegel both to mark and to be Reason's own highest development. This is to say, that when conceiving Reason, *we* have become "Reason-as-philosophy",[1] the element of Reason which has being and now has risen to the thinking of Reason. The "conception of Reason" is "Reason thinking itself".[2] In this rational "subjectivity"[3] of the philosopher, Reason attains its own self-knowing. Within this subjective knowing, the all inclusive "object" (i.e. Reason) has made itself its own "object" (Gegenstand). In "the conception of Reason", Reason knows itself. In Reason, the conceiving process has its all inclusive object while in "the conception of Reason", Reason has its own highest development as "subject". This subject is any human being who has achieved the philosophical knowledge of Reason.

In various ways, the above paragraph's discussion of 'Reason-as-the-conception of Reason' expresses the *reflexive* character which *Chapter Six* argued a theory must have before it might claim philosophical necessity. Hegel's "Reason" and his "conception of Reason" purport integrally to include the same theory of itself i.e. to include a theory of our theorizing process (i.e. an epistemology and methodology). Speaking more precisely, "Reason" can have this reflexiveness explicitly in Reason's conception of Reason only because "the conception of Reason" was already implicitly within "the Reason which has being" before philosophers came explicitly to conceive it. The reflexive return to itself which thus characterizes the movement of "Reason" and its special self-completing achievement are well represented by Hegel's image of a circle:

*Philosophie I*, S.46 (p.27):
This movement is a concrete sequence of developments or elucidations. We must not imagine these to be arranged into some spuriously infinite straight line but into a circle, i.e. into a line which turns back into itself. On the periphery of this circle are a great number of circles. The whole is a great, within-itself-bending-back series of developments and elucidations.[4]

The circle in FIGURE 1 portrays my interpretation of this reflexive, returning "movement" of Reason. While Hegel speaks above of the "great number of circles ... on the periphery", each presumably representing one "development" or one "elucidation" of Reason, my exposition will be initially simplified by referring instead to these as 'arcs'. Just as the "totality" of these arcs constitutes the circle, the totality of these developments and elucidations define Reason. Each arc represents a development, aspect, or "moment" of Reason. Again, these will be distinguished from the "Reason" which is their totality by various qualifiers, e.g. Reason-*as*-nature. Also we will consistently follow Hegel's occasional practice of referring to these aspects or arcs as "specific elements of Reason" (die bestimmte Ideen).[5] The human achievement of "the conception of Reason" is the closing reflexive arc portrayed at '12 o'clock' in FIGURE 1. FIGURE 2 again portrays this arc separately as that special circle "on the periphery" which reflexively completes Reason's circle. The arrows in FIGURE 1 start and end with Reason in order to recall that Hegel's Reason is "as much unmediated as mediated".[6] This is to say, that Hegel's "Reason which has being" first is "nature" (i.e. "intuited or ... unmediated Reason" or "Reason-as-nature").[7] From within nature, "Reason-as-the-human spirit" develops in history until, with the essential aid of the "elucidations" of the categories and distinctions which are given by "Reason-as-logic", humans begin to approach the achievement of an "adequate conception"[8] of the rational totality of nature and of human living, i.e. of "Reason". The "movement" which is traced by the arrows in FIGURE 1 relate to the *time* sequence of Reason's "development" from nature to philosophical consciousness, more precisely, from nature to the explicit "conception of Reason". In contrast, the arrows in FIGURE 2 portray the logical order in which Hegel's own elucidations of Reason are presented by him within his *Encyclopaedia*. As a *logical* "sequence", it starts with the most abstract and general categories

(1) *Enz*. III, PP577.
(2) *Enz*. I, PP36.
(3) *Enz*. PP215 and PP232Z.
(4) Hegel also uses this image elsewhere, e.g. *Enz*. I, PP15, PP17 and PP181An, and *Rechts* PP267Z. In a similar manner Kant uses the images of a "sphere", *Critique of Pure Reason*", op. cit. B780, and of "horizon" (B686, B787).
(5) *Enz*. I, PP213An.  (6)  *Enz*. I, PP213Z.
(7) *Enz*. I,PP244.  (8)  *Logic* II, S.271 (p.597).

FIGURE 1: Reason

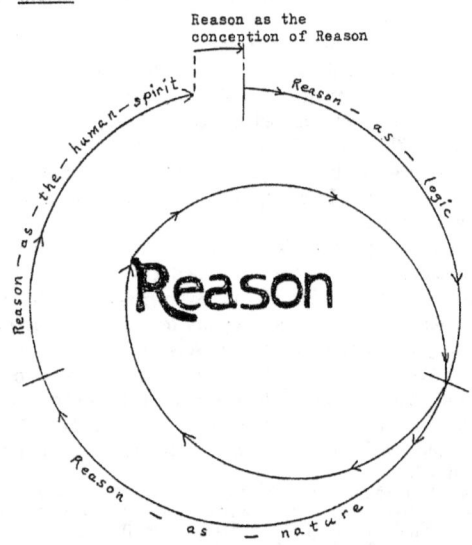

FIGURE 2: the conception of Reason

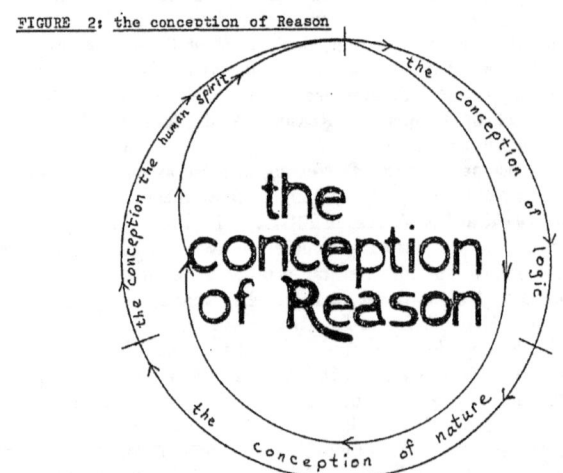

*System* 75

FIGURE 3: Reason-as- the-conception of Reason

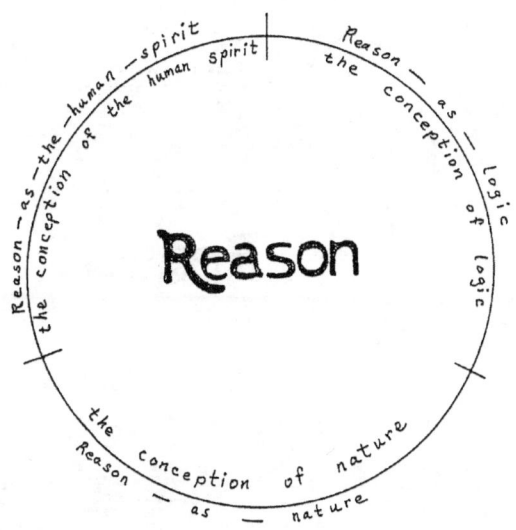

FIGURE 4:   Reason-as-the-monarchical-organ and
            the conception of the monarchical organ

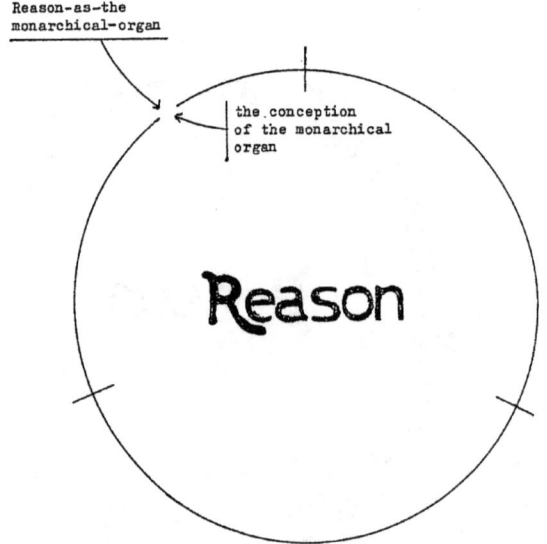

("being", "naught" and "becoming") and then moves eventually to the exposition of the most "rich" and "concrete" categories and distinctions (e.g. "constitutional monarchy"). This is to say, that it begins

1) with an outline of all the "elucidations" and "specific elements of Reason" which humans find they require even to think about thought (together, the several hundreds of these constitute 'the conception of logic', i.e. *Enz.* I: the "science", *or better, the 'philosophy'* of logic),
2) moves on to the analysis of the additional "specifications" required for the study of the physical sciences (together, the many hundreds of these constitute 'the conception of nature', i.e. *Enz.* II: "the philosophy of nature" and, finally,
3) moves on to expound an outline of the further categories and "actualities" required for a study of all the significant aspects of human living (together, the several hundreds of these make up 'the conception of the human spirit', i.e *Enz.* III: "the philosophy of spirit".

It is because a complete "elucidation" of human living must include an account of the human "development" of philosophical consciousness, that such elucidation discovers itself as already *being* an elucidation of philosophical consciousness by virtue of its earlier expositions of logic, nature and humankind. At this point, elucidation finds itself to be within a circle. It discovers that to go on is only to repeat, to correct, or to refine the account of the many hundreds of "specific conceptions" already traced. This is the discovery of the fundamental *reflexiveness* within "the conception of Reason". This is represented by the arrows in FIGURE 2 which both start and finish with "the conception of Reason".

It has already been suggested that Hegel's "Reason" and "the conception of Reason" respectively have the same emphases of "objectivity" and "subjectivity" as did the two phrases quoted much earlier: "the Reason which has being" and "self-conscious reason".[1] This difference of emphasis will continue to be employed throughout, i.e. "Reason" and every "specific element of Reason" mentioned will refer to *objects, beings* and *actualities* irrespective of whether they are yet seen by a given human consciousness while "the conception of Reason" and each "specific conception" of which it is composed will refer to a *consciousness*, a *knowing*, or a *theory* of such objects by human *subjects*.

This method of recording this useful distinction is followed with the support of the passages already quoted and with the wider support of Hegel's own exposition, e.g. his saying in *Rechts* PP272An., that "Reason" (Idee) is "more concrete" than "conception".

It must be stressed that this difference is only one emphasis. The mutual dependence of "Reason" and "the conception of Reason" and the self-mediating character of this dependence would make their separation false and requires that 'Reason-as-the-conception of Reason' become "grasped as Object-Subject".[2] The "objective" emphasis of Reason is recorded in FIGURE 1 by the three major "specific elements of Reason" being placed on the *convex* or outer side of the three corresponding arcs. In contrast, the "subjective" emphasis of conception is represented in FIGURE 2 by the three major "specific conceptions" being located on the *concave* or inner side of the three corresponding arcs. FIGURE 3 simplifies and incorporates these features of FIGURES 1 and 2 and thus portrays the complex reflexive or self-mediating unity of "Reason". FIGURE 3 also seeks to illustrate the point that, for every convex object or "specific element of Reason", there should be a corresponding concave "specific conception", i.e. a philosophical, subjective or rational theory of that object. FIGURE 4 offers an example of this 'hand in glove' relationship by locating "Reason-as-the-monarchical-organ" on the convex side of the absent arc of the "Reason-as-the-human-spirit" arc and by placing "the conception of the monarchical organ" on the concave side of that arc. In *Chapter Eleven*, FIGURE 9 will show more fully the way in which this 'absent arc' is made up of a chain of circles, each representing a "specific element of Reason" and each with a different level of "generality".

In the following passage, Hegel explicitly confirms, in a theological idiom, that Reason's full development is dependent on its rising to self-consciousness through the human attainment of "the conception of Reason", i.e. without this "knowing .... the Divine Spirit could not become the in-and-

(1) *Enz.* I, PP6.
(2) *Enz.* I, PP214.

for-itself General" (i.e. could not become 'Reason-as-the-conception-of-Reason'):
> *Philosophie* I, S.96 (p.75):
> The essence of my human spirit which is my "self-conscious reason" is my essential being, my very substance without which I could not be actual. This essence is the combustible material, so to speak, which can be kindled and illuminated by the general Essence as such (i.e. by "Reason") which is the object of philosophical study. Only in so far as this phosphorous is in humankind is the comprehension, the kindling and the illuminating possible. Only thus is the feeling, intuiting and *knowing* of God [i.e. of Reason] within the scope of humankind at all. Also, without this essence which is the divine spirit within humankind, the Divine Spirit could not become the in-and-for-itself General.

This is another statement of Hegel's view that the "teleological" aim of nature and of human history is the human attainment of the sort of knowing and willing which is contained within and demanded by "the conception of Reason". Such knowing and willing forms the core of "rational living".[1] This is both the inherent aim, and the eventually to become self-conscious aim, of human life and history. This aim implies my own, often repeated prime prescription: 'Act so as to maximize free, rational living'.

This chapter, has begun to outline the case for our seeing either Hegel's or my monarchical conclusions as 3) a *logically* integral "element" of a 1) *comprehensive* theory, a *reflexive* theory which claims to embrace all 2) *"experience"* and which accepts the demand of our 4) *comparative* tests that todays leading philosophy must "contain the principles" of all "previous philosophies". However, one more question remains to be discussed here. Hegel's frequent use of the adjective, "absolute", and his occasional reference to "Reason" as "the Absolute", might at first sight lead us to charge him with claiming something for his system which *Chapter Six* argued was humanly unachievable, namely, 'absolute necessity'. I have found no passage in which he either clearly claims this sort of 'absolute necessity' for his philosophy or in which he explicitly accepts the unavoidability of the residual 'vague doubts' in *Chapter Six*. Nevertheless, I *leniently* read such an acceptance to be implicit in his frequently saying that "every individual is a child of his time" and that it "is foolish to imagine that any one philosophy could go over and beyond its contemporary world",[2] in his saying that he has given "scepticism's demand that we "doubt everything" its appropriate place within his conception of Reason,[3] and in his plea to be excused from any inadequacy in his "execution" of the search for "the truth" about "the value of things, of insights and of human actions".[4] Such words also assist the *lenient* interpretation of Hegel's use of "absolute" so as *not* to indicate his view that he had achieved the 'absolute theory' but rather to refer to the reflexive or self-completing character of his philosophy. Such a gloss is also suggested by the phrase which he frequently used as inter-changeable with "absolute", i.e. "in-and-for-itself" (an und für sich), the feature outstandingly characteristic of 'Reason-as-the-conception-of-Reason'. This reading when added to the other findings of the outline of Hegel's philosophy within this chapter allows us modestly to assert that no obviously insurmountable obstacle has been found in his wider system to granting the status of 'philosophical necessity' to the model's monarchy. Also, Hegel's system seems to accord with the perspective defined in *Chapter Six*. The method by which "self-conscious reason" can become "reconciled" with "the Reason which has being" would seem to be the same as the method by which we search for 'philosophical necessity'. Its four criteria contain all of the "rational" demands that we can place upon a theory which purports to secure this reconciliation. In the modified words of the previously quoted epigram of PP6An., 'What is rational is philosophically necessary'. The search for philosophical necessity accepts Hegel's view that philosophy is only possible on the assumption that the object of its study (i.e. all experience) has a finite, knowable and rational structure. This structure, Hegel calls "Reason which has being" or simply, "Reason". The "conception of Reason" is taken merely to be Hegel's name for a 'philosophically necessary theory'.

The next chapter will explore whether Hegel's conception of "Reason" prohibits or allows the generation of *prescriptions,* e.g. the formulation of a *model* constitution.

(1) *Rechts,* PP270An. (S.422).
(2) *Rechts,* S.26 (p.11).
(3) *Enz.* I, PP7An.
(4) *Logik* II, S.243 (p.575).

# Chapter Eight:
## HEGEL'S PRESCRIPTION

*Chapter Six* argued that a theory would have to be evaluative as well as descriptive before it could hope to be comprehensive let alone philosophically necessary. It went on to argue that such a theory would also have to be evaluative in relation to any current or future choices of action which might be facing us, i.e. it must also be *prescriptive*. It was said that the axiom of non-contradiction logically leads us to prescribe actions which are calculated to help our present or future worlds to become more in line with the scale of values arranged within our currently leading theory, i.e. it enjoins us to act wherever possible in order to maximize the actuality of these values. *Chapter One* explained why this book is concerned only with the formulation of a 'general, prescriptive guide'[1] to action. It might be supposed that we would have had little difficulty in assuming that Hegel also saw his constitutional monarchy as offering such a prescriptive model given the previously quoted claims which he attached to it: "rational", a "hieroglyph of Reason", etc. This impression would be encouraged by a reading of the several clear prescriptions that Hegel offered on various occasions and which will be discussed shortly. This is to say, that the view that Hegel's philosophy had a prescriptive side to it might have been largely taken for granted if it were not for one of his paragraphs which plainly implies that prescription is a philosophical impossibility. This paragraph is the famous "owl of Minerva" passage in the Preface to *The Philosophy of Right*. It clearly denies that a philosophical "science of the state" can ever teach "the world" how it "ought to be". This passage will be translated and studied in a later section of this chapter. First, several passages in which Hegel is clearly offering some general and specific prescriptions will be considered. These later analyses will establish that an evaluative and prescriptive dimension is nevertheless inherent to Hegel's system, ordered as it is by his prime value, i.e. by "Reason". The first two are those which most obviously relate to constitutional questions:[2]

> *Rechts*, PP28OZ:
> Within a rational constitution, ... the monarch only has to do with the *formal* decision and thus he is only required to be a human being ... He need only .... say "yes" and to place the dot on the "i" ... The ... pinnacle ... *should* be such that the personal attributes of the monarch's character are not significant .... This specification for the monarch is *rational* because it accords with the conception of Reason-as-the-constitution ...
> *Rechts*, PP32OZ:
> The subjectivity of the monarch is by itself abstract but it *should* be a concrete ... ideality which spreads itself over the whole state.

By implication, these words clearly prescribe how each one of us should act when we have the opportunity: 'we should either maintain or build a constitution for the states in which a monarch would be seen as the *formal* "pinnacle" of decision making, i.e. the formal "subjectivity" which helps maximally to guarantee that this state will concretely secure for itself a unity of decision-making over time'.

With regard to the question of a monarch's role before a rational constitution becomes established, Hegel said that the independent intervention of the monarch is sometimes "required and *justified*" in order to remove an obstacle to the administration of justice which might be caused by

---

(1) Habermas would seem to call such a 'model' a "critical theorem", *Theory and Practice*, op. cit., p. 32.
(2) Under 'prescription', the *Glossary* lists additional passages which are clearly prescriptive, and some which are not so clear.

a "clique of officials". Hegel took "Friedrich II's "overruling of the lawyers' arguments in the "Arnold Case" to be an example of such an intervention.[1] In the context of another undeveloped constitution, Hegel clearly states his support for the King of Wurtemberg's proposals for constitutional reform:
> *Wurt.*, S.471 (p.254):
> Are not the quoted proposals nothing other than the sort of constitutional fundamentals which we *must* recognize and accept with the *highest approval?*

The next two clearly prescriptive passages make broader constitutional points:
> *Eng.*, S.86 (p. 297):
> ... when the aristocratic element in England as compared with the democratic element is the most significant force ... and when it finds its security and stability in the submerging of the people it rules into collective sensuality and into ethical depravity ... it is to be recognized as a *good* sign of the reawakening of the *moral* sense within the English people that they now have a feeling of the need for *reform* which involves a repugnance at that depravity. At the same time, we recognize that it *should* have become accepted that the *correct* way *to seek the improvement* is no more merely by the moral means of notions (Vorstellungen), by admonitions or by a union of isolated individuals in order both to avoid becoming beholden to the system of corruption and to work against it, but is *by the alteration of institutions*. The usual prejudice of laziness which always clings to the old faith in the goodness of an institution even when it hangs upon a wholly *depraved* set of circumstances has finally given way. Therefore, a thoroughgoing reform has become all the more demanded ...
> *Eng.* S.89 (p.300):
> Hitherto, the features which have an important part to play in those ... *glorious and fortunate advances* have been *lacking* in England. Among these features, the scientific codification of the law *stands the highest* ...

Hegel is clearly congratulating the English now that their "moral sense" has been reawakened. This is true in spite of the fact that Hegel disapproves of the specific reforms being proposed. However, he does go on to imply a prescription that the reformers work to alter the existing institutions and especially to seek "the scientific codification of the law".

The last passage to be considered below reveals Hegel's prescriptiveness by unambiguously showing him to recognize that the free will of humans, places upon them some "responsibility" both for the "good" and for the "evil" in the world. Unavoidably, his words imply that it is only because humans have the capacity "to know" and to will the good that they can be held "responsible". This view requires us "logically" to conclude that this responsibility enjoins a philosopher to try to offer the sort of knowledge which would help people to will the good in the present and future, i.e. that he should attempt to offer general prescriptions. Hegel starts out by taking great care to emphasize that "the cunning of Reason" which he has just discussed must not be interpreted to reduce us merely to the tools or "means" of "Reason":
> *Geschichte*, S.49 (p.33):
> While we may allow that the aims of most individuals and their satisfaction are sacrificed because an individual's happiness must in the main belong to the realm of chance, a view which accepts that for the most part individual's are to be seen as abandoned by Reason and to be considered under the category of means, yet there is one misreading of this view which we must oppose. It must not be taken to separate individuals in every respect from Reason, i.e. from the Highest. Immanent *within individuals, there is an eternal or divine property which is in no way subordinate* to Reason. This property is found, for example, in people's moral, ethical and religious lives ... (S.50). When we speak of a "means" to an end we at first imagine that the means stands outside the end or has no share in the end. In fact, even natural things at large must have a characteristic within them which accords with the rational end which is the conception of Reason. Less than other creatures, humans behave according to that wholly external relation while their freedom also provides them with the opportunity to satisfy personal aims which may be different from the aim of Reason. *Humans have a share* in that aim and that is why *they are ends in themselves.*[2] Humans are not mere formal ends in themselves as are living things ... whose properties are indeed *rightly* subordinated to human life and used as means. In contrast, humans are ends in themselves in the sense that they form the content of the *rational* aim ... It is only because this divinity is in humans that they can be an end in themselves. From the outset, this property is *self-conscious reason* and so far as it is active and self-determining, it is called *freedom* ... This property partially raises humans above the realm of external necessity and chance. However, it must also be said that to the extent that individuals can appropriately claim freedom, to that same extent *they are responsible* (Schuld) for ethical and religious corruption ... This is the mark of the absolute and high specific characteristic of humankind. *A human being can know what is good and what is evil* and this specific

---

(1) *Rechts*, PP295An. See Knox's explanatory note 61.
(2) This sentence reminds one of Kant's second formulation of the categorical imperative, *Grounding*, op. cit., p. 36.

characteristic is *logically the willing of either good or evil*. In one sense, humans can have the responsibility for ... all ... the good and evil in the world. Only animals are genuinely without responsibility ... (S.51).
(S.54) This may be enough discussion about the means which Reason or the world Spirit uses in history in orders to realize its own conception. Put simply and abstractly, this realization results from *the activity of human subjects* within which Reason is present as their immanent and substantial essence. At first, Reason is still obscure though it is their hidden foundation. (S.55)

The recognition of this "responsibility" helps to explain why occasionally Hegel did, by implication, clearly offer prescriptive guidance to his fellows as already exemplified both with regard to the role of the monarch and in relation to constitutional reform both in Wurtemberg and in England. Shortly, this recognition will lead us also to read Hegel's "Reason", "rational", "genuine Infinity", "actual", "right", and, thus, the many hundreds of other evaluative references within Hegel's theory, as logically helping to provide a systematic basis for such prescriptions. First, however, we must face the inescapable fact that in "the owl of Minerva" paragraph, Hegel clearly denies by implication that philosophy can offer any political prescriptions.

### Hegel's Denial of Prescription

Since the following quotation plainly limits philosophy to *retrospective* knowing by saying that "philosophy is always too late" to teach "the world" how it "ought to be", it also, by implication, unavoidably denies prescription to philosophy. This is why it is argued here that it must be altered if a similar paragraph is to be retained within the 'text' of a philosophically necessary political theory. Each of the following improving *modifications* is keyed to the points marked within the translation:

*1): insert the word, 'almost';
*2): insert the word, 'usually';
*3): insert the word, 'usually';
*4): insert the phrases, 'if philosophy's rational ideal world is to assist actuality's structuring process in any way, a citizen seeking to use this ideal must, more importantly, be aided by the empirically existent tendencies which are already strong within that process. Be that as it may, usually...';
*5): or instead of '*4', perhaps only insert 'alone' here; and
*6): insert the word, 'usually':

    *Rechts*, S.27 (p.12):
    One more word remains to be said about the teaching of how the world ought to be. Philosophy (*1) *always* comes too late to give it anyway. As the thought of the world, philosophy (*2) *first* appears in time *after* actuality's structuring process *has been completed* and has made itself ready to be conceived philosophically. The rationally ideal world as distinct from the empirically real world (*3) *first* appears within the ripeness of the relevant empirical actuality. This is a teaching of the conception of Reason, and history equally shows it to be necessary. This rational ideal grasps this same empirical world in its substance. This ideal builds this world up into an intellectual realm. Therefore, (*4) when philosophy paints its grey in grey, then has a shape of living become old. With this grey in grey, (*5) that shape *is not able* to rejuvenate itself but only to know itself: the owl of Minerva (*6) *first* begins its flight with the falling of the dusk.

If philosophy's "grey in grey" only comes *after* "a shape of living" has matured and if this shape cannot be "rejuvenated", why did Hegel attempt to offer the English the quoted advice on how to "reform" (i.e. rejuvenate) their corrupt constitution? Did he not *prescribe* the "scientific codification of the law"? Would not such codification be one result of the "science of the state" and did not these prescriptions in some sense attempt to help "to construct a state as it ought to be"? The argument in *Chapter Six* and Hegel's own clearly prescriptive practices (as listed in the *Glossary* and as exemplified above) stand irreconcilably opposed to this "owl of Minerva" paragraph and this is why it has been *modified*. If we were inclined to let Hegel off lightly for this bald contradiction within his work, we might conjecture that perhaps it was due to his calculation that if the Prussian censors read his owl of Minerva paragraph, they might be soothed away from reading on to discover the implied selective criticisms of the existing Prussian constitution, e.g. for its lack of a living representative assembly.[1] This conjecture could also be seen as fitting in with

---

(1) The fact that Hegel experienced censorship both earlier as editor of the *Bamberger Zeitung* and later with his article *About the English Reform Bill* gives this suggestion some plausibility. Also, T.M. Knox says about the publication of *The Philosophy of Right*, that the "reason why it was delayed 18 months can hardly have been anything except fear of the censor". See "Hegel and Prussianism" in *Hegel's Political Philosophy*, W. Kaufmann (ed.), New York 1970, p.16. Also see my report on Ilting's view on this issue in the *Preface*, page 7.

the Preface's last paragraph which might be interpreted as Hegel's attempt to alert the careful reader to this way of evading the censors. There he says that the Preface as such could only offer an "external and subjective ... introduction to the standpoint of the book". By implication, perhaps he is saying that it should not be seen as constituting a part of his "scientific exposition". Because we cannot be sure whether the presence of the Prussian censors did or did not have this significance for Hegel, we are still faced with the problem of the owl of Minerva paragraph's clear denial of any possibility of philosophical or scientific prescription. Clearly, it must be rejected or modified if we are to move toward a philosophically necessary political theory.

**Conflicting Readings**

This bald contradiction within Hegel's exposition could lead us to interpret many ambiguous passages in two conflicting ways depending on whether they were read together with the the owl of Minerva paragraph as it stands, or together with his prescriptive practice and the proposed modified version of this paragraph. One example of such possible conflicting interpretations is provided by a passage which occurs in the Preface a page earlier:

*Rechts*, S.26 (p.11):
This book, in so far as it contains a science of *the state*, seeks nothing else but to *conceive* and to present the state as an inherently *rational* entity. As a philosophical work, it must be as far as possible from the attempt to construct *a state as it ought to be*. The teaching which may be within this book *cannot* extend to instructing the state about what it ought to be. Far more, it teaches how the state or the ethical universe should become philosophically known ...

Hegel's own owl of Minerva paragraph would incline us to read the "cannot" in the above translation as resulting from the fact that "philosophy always comes too late". However, Hegel's prescriptive practice suggests that the "cannot", instead refers to the philosophical priority which Hegel and I give to the discovery of the "inherently rational" state, i.e. the "rational ideal" or 'model'. Hegel is perhaps saying here, that this task is difficult enough for one book and so "this book cannot extend to instructing" any one empirically existing "state about what it ought to be". A "science of the state" must *first* attempt "to conceive ... *the* state" as it ought to be and "be as far as possible from the attempt to construct *a* state, as it ought to be". While the conception of the rational state, no doubt, has many prescriptive implications for every existing state, the drawing of these implications are of secondary importance and are too numerous, detailed and subject to the contingencies recalled at the beginning of *Chapter One* to be included in one book. They are secondary in the sense that they would be impossible to see until we have built a model state within our "intellectual realm". They would be too numerous and contingent to the extent that they went *beyond the obvious* prescriptive extensions. While "Reason-as-constitutional-monarchy" is seen here as obviously implying the general prescription that we should help to maintain or to build constitutional monarchies in our world, it is a much more detailed and uncertain question to determine how best to do this in each, let alone in every, political system. For example, within the political environment of the United States, does the model of democratic monarchy prescribe that we should work for the institution of monarchy immediately or instead for a 'parliamentary' as opposed to the 'congressional' arrangements in the first instance? Even for the British case, the detailed prescriptive implications are not wholly obvious. While the model clearly suggests that we should support the monarchical system, only a much longer analysis might allow us to see whether or not the model (which combined with the relevant empirical evidence and arguments) also implies that the civil list should be reduced, that the Church should be disestablished, or that the electoral system should be made proportional without delay. These are important local questions but philosophically they are not the first questions. Prior is the search for a rational model which may serve as the general prescriptive goal. This model is certainly the primary concern of this work and may have been Hegel's also.

**By First Discovering the "Rational Ideal" State to Serve as the General Prescriptive Goal, Philosophy Escapes the Charge of Subjectivist Moralizing.**

'Subjectivist moralising' is what Hegel refers to as "negative fault finding" in the next passage to be translated. It is the sort of shallow criticism or prescription which results form what an "idiosyncratic individual ... spins out for himself in his isolation" from "ideals which phantasy has produced".[1] The sort of prescription which this chapter is affirming escapes the charge of subjectivist moralizing because it first seeks a philosophical ideal, a model discovered with regard to the "more comprehensive design" (für den allgemeinen Zweck) of Reason. This is why such a model can stand as a realistic general goal for the guidance of action.

(1) *(Geschichte*, S.51-54, (p.34).   (2)   Ibid., S.37 (p.22).

Returning to the above passage (*Rechts*, S.26), I see it also as rejecting the easy criticism of existing states which anyone can offer and which does not require the critic to judge any state against the standard of an openly formulated rational model. This view is more explicit in the following extract. The *rational* model is a formulation based on actuality, i.e. based on the discovery of "the genuine value" or the "positive aspect" of all past and present empirically existing states.

*Geschichte*, S.53:
It is easier to see the deficiencies within individuals, within states, and within the changes in the world than it is to discover their *genuine value*. While engaged in this *negative fault finding* ... one stands over events without grasping that these events themselves are predominantly shot through and through with *a positive aspect* ...

While *Enz*. I, PP6An. would also seem to be ambiguous in the sense that it leads to two conflicting interpretations depending on whether or not it is read together with Hegel's own owl of Minerva paragraph, it is glossed here as an elaboration of the above criticism of 'subjective moralizing'. It charges the "acuteness" of the "abstractive understanding" with criticizing without a rational model and thus of only being concerned with "trivial ... external and transitory ... political arguments". I understand Hegel to be saying that "such trivial objects" are not the *primary* "interest of a philosophical science". In the first instance, "philosophy has only to do with Reason and, therefore, with actuality". The "abstractive understanding may indeed rightly find in such cases, much that does not accord with ... definitions" which are popularly believed to be "correct". In this sense, "Who is not acute enough to see much in his environment which ... is not as it ought to be."

The next example of a quotation which lends itself to two conflicting readings is the "child of his time" passage that immediately follows the above "science of the state" extract from the Preface:

*Rechts*. S.26 (p.11):
Because some of what is, is Reason, the task of philosophy is to conceive what is. As for the individual, everyone is a child of his time anyway and therefore philosophy also is its time grasped in thoughts. It is ... foolish to imagine that any one philosophy could go over and beyond its contemporary world ... If, in fact, a theory goes over there and behind the world as it is to build a world as it ought to be, then, indeed, that world exists but only in an individual's intentions - a fluid area in which an individual is left to build anything that he might fancy.

While the owl of Minerva paragraph would lead us to read, "the task of philosophy is to conceive what is", as an earlier statement of the merely *retrospective* "knowledge" which that paragraph grants, Hegel's prescriptive practice and *Chapter Six's* requirement that a philosophically necessary theory be prescriptive leads this phrase to be construed as a restatement of the famous epigram first written two pages previously in the Preface:

Some of what is rational is actual and all of what is actual (or only part of what exists) is rational.

This is to say, that not every aspect of "what is" is "Reason" but only those features which are "rational", i.e. those which provide some of the "objective guarantees" [1] or conditions for the human achievement of "the conception of Reason" (i.e. the "teleological aim") which orders the whole of Hegel's system as mentioned near the end of *Chapter Seven*.

The Threat To Prescription From Determinism

On the other hand, if read together with Hegel's owl of Minerva paragraph alone, the statements that it is philosophy's task "to conceive what is", that every individual "is a child of his time" and that "it is ... foolish to imagine that any one philosophy could go ... beyond its contemporary world" might seem to confirm a 'total, external, deterministic' view of the world's "structuring process" which is only knowable in retrospect, i.e. "the owl of Minerva *first* begins its flight with the falling of the dusk". Exactly the same sets of conflicting interpretations would flow from the next section's five related translations. Similarly, they also might be read to threaten any rational prescription by asserting that the future is entirely outside the scope of deliberate, human control. They could be easily taken to assert a 'total, external determinism' if they were read in isolation from the above recognition on Hegel's part of human "responsibility" or read in isolation from his clearly prescriptive practice. In this recognition and practice, I see one of Hegel's voices fighting against the ambiguous, deterministic voice which is again exhibited in the next section. The first voice helps me to remove the threat posed by the second voice to prescription.

(1) *Rechts*, PP286An.

**Five Deterministic, Yet Equivocal Passages**

In the first of the five ambiguous extracts quoted below, it is suggested here that two *lenient* insertions be made: 'enduringly' and 'for the most part',[1] at the points marked *1) and *2) respectively:

1) *Enz.* I, PP209Z:
   Reason is as cunning as it is strong. In the main, cunning resides within the mediating activity in which the existing objects and people influence and wear each other down. They are left to follow their own natures. Reason does not directly interfere with this process. Nevertheless, only Reason's aim is *1) brought forth. One can in this sense say, that Reason or divine Providence as absolute cunning retains itself within the world and its process. Reason or God has left human beings with their particular passions and interests to continue to shape events even though what thereby comes to pass is the fulfilment of His intentions. What comes to pass is *2) other than that at first intended by the people involved.

2) *Geschichte*, S.52 (p.35):
   ... we say that universal Reason is *accomplishing* itself ... (S.53) Now, in contrast to those simple ideals, the insight to which philosophy *should* lead is that *the actual world is as it should be,* i.e. that the genuine Good, the general and divine Reason also has the power to *bring itself* to completion. The most concrete notion [2] of this Good, of this Reason, is God. *God governs the world.* The content of His governing, His plan, is world history. Philosophy wishes to grasp this plan because only that which is carried out according to this plan is actuality. What is not in accordance with this plan is only *foul existence.* Those who have those simple ideals seem to view the world as if it were only an appearance of mad or foolish happenings. This appearance fades before the pure light of this divine Reason (Idee). Reason is no simple ideal. Philosophy wishes to know the content of these happenings, i.e. to know the actuality of the divine Reason ...

3) *Enz.* I, PP234Z:
   The discontented striving fades when we know that the ultimate aim of the world is as much completed as continually completing itself.

4) *Enz.* I, PP6An.:
   Philosophy has only to do with Reason (Idee) and therefore with actuality. Reason is not so impotent that it only ought to be but is not actual.

In the light of the complications of the above arguments, it should be emphasized that while "the ultimate aim of the world" is somewhat dependent on human "self-conscious reason" and willing because humans are "responsible", this is not the same as saying that the achievement of this aim (i.e. the achievement of 'Reason-as-the-conception of Reason') is dependent on any one individual or nation. No, as Hegel says in the next translation, Reason or "the world Spirit" has "nations and individuals enough to exempt some from having to contribute to this achievement". Given limitless time and space, if some individuals, governments or peoples fail to assist the advance of Reason in the world, it is in the highest degree probable that others in other times or places will not so refuse.

5) *Philosophie* I, S.55 (p. 36):
   ... the length of time which Reason or the world Spirit requires to achieve philosophy can at first surely strike us as being as astonishing as the immensity of space of which astronomy has come to speak. We must recognize, however, that Reason is not in a hurry .... It has time enough just because it is eternal. It is not confined to any one time span. Exhausted and ephemeral beings ... do not have enough time. Who does not die before he has finished many of his aims. It is not time alone, however, which is used for the acquisition of Reason-as-the-conception of Reason. It costs much else. As a result, it does not matter that Reason has spent many races and generations in its labour to come to consciousness or that it has made a huge display within history of rising up and passing away. Reason is rich enough for such a display. It has produced its work on a large scale. It has nations and individuals enough to exempt some from having to contribute to this achievement.

This "time" and this "exemption" is taken to grant, by implication, the negative power of some individuals, governments or peoples to frustrate, *for a time,* some of the actualizations of Reason. If so, they also have the positive power to accelerate or at least not to retard "actuality's structuring process". That some "peoples" or "governments" may so retard this process is explicitly recognized by Hegel in the following text which directly relates to the aim of this book to help define the philosophically necessary model constitution. Here, Hegel speaks of the actual or "*true*

(1) This second phrase is present in the above mentioned "cunning of Reason" passage (*Geschichte*, S.49 (p.33)).
(2) *Vorstellung.* Hegel's reference here to "God" as *Vorstellung,* as opposed to his claim that "Reason" is a *Begriff,* would seem to lend Hegelian support to my own preference for replacing God by Reason as at the centre of the comprehensive theory which can be held to be philosophically necessary.

constitution towards which each people must move". That this is a prescriptive "must" rather than a deterministic 'must' is clear from his saying later that, while "a government *must* recognize when the time for constitutional change has come", in fact, it may not do so and this same government and its "inessential arrangements may retain the upper hand" for some time. From his prescriptive position, Hegel also says that "it *is essential* to know what the *true* constitution is" because "what may stand against the true constitution has no durability".

*Philosophie* II, S.112-13 (p.97-98):
Because every people falls within the historical process, the *true* constitution is certainly not suitable for every people at every time. Just as the individual human is raised by his education within a state from having a perspective of isolated singularity to that of adopting the view of the general interest, so each people is educated over time. Each nation as a child during its barbarian stage tends to move towards a more rational structure. Humans do not remain where they are but alter over time. The same is true of a people's constitution and it is in this context that we can ask the question of what is the true constitution towards which each people *must* move. This true constitution once discovered could be said to stand in front of each historically existing nation as that towards which it tends to go. With the passage of time, each people must alter its existing constitution so that it continually is brought nearer to the true constitution .... The constitution of a people *should* truly express that people's consciousness of its own spirit, its own living ethical practices. It should give these immanent structures the form of truth. A people's constitution should enshrine that people's knowledge of itself. If for a people that view is no longer true which its constitution still expresses as the truth and if its consciousness or conception of itself and its reality are different, the body and living spirit of that people are disunited and divided. In this case, one of two things can happen. First, the people may either by a violent internal eruption smash that law which is still valued by the existing constitution or it may alter those particular elements of the law which no longer express the truth of its ethical practices. A people may do this when its spirit has moved beyond its existing constitution. Second, a people may not have the understanding or strength of spirit either quickly or slowly to remove such elements. In this case, that people will either retain its *inferior* law or it will become subordinated to a *superior* people which has reached a *higher* constitution.

In this context, we can see why it *is essential* to know what is the true constitution. What may stand against the true constitution has no durability, has no truth, and it cancels itself out. It has a temporary definite existence but it cannot support itself. It has been valued but it cannot continue to be valued. That it *must* be repealed or abolished lies in the very conception of the constitution. This insight can only be reached by philosophy. A non-violent political revolution can occur only when a similar insight is widely held ....

A government must recognize when the time for such change has come. If, however, the government is tied to the temporary arrangements, ignorant of that which is the truth, taking the inessential, valued arrangements as a defence against the essential arrangements (i.e. against that which is contained within Reason (Idee)), then the government effectually over-throws itself under the pressure of this spirit of Reason. With the dissolution of its government, a people dissolves itself unless a new government becomes established. Alternatively, the existing government and the inessential arrangements may retain the upper hand.

Following this long passage and returning now to look at the second of the five ambiguous extracts translated above, Hegel is saying that "philosophy wishes to grasp this plan" so that it can better prescribe which aspects, if any, of the existing arrangements or institutions should be altered in order to make them more closely approximate to the "true constitution", to the rational model which philosophy sees as part of that "plan". Philosophy should recommend changes to the extent that they would tend to make the empirically existent institutions more "actual" and less examples of "foul existence".

### The Threat To Prescription From Merely Retrospective Knowledge

With regard to the before mentioned *retrospective* knowledge which the phrase, "child of his time", might be taken to signify and which is plainly accepted by the owl of Minerva paragraph, this limitation on philosophy is clearly removed by Hegel's own prescriptive practice and by his recognition of human "responsibility". It tends, also to be removed by the three passages summarized next which suggest that philosophy may attain the sort of knowledge which is relevant for the future as well. The first says that "philosophy does stand above its time in form" and "is the inner birth place of the human spirit which will later become an actual social or political formation".[1] The second says that "time was required before the principle ... of Socrates

---

(1) *Philosophie* I, S.74 (p.54). Haldane's translation is confused.

could become part of wider public self-consciousness".[1] The third says that philosophy, as "the thinking human spirit of world history strips off every restrictedness of the particular spirits of the nations ... and ... raises itself toward a knowing of Reason-as-the-conception of Reason".[2] Shortly, the evaluative and prescriptive implications of Hegel's "Reason" and "actuality" will be discussed, but first, we must return to the above "child of his time" extract in order to finish the examination of the set of conflicting interpretations to which it gives rise. While the owl of Minerva paragraph denies that we might help to "construct a world as it ought to be" for the present or near future, the proposed gloss does not exclude the possibility of our building up a realistic, "actual" or "rational" ought to be world "into an intellectual realm", i.e., a 'model' which would have prescriptive implications for the near future. Accordingly, the rejection of a philosophy's going "over [there] and behind its contemporary world", is interpreted only as a dismissal of subjectivist moralizing, e.g. a rejection of the ought to be worlds of the "abstractive understanding", or of the "phantasies" of naive utopians, or of a religious other worldlyness. In the same vein, the Preface rejects an "idle ideal".[3]

Previous and later chapters discuss the model constitution in greater detail. This chapter elucidates the general *evaluative* character of the whole of Hegel's philosophical system within which the model constitution is seen to have its place and from which its political prescriptions can be developed. Accordingly, it must finally be argued that Hegel's system is *evaluative* to its very core. First, Hegel recognizes the existence of an endless multiplicity of partly repetitive and thus boring experiences which he calls the "spurious infinity". This "infinity" can only be defined by contrasting it to what he calls the "genuine Infinity" or "Reason", i.e. to the finite number of specific elements of Reason of which the genuine Infinity is composed. *Chapter Seven* suggested how one such element (i.e. 'Reason-as-the-conception of Reason') enables this list of such elements to be finite by its reflexive completion of the circle of Reason. Each within this totality of elements is a *valued,* specific aspect of the indefinite multiplicity of possible experiences. However, each is valued only to the extent that it is seen either to be an "elucidation" or a "development" of Reason, only to the extent that it is seen to be a condition for, or a result of Reason's "structuring process". These specific elements of Reason are of three types:

1) those which compose "Reason-as-logic" ("categories"),
2) those which compose "Reason-as-nature" ("actualities"), and
3) those which compose 'Reason-as-the-human-spirit' ("actualities").

FIGURES 5 and 6, to follow, recall the pictorial interpretations in *Chapter Seven* and summarize the above elaborations. The very circumference of the circle in FIGURE 5 is composed of "the genuine Infinity" because it characterizes both the objective and subjective (i.e. the convex and the concave) aspects of Reason. All of the points on the rest of the page outside the circle represent the "spurious infinity". The claim is that "the genuine Infinity" as "Reason" expresses the *valued* "essence" or the "positive aspect" of all experience. Similarly, the circumference of the circle in FIGURE 6 is composed of "the logical categories", of 'the natural actualities' and of 'the human actualities'. Outside the circle, the spurious infinity is alternatively called "inessential appearance". The *Glossary* of these terms lists more of the many superfluous, because interchangeable, words which Hegel also uses to register these same distinctions.

*Chapter Six* claimed that a theory would have to be evaluative in order to be comprehensive because the desire to know what *ought* to be is one of our non-sensuous experiences. It is one of our motives for philosophical pursuit. In fact, it seems that no explicit theoretical attempt to reject this aim could escape self-contradiction. This is why there is a fundamental *evaluativeness* which is reflexively embedded in the very search for philosophical necessity. *If we value* this search, we must value the experiences or the particular arguments, perspectives and pieces of evidence which offer us any assistance in this search. For example, we must value the particular experiential, logical or comparative tests which may help us rationally to eliminate all but one of the competing theories. Also, to the extent that we value the achievement of philosophical necessity, to that same extent, we must logically value the natural, social, political, cultural or historical developments, structures or conditions which arguably encourage the success of this search. These

---

(1) *Rechts,* PP274Z.
(2) *Enz.* III, PP552.
(3) *Rechts,* S.24 (p.10).

FIGURE 5: Reason as the genuine Infinity which by contrast defines the spurious infinity

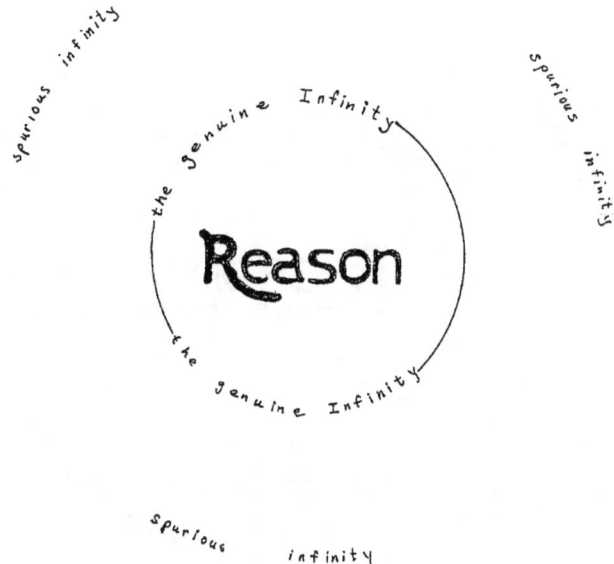

FIGURE 6: Reason as the categories and actualities which
by contrast define   inessential appearance

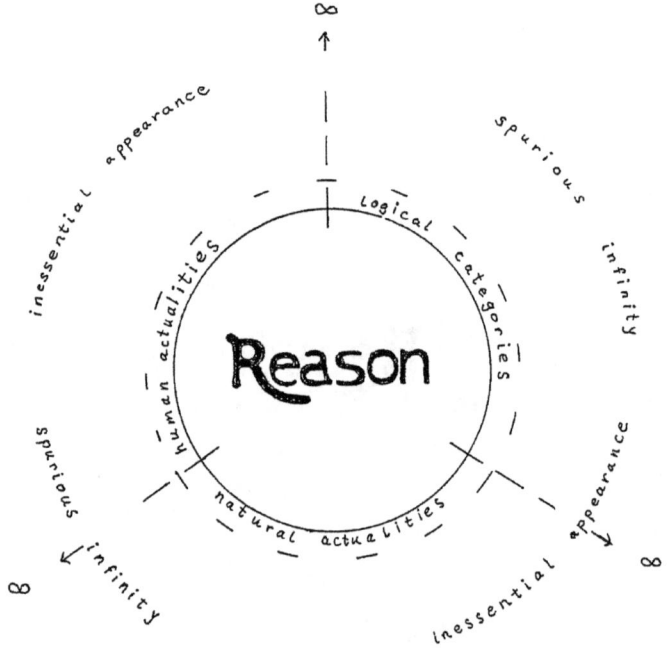

same conditions could equally be said to support 'the maximization of free, rational living'.  In this regard, for example, we might see the reduction of poverty; and the increases in literacy, in public education, in the freedom of speech, in the freedom of the press, and in the freedom of association; as historical developments which make the relevant philosophical dialogues more widely possible and thus more likely to succeed.  Speaking with a more precise reference to the concern of this book, it sees "the positive aspects" of constitutional experience contained within "Reason-as-the-constitution" as providing some of the "actual" political conditions for a people to approach a philosophically necessary theory.  The existence of a rational constitution would help to encourage a people to achieve the teleological aim defined by Hegel and summarized by another modified version of his epigram:

>'Some of what is philosophically necessary is rational living; and all of what is rational living is philosophically necessary.'

This chapter has re-written Hegel's owl of Minerva passage in line with the discovery that the offering of political prescriptions follows logically from the evaluative character of Hegel's wider system.  The next chapter examines Hegel's "necessity" and discovers that the meaning of his "inner necessity" is close to the 'philosophical necessity' of *Chapter Six*.  The next chapter will also secure the logic of his system against J.N. Findlay's charge that Hegel rejected 'the axiom of non-contradiction'.

```
C h a p t e r   N i n e :
```
**HEGEL'S NECESSITY**

*Chapters Eight to Eleven* have the task of elucidating those fundamental features of Hegel's wider system which will contribute to a sharper understanding of his constitutional monarchy. The previous chapter has prepared the way for seeing Hegel's constitution as having a prescriptive significance. The next chapter will examine the social and economic foundations, as Hegel saw them, for his political arrangements. *Chapter Eleven* explains how his system requires the rational constitution to display the three moments of "generality", "particularity", and "singularity". This chapter considers what Hegel means by the "necessity" [1] of constitutional monarchy.

**Hegel's "Inner Necessity" Is My 'Philosophical Necessity'**

Hegel uses "necessity" in two distinct but integrally related ways. One refers to the "objective" processes of the natural and human worlds which would make many things happen even if people had never chosen deliberately to shape events, i.e. "external necessity". The other use refers to the compelling character of the arguments and evidence for the human derivation and testing of theories about these worlds, i.e. "inner necessity".[2] While Hegel does not always explicitly use the two distinguishing adjectives, *external* and *inner*, the contexts usually make the two meanings clear. "The cause" and effect "relationships" [3] of "external necessity" initially are seen to characterize "the Reason which has being" or simply, "Reason", while "inner-necessity" is seen to characterize "self-conscious reason's" discovery of "the conception of Reason". The "conception of Reason" is a subjective "thinking" about "external necessity".[4] The "conception of Reason" includes a theory of external necessity, and is thus a "reconciliation of *inner* with *external* necessity. This thinking recognizes external necessity's "objectivity",[5] but holds that it must not be seen as "alien". Inner necessity "overcomes" the seeming difficulty of making "the transition from external necessity to freedom". The conception of the inner necessity of Reason secures the theoretical condition for our "liberation". 'Reason-as-the-conception of Reason' knows external necessity not to be "external" in the sense of a deterministic force, alien do our knowing and willing selves but as "the cunning of Reason" which provides this our rational subjectivity with its very being, its foundation, its material, and the medium for its exercising of its freedom. It finds a world which is life giving and intelligible. We find ourselves at home in the existing world in the sense asserted by the previously quoted epigram:
> Some of what is rational is actual, and all of what is actual (or only part of what exists) is rational.[6]

This is to say, that this discovery of "inner necessity" enables us, firstly, to see the sense in which the world as it exists is already rational enough to allow our rational selves to feel not utterly at odds with it. This makes despair rationally avoidable. Secondly, this discovery helps us to see those parts of our existing world which are not rational and, therefore, not actual; and, thirdly, to act freely and responsibly to assist the existing world become more rational. The prescriptive significance of this third result of our achieving a knowledge of this inner necessity is again clearly given voice by Hegel himself in the following extract which distinguishes between

---

(1) *Rechts*, PP279Z.
(2) See the *Glossary* for lists of references to these terms.
(3) *Enz*. I, PP153.
(4) *Enz*. I, PP159An.
(5) *Enz*. I, PP158Z.
(6) *Enz*. I, PP6An.

"natural" and "human" external necessity. Here he is discussing the difference between "the laws of nature" and "human laws". He writes that "an inner voice says what human laws *should* be" [1] because "humankind finds within itself the test of what is to be accepted as valid":

> *Rechts*, Zusatz S. 15 (p. 224):
> There are two kinds of laws, laws of nature and human laws. The laws of nature simply are and are thus accepted .... We become acquainted with both sorts of laws as those laws which are simply there. Thus the citizen and the positive jurist ... stand and remain no less than the natural scientist by what is given. However, the difference is that the human spirit of critical study is aroused by ... the variety of human laws as between peoples and times. This calls our attention to the fact that these laws are not absolute ... Here, there **necessarily** enters the possibility either of a clash between one of these laws and our **inner** voice or of their agreement. Humankind does not remain satisfied with what has definite existence, but it claims to have the standard of what is **right** within itself. While humankind can have a sense of being subjected to an alien governmental authority by **external necessity** and force, in no case can we feel the same way in relation to **the necessity of nature**. An inner voice says what the human laws should be and within itself humankind finds the test of what is to be accepted as valid .... Here, therefore, is the possibility of a conflict between what is and **what ought to be**, between a human law which has been determined arbitrarily and the **right** that has being in-and-for-itself and which remains unaltered .... Humankind **must** meet its own reason within the laws it accepts as **right**. Humankind must, therefore consider the **rationality** of the laws which pass for right and this is the subject-matter of our science of the state .... The present world has a pressing need for this science because the culture of the time ... has placed thought at the pinnacle of all that **should be valued**. Theories have placed themselves over against the definitely existing human laws and each theory wishes to appear as in-and-for-itself correct and **necessary** ....

Based on the perspective recalled in FIGURE 6, FIGURES 7 and 8, to follow, attempt to summarize the above interpretation of the relations between these various sorts of necessity. FIGURE 7 seeks to remind us both that "external necessity" has a shaping power before any humans become free actors and, yet, that it helps to foster the development of this freedom. FIGURE 8 shows how the liberating "inner necessity" retains external necessity by thinking it within "the conception of Reason". FIGURE 8 replaces the labels of "external necessity" with 'natural necessity' and 'historical necessity'. 'Historical necessity' is taken more accurately to express the "human" necessity which was implicitly present in the "human laws" discussed in the above passage. Another version of the above epigram may also help me to summarize this section's findings:

> 'Some of what has inner necessity has historical necessity, and all of what has historical necessity has inner necessity'.

**Findlay's Criticisms**

While J.N. Findlay's *Hegel: A Re-examination* usually offers an accurate and sympathetic account of Hegel's system, several parts of his commentary need to be considered in the light of an elaboration of Hegel's "inner necessity". The "inner" or 'philosophical' necessity interpreted in FIGURE 8 represents the claim that the *Encyclopaedia's* discovery and elucidation of the many hundreds of "specific conceptions" together constitute "the conception of Reason". *Chapter Seven* said that Hegel's philosophy of logic [2] seeks to outline all the categories which we require in order to think about thought, and that his philosophies of nature and of the human spirit [3] seek to expound the additional distinctions and relations required for the study of nature and humankind. To be more specific, Hegel's plan was to start with the most general yet abstract and thus the most empty and vague requisite elements and to go on to show how a study of these necessarily leads to the discovery of all the others which are less and less abstract and more and more concrete until an outline of the whole of experience is secured. Following this "methodical" [4] plan, Hegel begins with *vague* "being" (Sein) and finishes with the complex yet *precise* "conception of Reason".

(1) This passage will also be seen to provide additional support for the claim that Hegel himself must have recognized that his *Philosophy of Right* would have a prescriptive significance.
(2) *Enz.* I.
(3) *Enz.* II and III.
(4) *Enz.* I, PP24Z, PP42An., PP88An.

*Necessity* 93

FIGURE 7: external necessity

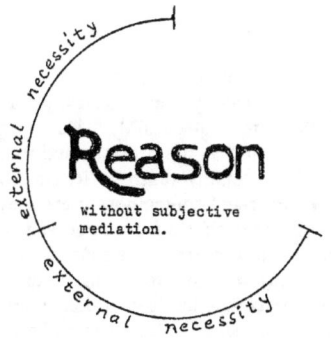

FIGURE 8: inner necessity with natural and historical necessity

What does it mean to claim "inner necessity" for the derivations of the many hundreds of these specific conceptions? If these derivations are taken to have 'philosophical necessity', we can say exactly what this claim means. It would mean that we can see how every category and distinction is discovered from within the preceding discussions (i.e. that they are logical) and that the resulting interconnected list of categories appears to capture the essence of all our experience, including the non-sensuous experience of competing philosophical systems. The chain of derivations would be seen as philosophically necessary if it seemed:
1) to be comprehensive,
2) to be compatible with all known experience,
3) to be logical, and
4) to defeat or absorb all known competitors.

This is what Hegel is taken to mean by "inner necessity". He makes much the same claim for these derivations by saying that they are "dialectical".[1] This adjective both emphasizes that each category is in some sense "*contrary*" to the previous and following categories and yet is only an element within the differentiated totality which is "Reason", and that they all are the surviving results of *dialogues* with previous and contemporary theories.

J.N. Findlay's reading of Hegel differs from mine at several points. While I agree with him that Hegel holds his derivations to have a greater "rigour" than can be claimed for merely mathematical deductions, Findlay does not say with me, following Plato, that this is because a "dialectical" system also must scrutinize the competing assumptions upon which rival theorems are based. Findlay and I disagree even more sharply, however, when he says that this "rigour" requires a "unique starting point" and a "unilineal dialectical chain":[2]

> Hegel assumes ... that a dialectical system is in a sense more rigorous than a mathematical system. For whilst in the latter there are many starting points and many alternative directions that proof may take, in a dialectical system there are both unique starting-points and a single line of proof.[3]

Hegel himself shows some flexibility on the question of his "starting point".[4] The reasons why he chooses to begin with the most abstract category is because it is more efficient to start with the simple and then to work up gradually to the complex. With this plan, the dominant direction of elucidation can always be toward the more and more concrete. Any other starting point would require us first to analyse it into its simpler conceptual pre-conditions, i.e. require us, in fact, to *go back* to Hegel's point of departure before we could *go forward* to the richer and more complex derivations. Having said this, however, I do not see, for example, how the system would have been altered if he had begun his exposition with "naught" (Nichts)[5] rather than with "being" (Sein).[6] Both seem equally abstract and each seems equally capable of being discovered within our thinking about all experience, including within our thinking about the other category.

As for the claim that Hegel's system is "unilineal", Findlay neither cites nor do I know of any text in which Hegel says this himself. In any case, such a claim would have been impossible to sustain for the reasons that Findlay himself points out.[7] We have only to think,for example, of the ease with which Hegel could have discussed the monarchical organ after, rather than before, the other two organs. This is illustrated by the order of the presentation in *Chapter One*. I must also differ from Findlay's view in the following extract where he says that the derivations or "transitions" are only "necessary ... in the rather indefinite sense" which is present in "a work of art". Neither do I read Hegel as ever claiming that every category is part of a "triad" or that "absolute rigour" characterizes his system, if this means claiming more than the rigour of philosophical necessity or more than the "in-and-for-itself" or reflexive rigour present within "the conception of Reason":

> A study of Hegel's dialectical practice will show, further, that in spite of anything he may say regarding their necessary, scientific character, his transitions are only necessary and inevitable in the rather indefinite sense in which there is necessity and inevitability in a work of art. His dialectical triads certainly reveal a community of style, but ... There is not ... one continuation which alone seems obligatory, but rather a number of possible continuations, some of which seem more fitting than other ... To look for absolute rigour in the Dialectic is to ignore the illumination it has for the sake of some quasi-mathematical interconnection which it does not and cannot possess.[8]

(1) See *Glossary*.
(2) J.N. Findlay, *Hegel: A Re-examination*, London 1959, p.71.
(3) Ibid., p.70
(4) See *Enz*. I, PP17, PP86An., PP159Z and PP186Z.
(5) *Enz*. I, PP87.   (6)   *Enz*. I, PP86.
(7) Op. cit., p.73.   (8) Ibid., p.73.

In the next passage to be quoted, Findlay discusses what Hegel calls his "theory" of "contrariety". It has already been said that all the elements within Hegel's "dialectical" system are in one sense "contrary" to each other. In contrast and without giving his source, Findlay asserts that Hegel's exposition of contrariety "plainly" rejects "the law of contradiction" (i.e. 'the axiom of non-contradiction' discussed in *Chapter Six*):

> Hegel's ... doctrine ... is that ... contradiction enters into all our notions and ideas, even those that are most securely founded and in most constant use, that it also enters all things in the world, that is the moving soul of scientific method ... Hegel further emphasizes that he is not talking of "contradiction" in some half-hearted or equivocal manner; he is not saying that X is A in one sense but not in another, that it is A in so far as it is X but not in so far as it is something else. All these devices are *explicitly disowned* by Hegel ... Hegel makes it as *plain as possible* that it is not some watered down, equivocal brand of contradiction, that he believes to exist in thought and the world, and to be an ineliminable component in self-conscious spiritual reality.[1]

Findlay's next words, with which I agree, would seem effectively to cancel the above claim that Hegel "is not saying that X is A in one sense, but not A in another" or offering "some ... equivocal brand of contradiction", but soon I will examine Hegel's own words so we can test this for ourselves:

> ... it is plain that he cannot be using it in the self-cancelling manner that might at first seem plausible. By the presence of "contradiction" in thought or reality, Hegel plainly means the presence of the opposed, anti-thetical tendencies, tendencies which work in contrary directions, which each aim at dominating the whole field and worsting their opponents, but which each also require these opponents in order to be what they are, and to have something to struggle with. .... Hegel's doctrine of contradiction as present in all our concepts does not mean that such contradiction will impede their working in ordinary contexts, or in the well drilled precision of deductive systems. Hegel is no philosophical (p.79) anarchist concerned to disrupt orderly processions by hurling dialectical bombs ...[2]

Findlay does not refer directly to any of Hegel's texts on this issue yet when these are examined we see that they need not be read to support his assertions. Far from denying the axiom of non-contradiction, Hegel's own words can be interpreted instead as attempting to correct various modern uses or reformulations of Aristotle's "laws of contradiction and excluded middle".[3] He seems to be explaining how their merely formal and isolated applications cannot be sustained within philosophy. He argues that the philosophical examination of these "laws" shows them to be a part of the complex system of "contrarieties" of which Reason is composed. For example, in his larger *Science of Logic,* he is concerned to discuss "ordinary abstractive thinking's ... so called",

1) "law of identity" which in its "negative form" is "*the law of contradiction*",[4] i.e. "A cannot be at the same time A and not-A;
2) the "law" of "diversity", i.e. "All things are different"[5] and;
3) "the law of the excluded middle", i.e. "Something is either A or not-A, there is no third" classification.

Hegel implies that, while abstractive thinking uncritically assumes that these three "laws" are separately valid and are indifferent to one another, they all could be derived from any one of them when they are "transformed" or considered within his own "theory" (Satz) of "contrariety" (Widerspruch) which is summarized by the following "proposition" (Satz): All things are themselves inherently contrary".[6]

Two pages later, Hegel's examples make it entirely clear that these words are not intended to violate the axiom of non-contradiction. There, he implies that "the father" is in one sense *identical* with "the son" (e.g. their common biological link), in another sense they are *different* (e.g. one must be born before the other), and in a third sense, one must *either* be the father *or* not of a given boy. The clarity of Hegel's position so far has admittedly been enhanced by the *free translation* above of *Satz,* first as "law" and then as "proposition" and "theory", and of *Widerspruch,* first as "contradiction" and then as "contrariety". In spite of this clarity, it is possible to see why Hegel's intervening discussions might easily have been read *in isolation* by Findlay "plainly" to reject the axiom of non-contradiction. These intervening words analyse how both physical "movement" and human "impulse" exemplify this all pervading contrariety within the empirical world.

(1) Ibid., pp;. 76-77. The emphases are mine.
(2) Ibid., pp.77-79.
(3) Aristotle, *Metaphysics,* translated by John Warrington, London 1966, p.123.
(4) *der Satz des Widerspruchs, Logic* II, S.45, P.416.
(5) Ibid., S.52, p.422.
(6) Ibid., *widersprechend,* S.74, p.439.

In the extract translated below, the first bold segment (i.e. "... it is at one and the same instant here and not here, or ... in this place it is and is not at the same ...."), could easily have fostered Findlay's 'harsh' interpretation.[1] Similarly, the later bold phrase (translated as "... any positive impulse is at the same time the negative of itself"), could be more readily translated as "...something ... is the negative of itself in one and the same respect or sense" (Rucksicht). Again, out of context, Findlay might have seen this as evidence of Hegel's "plain" denial of the axiom of non-contradiction.

> Logic II, S.75-76 (p.440):
> The common experience of physical motion itself enunciates that at least there exists in the empirical world a multitude of contrary things, contrary arrangements, etc. This experience demonstrates that contrariety is not just outside such motion, occurring merely within the reflexions of observers ... This contrariety is the negative in its essential specification. This is to say, that contrariety is the principle of all self-movement. Within physical motion, self-movement has established itself no further than to display itself empirically. Sensuous motion is the unmediated and definite existence (Dasein) of this principle. Definite existence moves itself in this way only, not in the sense that it is here in this instant and in another instant there, that is only a definition of motion, but in the sense that **it is at one and the same instant here and not here, or in the sense that in this place it is and is not at the same time** .... Movement is itself a definite existence of contrariety. Similarly, is not the distinctively inner self-movement of an impulse ..., e.g. the impulse to eat, nothing other than something which contains within itself a deficiency? This is to say, that any positive something is both self-contained and a deficiency, e.g. **any positive impulse is at one and the same time the negative of itself.** An impulse is a dependence on a something which is not this impulse, e.g. hunger is impossible without food. The abstract identify of A = A by itself has as yet no life, but a definitely existing positive something which has negativity immanent within itself must go out of itself into the world which alters it, e.g. hunger drives an animal to move and to shape and be shaped by the other beings in the world. Therefore, something is living only in so far as it can embrace negativity within itself, in so far as it has the strength to seize and sustain contrariety within itself .... Without this strength it perishes rather than lives by its contrariety. Speculative thinking or philosophy resides in thinking by thinking this contrariety and holding it fast within thought ...

The first bold segment is not taken to require that we read Hegel here to be denying the axiom of non-contradiction. He need *not* be interpreted as saying that, at exactly the same time and in exactly the same sense, every definitely existing being is both here and not here. Instead, I understand him to mean that an existent being as such is within an existent world, i.e. within a complex and dynamic system of contrarily defined beings. So placed, it is pushed and pulled this way and that. The definitely existing world as a complex of somewhat differently defined beings must have the property of motion. As a whole it must have self-movement even though merely physical "motion" is not yet the full actualization of self-movement, but all motion is inherent in the contrarieties which must define the "place" of every existing being with reference to its environment. Thus, with respect to a given existing being, while at one "instant" it is "here", at the same instant its definition includes the contrary beings in its environment which are "there". It is "in this place" now, but it is true that "at one and the same time", it is residing within a world of contrarieties which make it subject to being removed from "this place". At one and the sane time, it is actually "here" and potentially "not here". It is this gloss which led me to *add* the above clarifying phrase: 'that is only a definition of motion'.

It may be helpful to note that this reading is assisted by an awareness of the literal meaning of *Dasein:* "being-there", e.g. existing in a specific way within a world bound by time and space. This meaning is reinforced on Hegel's next page which talks about the world of "above and below, right and left", i.e. a world which is itself all the conditions for the contrariety of motion. Having all the conditions for motion means that, as a whole, this world is "self-moving".

---

(1) The opposite of a 'lenient' interpretation.

# Necessity

If Hegel's own acceptance of the axiom of non-contradiction needed any further proof, it should finally be recalled that he took care to say, that, while a "cause" precedes its "effect" and is also "the cause of itself", it is not both cause and effect in the same "connection".[1]

Returning to Findlay's account of Hegel, he seems to offer in "mitigation" an *improving* interpretation of his own which agrees entirely with my own lenient readings:

> Ordinary thought steers clear of contradiction by refusing to apply its concepts in unwanted cases, and a deductive system avoids them by the sheer precision of its abstractions, in which all factors that might lead to hesitation or conflict have been deliberately excluded. Contradiction will not arise as long as one remains resolutely at a single level of discourse, which one does not seek to connect, nor to see in relation, with other forms of discourse. It arises only when one tires of the deadness and sheer senselessness of such one-level discourse, and tries to pass on to something deeper; its point of emergence is not within smoothly functioning patterns of discourse, so much as between them. Hence the hesitation, the conflict it involves does not lead to the demoralizing paralysis it would engender were it injected into a well-oiled conceptual system, but provides the spur to that deepening of our conceptual grasp which is the essence of philosophy. The contradictions in ordinary concepts are, in fact, only contradictions [i.e. contrarieties] to those concerned to see the facts completely and from every conceptual angle ...[2]

Another modification of the much used epigram will serve to recall the findings of this section: 'What is rational must embrace all of what is contrary within itself, and some of what is contrary but not contradictory is rational'.

This chapter has argued that Hegel's "inner necessity" can be construed as another name for 'philosophical necessity'. It sought also to elucidate the necessity of the "contrarieties" which together are Reason's life. This argument and elucidation should help the next two chapters to explain the necessity and contrariety contained both in Hegel's social theory and in the three "functions" and "organs" of his constitution.

---

(1) *Beziehung, Enz.* I, PP153Z. For confirmation, also see *Enz.* I, PP1An.2, PP67An, PP115A., PP119An PP24Z2&3; *Philosophie* I, S.528 (p.459) and S.531 (p.461).
(2) Op. cit., p .79.

# Chapter Ten:
## HEGEL'S SOCIAL THEORY

The previous three chapters have examined some of the foundations which should help us to assess the extent to which democratic monarchy is or is not based on Hegel's own arguments. These chapters have addressed themselves to the wider issues of Hegel's system, prescription, and necessity. This chapter will examine what might be broadly called the social basis of Hegel's constitutional conclusions. More exactly, it offers an interpretation of how his conception of the "rational state" in the *Philosophy of Right* is the highest objective synthesis *(Rechts* PP257) of the many "affirmative" [1] yet subordinate elements which have emerged in social history. However, before proceeding with this account, it should again be made clear that it would be unrealistic to expect that all will find the interpretations here to be *obviously* 'correct'. The complexities and obscurities of Hegel's formulations too easily invite conflicting yet plausible readings. For example, some may want to question the suggestion that, by the application of Keynesian or Marxian methods, Hegel's state could solve the problem of poverty which he claims a market society tends to produce. Of course, all of the possible, real and imagined, objections to such an observation could not explicitly be met here in advance even if one had unlimited space. This problem is aggravated, for this chapter, however, by its greater relative brevity. The *political* focus of this book requires that less time be spent on economic and social issues. Still, this chapter endeavours to face the most important arguments and it is hoped that its suggestions would at least provide part of an agenda for any more extended disputations. In line with the method of seeking 'lenient interpretations' mentioned in *Chapter Six,* the search for those constructions of Hegel's text which make his argument as strong as possible is continued.

We shall begin with Hegel's account of the social foundations of constitutional monarchy. It was suggested earlier that Hegel sees his rational state as the highest objective synthesis of the varied "affirmative" elements which have emerged in human history, i.e. "elements of Reason as the human spirit". Alternatively expressed, Hegel's implicit plan in *The Philosophy of Right* was to outline the human conditions for a rational state. Correctly, he makes a distinction between the "subjective" and the "objective" conditions. Some are *subjective* in the sense that they reside in the developing feelings and thoughts of human individuals and groups. Others are *objective* in the sense that the relevant generation finds them already there in its empirical world as shaping forces (e.g. natural, crafted or manufactured "things" [2] and certain social habits, customs, traditions and institutions). They are already there before they could have come to the reflective consciousness of the generation concerned. Of course, this does not deny that some of these objective conditions were partly the result of the subjective thoughts and wills of individuals and groups in previous generations. The *Introduction* [3] to *The Philosophy of Right* explains how the human individual's ability over time to develop from "sense" consciousness and willing, to "reflective" consciousness and willing, and finally, to "rational" consciousness and willing provides a fundamental subjective condition for a rational state.[4] People would need to be able to grow in this way before a state with a rational constitution would be possible.

---

(1) PP258Z, cf. "positive aspects", *Geschichte*, S.53, mentioned in *Chapter Eight.*
(2) *Sache, Rechts,* PP42.
(3) *Rechts,* PP1 - PP33.
(4) *Rechts,* PP19, PP20, PP21An, PP24An., PP26An., PP31An.

### Abstract Right [1]

The first of the three parts of *The Philosophy of Right*, "Abstract Right",[2] considers the quite obvious *objective* condition of the rational state that "persons" must relate to the non-human world, to the range of "things" mentioned earlier. People must use their power to possess, control, use, and transform certain items of that world. They must not only eat food, build houses, make tools, etc., but by so doing, they will be educating themselves about their own free wills as powers over "things" which do not have independent wills. This relation helps each person to arrive at an adequate theoretical awareness of himself. For Hegel, the appropriate relations of persons to things are regularized in "property" rights. The relations between persons and other persons concerning property are formalized by "contracts". Possible violations of these "abstract rights" give rise to distinct categories of "wrongs". These, in turn, require different "punishments". This part of *The Philosophy of Right* is interpreted here as summarizing what Hegel takes to be the "affirmative" ways (the most rational ways), that humans in history have found to regularize both their relations to things and their relations to each other when "things" are concerned. While a person initially might need to have only sense consciousness in his encounter with things and other persons, the ordered, complex and repeated character of these relations when established, encourages each new generation to develop a reflective consciousness which is concerned with these substantive entities and relations, these objective conditions of rational political life. At the same time, the reflections of different people from somewhat different circumstances also tend to produce contending views, e.g. about the meaning of "wrong". Such controversy, in turn, fosters "rational consciousness", i.e. the subjective search for rational solutions to such conflicts. This search marks an advance in the level of subjective thinking but at first yields only what Hegel calls "moral consciousness" (Moralität). This is the concern of Part II of *The Philosophy of Right*.

### Moral Consciousness [3]

Hegel argues that moral consciousness provides another subjective condition of the rational state. Nevertheless, he sees it as insufficient because at its highest point of development it still fails to get beyond formal "conscience" [4] and an abstract representation of "the Good",[5] a stage of subjective consciousness which Hegel thought Kant had clarified and formulated in his conception of the "categorical imperative".[6] Hegel argues that this moral consciousness is inadequate because it is, on its own, unable to reach beyond its own merely subjective reflections about the objective world, a world which is only considered abstractly and not concretely. Moral consciousness as such does not go on to grasp any of the detailed contents of the objective "Good". Hegel argues that many of these contents were, in a sense, already present in human history, that many of the objective conditions for rational human living already existed (i.e. "the rational is actual"). He thought that these contents were capable of being brought explicitly to theoretical consciousness by an analysis of the long and varied history of human life and relations on this planet. Such an analysis of history would have to be a philosophical examination which would seek to discover examples and intimations of practices, institutions and attitudes which could be judged to provide some of the detailed conditions for the rational state. *The Philosophy of Right* is seen here to be a summary of the results of such an investigation on Hegel's part. He correctly selected as "affirmative" elements only those historically existent contents which also passed the test of moral consciousness (i.e. those that conformed to the "categorical imperative").[7] The range of such contents is what Hegel calls "ethical practice(s)" (Sittlichkeit). This is also the title for Part III of *The Philosophy of Right*.

### Ethical Practice [8]

"Ethical practices" are a synthesis of the elements previously discussed under the headings of "abstract right" and "moral consciousness". These earlier factors are thus seen both as conditions for, and as elements of, the ethical practices which together help to make up Hegel's rational state. In this third part, Hegel explains how living, *firstly*, in families issuing from monogamous marriage and, *secondly*, in post feudal market societies ("civil society"), provide some of the additional complex layers of conditions for the emergence of rational states.

(1) *Rechts*, PP34 - PP104.  (2) *Abstrakt Recht*.
(3) *Rechts*, PP105 - PP141.  (4) *Gewissen*, Ibid., PP136.
(5) *das Gute*, Ibid., PP129.  (6) Ibid., PP135An.
(7) Compare *Chapter Four*. It may be recalled that the earlier formulation of my own prime prescription (which I take to be an equivalent of this one) implies that each such element selected must be seen as the best one available for the promotion of 'free, rational living'.
(8) PP142 - PP360.

*Family* [1]

Briefly interpreted, Hegel argues that monogamous love between two people and the resulting family tends best to provide members with their first direct and intense experience of a *felt* "unity" [2] between persons. Thus, each tends to widen his circle of caring beyond himself or herself. One comes to see that not only isolated individuals but families can have property. Family life based on "love" fosters a sense of *sharing*, e.g. in the family's wealth. Also, the intimate relations and experience of others within a family when young help to give each member a realistic and concrete content to his or her developing moral consciousness. Hegel argues that the ethical practices of family life help to give substantive meaning to the moral imperatives which might otherwise be unable to reach beyond abstract consciousness. Being a member of a family gives us a pre-intellectual understanding of human nature which later can be widened and refined in more philosophical formulations. Consequently, the "rational being" which tends to be discovered comes not to be seen merely as an isolated computing or judging power. Instead, a human being's "rationality" is seen only as the highest of his faculties, the distinct power which must recognize and seek to reconcile the multiplicity of different stimuli, emotions, reflections, etc., which are also part of the being of any real and rational person's living in the world with other people. Thus, even if rationality is appropriately seen as the final subjective arbiter, it will also tend to be appreciated that it depends, up to a point, on certain biological, environmental, sensuous and emotional conditions for its development in each person. This does not deny but complements *Chapter Seven's* point that, for Hegel, these conditions for subjective reason are themselves made possible only as elements of "Reason". Subjective reason relies on them to provide the concrete problems and applications which enable one's moral reflections to have more than just a cerebral field of operation. The felt unity which tends to be experienced in families provides a pre-theoretical basis for any later moral and ethical consciousness, e.g. it generates a foundation for the later development of "patriotism",[3] i.e. the emotional or intellectual solidarity which each citizen can develop with their rational state. My own theory of the family largely agrees with Hegel's but mine rejects the male chauvinist and overly simple sexual types which he understandably yet unfortunately outlined.[4]

*Civil Society* [5]

In one sense, "civil society" (bürgerliche Gesellschaft) is seen by Hegel as fostering the very antithesis of the felt unity and ethical practices which are rooted in family life. This is because it initially engenders a focus upon "particular" [6] interests, "division" [7] and "self-seeking".[8] In civil society, the felt *inner* unity of family life tends initially to be replaced by a sense of competition of each against all and all against each. The dominance of this view that the interests of each person are mutually *external* to the interests of others seems to have led Hegel also to characterize civil society as "the external state".[9] This "creation which belongs to the modern world",[10] is largely what Marx later called "capitalist society", a market society, a "social formation" in which most of the labouring hours of its population are bought in a competitive labour market from those who do not own the means of production by those who do. This labour is employed to produce goods and services for exchange in a competitive market. In this way, Hegel's civil society is fundamentally different from feudal society. In feudal society, the *distribution* both of most of the labouring hours and the goods and services produced were largely predetermined by fixed formulae which were passed down to the progeny of each family from one generation to the next. Hegel saw civil society as marking an advance in human history for reasons which will be detailed more fully later but the thrust of his claim is that market society greatly expands the scope for individual liberation. Presumably, this new society was called "civil" (bürgerliche) and was seen as offering this extra field for "subjective freedom" [11] principally because of the sort of economy and classes which grew in the *towns* and *cities* in feudal society and which by Hegel's time, had expanded to the point were they were removing the dominance of feudal relations outside the towns. This *urban* (bürgerliche) economy tended to make each view himself as one in competition with all others. In these towns, contracts of many kinds became subject to many renegotiations in a life time. This tended to generate a greatly expanded urban population which had to live by its wits and skills. This fostered the development of an

---

(1) PP158 - PP181. (2) PP157. (3) PP257 and PP268. (4) PP166.
(5) PP182 - PP256. (6) PP250. (7) PP256An. (8) PP199, PP236An and PP253An.
(9) *äusserliche Staat, Enz.* III, PP523, *Rechts,* PP157, PP183.
(10) *Rechts* PP182Z. (11)   PP204Z, PP258An. PP350An., PP262Z, and PP301.

increasing variety of enterprising occupations and professions "or urban skill".[1] Hegel called the resulting population of of urban producers, "the classes motivated by skill" or "the section of skill".[2] While Hegel presumably also included doctors, lawyers and other professionals within this "skilled section" of post feudal society, he explicitly only listed three subsections: [3]
- A) "the craft section" (Handwerkstand),
- B) "the manufacturers section" (Fabrikantenstand), and
- C) "the trading section (Handelstand).

In spite of the seeming limitations of this list, it would appear that Hegel intended this category to include all those who, in contrast to the rural population with its largely feudal outlook and life style, rely for their subsistence on their own shrewd resourcefulness, talent, "work, reflection and understanding mediated by the wants and work of others".[4] Thus, Hegel also called this class the "reflective section".[5] However, the following three segments of the urban population seem not to have been included in this category by Hegel:
1) the "class" of workers which were "tied" [6] to the growing number of mindless jobs within the expanding processes of "mechanized" [7] mass production,
2) the "day-wage earners",[8] and
3) the unemployed.

Later, the significance of these probable omissions will be considered. Hegel was aware that the material or cultural deprivation of these segments of the population might lead them to develop into a disaffected and hostile" rabble" [9] which could threaten the very existence of a civil society. First, however, the natures of the other two "orders" (Stände) of which civil society is composed, namely,
- a) "the *agricultural* section,[10] and
- b) the official or "general section",[11] i.e. the *public servants* of the "general interest",[12]

must clearly be differentiated from that of the skilled or "reflective section" of the population. In contrast to the skilled class, Hegel's "agricultural section" of civil society seems very much to be a remnant of feudal society.[13] More than the reflective urban producers of market goods and services, the rural population tends to be confined to its family orientations and to its dependence on the processes and gifts of nature. Because its subsistence does not depend so crucially on its own creative intelligence and adaptability to new circumstances, because it "owes comparatively little to reflection and its own will",[14] it is less inclined to develop beyond feeling or sense consciousness. Indeed, to call it the '*feeling* class' in order to contrast it to the urban *reflective* population, would seem to accord with Hegel's analysis and with the other names which he uses more frequently for the "agricultural section": "the *substantial* or unmediated section".[15] As a result of the fact that rural life tends to be more "patriarchical", a "member of this class accepts unreflectively what is given to him and takes what he gets, thanking God for it and living in faith and confidence that this goodness will continue".[16] Hegel implies that this "simple attitude of mind" in the agricultural section inclines it to accept almost any state authority. This is in contrast to members of the "classes motivated by skill" who are reflectively inclined *initially* to view all established authorities (even those in objectively rational states) as "external". Unlike the rural population, therefore, they need to be "brought back to and welded into unity in the constitution of the [rational] state".[17]

Shortly, Hegel's analysis of how this process of re-integration tends to take place through the organization of "corporations" will be examined. These are the associations which the reflective producers of goods and services will tend to form in order to protect their various interests. First, however, we must see how Hegel's *public service* or "general" section of the population is to be distinguished from the above agricultural and skilled sections. The *general* section is that part of civil society which is made up of the public servants or career officials who serve in the government's courts and bureaucracies according to merit,[18] i.e. judges and civil servants. Hegel says that this class tends more than the other two to develop *rational* [19] consciousness, i.e. it tends "explicitly to have the general [interest] as its ground and as the aim of its activity".[20]

(1) *des bürgerliche Gewerbes*, PP256An.
(2) *der gewerbetriebenden Klassen*, PP253An., *der Stand des Gewerbes*, PP204, translated as "the business class" by Knox.
(3) PP204. (4)PP204. (5)*der reflektierende ... Stand*, PP202. (6) PP243. (7) PP253An.
(8) *Tagelöhner*, PP252An. (9) *Pöbel*, PP24OZ,PP244, PP253An, PP301An.
(10) *der ackerbauende Stand*, PP250. (11) *der allgemeine Stand*, PP202.
(12) PP205. (13) PP203Z. (14) PP203. (15) PP202, PP203, PP307. (16) PP203Z.
(17) P157. (18) PP308An. (19) PP301An. (20) PP250.

By contrast, the agricultural class tends more to have the *"general* [interest] *within itself"* so to speak, namely, in an unreflective or "unmediated" way in the *"substantiality of its family and natural life"*.[1] On the other hand, the skilled urban class tends initially to lose sight of the general interest altogether as each of its members becomes absorbed by the challenge of carving out their own *"particular"* [2] interests in the face of the competitive market. My own preferred *names* for Hegel's three sections of civil society, the sorts of *consciousness* by which each tends to be distinguished, and the primary content of their *concerns* are summarized in the following table:

| NAME OF SECTION | CONSCIOUSNESS | CONCERNS |
| --- | --- | --- |
| agricultural | sense | the general interest as felt |
| skilled | reflective | initially: particular interests as reflected and willed |
| public servant | rational | the general interest as thought and willed |

Having completed the broad outline of Hegel's analysis of the three sections of the population in civil society, we can now turn to his account of how the skilled class will tend also to be "brought back ... into unity" [3] with the general interest as formulated and willed by a rational state. We can now consider more carefully the section of the population which gives "*civil* society" its name, i.e. the *urban* producers of goods and services in a market economy.

What has already been said about "the classes motivated by skill" in a civil society provides the basis for an understanding of Hegel's account of how a *typical* individual's consciousness in a market society tends to develop from the felt unity of the family of his childhood to a reflective "division" as he first encounters market life as a young adult. Thus, he first tends to be driven beyond feeling to *reflection* by the contrasting experiences of the loving membership of his family and of the atomistic "externality" of the competitive economy. Here estrangement fosters education. At the same time, the market pressures encourage him to sustain an ever greater development of his reflective skills in order resourcefully to identify and to exploit any new market opportunities which may present themselves. They foster "the passion for gain" which "involves risk, industry" and the embracing of the "element of flux, danger and destruction".[4]

If this tendency to generate such clever self-seeking in its population were the only feature of civil society noticed by Hegel, he would have continued to see this "external state" as a retrograde step in human history. However, in *The Philosophy of Right* he came to heralded it as an advance, as a "creation which belongs to the modern world" [5] and which indeed allows greater scope to "subjective freedom". Hegel does this because he sees how the inherent dynamic of this society also tends to educate this subjective reflection so that it comes in the end freely to subordinate itself within the order of general freedom which is the rational state. He argues that the very "system of wants" and the "system of work" [6] in a market economy tends to encourage such modifications to reflective wills. First, it does this by generating an evolving series of distinct yet related "branches" [7] of production and distribution. Each such branch inherently has its own set of interests and concerns. It is these which provide the objective conditions for each member of society who finds himself earning his livelihood within one of these conglomerations to come consciously to identify with its set of concerns. Thus, when enough individuals within a given branch arrive at this appreciation, the subjective as well as the objective conditions are present for them to shape a formal organization to protect its common interests. Hegel calls such a voluntary association a "corporation".[8] He argues that these, in themselves, offer a partial home grown antidote within civil society to the degree of selfishness and isolating estrangement which the market economy also continues to foster in many young adults. He holds that participation in a corporation allows a person a field for "ethical" [9] activity which was previously absent from his life with the loss of the dominant influence of the family of his birth as he became an adult.

(1) PP250.  (2) PP250.  (3) PP157.  (4) PP247.  (5) PP182Z.
(6) *System der Bedürfnisse*, PP188; *Arbeitswesen*, PP251.
(7) *Zweige*, PP251.
(8) See "sections" in the *Glossary* for references.  (9) PP255Z.

This is a partial antidote which takes effect as person matures through his working in one sphere of civil society or another.

Hegel argues that corporations lead subjective freedom away from merely reflective egoism and thus help everyone to appreciate how the interests of these "relative unions" [1] are dependent on the general interest which is best formulated and protected by the still wider union which is the rational state. This recognition is additionally fostered by Hegel's later provision for the corporations to be represented directly within the constitution of a rational state. The acquisition of this subjective consciousness by those living in civil societies is both reflected and fostered by a rational state's "representative assembly".[2] In Hegel's constitutional monarchy, all of the larger associations in civil society are "summoned" [3] to elect deputies to such a deliberative assembly in order to "augment" [4] and to test the opinions, insights and knowledge of the government ministers and of their civil servants concerning the general interest. This assembly, therefore, helps to guarantee that the laws and policies decided upon will be seen, at least by the many voluntary associations which are represented, as either positively supporting their respective interests or as restricting them but in ways which they have come to understand as "right".

Hegel's characterises civil society as an "external" state because the individuals, families, and associations, of which it is composed initially view themselves as "self-dependent" [5] and others as *outside* their concern. Any existing judicial courts and other departments of government tend to be viewed only as either serving or as frustrating their respective *particular* interests. Therefore, these institutions of government initially are seen as impinging on these interests from *outside*. However, the apparent externality of government fades as individuals, families and associations came consciously to appreciate the full extent of their mutual dependence, as well as the "general" [6] interest which actually unites them and which is best formulated and cared for within a rational state, a state organized as a constitutional monarchy, a state in which they can directly and indirectly participate. Accordingly, subjective consciousness through the experience of corporations and their representation comes to see the governing agencies *not* as *external*. Individuals and associations come to see the government and the whole organization of the rational state as *their own*. "Patriotism" or the subjective side of the rational state becomes actual.[7] While life in early civil societies tends to be the ethical antithesis of life within families, Hegel argued that both would find their appropriate and subordinate places within rational states.

Before going on to examine some of the additional problems and deficiencies in Hegel's analysis, the thrust of Hegel's correct view concerning the historical relation between civil society and the rational state should be summarized. He says that civil society must exist before the fully rational state because this society generates some of the essential subjective and objective conditions for constitutional monarchy (e.g. a greater expansion of sophisticated reflective consciousness and the growth of corporations). Using Marx's terminology, the prior existence of the "capitalist mode of production" was a condition for the rise of the "bourgeois state". Thus, while early civil societies tended to be ruled by "external" governments, later civil societies and governments will tend to be incorporated into rational states. This does not deny Hegel's other point on a different level that "the rational state" as an "eternal" [8] element of Reason, is *logically* prior to every historically existent state: patriarchical, despotic, ancient, feudal, external, or rational. This is because the actuality of a rational state entails the concept of its potentiality. Every actuality must be conceived to have been a potentiality.

## Problems

We are now in a position to examine some problems in Hegel's social theory. We have already explained how *externality* tends to characterize early civil society. Individuals, families and associations in market society are initially inclined to view the private interests of others as well as the operations of any governmental agency or "public power" [9] as outside their own private

---

(1) PP229. (2) See *Glossary* for references. (3) P308. (4) PP301An. (5) PP157. (6) PP249.
(7) PP257 and PP268. (8) PP258An.
(9) *Öffenliche Macht*, PP234Z, PP252. I take the following references to be interchangeable with "the public power": "the police" (Polizei, PP230, PP256), "the securing power of the general [interest]" (die sichernde Macht des Allgemeinen, PP231), "the general caring and directing [agency]" (allgemeine Vorsorge und Leitung, PP236S), "the general power" (allgemeine Macht, PP241) and "the policing caring [agency]" (polizeiliche Vorsorge, PP249).

concerns. Their *feeling* for the general interest awakened in early family life has got lost in the egoistic *reflections* of young adulthood. Thus, the public powers are perceived as "external ordering and managing"[1] agencies. Because each executive or judicial agency is encountered one by one, each is at first *subjectively* seen as a separate entity whether or not it is *objectively* organized as a department of one government. Each is seen as one of a series of uncoordinated and *ad hoc* institutions. This would initially tend to be the case whether a government is in a republic or in a monarchy (feudal, absolute, or constitutional). Thus, members of civil society may view a government as "external" even when it acts to defend the very principles upon which market society rests, i.e. "abstract rights" or "the general [interest] which is immanent in the interests of particularity".[2]

Whether perceived as external or not, Hegel implies that "abstract right" places a rational obligation upon government also to perform certain other *functions* for civil society. He does not examine these systematically but starting with the two already discussed he mentions the following:
1) judicial,
2) policing,
3) to undertake "the regulation of ... the large branches of industry"[3] and to supervise the corporations in order to act when necessary "to moderate the convulsions" which may result from the "collisions of interest" between them,[4]
4) to regulate the market, e.g. by fixing the prices for the basic necessities and by inspecting food,[5]
5) to superintend a public education system (e.g. requiring parents to send their children),[6]
6) to provide "subsistence"[7] and health services to those living in civil society when individuals and corporations fail to do so themselves,[8] and
7) to attempt to reduce the growth of "poverty",[9] both by the use of the above measures and,
   a) by supervising the welfare schemes which corporations may provide for their own members,
   b) by facilitating trade with "other peoples",[10] and
   c) by directing plans for the systematic colonization of other lands".[11]

An examination of Hegel's discussion concerning the obligation to reduce poverty seems to reveal a *contradiction* in his analysis. To begin with, his recognition of the problem followed from his relatively simple, classical [12] economic account which nevertheless contained some remarkable anticipations of Marx's analysis.

Hegel recognized the inherent tendency in a market economy to generate both the accumulation of "excessive wealth" in fewer hands and a "growth of poverty" at the other end of the social scale.[13] He also recognized that such poverty provided one of the conditions for the development of a "rabble",[14] a section of the population which potentially constitutes a disruptive force within civil society. A person becomes a part of a rabble when, in addition to being poor, he has lost "a sense of right and wrong, of honesty and ... of self respect which makes a man insist on maintaining himself".[15] Another condition for the growth of a rabble is "a disposition of mind, an inner indignation against the rich, society, government, etc.", i.e. when poverty is seen as "a wrong done to one class (Klasse) by another".[16] Although Hegel does not say so explicitly, at one point he might be read to imply that the "working class"[17] might also become part of the

(1) "aussere Ordnung und Versanstaltung, PP231, PP249.
(2) PP249. (3) PP236. (4) PP236An. (5) PP236. (6) PP239.
(7) I take this obligation to act as the "trustee" (PP240) of such subsistence as following from Hegel's earlier recognition of "the right of distress" (PP127An.).
(8) PP240, PP241, PP242An. PP245An, PP253An.
(9) *Armut* PP244Z.
(10) PP246. (11) PP248 and Z, PP249.
(12) Raymond Plant discusses the influences which Adam Fersguson and Adam Smith had upon Hegel's analysis in his *Hegel*, Allen & Unwin, London 1973, pp.22 and 113.
(13) PP244, PP245. (14) Pöbel, PP24OZ,PP244, PP253An. (15) PP244. (16) PP244Z.
(17) As early as 1801 Hegel displayed an acute awareness of the "misery" (Elend) of *die arbeitende Klasse* which was abandoned to the "mechanical labour of factory work" (Fabrikarbeit), *Shriften Zur Politik und Rechtsphilosophie*, S.495, S.496 & S.498. (quote by Schlomo Avineri, *Hegel's Theory of the Modern State*, pp.96 & 100.

rabble. He observes that the "class" of workers who are "tied" to the "subdivided and restricted jobs" [1] which increasingly characterize the "mechanized" [2] processes of mass production are "unable to feel and enjoy the broader freedoms and especially the intellectual benefits of civil society".[3] If a large portion of the population were to become a rabble, this would pose a threat to the property rights which are seen by Hegel as an essential basis for civil society. The removal of this danger is presumably one of the main reasons why Hegel charges the government with the task of solving or reducing the problem of poverty.

While his preference is clear on this question within the above references, his analysis suffers from confusion and ambiguity elsewhere. At one point, he seems to undercut the government's obligation to reduce poverty by claiming that civil society does not have the capacity to do it. Still later, this revised view *might* be changed back again when he expresses his confidence that a combination of world trade, systematic colonization and corporate welfare may solve the related problems of poverty and of the rabble. If these views prove not be bald contradictions of one another, at least they suggest an *incompleteness* or *confusion* in Hegel's analysis which must be eliminated from the model's social theory. Whether or not Hegel mistakenly thought trade, colonization and corporations could dispel the otherwise inherent tendency of a market economy to propagate a rabble, it will be argued that Hegel could have tacitly assumed that his rational state would provide the best organization of sovereignty to solve this problem with these or perhaps with other measures. In any case, this is the claim made for the model constitution.

It was reported that Hegel suggests that civil society cannot solve the problem of poverty. He writes that the question of "how poverty is to be abolished is one of the most important problems which agitates modern society".[4] Immediately after this, in the next paragraph, he rejects two different strategies for its elimination and concludes that civil society does not have "the capacity (Vermogen) to check poverty and the growth of the rabble".[5] The *first* proposal was that the "richer classes" [6] or public "foundations" like "hospitals" or "monasteries" should provide the poor with subsistence, without requiring them to work for it. He rejects this because it inherently "violates the principle of civil society" which is built on the attitude that each must earn his own way. Such free gifts would thus tend to undermine the sense of "self-respect" (Ehre) which is itself a barrier to the "condition of mind" that inclines one to fall into the rabble. Thus, Hegel plausibly argued that such assistance would help cause, rather than help cure the problem. The *second* proposal which he rejected was that the unemployed be given paid work by the government. Hegel's mistaken conclusion rests on his correct assumption that market economies with the growth of mass production and with other advances in technology will be able to produce an over "abundance" [7] of goods and services. It is this increase in productivity which tends to generate first unemployment, then poverty, and finally, a rabble. However, Hegel incorrectly claims that giving the unemployed paid work would necessarily increase rather than reduce the problem of over production. While he seems appropriately to grant the advantage of this proposal that such *public* sector work would help to sustain the "self-respect" of those formerly unemployed, he seems to overlook the possibility that the government could plan this sector so that it would produce different goods and services in order to complement rather than to compound the abundance already generated in the *private* sector. Moreover, the additional income received by these public sector workers could enhance the effective demand for the presumed excess of products in the private sector. This would especially be possible if this excess largely resulted, as it might well do, not from a lack of *desire* in the populace to take advantage of such goods and services but from their lack of sufficient *money* to pay for them. In effect, this is a Keynesian [8] argument which either refutes or casts into doubt Hegel's claim that such public sector work would only worsen the "evil ... of the lack of a fitting proportion of productive consumers".[9]

These rejections on Hegel's part, of the wisdom of providing for the unemployed by either supplying them gifts or work present us with the dilemma of making sense of his earlier claim that the government has the obligation maximally to overcome poverty. This is the clear

---

(1) PP243.  (2) PP253An.  (3) PP243An.  (4) PP244Z.  (5) PP245.
(6) *der reicheren Klasse*,PP245.  (7) *Überfluss* PP245.
(8) Raymond Plant makes a similar point in his "Economic and Social Integration in Hegel's Political Philosophy", a paper published in the proceedings of the 1976 meeting of the Hegel Society of America, D.P. Verene (ed.), *Social and Political Thought: The Philosophy of Objective Spirit*, Humanities Press, 1980, p. 86.
(9) PP245.

implication of the combination of the following passages:
1) "... the possibility of sharing in the general wealth ... is assured by the public power ... (even though) this assurance must remain incomplete ... ; [1]
2) "The general power takes the place of the family where the poor are concerned in respect not only of *their immediate wants* but also of laziness of disposition, malignity, and other vices which arise out of their plight and their sense of wrong"; [2]
3) "... society struggles to make [moral or subjective aid] less necessary by discovering the general causes of penury (Notdurft), the general means for its relief, and by *organizing* relief accordingly ... [i.e.] general regulations and ordinances which are *obligatory*. Public conditions are ... to be regarded as *all the more perfect* the less (in comparison with what is arranged publicly) is left for individual [charity] to do"; [3] and
4) "Since civil society is responsible for feeding its members it also has the right to press them to provide for their own livelihood".[4]

Hegel's rejection of the two strategies for removing poverty even makes one wonder if he meant to imply his own approval of the contemporary policy in Scotland when he reported it without comment. Apparently, this policy was to "leave the poor to their fate, and to instruct them to beg in the streets".[5]

It is difficult to see how he could have thought begging would be more likely to produce "self-respect" in the poor than gifts. Perhaps he did not believe this but his words face us with the question of what other policy would be left if the provision of gifts and jobs is denied? Again, if the poor are to be forced to "beg in the streets", this would conflict with Hegel's earlier argument that "society" through its government should "struggle" to discover "the general causes of penury, the general means for its relief" and *organize assistance* accordingly. More specifically, it would conflict with the examples of such "general means of relief" which he listed, e.g. "public almshouses, hospitals ..." [6] Be this as it may, Hegel's rejections of the two remedies seem to imply that he had become resigned to the insolubility of the problem of poverty which he admitted may grow to afflict a "mass" [7] of the population. His conclusions *seem* further to be confused, however, by his going on later *to imply* that these problems might either wholly or partly be alleviated by a combination of world trade, "systematic colonization" [8] and a system of welfare self-administered by the corporations.[9]

Hegel did not make it clear whether or not he expected that such trade, colonization and corporate welfare would fully solve the problem of the rabble. It could be argued, however, that the most that international trade and colonization could do is to provide a *temporary* remedy. After all, these measures would only tend eventually to make the whole world into a competitive market. If so, the same tendency to produce the extremes of wealth and poverty which Hegel had noticed within a "particular civil society" [10] would again re-assert itself in a world civil society. Therefore, *if* Hegel saw world trade and colonization as offering an adequate long term solution for the "distress" [11] of the class tied to mass productive work, to the problems of poverty and of the growth of a rabble, he was mistaken. This inadequacy in Hegel's analysis requires Keynesian, Marxian, or other remedies to be attempted by the model social theory.

To some extent, Hegel also hopes that each corporation could be organized to provide a more direct, sensitive, and efficient means of securing the welfare and self-respect of its members than could the more distant government in civil society. He says,
1) that a corporation can become a "second family" which can better serve an individual's precise, general and particular needs than could the more remote "public power" [12] on its own;
2) that under the "supervision of the public power, the corporation has the right ... to protect its members against particular contingencies" [13] -- presumably, this means to guard them as well as it can against the destructive effects of unemployment, illness and old age; and

(1) PP241. I see the translations which appear in this chapter as being sufficiently 'literal' so as not to warrant their repetition in the *Appendix*.
(2) PP242. (3) PP242.
(4) PP24OZ. This last passage, could be interpreted as a crude way of expressing the famous principle which Marx adopted as the one which would distinguish an "advanced communist society" from all previous epoch: "From each according to his abilities, to each according to his needs", "Critique of the Gotha Programme", in *The First International and After*, op. cit., P.347.
(5) PP245An. (Knox.) Bernard Cullen reads Hegel to support this policy, *Hegel's Social and Political Thought: An Introduction*, Gill & Macmillan, 1979, P.88
(6) PP242An. (7) PP245. (8) PP246 and PP249. (9) PP252 to PP253An. (10) PP246.
(11) PP243. (12) PP252. (13) Ibid.

3) that "in the corporation, the family has its subsistence better assured".[1]

Presumably, it was on the understanding that the very emergence of a corporation presupposes that its members have acquired and continue to maintain mutual respect and a sense of responsibility for each other's welfare, that Hegel made the following claim which otherwise would seem very doubtful:

4) "Within the corporation the help which poverty receives loses its accidental character and the humiliation wrongfully associated with it. The wealthy perform their duties to their fellow associates and thus riches cease to inspire either pride or envy, pride in their owners, envy in others".[2]

*Perhaps*, Hegel had in mind that each corporation, as an "authorized" [3] association by law, would be required to levy a graduated income tax on its own members in orders to produce sufficient revenue to enable it to administer its own health, unemployment, and retirement insurance schemes. Thus, every corporation would also have to be this sort of comprehensive 'friendly society', 'a welfare authority' within the "rational state". If this is what Hegel had in mind, the health and welfare functions which he may still require of the central government would only *directly* apply to the members of civil society who were not members of such corporations.

## Comparisons

We have now reached the point where some of the possible similarities between Hegel's and the model's social theory can be outlined. *If* his earlier ambiguous suggestions concerning world trade and colonization can be interpreted only to claim that these could temporarily inhibit the growth of a rabble; and *if* his relatively incomplete and obscure words about the welfare which should be administered by corporations, can be elaborated upon as has been suggested; then, there would seem to be no obstacle to accepting these elements into the model's social theory. We would find it difficult to criticise a conception of a society which was largely made up of self-managing, voluntary associations within a legal framework; a society whose elected assembly represented the corporations of the time; and a society which by such deliberative procedures and with working majority support could decide in the face of any remaining or re-emerging poverty and estrangement in its population to experiment with Keynesian, Marxian or other solutions in an attempt to solve these problems. Such a society would not only nicely complement democratic monarchy but might plausibly be interpreted to be a *lenient* elaboration of Hegel's own social theory. The *way* this society generates some of the necessary conditions and elements of both Hegel's and the model's somewhat different constitutional monarchies is obscurely referred to when Hegel asserts that "civil society passes over into the [rational] state".[4]

Of course, it is not claimed that Hegel explicitly contemplated the sort of Keynesian remedies suggested, nor that he anticipated the sort of Marxian plans outlined in *Chapter Five*. Instead, what is being claimed is that Hegel's own rational state would be well organized to experiment with such remedies for unemployment and alienation. It could attempt these, as it *should*, to the extent that they proved pragmatically necessary in order maximally to guarantee to each person an equal opportunity to enjoy both the just fruits of his or her labour, and the cultural benefits of society. It should adopt any policy which has the prospect of increasing the quality and quantity of free, rational living. A lenient interpretation of Hegel's constitutional monarchy provides such a framework for a society's deliberations. However, the claim for democratic monarchy is greater. It would be even more able to face and cope with these problems. In order to explain more exactly why this should be so, first, we must compare and contrast Hegel's definition of "corporation" with that of the model's 'electoral association'. Second, we must return to examine the flaw claimed earlier that Hegel failed explicitly to recognize the possibility that factory workers, day-wage earners and the unemployed could form their own electoral corporations and thus become recognized subsections of the "reflective" class of civil society. Other advantages of the model will be spelled out in later chapters.

Hegel's chapter on civil society explicitly mentions "corporations" whose respective common interests relate to their different material concerns, each with a distinct "branch" of craft production, manufacturing production, and trade.[5] It is because these corporations are rooted in a market society that continually some branches rise and others fall. Consequently, he referred to the elected chamber made up of deputies from these corporations as representing the "fluctuating" [6] element in civil society. While Hegel's words are not entirely clear on this point, they could easily be interpreted as antagonistic to one of the features of the model constitution. They could

(1) PP253. (2) PP253, Knox. (3)*berechtigten*, PP253An.
(4) PP256. (5) PP204. (6) PP308.

exclude deputies from being elected by the less fluctuating elements in civil society, e.g. the agricultural or public servant sections. Democratic monarchy, with its A.P.R. provision, would not exclude deputies from any such voluntary association as long as it had sufficient numbers of members registering their preference to be so represented. The dispersed locations of agricultural workers or farmers might make it too difficult for them to organize to form an electoral association. Also, while public servants could more easily organize, they might well judge it to be unwise *openly* to engage in the party political fights and alliances into which they would tend to be drawn if they were directly represented in the chamber which produces the government, i.e. their cabinet supervisors. However, if a farmers' or a farm workers' union, or if a union of public servants wished to be directly represented, democratic monarchy would allow this. At the same time, its A.P.R. system would equally allow these groups or their individual members instead to choose to channel their votes through either their geographical constituency or through any other electoral association, e.g. one of the political parties.

This raises another difference between Hegel's and the model's constitution. The latter's acceptance of *mass political parties receives no explicit support* from Hegel's words. Later chapters will return to the details of this issue but the greatest support for the model's electoral arrangements which can be claimed from Hegel's words are that,

1) he explicitly favoured parliamentary "parties",[1]
2) *may* have included municipal or "community",[2] "professional",[3] and "religious"[4] corporations among the list to be represented in addition to the craft, manufacturer, and trade corporations, and
3) explicitly declared his preference for the as yet atomized "multitude"[5] to be organized so they could share power.

It is argued here that A.P.R. satisfies or complements all of Hegel's arguments but it explicitly goes beyond them. While similar, an 'electoral association' may still differ from Hegel's conception of an "authorized" association (i.e. a "corporation") because the model openly invites all adults to secure a voting participation in the constitution by registering with any of a wider range of electoral associations. Perhaps more importantly, however, it would openly encourage the unemployed, the day-wage earners, and the mass production workers either to join existing associations or to organize their own "corporations". Again, perhaps a little implicit support for this provision from Hegel's own words might be claimed when he said that the "multitude" must become "organized". However, this need not necessarily be taken to imply that they should form themselves into electoral associations. Nevertheless, the thrust of his whole argument that the "difference"[6] and "division"[7] generated by market society has to be "brought back" to the articulated "unity"[8] of a rational state, when combined with his desire to inhibit the growth of a rabble, could plausibly be read to give broad support for the representation of all segments of the population. Arguably, all groups should be represented, according to Hegel, as long as they had *reflectively* developed sufficient solidarity with a sizable enough portion of their fellows to have enabled them to organize and sustain an 'electoral association'.[9] I see no reason to doubt that the stresses of being unemployed or of doing factory or casual work would stimulate the development of "reflection" in some just as Hegel saw the required levels of sophisticated reflection being fostered by life within other "branches" of market society. Thus, when day-wage workers, industrial workers, or the unemployed reflect on their respective common problems, they may well be able to form "corporations" like those formed by others in "the system of work".

If so, these electoral associations, like the other organized parts of civil society, could play a constructive role in the deliberations in the elected chamber. While Hegel does not *explicitly* support corporations for workers and the unemployed, neither does he explicitly rule them out. *Leniently* interpreted, his formulations might suggest that he had just not yet come to see how these segments of the population could acquire the necessary reflective solidarity with others

---

(1) See *Glossary*. (2) *Gemeinden*, PP288. (3) *Gewerbe*, PP288.
(4) PP270An. (5) PP290Z. (6) PP182Z. (7) PP256An. (8) PP157.
(9) I.e., an association which also functions between general elections to promote and protect its common interests, whatever they might be - an association with a "wider posture" (PP308) than the collection of votes at election time.

which would enable them to form corporations. *Harshly* interpreted, he might be said either to be a proponent or a victim of the dominant "bourgeois ideology" which endeavoured to minimize the power of the working class to resist the exploitative conditions of capitalist society.

**Market Society vs. Communist Society**

One last issue remains to be faced in this chapter. It might easily be supposed that the broad acceptance of Hegel's market society within the model social and political theory conflicts with the similar acceptance in *Chapter Five* of Marx's communist society. However, there is no logical contradiction here because democratic monarchy provides the most rational decision-making framework for either society. It complements and thus could be supported by either society. It also could help either deliberatively to decide to modify itself into the other. Thus, it is argued that Hegel's and the model's justification of private "property" rights could be equally satisfied either in a market or in a Marxian communist society. Marx recognized the appropriateness of "personal" property even if he rejected "private" and "bourgeois" property for communist society. He argued that when most of the means of production are collectively and democratically controlled, the remaining "personal property" would lose its "class character".[1] Similarly, it is argued that life within communist society could be at least as conducive to the generation of the required level of sophisticated reflective consciousness which is a condition of a maximally rational society, constitution, and state.

To the extent that the stimulation of reflection may be uniquely dependent on people's participation in a market economy as Hegel might easily be read to argue, no reason as yet is seen here why a restricted market economy should not be retained for the production of 'luxuries' within a communist society. *Luxuries* are all the goods and services which are not deemed to be basic for all humans to 'live', i.e. what are not seen (by the democratic deliberations of the hierarchy of communal assemblies) to provide the necessary conditions which give genuinely equal opportunity to all. In contrast, for the production of these basic necessities (e.g. food, shelter, education, recreation, health services), the means of production would have to be collectively owned, controlled, and worked. All would be expected to contribute his or her equal share, within the limits of administrative possibility, of the labour required for this production. Fairness might also counsel the rotation of both the unpopular and the popular jobs within the sphere according to a plan agreed to by the elected assembly. Alternatively or additionally, such a plan might require an agreed system of differential rewards for the performance of some functions: more reward per hour for the unpopular and less for the popular jobs. If all had the *right* to share in the consumption of these necessities according to their assessed needs, then each would be in a position freely to choose or not to choose to participate in the production and consumption of luxuries. Such a market economy within a communist society when combined with the other objective features (principally its provision for genuine equal opportunity), could arguably foster at least as much sophisticated reflection as might tend to be generated within Hegel's own civil society.

Apart from my rejection of Hegel's male chauvinism, this chapter has tried to show how the model's social theory may be seen as compatible with Hegel's even though it does clearly go beyond his own formulations at certain points. The model theory explicitly widens Hegel's definitions of "corporation" and of the "reflective section". Also, while Hegel seems understandably to have assumed that only a dominantly market society could be complemented by his rational state, the model constitution could equally provide the sovereign organization for a dominantly communistic society. The next chapter will expound the three moment structure of Hegel's conception of the state while the last chapter will compare Hegel's own constitutional monarchy with democratic monarchy.

---

(1) Op. cit., p.81. Similarly, Marx seems to want "individual property", op. cit., "The Civil War in France", p.213

# Chapter Eleven:
## The Three Moment Structure Of Hegel's State And System

Just as the previous chapters have helped to explain the way in which democratic monarchy largely rests on Hegel's Reason, necessity, and social theory; this chapter will outline the three moment structure which shapes both his constitution and the model. Thus, here I will continue to sketch the argument that could be made for seeing democratic monarchy *logically* as an integral element of a comprehensive theory. This common foundation for Hegel's and the model's constitutional monarchies will help the next chapter to elaborate the differences between the two. One superficial difference, however, should be noted immediately. While both refer to "the law-giving function", Hegel more usually names the other two functions as the "governing", and as the "monarchical" or "finalising" functions, respectively. The model's two different labels (the 'particularizing' and 'unifying' functions), offer clarifying interpretations of Hegel's own argument. Both constitutions agree that the three functions of the ideal organization of the state are manifestations of the wider three moment (Moment) structure which also characterizes the many other elements of Hegel's system. According to Hegel, all the specific categories and actualities of Reason have the moments of "generality", "particularity", and "singularity".[1] "Reason", "the conception of Reason", all of the other "specific elements of Reason", and all of their corresponding "specific conceptions", are each composed of these three "moments".

### Generality, Particularity, and Singularity

Hegel uses *Moment* more widely to signify a distinguishable feature or aspect which is an inseparable constituent of a larger totality. Thus, while he does use it to refer to generality, particularity and singularity, he also uses it to name what has thus far been translated as "element". This use of "element" and the later uses of "function" and "organ" as some of the translations of *Moment,* seek to make the exposition of the model more precise than Hegel's own. The following passage confirms the reading that, for Hegel, Reason and each specific element of Reason have the three "moments" of generality, particularity and singularity:

> *Rechts,* PP272An.:
> How the *conception* of a specific element of Reason (Idee) and thus how, in a more concrete way, the specific elements of Reason themselves immanently define themselves, and therewith how their moments of generality, particularity and singularity are abstractly established is discovered in the philosophy of logic.[2]

Previous chapters have silently recorded this reading of Hegel by dividing the circles in the various FIGURES into three arcs, each arc representing one of these three moments. Shortly, I will explain, for example, why the arcs in FIGURE 3 labelled "Reason-as-logic", "Reason-as-nature" and 'Reason-as-the-human spirit', respectively, are called Reason's moments of generality, particularity and singularity. The meaning of these terms will be made clearer if their formal association with 'all', 'some' and 'one' are recalled. A truly universal or *general* statement applies to *all* the cases without exception defined by that statement. The list of these cases is that statement's *particularity,* i.e. each such case is a *particular* instance or is a *particularization* of that general statement. Any list of particularizations could include only *some* not all experiences. Moreover, it could not include any irrelevant experiences or cases. A general statement, one of its particular cases, or their consistent union, can be said to have *singularity* because each is *one.* To summarize, a statement has *generality* if it applies to *all* such cases. *Some* finite number of such

---

(1) *Allgemeinheit, Besonderheit, Einzelheit.*
(2) Also see *Enz.* I, PP163, PP164 and An., and *Logik* II, S.263-301 (pp. 600-622).

cases constitutes its *particularity*. The fact that either or both can be contained in *one* statement constitutes its *singularity*. The way Hegel sometimes uses these terms also makes them signposts for moving within his system. As a "system", Hegel's philosophy is a reflexive *hierarchy* of *general* statements or conceptions. "Reason" is at the top of this hierarchy because it is the general conception which organizes and includes all others. It is the general of generals and together they seek to outline the truth of all experience. Each of the elements within this hierarchy of generality refers to a distinct aspect of experience, some being more limited in scope than others. Occasionally, Hegel refers to the *generality* of a given element and at other times speaks either of the *particularity* or the *singularity* of the same element. In such contexts, "generality" directs us to move *up* the hierarchy in order to recall that this element is part of a wider system which seeks to outline *all* experience. Similarly, its "particularity" is a signpost directing us to move *down* the hierarchy by recalling that this element itself contains *some* more limited elements. Its "singularity" is a signpost directing us to *stop* for an instant within the hierarchy to notice that this element is *one*, is one element of the whole or is one integration of more limited elements. Recalling again the formal association of the three moments with *all*, *some* and *one*, the same "element" can be said to be a *general* conception (i.e. that it refers to *all* defined cases), a *particularization* of Reason (i.e. is one of the *finite* number or a particular element within the hierarchy of generality), and a *single* point within that hierarchy. In different senses, this same hierarchy could be called a hierarchy of particularity, of singularity, or of generality. The articulated identity of these three moments is asserted by Hegel in the following brief but difficult passage:

> *Logik* II, S.298 (p.620):
> Because it is only a specific and *general* conception, a particular conception is on the same basis a *singular* conception. And conversely, because a singular conception is a specific and general conception, it is as much a particular conception.

We are now in a position to explain why the three arcs in *Chapter Seven's* FIGURE 3 labelled "Reason-as-logic", "Reason-as-nature" and "Reason-as-the-[human]-spirit", are respectively called Reason's moments of generality, particularity and singularity. When it is said that the philosophy of logic expounds Reason's moment of generality, what is being claimed is not that the categories which are the objects of the philosophies of nature and of human living do not also have generality but that the specific elements within the conception of logic are more obviously at the top of the hierarchy of generality. The ready implications of thinking about thinking are wider than the implications of thinking about either plants or political constitutions, for example. Equally, the identification of "Reason-as-logic" with generality does not deny the truth that it is both composed of *single* or specific elements of Reason which are the logical *particularizations* of Reason, nor that, as a whole, it forms a complex totality, a unity, a *singularity*.

Similarly, while "Reason-as-nature" is said to be the moment of particularity, this only means that the single actualities which are the *general* objects of the philosophy of nature are less general in scope and thus are less obviously within, let alone at the top of the hierarchy of generality. They are more obviously near the bottom of the hierarchy of generality. They less obviously form a *single* whole. Also, while "Reason-as-the-[human]-spirit" is the moment of singularity, this does not deny that the actualities which compose it are equally *general particularizations* of Reason but only marks the relative transparency with which they display "Reason" to be *one*, complex, reflexive system of logical, natural and human realities, i.e. a unity. Of course, this display is most clearly achieved within Reason-as-the-human-spirit by philosophy when it thinks through "the conception of Reason".

**Essential Particularity Versus Inessential Particularity**

At this juncture, it will be helpful to distinguish another way in which Hegel uses "particularity". Its use as a signpost to move down the hierarchy of generality and as signifying the finite number of categories or actualities which are particularizations of a more general conception have already been noted. Sometimes, however, Hegel seems to use "the particular" or "particularity" to refer to items of reality which are, so to speak, below the bottom of the hierarchy of generality. In such cases, he is referring to the indefinite multiplicity of past, present, or future manifestations of, and deviations from, the "actualities" of which the "genuine Infinity" is composed. These entities are 'below the bottom of the hierarchy' because they are thought to be wholly reducible to these actualities and thus to the finite circle of the reflexive hierarchy which these help to make up. Such "particularity" relates to items for which we need proper nouns and names in addition to the terms already defined within Reason's hierarchy of generality in order to give them a fully adequate account. FIGURE 6, in *Chapter Eight,* called this indefinite multiplicity the "spurious infinity" or "inessential appearance". Following this lead, these two uses of "particularity" will be distinguished by naming the latter one, *'inessential* particularity'; and the former one, *'essential* particularity'. Later in this chapter, this distinction will help us to make sense of *Rechts*, PP259 and Z, which outlines the three moments of "Reason-as-the-state".

### The Hierarchy Which Joins the Monarchical Organ To Reason

FIGURE 9 seeks to summarize the way in which the foregoing discussions relate to the special concern of this book. It displays the hierarchical chain of derivations or "elucidations" which link "Reason-as-the-monarchical-organ" to "Reason". This FIGURE could be said to put the 'absent arc' in FIGURE 4 *(Chapter Seven)* under the microscope. Because "Reason" is at the very top of the hierarchy of generality, it is represented by the largest circle. The scope and thus the size of each of the connecting elements of Reason gradually decreases until the most limited is reached. This is to say, that while "Reason" claims to be the essence of all logical, natural, and human realities, "Reason-as-the-monarchical-organ" claims only to define the essence of all past, present and, perhaps, future heads of state. Thus, this smallest circle would seem to be at the very bottom of the hierarchy of generality because beyond it, nothing else can be said of *general* significance about heads of state. All additional talk could only describe and evaluate the indefinite multiplicity of historically existent heads of state with the additional aid of the relevant proper nouns such as the local titles for the office. Remembering the thoroughly evaluative character of Hegel's system *(Chapter Eight)*, the eight circles, from the smallest to the largest, also represent eight prescriptive *models,* each relating to the following different but overlapping areas of experience:

1) heads of state ('Reason as the monarchical organ')
2) the finalising or uniting of state decisions ('Reason as the finalising function')
3) constitutions ('Reason as the constitution')
4) politics ('Reason as the state')
5) ethical practices ('Reason as ethical practice')
6) empirical relations between people ('Reason as the objective human spirit')
7) humankind ('Reason as the human spirit'), and
8) all experience ("Reason").

As in previous FIGURES, each of the eight circles drawn in FIGURE 9 is divided into three arcs, each arc representing one of the three moments of the specific element of Reason whose name appears in the centre of the relevant circle. As previously, the arc now labelled 'g' for generality is represented by the arc between 12 o'clock and 4 o'clock, 'p' for particularity is between 4 o'clock and 8 o'clock, and 's' for singularity is between 8 o'clock and 12 o'clock.

In FIGURE 9, each smaller circle is meant to be a magnified version of one of the arcs in the next larger circle, i.e. each arc, so to speak, is seen as itself another complete circle when looked at under a microscope. The arrows relate each smaller circle to the arc in the next larger circle of which the smaller circle is a magnification. In each case, the next larger circle represents the next higher specific actuality in the hierarchy of generality. In this way, the arrows direct us toward Reason, i.e. "toward higher and the highest genus".[1] FIGURE 9 portrays only one of the several possible exact ways in which the arcs of these eight circles might be labelled [2] and the connecting arrows drawn. While the smallest four circles are explicitly expounded by Hegel in *The Philosophy of Right* through a discussion of each of their three moments (generality, particularity and singularity), the largest four circles are only rarely or obliquely elucidated in this way. Thus, with regard to the largest circles, Hegel's use of "unmediated" has been read to be an indirect reference to "particular". The relevant paragraphs for the smallest four circles are translated and discussed later, while the relevant passages which suggest the drawing of each of the largest four circles are listed in the *Glossary* under its appropriate name, e.g. 'Reason-as-the-human-spirit'.

---

(1) *Logik* II, S.296, p. 619.
(2) For example, while I have drawn the 'Reason as ethical practice' circle on the basis of Enz. III, PP517, two other paragraphs might easily be read to suggest a different labelling (*Rechts*, PP157 and PP263).

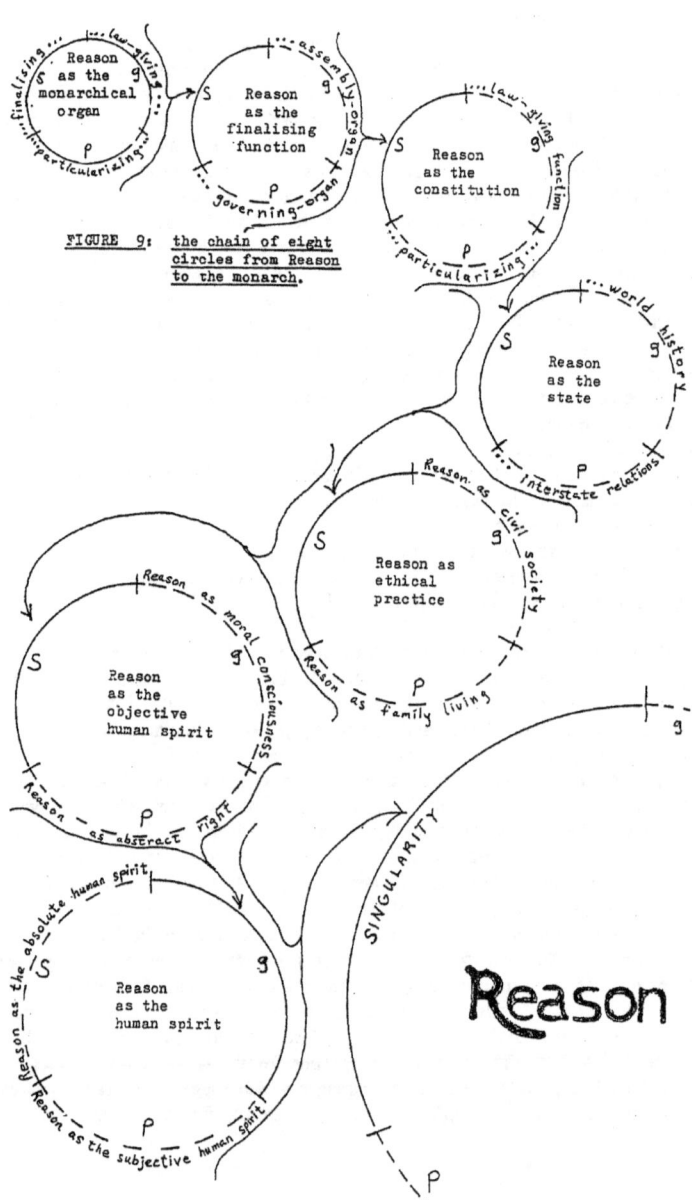

FIGURE 9: the chain of eight circles from Reason to the monarch.

### An 'A to Z' Map Of Reason

The map of the hierarchy in FIGURE 9 provides a pattern which might allow the production of a complete and precise pictorial representation of the hierarchical relations between the many hundreds of specific elements which compose Reason.[1] This would be a sort of 'A to Z' book composed of as many pages as there are specific elements of Reason. On each page there would be one circle divided into three arcs with the name of the specific element of Reason in the centre and with the name of each of its three moments written on the convex side of each arc, the concave side of each arc being marked with a 'g', 'p', or 's' as described above. The number in the centre by the name of the circle's name would refer back to the earlier page upon which it had first appeared as one of three arcs on a 'larger' circle, while each of the three numbers on the three arcs would refer to the later pages upon which these arcs would be themselves magnified and thus appear as complete circles.

On the very first page would appear the circle of Reason (i.e. FIGURE 3) and thus on pages 2, 3 and 4, respectively, would appear the circles of 'Reason-as-logic', "Reason-as-nature" and 'Reason-as-the-human-spirit'. This guide book and summary would be divided at least into eight sections corresponding to the eight levels of generality portrayed in FIGURE 9. More sections would be required if in some cases more than six circles linked elements at the bottom of the hierarchy of generality with the top (i.e. with Reason). However, if six and only six were always required, then the numbers of pages and circles in each of the eight sections would be as follows:

```
Section One:              1 page
Section Two:              3 pages
Section Three:            9 pages
Section Four:            27 pages
Section Five:            81 pages
Section Six:            243 pages
Section Seven:          729 pages
Section Eight:        2,187 pages
              Total   3,280 pages
```

This map is suggested in order to emphasize the three moment structure of Reason. Its plan is offered in spite of the fact that I have not yet fully worked out whether every part of Hegel's system could equally be summarized in this way, e.g. the relations between "being", "naught" and "becoming". Another questionable implication would seem to be that Hegel's philosophy when systematically and efficiently expounded in this way, would always have to take the form of *triads*. While it is clear that Hegel's own practice in the *Encyclopaedia* did not always do this, it remains an open question whether his exposition could appropriately be recast so as to directly provide the terrain for such an A to Z book.

FIGURE 10 pictorially represents the three moment structure of both Hegel's and the model constitutions. It does this by again depicting the three smallest circles of FIGURE 9, but draws the additional requisite circles so that all the arcs which constitute them are made visible. Because the rational need for the organs must be given in terms of the required state functions, each organ is defined by the way it jointly performs these functions. Thus, FIGURE 10 shows that the three sets of three arcs which constitute each of the three "organs" refer to the same three "functions" of the constitution which are already pictured as larger circles. This sort of *reference back* to specific elements of Reason which are at a higher level of generality in the hierarchy illustrates just how there can be a *bottom* to the hierarchy. It is assumed that such a *looping back* always occurs at some level of generality so as eventually to *terminate* every hierarchical chain of derivations throughout the system. This is another example of the 'reflexiveness' which is a pre-condition for our conceiving of "Reason" as a closed circle of a finite size.

---

(1) Michael Kosok offers an alternative notational system for Hegel's system. While mine might be said to be 'geometric', his might be said to be 'algebraic'. Also, while offering many interesting suggestions for interpreting the dialectical structure of Hegel's philosophy, he mistakenly assumes that Hegel's system could not be complete: Hegel's "logic has an indenumerably infinite number of 'truth' values (p.247), and that "this process cannot be completed at any single stage for new indeterminacies always appear" (p.249). "The Formalization of Hegel's Dialectical Logic", in Alasdair MacIntyre (ed.) *Hegel: A Collection of Critical Essays*, Anchor Books, 1972, pp. 237-289.

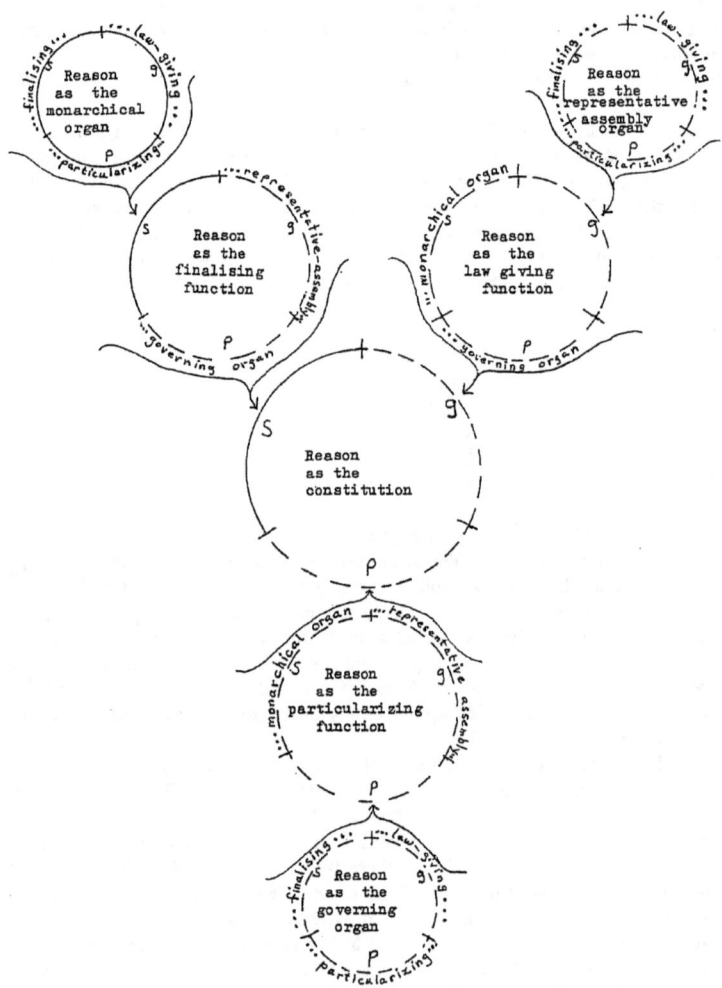

FIGURE 10: the three sets of moments, functions and organs of Reason-as-the-constitution.

With respect to some of the other perspectives developed in earlier chapters, this A to Z map would chart the layered character of all of the "great number of circles ... on the periphery"[1] of Reason's circle. Such a map would attempt to include all and only the terms which have a *general* significance for the understanding of all experience. It would exclude, except perhaps for the purposes of illustration, all proper names and all the other additional terms which one needs in order to give a fully adequate empirically accurate account of any entities within the indefinite multiplicity of beings which existed or exist in nature or in history and which would appropriately be plotted in the area outside of the circumference of the circle drawn in FIGURES 5 and 6. FIGURE 10 shows how each of the three functions or organs is derivable from the conception of the constitution, and conversely, how this conception can be derived from any one of the functions or organs. It illustrates how throughout Hegel's system the three moments of generality, particularity and singularity are both distinguishable and inseparable. This also makes the following two statements by Hegel more easily intelligible:

*Logik* II, S.273 (p.600):
Each of these three ... moments is as much the whole specific conception of which it is a moment as a specific conception itself. As such, it is one specification of the conception of Reason.
*Logik* II, S.295 (p.618):
The specifications of generality, particularity and singularity are specific conceptions which are themselves essentially the totality of all specification.

Before elucidating further the third smallest circle in FIGURE 9 (i.e. Reason-as-the-constitution), the next section will discuss and then translate the paragraph which suggested the drawing of the fourth smallest circle: Reason-as-the-state.

### The Singularity, Particularity, And Generality Of Reason-As-The-State

In line with the previous discussion of the signpost meanings of the three moments, the phrase, 'the *generality* of the state', could be interpreted in either of two ways. *Firstly*, it could be referring us to one of the elements of Reason higher in the hierarchy of generality, (e.g. Reason-as-the-objective-human-spirit) for which Reason-as-the-state is one of nine essential constituents. *Secondly* it could be recalling the fact that Reason-as-the-state is more general or higher in the hierarchy than the more particular elements or entities which it integrates into itself, e.g. 'Reason-as-abstract-right'. Paradoxically, the phrase, 'the *particularity* of the state' could be read to express the same two sets of relationships between elements in the hierarchy but from a different direction. Thus, this phrase could be read to say either, that Reason-as-the-state is more particular (i.e. less general) than Reason-as-the-objective-human-spirit, or to refer us to the many less general (i.e. more particular) elements which it integrates. Both phrases could also have a *third* meaning. The distinction will be recalled between '*essential* particularity' and '*inessential* particularity'. With this in mind, 'the generality of the state' could be reminding us that Reason-as-the-state is the specific element of Reason which purports to reduce to itself all of the indefinite multiplicity of historically existent or inessential particular states, i.e. 'the particularity of the state' could be referring us to the inessential particularity of the state - the indefinite multiplicity of states which Reason-as-the-state reduces to itself. The phrase, 'the *singularity* of the state' could similarly have three meanings:

1) Reason-as-the-state is *one* among the many hundreds of specific elements within the circular hierarchy of generality which constitutes Reason.

2) As such, it is the *one* which reduces to itself all of the indefinite multiplicity of historically existent states.

3) To be actual, Reason-as-the-state must be present within at least *one* historically existent state. As historically existent, such a state must continually integrate the multitude of essential and inessential particular entities which comprise it into *one* complex whole, into a unity.

With regard to this third meaning, it will be shown how Hegel argues that the organization by which a state can best continue to achieve this living integration is "the rational constitution", i.e. 'Reason-as-the-constitution'. Thus, the next section will return to a consideration of the functions and organs which this singularity of the state has interpreted to require a rational state to integrate within itself.

In effect, the previous chapter suggested how the rational constitution would integrate some of the other 'essential particulars' listed in FIGURE 9, i.e. Reason as abstract right, as moral consciousness, as family living, and as civil society. Of course, there is also an indefinite

(1) *Philosophie I*, S.46, P.27.

multiplicity of 'inessential particulars' which must be knitted within its fabric ranging from the specification of which language is to be used on official occasions to determining whether firemen will wear green or blue uniforms. While at one or another time Hegel seems to use these three phrases and their derivative terms in all of the above nine ways, the paragraph which forms the basis for the drawing of the fourth smallest circle ('Reason as the state') in FIGURE 9 employs only three of these nine. Accordingly, *Rechts*, PP259, shortly to be translated, is divided into three sections. Section (a) briefly speaks of 'the *singularity* of the state' in the sense of the above third meaning. This is to say, that as actual, Reason-as-the-state must in some measure be present within "every *single* historically existent state" and this requires each to a degree to be a "self-relating organism" or to have a "constitution". Section (b) asserts that Reason-as-the-state must include "interstate relations" because the indefinite multiplicity of 'inessential *particular*' states which Reason-as-the-state reduces to itself, at the same time marks at least the potential, and the probable empirical truth, that every state must live, fight or die among other historically existent states. Section (c) recalls that the rational state is a model, an "effective genus" towards which all particular states incline, or by which, they are judged. It is one element of the ultimate teleological end of the natural and human worlds which is to achieve and to live according to "the conception of Reason". This is to say, that section (c) says that Reason-as-the-state is one 'essential particular' within the ultimate aim of "the process of world history". One could not live in full accordance with "the conception of Reason" unless one lived within a rational state. Thus, section (c) also directs us to move *up* the hierarchy of *generality* by seeing that Reason-as-the-state is an essential part of the highest possible human life as defined by the conception of Reason at the very top of that hierarchy. A reading of the 'literal' translation in the *Appendix* of the following paragraph and of the comparable paragraph in Enz. III [1] will show that more liberties than usual were taken in order to make the following free translation more readily intelligible than the relatively brief and obscure original.

*Rechts*, PP259:
Reason-as-the-state,
a) has at least intellectually unmediated actuality in every *single* historically existent state because of each state's self-relating organism, i.e. because of its *constitution* or internal state law;
b) has *interstate relations* and law because each historically existent state has been and always will be, at least potentially, only one among an indefinite multiplicity of such inessential *particular* states; and
c) has an absolute power over such individual states in the sense that it is their teleological end (i.e. it is the *general* element of Reason, it is the *genus* or it is the specific element of Reason-as-the-human-spirit which gives itself actuality in states in the process of *world history*).

*Rechts*, PP259Z:
To be actual, Reason-as-the-state must be present in at least one *single* historically existent state and an historically existent state is by definition, moreover, an inessential particular state. This *singularity* is to be distinguished from this *particularity*. Singularity is an essential moment of Reason-as-the-state while inessential particularity belongs to history.[2] The inessential particular states are independent from each other and, thus, their *relations* can only be externally mutual. In this context, the third principle which we must see as binding them together is their common teleological end which is Reason-as-the-state, the political element of the human spirit which gives itself actuality in *world history* and which constitutes their absolute arbiter.

Indeed it is possible that several states by forming a confederation may be able to establish a jurisdiction over other states. It is possible that combinations of states can arise, as, for example, the Holy Alliance, but these are always only relative and limited, as is also so-called "perpetual peace".

The only absolute arbiter which ultimately makes itself good, either because or in spite of inessential particular states, is the rational state (i.e. the element of the in-and-for-itself human spirit which has being, that which establishes itself within history as the *general* principle, the *effective genus*).

### The Generality, Particularity, And Singularity Of Reason-As-The-Constitution

The paragraph which suggested the three smallest circles in FIGURE 9 and which also prompted the whole of FIGURE 10, is *Recht*, PP273. This paragraph lists the three essential functions of the rational constitution (law-giving, governing or particularizing, and finalising or uniting) each

---

(1) PP536. (2) Also see *Appendix B's Rechts*, PP258An.

"articulating" the moments of generality, particularity and singularity as now understood.
> *Rechts*, PP273:
> Reason-as-the- constitution appropriately tends to articulate itself within actuality into the following three substantial functions:
> a) the function of defining and firmly fixing the laws to have *general* application, i.e. *the law-giving function;*
> b) the function of subsuming the *particular* spheres of interests and singular cases under these general laws, i.e. *the governing* or *particularizing function;* and
> c) the function of subjectivity (i.e. the human ability willingly to finalise both the above general and particular decisions into one coherent package), i.e. *the monarchical* or *finalising function*. In the performance of this *finalising function*, the three differentiated *organs* of the rational constitution are held together in a *single unity*. The finalising function should thus be seen as the pinnacle and the beginning of the whole which is *constitutional monarchy*.

Section (a) says that "law-giving" is the constitution's *general* function. Laws seek to embrace and to integrate *all* of the current and foreseen interests into general statements of principle. These formulations seek to promote and to protect the ways of human life which either are themselves rational or which provide some of the conditions for the citizenry to live rationally. This is to say, that rational law (i.e. *Recht*) fosters rational living through the formulation and following of *general* principles. Law-giving is the most general of the three functions because it cannot be performed without the legislators rising in thought to the relatively abstract categories which allow clear principles to be formulated without the use of proper nouns. In contrast, a great deal of particularizing and finalising can be done in existent states on a purely *ad hoc* basis. Inherently, laws result from intellectual "mediation". Law-giving is the factor in political living which most pointedly directs the consciousness of citizens to move *up* the hierarchy of generality toward the conception of Reason.

The characterisation of the "governing function" of *section (b)* as the 'particularising function' probably needs no explanation both in the light of previous discussions and of the partial textual basis for this translation. A people rationally needs not only to formulate the *general* principles upon which it will seek to integrate and to reconcile the changing inessential particulars of its collective life, it must also actively apply these in practice to the indefinite multiplicity of cases and disputes which arise daily in the changing life of a state. The "finalising function" of *section (c)* as referring both to the 'royal assent' which must be given to every bill before it becomes law, and to the form which requires every governmental decision (executive or judicial) to be taken in the name of the monarch. The model calls it the 'uniting function'. It helps to ensure that the many laws and their many more applications will avoid self-contradiction and will continue to form *one* dynamic package of principles and particularizations over time. When this section says that,
> In the performance of this finalising function, the three differentiated *organs* of the rational constitution are held together in a *single unity*,

this is illustrated by the second smallest circle in the top left hand corner of FIGURE 10. The monarchical organ helps maximally to guarantee that this uniting function, which should be jointly exercised by all three organs, will be consistently performed. That the other two functions are also to be jointly exercised is perhaps only obliquely suggested by this paragraph. The truth that, like the three moments, the three functions are conceptually connected as well as being conceptually distinct is perhaps clear from our recollection that every *general* law if actual has both been finalised at least for the time being and is being applied to the existing particular cases which are its concern. Similarly, every decision on a *particular* question both marks a momentary finalisation and is an application or particularization of at least some implicit general principle. Again, every *finalisation* at least implicitly begs some general principle which relates to an indefinite number of particular cases.

In spite of these points, however, Hegel regrettably varied his terminology sometimes and this confuses somewhat the sharp distinction between a "function" and an "organ" which the six smallest circles in FIGURE 10 graphically record. In any case, this distinction must be made if we are to make sense of Hegel's exposition. The *Glossary* lists the various other German terms which Hegel uses and which are freely translated here only as either "function" or "organ".

In effect, previous chapters have developed this book's understanding of these functions and organs. However, the following table summarizes the connections between the moments, functions, and organs and thus helps prepare the way for the next chapter's comparison of the model constitution with Hegel's own formulations. Both sets of arrangements might be said to associate the performance of each function *mainly* with one of the three organs as follows:

|     | MOMENT | FUNCTION | ORGAN |
| --- | --- | --- | --- |
| (a) | generality | law-giving | representative assembl |
| (b) | particularity | governing (particularizing) | government |
| (c) | singularity | finalising (uniting) | monarch |

This association is inherently determined by the character of each organ. Thus, each is inclined to spend most of its time on one function. Hegel's position is not so clear on this point and thus the model's is again the result of a lenient interpretation of his ambiguity. Perhaps I have only read my own conception,
1) into the fact that each organ is mainly discussed by Hegel under the sub-title of its respective function, and
2) into his own confusion of "functions" and "organs" as suggested by his usually calling them both, "powers" (Gewalten).

It has also already been explained how the internal structure of each organ peculiarly suits it to perform the function for which it is mainly responsible. This understanding can be briefly restated using some of Hegel's terms:
1) The "assembly" as "representative" [1] of *all* interests should be best placed to formulate the *general* principles which will apply to all "sections" of the citizenry.
2) The government or "cabinet" as a smaller body can more efficiently act to apply the law to the indefinite multiplicity of essential and inessential *particulars* which arise daily and to formulate and execute policies both within the state and with regard to "interstate relations".
3) The "monarch", being *one* hereditary human "subject", is best placed to help "guarantee" the complex unity or *singularity* of the state through his or her performance of the finalising (uniting) function while performing either the figurehead or caretaking roles.

**Constitutional Monarchy Is Rational**

The justification for democratic monarchy largely follows the interpretation of why Hegel claimed that constitutional monarchy offers the most "rational" set of arrangements. In political life, it best encourages the reconciliation of "self-conscious reason with the Reason which has being".[2] Reason-as-the-constitution both as an institution and as a conception is itself part of this "reconciliation" because its *three organs* are tangible demonstrations of Reason's *three moments*: generality, particularity and singularity. The three organs help "reason" to recognize the philosophical necessity of the three less tangible yet distinct and certainly essential *functions*. On the other hand, the way the three organs jointly exercise the three functions empirically demonstrates their conceptual inseparability, their unity or their singularity. It demonstrates that each organ "must build itself into a whole and contain in itself the other moments".[3] This is most simply personified by the uniting activity of the monarchical organ. Constitutional monarchy is the most rational organization of the state because it tends best to ensure that the three vital functions will be consistently performed within the empirically real world. If they are performed, this in turn maximizes the empirical chances that the cultural, social, economic and political activities of a people will also become a self-conscious part of a life of Reason. These institutions are better than any others in helping the citizenry both to *act* and *think rationally*. He says, for example, that they raise "particular self-consciousness to its generality".[4]

This chapter has attempted to elucidate the way Reason's three moments also characterize the rational state and its constitution. The next chapter will examine the extent to which democratic monarchy is a reconstruction of Hegel's words.

(1) See *Glossary*.
(2) *Enz.* I, PP6.
(3) *Rechts*, PP272Z.
(4) *Rechts*, PP258.

## Chapter Twelve:
## From Hegel's Constitutional Monarchy
## To The Prescriptive Ideal

Previous chapters have elaborated democratic monarchy as the prescriptive ideal, defended it against republican attacks, and sketched how it might logically claim to be rooted in Hegel's wider system. This chapter will examine the extent to which this model conforms to Hegel's own constitution. It is argued that no conflict *need* be read into the differences between his and the model's formulations *except* at two points in *The Philosophy of Right*. These arise from Hegel's paragraphs, to be translated shortly, in which his monarch is given the "unconfined discretion" to appoint ministers and the right, "directly and solely" to conduct "interstate relations". With the exception of these two passages, Hegel's paragraphs are either plain enough or equivocal enough to allow us leniently to interpret him largely in support of the model. In addition to the previous chapter's showing of how PP273 can be read to provide the three function and three organ structure of democratic monarchy, this chapter will discuss how other paragraphs can be read either clearly or leniently to agree with the prescriptive ideal proposed here. It is not denied that Hegel's ambiguity may easily lead others to draw different conclusions in the first instance. Nor do I deny that democratic monarchy, as an institution for working majority rule, clearly *goes beyond* Hegel's words. Sometimes, his words are either too brief or too equivocal for us to say whether he would or would not support it. The features which seem to fall into this category are the following:

1) associational proportional representation (A.P.R.),
2) the procedure for constitutional change,
3) universal adult suffrage,
4) the procedure for recalling deputies,
5) no legislative veto for the non-elected chamber,
6) the 'figurehead' and 'caretaking' roles,
7) the 'state prerogative council',
8) some 'life peers' in the non-elected chamber,
9) the 'constructive vote of no confidence' provision, and
10) the procedure for impeaching and replacing a monarch.

This chapter will not discuss the last four items because nothing has been found in Hegel's words of direct relevance to them. The very last item, however, should be seen as quite obviously connected to the rejection of Hegel's two phrases discussed below. Both that rejection and this procedure follow necessarily from the principle of working majority rule.

In relation to the first six items, many of Hegel's ambiguous passages which might be read as concerning them will be examined. His words relating to the first two provisions will be assessed shortly, together with the discussion of Hegel's arguments concerning the *quantitative* and *majoritarian* features of the model. First, however, the two phrases which the model rejects will be studied. These are the passages which have required a *reconstruction* of Hegel's constitution in order to formulate democratic monarchy. It will be recalled that the model provides, whenever possible, for the monarch's will to be subordinated to the will of the 'working majority' and its elected officials. This requires the monarch to perform only the figurehead role as long as such a majority is in existence. Accordingly, he or she would be bound to appoint the leader of that majority as prime minister. Also, for example, the conduct of foreign affairs would be left *mainly* to the foreign minister and "cabinet". The monarch's role would be purely *formal* in these and all other matters provided that a working majority was present.

In sharp contrast, Hegel's words concerning these two cases do not make the monarch subordinate in this way. Instead, they give him unrestricted priority. While my monarch's discretion would be *confined* by that of such a majority, in PP283, Hegel grants his monarch the right to appoint his ministers at his own "unconfined discretion".

*Rechts,* PP283
[While the paragraphs starting with PP275 have discussed the prime, singularizing responsibility of the monarchical organ, i.e. the function of "finally deciding"], the second function of the monarchical organ is to particularize, i.e. to subsume the empirically exact details of its state's life under the general, constitutional and statutory law. The monarch's "cabinet" or council of the highest counselling positions forms this moment of the constitution's *particularity* in so far as it exists as an organ which is separate from the monarchical organ. The cabinet brings its *advice* concerning the changing affairs of state, including any proposed modifications to current statutory provisions, before the monarch for his finalising decision. This advice should be presented objectively, i.e. with a clear statement of the relevant empirical facts, and of the legal, circumstantial and other grounds for deciding one way or the other.¹ Because these highest advisors or governmental ministers deal directly with the person of the monarch, their appointment and removal falls within the monarch's *unconfined discretion.*

Not only is this "unconfined discretion" incompatible with the model, it would also seem to conflict with Hegel's own earlier claim, contained in the passage next to be translated, that because "the monarch only has to do with the *formal* pinnacle of decision", the "personal attributes of the monarch's character" are not "significant".

*Rechts,* PP280Z:
Men often say against monarchy that it is through such an institution that a state becomes unnecessarily dependent upon contingency. For example, it may be alleged that a monarch is improperly educated or perhaps that he is not worthy of standing at the very pinnacle of the state's decision taking and that it is indeed *irrational* that such arrangements exist. When such arguments are used against monarchy, they can be clearly refuted by pointing out that their assumption is *nugatory* which sees the *personal attributes* of the monarch's character as *significant.* Within a rational constitution or completed organization of the state, the monarch only has to do with the *formal* pinnacle of decision ... Wrongly, therefore, do men demand objective qualities like education and skill of the monarch. Usually, he need only be a quite ordinary human being in order to say, **"yes",** and to *place the dot on the "i"* **of the advice given by the representative assembly and the government of the day.** The structure of the *finalising pinnacle* of state decisions should be such that the personal attributes of the monarch's character are not significant. This specification for the monarch is *rational* because it accords with the conception of the constitution.

This same account of the monarch as only having to "say, 'yes', and ... place the dot on the 'i' of ... advice given" would also seem to conflict with the second passage which the model rejects. Hegel says that the "conduct" of the rational state's relations with "other states falls ... *directly and solely* to the monarch".

*Rechts,* PP329:
The state has an orientation towards the world outside just because it is an individual subject. For that reason, its relation to other states falls to the monarchical organ. This is to say, therefore, that the conduct of these relations, *directly and solely,* accrues to the monarch to command the armed might of the state, to maintain the relations with the other states through envoys, to conduct war, to conclude peace and other treaties, etc.

The same unacceptable point is made by Hegel in his *Encyclopaedia.*

*Enz.* III, PP544:
Broadly speaking, the representative assembly is concerned to take part in all that belongs to civil society. As the representative of private persons, it is concerned to shape the operation of the particularizing function especially by the giving of laws, i.e. by defining the generality of interests (which do *not* have the character of conducting and handling the state as an individual, e.g. war and peace, and thus *not* with what belongs to the monarchical organ *exclusively).*

These passages might also easily lead one to suppose that Hegel granted his monarch the power to decide between the organs of the state when they found themselves in any unresolved disagreements. In fact, Hegel never made his own plan for this contingency clear. Of course, the model gives clear priority to the working majority in such cases, when it exists, and to the 'state prerogative council' headed by the monarch, when it does not exist. This provision fills an important gap in Hegel's constitutional theory. The model's provision helps maximally to guarantee the "unity" of the state which Hegel so highly valued.

---

(1) The parts of these free translations marked by bold print are quite different from Knox's. See Glossary under "Knox" for a summary of the main differences between his and my translations.

The rest of this chapter examines Hegel's passages which either clearly or equivocally support democratic monarchy. It will be recalled that the explicit value behind the model is that of maximizing the *quality* and *quantity* of free, rational living. Especially the 'quantitative' part of this formulation is seen to carry a democratic implication. Hegel can be leniently read to support both this value and this implication in a number of his phrases, e.g.

a) the three organ constitution is "rational";
b) the rational state helps to raise "particular consciousness to its generality";[1]
c) "self-conscious reason" or "subjective freedom" [2] tends to be raised by the higher quality and publication of the debates in the representative assembly,[3] and by the fact that "the assembly has the character of appropriately being a living, mutually teaching, convincing and collectively advising assembly";[4]
d) this publication "is the greatest means of education concerning state interests" by which "public opinion first approaches true thoughts and insights into the conditions and the conception of the state, ... approaches an ability to judge more *rationally* about state affairs";[5] and
e) he also sees the deliberations of the representative assembly as tending to "augment" the civil service's "insight" [6] into state interests and thus to assist "the state" in its "aim" of "knowing ... the theorized, objective truth of Reason (Vernünftigkeit)".[7]

That this "knowing" in Hegel's view best follows an energetic debate or *dialogue* between sophisticated points of view is marked by his referring to the representative assembly as "a great assembly where one intelligent position devours another".[8] All this can be true even if we admit as Hegel does that most people have not yet fully attained "the conception of Reason". The knowledge of "the will of Reason", is *'currently'* not "possessed by the people":

Rechts, PP301An. (S.469):
... the in-and-for-itself Will which has being, i.e. the will of Reason, is the fruit of a deeper knowing and insight which is plainly not currently possessed by the people as a whole.

However, as *Chapter Six* argued, to the extent that the model's democratic institutions engender an extension of the quantity of rational thought and action, the more deliberative participation in communal decision-making would conform to the criteria of philosophical necessity. The state's policies would be more likely to result from a *comprehensive* theory which had integrated within itself the full range of available *experiences* and *competing* views. On the other hand, the more people might be arbitrarily excluded from a state's collective deliberations, the greater would be the *prima facie* case for seeing their procedures and conclusions as less than fully rational. In this way, a greater *quantity* of rational living would also tend to enhance the *quality* of thought and action. Rational quality and quantity tend to complement one another.

Previous chapters have derived the argument for majority rule from the philosopher's assumption that others may also be, or have the potential to become, rational beings. However, the above argument also accounts for the rational preference for majority rule over minority rule. The sheer existence of an enduring, working majority is evidence that *more* deliberative reconciliation of conflicts has taken place within this majority than has been achieved by any opposing voting block. Of course, as empirical, such evidence could not give conclusive proof that such rational unity had been attained. For example, the unity might instead be based on the anti-rational charisma of a fascist leader. However, a model constitution can only be constructed on the basis of such *empirical* presumptions. No constitution can protect a community absolutely from the possible emergence of anti-rational majorities or minorities. The model can only claim to minimize these risks. Therefore, when a working majority exists, it has the constitutional right to rule, because empirically or *quantitatively* speaking, it is presumed to be the most rational.

For readers so inclined, some of Hegel's own passages might be interpreted to show his interest in such wider popular 'participation' [9] and popular sovereignty. For example, he equivocally expresses his interest in popular participation by referring to the citizens' vote as "a high political right" and as "one of the most important political functions".[10] Hegel also observes that,

Rechts, PP317Z:
The principle of the modern world demands that what *everyone* should acknowledge must prove itself to be justified ... *everyone* wishes to have a share in discussing and advising ...

That it is of "the highest importance" for as *many* citizens as possible to "organize" themselves into the sorts of 'associations' which could be represented in the elected chamber could clearly be

(1) *Rechts*, PP258.  (2) PP316Z.  (3) PP315.  (4) PP309.  (5) PP315.
(6) PP301An.  (7) PP270An. (S.426).  (8) PP315.
(9) See *Glossary*.  (10) *Wurt.*, S.482 and 483 (p.273 and 263).

the prescriptive implication of the next quotation:
> *Rechts,* PP29OZ (S.460):
> ... The lower part of society or the multitude has clearly been left more or less unorganized. Yet it is of the *highest importance* that it become organized because only then can it become politically strong and powerful. Otherwise it will continue to be only a crowd, a multitude split into atoms.

The next two passages might lend Hegel's support to popular participation by referring to the greater "liveliness" of the "people" and to the "representative assembly" as the "empirical generality" of "the many":
> *Rechts,* PP315Z:
> ... The publication of the proceedings of the representative assembly is the greatest means of education concerning the wider state interests. Within a *people* where this takes place, they display a wholly other *liveliness* in connection with the state than where the representative assembly is absent or is not public. Only through this familiarity do the representative chambers keep in tune with the changes in public opinion at each and every step ...
>
> Rechts, PP301:
> ... Within the representative assembly ... public consciousness as an *empirical generality* of the views and thoughts of the *many* comes into existence ...

Of course, there is a sense in which democratic monarchy claims to be an articulation of the optimal constitutional conditions for "the sovereignty of the people".[1] In *Rechts,* PP279An., Hegel himself makes it clear that he is only opposed to the "superficial notions" of "the people" and its "sovereignty" which speak of it as if it were necessarily opposed to the sovereignty articulated in constitutional monarchy. Following this lead, his pejorative use of the term, "democratic",[2] is not taken to require the rejection of the model's representative, parliamentary, constitutional and monarchical 'democracy' but only the direct, mass, institutionless, lawless, mob-rule, or formless "democracy" which many of his conservative and liberal contemporaries also feared. Some of the other passages which are critical of "public opinion", and of "the people" and their assemblies can be *leniently* read to deny only, for example, that such a people or its assembly *without an already existing constitution* could "make" a constitution from scratch.[3] While *Rechts,* PP273An. and Z, allow only for the "indirect" or unintentional and gradual "modification" of the constitution, the model even recommends 'constitutional change' when this is seen to help move an existing constitution closer to the model. *Chapter Eight* showed that this view could be held to agree with Hegel's own practice when he supported constitutional changes for the less well organized states of Wurtemberg and Britain. At the same time, there are several points, where Hegel charges the electorate with apathy, inconsistency and "ignorance".[4] These charges do not have the effect of denying rationality to democratic monarchy, however, because its electoral and representative system does not share the apathy making features of 'the first past the post' electoral systems which he had in mind when he offered this sort of observation. The model would make such inconsistency less likely. Its operation would tend to minimize such ignorance and would best foster the public "education" for which Hegel has already been quoted in support.

Before discussing the passages in which Hegel might be read by some as rejecting the maximization of the numbers of citizens participating, it should be noted in passing that Hegel supported many of the other provisions which are appropriately assumed to be both conditions and features of a genuine liberal democracy in operation, e.g. "freedom of speech"[5] and the freedoms of the press, association, movement and occupation. At one point, he explicitly declared his support for a proposed "bill of rights" which he said "are simply the organic provisions which speak for themselves and make up the rational and basic principles of a constitutional condition".[6] The criticism of the limitations which Hegel nevertheless placed upon speech and the press will not be developed here.[7] Suffice it to suggest that these limitations could not be philosophically sustained against J.S Mill's eloquent case for the freedoms of speech, press, and lifestyle in *On Liberty.* "Liberty" is seen here as a condition for the maximization of the *quality* of everyone's "self-conscious reason".

---

(1) See *Glossary.* (2) See *Glossary.*
(3) See 'constitutional change' in the *Glossary.*
(4) Apathy: *Wurt.* S.484 (P.264), *Eng.* S.1114 (p.319), *Enz.* III, PP544An. (S.343) and *Rechts,* PP311An. (S.481); inconsistency: *Eng.,* S.84 (p.295); and "ignorance": *Eng.* S.90 (p.300).
(5) *Rechts,* PP317Z. (6) *Wurt.,* S.491 (p.270). (7) *Rechts,* PP319An. (S.488).

In spite of the implicit value placed on the *quantity* of rational living which might be read into the above Hegelian encouragements to popular participation and sovereignty, at several points, Hegel's tone toward "numbers" is dismissive to say the least. This is exemplified by his above mentioned discussions of electoral apathy. In these, he makes the point that apathy tends to be induced in large electoral districts when each voter can easily calculate his own negligibility. Read in isolation, such comments could imply that the quantitative features of *democratic* monarchy are not compatible with Hegel's own words. Another example of Hegel's ambiguity on this question of *numbers* is provided by the next extract. In isolation, some might see its reference to the "externality" of "great numbers" to mean that the differences between the numbers of members of each 'electoral association' should be ignored. This could suggest a 'one association, one vote' system within the elected chamber of Hegel's representative assembly. In contrast, this passage is leniently read here as making two points: that the great numbers could not be directly involved at the highest levels and that numbers *alone* are not important. Instead, numbers must be constitutionally recognized within a system which invites "associations" to be represented "essentially" because voluntary associations constitute "the very character ... specificity and structure" of "civil society". This construction does not exclude the *lenient* addition of *proportional* voting to the elected chamber.

> Rechts, PP308:
> The fluctuating side of civil society falls within the elected chamber of the representative assembly. It can enter this chamber only through representatives *essentially* because of the very character of civil society's specificity and structure and *externally* because of the great number of its members ...

Similarly, using and without violating some of the quantitative terms which Hegel defines in a broader context within his philosophy of logic, it can be argued that the way specific quantities of citizens are recognized by the model through their associational representatives does not introduce "sheer quantity"[1] into the proposed political arrangements but "qualitative quantity"[2]. Each electoral association within the model is seen, as Hegel *might*, to be a "qualitative structure of number".[3] This recognition of "numbers" within structures would not seem to "exaggerate quantity's radius of validity"[4] and, in fact, might be seen as one possible implication of Hegel's claim that "quantity must also come into its right in the objective world, as much in the natural as in the human world".[5] A.P.R.'s recognition, therefore, of the differences between the numbers of voting members within each electoral association might also be seen to be in line with the broad assertion that "philosophy is the very discipline which equally strives to distinguish both that which according to conceptual thinking and according to experience is differentiated".[6] It is in this sense that the highest prescriptive goal and thus the model constitution seeks to foster 'the maximization of both the *quality* and *quantity* of free, rational living'.

At the same time, it might be supposed that Hegel had a fully developed theory about what "corporations" are and about which ones should be "authorized" to send deputies to the elected chamber. In fact, Hegel says very little about these questions. *Chapter Ten* has already outlined Hegel's view that corporations tend to grow out of the pressures and divisions in civil society. Those individuals with common interests will be inclined to band together in order officially to promote these interest. Without sufficient elaboration, he also said that each corporation would be a "coherent group"[7] and that the number of its members would depend on the "character"[8] and intensity of the common interests which spurred its formation. Presumably, the numbers would have to fall within a certain "range".[9] Its numbers would have to be great enough to enable it to act effectively within society at large and yet each must be small enough so that it would not loose its sense of identity and become a "multitude, split of atoms".[10] Hegel did not say what the objective "measure"[11] of this "coherence" and "number" might be. He only specified that an electoral association would have to have a "wider posture"[12] than simply to meet every election

---

(1) *Enz.* I PP99 and Z.  (2) *Enz.* I, PP106Z (S.224).  (3) *Enz.* I, PP102An. (S.215).
(4) *Enz.* I, PP99An. (S.210).  (5) *Enz.* I, PP99An. (S.211).  (6) *Enz.* I, PP103Z (S.217).
(7) *Rechts*, PP252.  (8) Ibid.  (9) *Enz.* I, PP106Z.  (10) *Rechts*, PP290Z.
(11) *Enz.* I, PP106Z (S.2240 & PP108Z (S.22).  (12) *Rechts*, PP308.

time to cast and collect ballots.¹ A.P.R. fills this gap left by Hegel. Its recognition of the comparative "strengths" ² of the corporations by giving them weighted votes could even be seen as an example of what Hegel called a "qualitative ratio".³ Without such an objective measure, Hegel's few words might easily lead to the harsh interpretation that he intended the choice of corporations and their representatives to be left to the arbitrary will of the monarch. Hegel says that "each particular great section (Zweig) of society, e.g ... commerce, ... industries, etc. ... has an *equal* right to become represented ...".⁴ He also says that he agrees with the traditional European view that all "the various great interests of the nation should be represented in the nation's great assembly".⁵ One implication of the above quotations is that the small interests need not be or could not be represented directly, but how is it to be decided which are "great" enough to be "summoned"? We are simply left to guess whether Hegel might not have accepted that these "great interests" should be represented in *proportion* to their greatness (i.e. "equal" in proportion to their respective voting memberships) rather than "equal" in the sense of 'one association, one vote' within the elected chamber.

The *lenient* interpretation that he could support 'proportional equality' might also be read into several other points which Hegel makes:

1) He suggested, in his *Constitution of Germany,* that some districts might be summoned to send representatives to the "Imperial Representative Assembly" (Reichstag) in proportion to their inhabitants. These representatives were to be elected from the territorial and population subdivisions of the Empire which would have already been established for the military convenience of the armed forces. These representatives were to vote within the existing "Cities Bench" of the assembly, at least for the purposes of levying taxes for the support of the Empire's armed forces: "... representatives could be elected from the sub-divisions *according to the numbers* of their inhabitants".⁶

2) Shortly after offering that suggestion, Hegel expressed his dismay at the existing constitution's allowing "the *smallest* Imperial city" a vote while *whole* provinces such as "Bohemia" and "Saxony" were excluded.

3) Hegel's criticism of the pre-1831 "inequalities" between the English parliamentary constituencies, and his complaint that one "section" plays "an *overbearing* part in state operations".⁷

4) Less relevantly, we might note that Hegel did accept a principle of proportionality in the payment of taxes: "... public taxes proportionately equal for all".⁸

In the face of these ambiguities, however, we are left plainly to assert for the model, that the principle of 'maximizing the quality and quantity of free, rational living' prescribes 'proportional equality' for the 'associations'. It must be stressed that the above uses of Hegel's own terms are not regarded here as proof that he would necessarily agree with A.P.R. Nevertheless, they exclude the charge that a democratic, associational, proportional, representative, majority-rule constitution is *obviously* incompatible with his wider conceptions of "quality" and "quantity".

So far, we have studied some of the respects in which the model constitution goes beyond Hegel's. The suggestion that the value of the *quantity* as well as the *quality* of rational living might be read into Hegel's words prepared the way, first, for the further elaboration of the defence of the principle of majority rule. This, in turn, provided the settings both for discussions of constitutional change and of A.P.R. The model's procedure for changing a constitution was seen

(1) It will be recalled that in *Chapter Ten,* it was made clear that the model explicitly invites trade unions as well as mass political parties to register as 'electoral associations'. Hegel's words and phrases already listed are vague enough to allow these additions. They do not seem to require us to agree with Knox's assurance that Hegel "is *of course* not thinking of what we know as Trade Unions *since his Korporationen* are only societies of which both *employers are employed* are members" (note 83 to *Rechts,* PP229). Given that not many trade unions existed when Hegel was writing, it may well be that he did not have them in mind as possible examples of "associations", there is no Hegelian or philosophical reason to exclude them and, in fact, they could be seen as precisely the means by which the "lower part of society or the multitude" (*Rechts,* PP29OZ) might become "organized" as we saw Hegel prescribing earlier. While, both Hegel's and the model's electoral associations could well include some "relative unions" of employers and employed, no Hegelian or other reasons are seen to limit them to associations of this sort.

(2) *Rechts,* PP255Z. (3) *Enz.* I, PP105 and Z. (4) *Rechts,* PP311An. (S.480).
(5) *Eng.* S.106 (p.313). (6) *G.Cons.,* S.578 (p.239).
(7) *Eng.* S.85 (p.296), *Enz.* III, PP544An. (S.342); *Wurt.,* S.575 (p.293).
(8) *Wurt.,* S.467 (p.251) and S.491 (p.270).

as probably conflicting with one of Hegel's paragraphs but as perhaps implicitly supported by some of his own prescriptive practices. We also saw how the A.P.R. system might be read into Hegel's brief discussions of the principles which should govern both the formation and representation of "corporations". Therefore, of the ten provisions which were listed as going beyond Hegel's own constitution, the following are yet to be discussed:

3) universal adult *suffrage,*
4) *recall* of deputies,
5) no *legislative veto* for the non-elected chamber, and
6) the *figurehead* and *caretaking* roles.

After these remaining points have been compared with Hegel's words, some additional passages which might be read either to support or to undermine the *ultimate* control over the three functions which democratic monarchy gives to the 'working majority' will be considered. Finally, the most obscure terms and phrases which Hegel uses within his most difficult paragraphs dealing with his monarch will be elucidated.

### (3) Universal Adult Suffrage

To say the least, Hegel's words give us no reason to think that he favours the inclusion of women in his electorate.[1] Nor is it even clear that he included all adult men. His few comments neither categorically affirm nor reject it. They are critical of the contemporary theories which were proposing universal suffrage but his objections may not have been based on a preference for a smaller electorate as such. Rather, he may have opposed these theories only because they were grounded on superficial notions of "the sovereignty of the people", i.e. they ignored the actual, rich and organizationally structured will of the people which was already articulated through the "associations" in society. Hegel says also that age and property qualifications for voting are only "negative ... and ... merely presumptive" and do not provide a "positive guarantee" of electoral rationality. He says that such qualifications *might* be valid only if they are additions to the essential qualification which is that a subject be a member of one of the associations which has been "summoned" to send representatives to the elected chamber of the representative assembly.[2] The model's electoral system also accepts Hegel's suggestion that each new candidate for election to the representative assembly should have already had the experience of being an official of his or her association, or perhaps alternatively, of being a state civil servant.[3]

### (4) Recall Of Deputies

The scheme which would allow voters in an electoral association to inaugurate a new election for their deputy(s) has no explicit support or opposition within Hegel's own words. However, two phrases in *Rechts,* PP309Z might be read to pull against each other on this question. Near the beginning, Hegel speaks of the deputies as "plenipotentiaries" (Bevollmachtigte) whose offices are based on "trust". However, later he says that the electors require a "guarantee" that their deputy will promote the general interest. If all deputies could be *trusted* completely there would be no need for a guarantee. It is because there is need for such *guarantees* that the model's 'recall scheme' provides one. In the middle of the same passage, a sentence appears which might seem to create another unbridgeable gulf between Hegel's and the model's constitution. Read in isolation, it might easily be interpreted to reject the principle of "majority voting" as such: "Hence *majority voting* runs counter to the principle that I should be personally present in anything which is to be obligatory on me". In its context, however, this can be leniently read only to mean that obligations are better formulated and negotiated by trusted deputies than determined without deliberation by the counting of citizen's heads. Laws would be more rationally found by a deliberative, representative assembly than by plebiscites.

### (5) No Legislative Veto For the Non-Elected Chamber

Disregarding the fact that the model's "upper house" is partly composed of 'life peers' while Hegel wrote only of hereditary members, he said very little about this chamber. He gave it the tasks of "mediation",[4] of ensuring the "ripeness of decision"[5] or it helps to secure the state against the destructive effects of being ruled by "momentary majorities".[6] These words are vague enough to be compatible either with the view that the upper house should have a veto power or that it should not. It will be recalled that the model's non-elected chamber can at the most require the elected chamber to vote again. Perhaps Hegel's own support for this kind of

---

(1) See, for example, *Rechts,* PP171.
(2) *Rechts,* PP308An. (S.477), PP310An. (S.479), and PP311An. (S.480); *Wurt.,* S.482(p.262), S.483 (p.263) and S.484 (p.264).
(3) *Rechts,* PP310; *Wurt.,* S.485 (p.265). (4) *Rechts,* PP312.
(5) PP313. (6) Ibid.

subordination of the hereditary to the elected chamber could be *read into* his broad approval for the King of Wurtemberg's proposed constitution which included a one chamber assembly in which the elected members were to out number the hereditary members, 73 to 59.[1] This implication is less certain, however, because in the next several sentences, without making his own preferences explicit, he contrasts this proposal with other constitutions which either grant the hereditary numbers "one more vote" than the elected members or arrange them into separate chambers.

### (6) The Figurehead And Caretaking Roles

While these two roles for the head of state are certainly not explicit in Hegel's words, some of the apparent contradictions in his formulations could be removed by this distinction. Two passages quoted near the beginning of this chapter are examples of this. If the "unconfined discretion" of PP283 could be taken only as referring to the caretaking role, it would not have had to be rejected. When he said, in PP280Z, that the monarch "need ... only ... say, 'yes' and place the dot on the 'i' of ... advice", this could easily be read as a characterisation of the figurehead role. Both roles might be similarly read into some later sentences from the same *Zusatz*:

> *Rechts,* PP280Z:
> Indeed, there can be circumstances in which the personal attributes alone of a monarch come to the fore, but then the state is not yet fully formed or not well designed. In a well ordered monarchy, only the objective side of his and of the state's personality becomes constitutionally operative, i.e. only the concrete "advice" formulated by the other two organs becomes the law of the land. In a rational state, the monarch only has to add his subjective "I will" to this advice.

The figurehead role may be implicit in the following extract in which the monarch's royal assent or "I will" added to the "law-giving and particularizing initiatives taken by others" is seen by Hegel as symbolic of "the attainment of general human decisiveness":

> *Rechts,* PP279Z:
> ... when the rational constitution is secure, the monarch often has nothing more to do than to sign his name to the law-giving and particularizing initiatives taken by others. This *name,* however, is important. It is the pinnacle beyond which collective decision making cannot go. One might say that an organic constitutional structure was definitely present within the beautiful democracy of Athens. However, we see at the same time that the Greeks had to extract their final decisions from wholly external appearance, from the oracles, from the entrails of sacrificial animals and from the flight of birds. Also, we see that the Greeks took their relation to nature to be that as to a force which acts through these appearances to promulgate and express what is good for humankind. In that time, self-consciousness had not yet come to the abstraction of subjectivity which experiences its self-relating negativity. Nor had it yet come beyond that self-consciousness to the attainment of *general human decisiveness,* to the attainment of an "I will" which must become proclaimed by humankind itself. This "I will" constitutes the great difference between the ancient and modern world and so it must have its own distinctive existence within the great structure of the modern state.

Again, the caretaking role might be seen as suggested by PP320 which characterizes the "subjectivity" of the monarch as an objective guarantee against the haphazard and destructive subjectivities which can threaten to dominate the citizenry from time to time:

> *Recht,* PP320:
> Subjectivity has its most external appearance in the isolated individuals and groups which tend to exist in civil society. This subjectivity is characterized by the haphazard wants, and the self-destructive beliefs and analyses which tend to disintegrate a state's life. Paradoxically, this sort of subjectivity has its enduring, objective guarantee in its opposite, in the uniting subjectivity of the monarch. The monarchical organ's subjectivity is identical with Reason's substantial will when it is conceived as the final, united, self-knowing structure or as an "ideality" of the whole state.

The previous chapters associated each of the three organs *mainly* with one of the functions. Yet, both Hegel and the model see that the three functions should be jointly performed. The monarch, for example, by finalising all general and particular decisions, is seen as *formally* performing the uniting function. In order for the model to be democratic, *ultimate* control over all three functions regarding legislative and executive decisions had to be given to the assembly's working majority between general elections. That this ultimate authority must be given to one of the organs, is one implication of Hegel's discussion of "internal sovereignty":

> *Rechts,* PP278:
> The internal sovereignty of the state is secured by the two provisions that,
> 1) the particular functions and organs of the state are not to be rigidly isolated, and
> 2) the wills of state officials are not to be made entirely self-dependent.

---

(1) *Wurt.,* S.472 (p.254).

Both are implemented by requiring the organs and the officials to have their root within the *formal* will of the monarch. This organization of internal sovereignty constitutes their single self.

One plausible reading of this paragraph would simply locate this sovereignty with the monarch. However, the equally possible and preferable interpretation is that the *"formal* will of the monarch" refers only to the figurehead role.

The next three sections will consider some other of Hegel's words which might either confirm or deny the model's majoritarian sovereignty over the three functions.

**The Law-Giving Function**

While Hegel's conception of "sovereignty" might logically demand that ultimate control be vested in one of the organs, Hegel fails himself plainly to specify which organ. The model clearly gives it to the elected chamber when it has a working majority and to the monarch in the context of the 'state prerogative council' when it does not. However, Hegel's words are vague enough at different points perhaps to suggest that he gives this sovereignty either to the monarch or to the government instead. One example of this is provided by the next free translation. If *endlich* were rendered as "last", meaning last in importance, rather than as "third", meaning the third organ to be mentioned but without attaching any special significance to the order, this would reverse the priority the model gives to the elected chamber of the "representative assembly":

*Rechts,* PP300:
Three organs are active within the law-giving function as a totality:
*firstly,* the monarchical organ to which *formally* the highest finalising decision belongs;
*secondly,* the governing organ which both has a concrete acquaintance with, and oversight of the whole state in its many sidedness (The governing organ oversees the whole both according to the fundamental principles which are already established by the constitution and by the law, and according to its acquaintance with the requirements of state power. This acquaintance especially characterizes the advising part of the governing organ, i.e. the cabinet.); and
*thirdly (endlich), the representative assembly organ.*

Hegel's above reference to the "monarchical organ" literally reads, "to which the highest decision belongs". These words when read in isolation or read together just with similar phrases like the ones following could easily suggest that Hegel sees the monarch in all cases not only as the formal but effective, *ultimate* authority in his constitution:

*Rechts,* PP284, PP279, PP292 and ÞÞ286An., respectively:
1) "...the monarch as the finally deciding subjectivity which is ... raised above all accountability ..., is
2) "the absolute ... deciding" and
3) "sovereign organ", i.e.
4) "the absolute pinnacle ...".[1]

Such phrases could easily *mislead* us to think that plainly for Hegel, the monarch's "finalising function" includes the constitutional right absolutely to *veto* any item passed by a working majority. This impression would again tend to be encouraged,
   a) by Hegel's broad support for the King of Wurtemberg's proposals which included a final veto for the monarch, requiring him only to give his reasons after he had refused for the third time to sign his name to a measure;[2]
   b) by Hegel's expression of regret that the power of the British monarchs had long since become "more illusory than real",[3]
   c) by the before mentioned monarch's appointment of his ministers at his own "unconfined discretion",[4] and
   d) by the before mentioned references to the monarch as having the "direct" and "exclusive" right to conduct "interstate relations".

However, one passage tends to support the model and thus dramatically to reverse these strong impressions that Hegel intended the monarch's finalising function with regard to legislation to be substantive rather than formal. This passage was the one translated earlier and which asserted that,

Within ... a completed organization of the state, the monarch only has to do with the *formal* pinnacle of decision ..., he need only be a quite ordinary human being in order to say "yes" and to place the dot on the "i"...[5]

The model removes these equivocal voices of Hegel by clearly 'confining' the monarch to symbolic or

---

(1) Also see *Rechts,* PP275.  (2) *Wurt,* S.470 (p.253).
(3) *Eng.,* S.117 (p.322). Also see S.90 (p.300), S.101 (p.309) S.103 (p.311), S.118 (p.322), S.123 (p.326) and S.128 (p.330).
(4) *Rechts,* PP283.  (5) *Rechts,* PP28OZ.

*formal* functions as long as a working majority exists. Accordingly, the above "highest", "finally" and "absolute" phrases are glossed as referring to the monarch's *main* responsibility *formally* to finalise the general and particular decisions which effectively have already been taken by the working majority and its elected council of ministers, *not* as referring to the monarch's *ultimate* substantive authority over the other two organs. Similarly, Hegel's support for the King of Wurtemberg's veto and his regret at the weakness of the British monarch are construed both as only referring to states which had not yet attained a fully representative constitution or did not yet have a "completed organization" and thus could not yet afford the monarch to be 'confined' to "the pinnacle of *"formal* decision". As already mentioned, some of Hegel's other ambiguous words if read in isolation might suggest that he gives the governing organ more authority in cases of conflict than he does to the 'working majority'. These are considered in the next section.

### The Particularizing Function

If working majority *rule* is also to mean that it controls particularising, this requires the elected chamber ultimately to have constitutional power over the governing organ. In the last resort, this demands that the majority in the chamber be able effectively to replace government ministers (and judges) who refuse to particularize in accordance with its will. It has already been argued that the monarch's "discretion" to appoint his ministers would have to be 'confined' rather than "unconfined". Similarly, his "conduct" of foreign affairs would have to be seen only as "accruing" to him *formally,* to the foreign minister and the cabinet *mainly,* and to the 'working majority' indirectly but *ultimately.* Both of these 'improving' changes would have to be made before working majority control over the particularizing function could be read into Hegel's other words. Hegel does not explicitly inform us whether he is assuming that the monarch will usually appoint civil servants or members of the representative assembly to be his "ministers". From *Rechts,* PP315Z, we know that ministers are *speaking* members of the assembly but in which of its chambers Hegel does not say. Neither does he explicitly say whether they would be *voting* members of either chamber. At the same time, perhaps we could *read into* some other of Hegel's words the view that the representative assembly should control the appointment of ministers:

1) He speaks with approval of the "opposite party" in the British Parliament seeking to replace the government of the day with its own leaders. Hegel clearly implies here the general prescription that 'a loyal opposition *should* attempt to replace the government with its own men' by saying that this "struggle ... is precisely its *greatest justification*".[1]
2) He speaks of the "accountability"[2] of the governing organ as opposed to the monarch's unaccountability which *might* also imply the *replaceability* of ministers if they are *accountable* to the will of the representative assembly.
3) He speaks of the members of the elected chamber as being preoccupied with "the seeking of higher state office"[3] which might mean cabinet posts.

Equivocal passages which might be read as asserting the government's priority in any conflict with the elected chamber, are construed here instead as asserting the government's *main* responsibility and not as excluding the *ultimate,* if indirect, authority of the working majority in these and in all other areas of particularizing, e.g.

a) Hegel speaks of the "budget" as being "a governmental concern" in "a cultured state";[4] and
b) of "the representative assembly's government" as being "superior" to the assembly in its "influence over war and peace and over external politics".[5]

Still another passage[6] says that the elected chamber could be "strengthened" while "directly confronting the government" by the agreement of the hereditary chamber. Such "strengthening" could also occur and would be welcomed within the model constitution, but it makes it clear as Hegel does not, that the majority in the elected assembly can insist that such a government be replaced by its own elected leaders, with or without the agreement of the hereditary chamber, of the reigning monarch, let alone of the government being "confronted". Finally, when Hegel says that the representative assembly does not need "a means of coercing" the government, this is construed not to exclude the assembly's ultimate constitutional right to coerce the government. It is read only to report that this is rarely needed in a rational state, either because the two usually voluntarily cooperate or because the threat of such coercion in the background is enough to secure the government's compliance.

---

(1) *Wurt.,* S.476 (p.258). (2) *Rechts,* PP284. (3) *Enz.* III, PP544An. S.343).
(4) *Enz.* III, PP544An. (S.43). (5) *Wurt.,* S.489. (6) *Rechts,* PP313.

## The Uniting Or Finalising Function

The most relevant passages concerning the majority's ultimate control over the uniting function have already been discussed. It has been explained why his "unconfined discretion" and "directly and solely" phrases have been rejected. His "place the dot on the 'i' ...." *Zusatz* was leniently interpreted to allow the working majority constitutionally to be the *ultimate,* if not the *formal,* finaliser and uniter.

## Difficult Paragraphs

What remains to be done is to sketch how Hegel's difficult paragraphs in *The Philosophy of Right* concerning the monarch are interpreted in order to elaborate the model's monarchy. The following is a list of summarizing and simplifying, interpretive titles for each of these paragraphs and parts of paragraphs. The *Appendix* offers *literal* translates of these paragraphs in full. Refer to these if any obscurities remain in spite of the attempts following this list of titles to elucidate what are taken to be the most problematic terms and phrases contained in these paragraphs.

PP273: The rational constitution has three *functions* (law-giving, governing or particularizing, and finalising or uniting). The monarch's finalising function helps to hold the three *organs* together.

PP275Z: The sovereignty of the state is best guaranteed *formally* by the single, human self of the monarch.

PP276: Sovereignty is the basic, united, self-knowing structure of Reason-as-the-constitution, a single unity of the state's functions and organs.

PP278: Internal sovereignty is the single self of the whole in which all of the functions, organs and officials are rooted.

PP278An: Sovereignty both in regard to internal and external affairs is a united, self-knowing structure whose actuality is fostered by governmental activity in times of peace, but especially in times of crisis. The human will's self-relating negativity is the absolute foundation of this singularity called sovereignty.

PP279: Sovereignty or collective subjectivity is best secured by a constitution in which formal finality of decision rests with the subjectivity of one human individual, the monarch. Subjectivity is the groundless self-determining capacity of the human will which is certain of itself.

PP279An: Sovereignty is best secured by the monarch's personality and by his or her formal, final "I will".

PP279An: The rational state does not leave the function of *formally finalising* decisions to a corporate or "moral person".

PP279An: While purely analytical understanding may see the monarch as deduced, monarchy is that which originates out of itself.

PP279An: It is a confusion to oppose the sovereignty of the people to the sovereignty of the rational state.

PP279An: Even in non-rational but enduring states, there must be a singularizing pinnacle of decision which tends to arise in the person of a chance leader.

PP279An: If such pinnacles of self-determination are blunted, the requisite unequivocal and clear final decisions can still appear to come from oracles or from other sources outside the circle of human freedom.

PP279Z: The model constitution organizes the state as a great architectonic structure which is a hieroglyph of Reason.

PP279Z: The "I will" of the monarch is not permitted to be capricious. When the rational state is secure, the monarch often has nothing to do other than to sign his name.

PP280: Since monarchy is "raised over all ... agreement", in the sense that hereditary succession does not depend on the prior intellectual or political mediation of others but "originates out of itself", monarchy tends to guarantee that a state will at least enjoy natural or "unmediated singularity".

PP280An: Like the so-called ontological proof of the definite being of God, the derivation of why the formal finalising function should be left to the unmediated naturalness of a monarch can only be appreciated from the speculative perspective of the philosophy of logic.

PP28OZ: Because within a completed organization of the state, the monarch is only the formal pinnacle of state decisions, he or she need only be quite ordinary to say, "yes", and to place the dot on the "i" of the objective "advice" given by the representative assembly and the government of the day. Therefore, the personal attributes of the monarch, say, his education or his worthiness, are not significant.

PP281An: A truly philosophical treatment grasps how the monarch's legitimacy is grounded in birth and the right of descent. In contrast, purely analytical thinking abolishes this in-and-for-itself character of the monarch's majesty.

PP281An: There is an inherent flaw in the practice of electing a head of state.

PP281Z: Monarchy cannot be firmly justified either by pure theology or by arguments based on sheer utility or positive law.

PP282An. & Z: The state's ability to offer pardons, reprieves or amnesties to criminals is rooted in the strength of the human spirit to forgive and forget. A pardon is an example of a particularization which the monarchical organ *formally finalises*.

PP283: The monarch's particularizing function is exercised through his cabinet, the council of his highest advisors. The monarch appoints and removes these ministers at his own "unconfined discretion". [These appointments by the model's monarch are 'confined'.]

PP284: Not the monarch but his ministers are accountable to the representative assembly for governmental actions.

PP285: The third constitutional function of the monarchical organ is to help maintain the general actuality of its state.

PP286 & An: The "objective guarantee" of each of the three organs is the rational structure of the constitution.

PP286An: Objective guarantees of rational living are those offered by "institutions" and it is these alone which the conception of the rational constitution seeks to define. Such subjective guarantees as a people's patriotism and the personal characters of the monarch and of the other state office holders, therefore, are not relevant to an exposition of the model constitution.

PP320 & Z: The subjectivity of the monarch is an objective guarantee against the haphazard and destructive subjectivity which can characterize the citizenry from time to time.

PP321: As a mediated singularity, a state is an individual among other states. In a rational state's monarch (or sovereign), singularity appears as an actual, unmediated individual.

PP322An: A self-dependent collectivity with its own self-determining centre does not aspire to join with another to make up a larger collectivity with a different centre. This self-dependence was first shaped by the force of a self-dependent leader at the pinnacle, a patriarch, a chief, etc.

PP329: The state, as an individual subject in relation to other states, requires the conduct of interstate relations to accrue, "directly and solely to the monarchical organ". [The model's improving modification to this paragraph says that, in a rational state, it should fall *mainly* to his foreign minister and cabinet, *ultimately* to the elected chamber, and only *formally* to the monarch.]

PP329Z: The many and delicate relations with other states can only be handled from out of the pinnacle. Monarchs and cabinets are not subject to the passions of war any more than are peoples and their elected assemblies.

**Elucidations**

First, the relations between Hegel's "singularity", "sovereignty" and "subjectivity" will be discussed. In PP279, it is made quite clear that *subjectivity* is one of Hegel's names for that general, individual and collective, human capacity to shape the many distinct details of human sensuous and non-sensuous experience into *one* self-conscious life, i.e. into one coherent system or totality however complex and dynamic that *unity* might be. Subjectivity names the human capacity, individually or collectively to achieve a *singularity* both in theory and in practice. *Sovereignty* is understood to be the special name given to the self-knowing, constitutional capacity of a people to achieve a collective singularity both in relation to internal and external affairs. It is Hegel's and the model's conclusion that an hereditary head of state supports sovereignty by helping maximally to guarantee the capacity of a collectivity repeatedly to achieve a complex unity over time. Hegel and the model also claim that the constitutional finalising function of the monarch rests most basically on his or her own "natural" capacity for subjectivity. Thus, the monarch's subjectivity helps to guarantee the collective's subjectivity and therefore its unity. The individual subjectivity of the monarch is seen as one factor within the system of constitutional "guarantees" which defines sovereignty. However, PP278An. might unfortunately be read to go so far as authorizing the monarch to use his subjectivity to become a dictator in an emergency. Hegel writes that in "a crisis, ... it is to sovereignty that the saving of the state is entrusted", requiring as this does, "the subordination or sacrifices of the otherwise authorized particular concerns and associations". Knox's translation of this passage's *Souveränität* as "sovereign", rather than as "sovereignty", leads the English reader to jump to this more authoritarian interpretation even more readily. It is true that elsewhere, Hegel sometimes referred to the monarch as "the sovereign", [1] but this passage is leniently taken here simply to be saying that the sacrifice of private interests is sometimes necessary. Because Hegel clearly sees the monarch only as an organ of the whole constitutional system of sovereignty,[2] he is not implying here, as might be thought, that both the representative assembly and the government should be dissolved in a crisis leaving the monarch to deal with the emergency as a benevolent despot. Instead, the gloss followed here understands Hegel simply as asserting that many of the "particular associations and their concerns" within civil society must be subordinated to "the aim of the whole" as defined *jointly* by the office holders in the *three* organs of the constitution. Thus, these private interests of civil society may be subordinated by the *three* organs of "the organism" of Reason-as-the-state, not by an absolute monarch.

### Subjectivity

In PP279, Hegel recalls some of the characteristics of the human will's *subjectivity* which he had explored earlier in PP4-PP7 of the Introduction to *The Philosophy of Right*. He says that subjectivity is "the abstract, and to that extent, the *groundless* self-determining of the human will". Hegel's use of "groundless" here recalls his argument in the Introduction and elsewhere, that when the will discovers its capacity for "self-relating negativity" [3] (i.e. when it discovers its capacity for consciously dwelling at least for an instant within its "I = I"),[4] it discovers an "absolute" limit to the extent to which it can empty its consciousness. Within this maximally but not quite empty consciousness, the will discovers that it can no longer be naive about its choices. Each new "content" (Inhalt) that might be willed cannot now be willed on the basis of "grounds", i.e. *externally* given foundations whose validity is unconsciously taken for granted. In the "I = I", one has emptied one consciousness of all presuppositions, e.g. no externally *given* moral axioms are left from which to *deduce* the way of life which one should follow. From now on, these will have to be generated from within, if at all.

When Hegel says that willing within such a context is *groundless*, he means that it is 'presuppositionless'. This is not to say that the content willed in this way is necessarily incapable of receiving rational justifications as one might supposed from his unfortunate choice of the word "groundless". On the contrary, for example, the constitutional will of the monarch is in this ordinary sense 'grounded' in "the infinite, within itself *grounding* Reason".[5] The same interpretation applies to the paragraph which refers to the "majesty" of the monarch as "characterized" by *"groundless* unmediatedness".[6] Because this content is presuppositionless, pure *deduction* is not sufficient. Dialectical reason sees no self-evident, *externally* given first principles which would allow us by deduction responsibly to will additional content. All externally given principles have been cast into doubt by such reason. Because this context is the result of our own thinking which now sees that *if* your or my "I" is to be anything more than the simple "I" contained in the 'I am I', then you and I have to draw additional contents out of this maximally empty context itself. We cannot draw them out of any *unquestionably* grounded and externally based premises. Our questioning has driven us to this maximally empty juncture and our "self-conscious reason" [7] sees that *if* we are to get beyond the 'I am I', *then* any additions will be deliberately willed either arbitrarily or by 'reason'. It is to this context that PP278An. refers when it speaks of the "abstract conception of the human will", i.e. of the conception of the will as purely "I = I". The experience of the "I = I" is a result of the "will's self-relating negativity", the human capacity to negate or reject any content immediately found within our consciousness, i.e. the human ability "to put into question ... all particularity and determinateness" (e.g. any presuppositions, assumption, axioms, practices or habits). It is through such an abstracting process that we discover that we ourselves may be able deliberately to transform all unmediated and mediated "particularity and determinateness" into a unity consciously willed by us. This is the human will's "self-determining generality moving toward a singularity".

Subjectivity in general and the subjectivity of the monarch in particular is *absolutely grounded* in "the will's self-relating negativity" and "self-determining generality", and it need *not* be grounded in externally given principles or presuppositions. Rational subjectivity is internally *grounded* but externally *groundless*. It is grounded in the will's "negativity" and "generality".

(1) PP321  (2) PP279An.  (3) PP278An.
(4) *Enz.* I, PP86An. and Z; *Enz.* III, PP424 and Z, PP425 and Z, and PP426Z.
(5) Idee, *Rechts,* PP281An.  (6) Ibid.  (7) *Enz.* I, PP6.

Paradoxically stated, 'the grounded is groundless'. The will's 'grounding' in the "I = I" is taken here to be "absolute" in the Cartesian sense that I cannot sustain the doubt that 'I *am*', or that 'I *am* in some sense'. Thus, the 'I am I' or the "I = I" seems to provide us with a philosophically necessary internal foundation for our subjectivity, "the pinnacle beyond which ... decision making cannot go".[1] In the context of its "negativity" and "generality", subjectivity discovers that it has the *option* either,
1) of remaining frozen within the abstraction which is the simple "I = I", i.e. each has the option of remaining purely within the attitude of seeing oneself as being able to will anything but not willing anything in particular (i.e. not defining one's "I" other than by saying that it equals "I"), or
2) of willing to add to the contents or specifications of one's "I", i.e. the option of willing to be a more complex and definite unity when social, political and other opportunities present themselves, e.g. to become married, a teacher, an artist, a supporter of a particular political party with a specific ideology, etc.

The willing of such additional contents in this context can either be entirely the result of a rational thought process or it can be somewhat "arbitrary". To the extent that it is rational, it issues from deliberations which assess each alternative by the tests of 'philosophical necessity'. *Rational* willing would seek to actualize the contents and specifications which tend to maximize the quality and quantity of free, rational living. *Arbitrary* willing can proceed from an ignorance of this rational aim or by deliberately disregarding it. Hegel's and my more precise adjective for the second sort of willing is "evil". However, *unavoidable* arbitrariness arises when reason requires a decision to be made before reason has found an exact means for determining the answer by reason, or when reason concludes that more than one answer would always seem to be available. For example, Hegel correctly explained, in his earlier discussion of "punishment", that reason alone could not specify the exact fine that would be appropriate for any given crime (e.g. £100 or £101), yet reason sees that some fine is necessary. Also, reason alone could not determine whether policemen should be given blue or green uniforms, yet some uniform is necessary. While pure reason can determine that there should be three constitutional organs, it cannot decide whether there should be 500 or 501 members in the elected assembly, or that the income tax should be fixed at 29% or at 30%. In spite of such limitation of reason, reason sees that we can and must decide such questions if we are to survive and thrive.

Both Hegel and the model take the monarch's arbitrary origins [2] as helping to symbolize the above truth that some questions demand arbitrary but human answers. The hereditary succession to the throne helps to remind all concerned, that if they fail to generate a working majority with a united package of general and particular decisions (including as it must, some arbitrary components), then they will be ruled by the wholly or partly arbitrary will of the *one* or of the *few*. Such a monarch also represents the truth that whether one recognizes it or not, no content in principle is entirely beyond the scope of human shaping power. Each "human singularity", e.g. each individual, each community, each association, or each state has this subjectivity, the capacity to will either a fixed or a changing unity for itself over time. Accordingly, a state in order to remain a state must continue to actualize this capacity to will its own unity. Hegel argues as does the model that the distinctive subjectivity of the monarch helps maximally to guarantee the actualization of this self-knowing unity of the collectivity over time.

On a personal level, I have found it philosophically necessary to follow Hegel's own implicit choice to will the maximization of rationality in the world *if* I am not simply to remain at the 'I am I', and *if* I am to avoid either the ignorant or evil sorts of arbitrary willing. This means seeking both to know Reason's specifications and to live accordingly. With this in mind, Hegel's exposition of his system within the *Encyclopaedia* is seen as a report of the attempt of his own "self-conscious reason" to extract all the essential additional contents from the maximally empty context of the 'I am I'. Accordingly, it starts with a close examination of the meaning and implications of the 'am' within the 'I am I', i.e. it starts with "being".[3] At the same time, I have resolved to test this attempt of Hegel's with my own "self-conscious reason", i.e. against the four criteria of philosophical necessity. Here, his constitutional monarchy has been found not to be entirely adequate.

(1) *Rechts*, PP279Z.
(2) Heredity is 'arbitrary' in the sense of being non-rational. The procreative process need not depend on any self-conscious philosophical mediation.
(3) *das Sein*, Enz. I, PP86.

The point served by Hegel's recollection of subjectivity's capacity to will one unity rather than another, even in the maximally empty context in which there are no externally given *grounds* for doing so, is to help secure his view that *if* a people is to achieve a collective "singularity" over time, it will be achieved intentional or not, by *human* willing. Neither gods nor priests nor oracles ultimately offer us any guidance other than that which humans consciously or unconsciously allow. These vehicles are properly seen by Hegel as only various forms of human willing. It follows from this that, *if* an externally "groundless" yet internally grounded unity of the collectivity is to be maximally secured by us, *if* sovereignty is to be secured, *then* we must develop procedures for making binding decisions about any questions which may come into dispute. By definition, a rational constitution does this by authorizing the use of coercion as a last resort while providing all of the possible legal supports for deliberative resolutions of conflicts. Therefore, it maximally assists a people effectively, collectively, and repeatedly to will its own sovereignty, i.e. freely to live and to will rationally. Accordingly, the subjectivity of a monarch is a necessary part of a rational constitution and PP279 is taken to record Hegel's view that "the finality of deciding", when it is guaranteed by the monarch's subjectivity, helps maximally to secure the repeated capacity of a people to will its sovereignty.

If this claim proves to be successfully defended against all known criticisms, then we will have come to agree that such a role for a hereditary head of state is rational, i.e. satisfies the criteria demanded by our search for philosophical necessity. It should again be made clear that neither Hegel nor I are expecting, let alone requiring the monarch personally to be conscious of his or her own "self-relating negativity" and "self-determining generality". The rational constitution does not require a philosopher to stand at its finalising pinnacle. The model constitution can function well with a monarch who only has the quite ordinary subjectivity [1] which all normal humans have potentially by nature and which has been developed in almost all adults by the ordinary formal and informal educational processes of modern societies. This quite ordinary "subjectivity" is still "certain of itself".[2]

Hegel frequently assumes and asserts that the head of a rational state must be hereditary but only explicitly and in piecemeal fashion develops his arguments for this conclusion.[3] His central argument is that the institution of hereditary succession, better than any other arrangement, both

(1) displays, and
(2) secures

the collective, single subjectivity of the rational state. As head, he is *mainly* charged with the task of helping to guarantee the *singularity* discussed above. He or she unites all by performing the finalising function. That the single subjectivity of a state is best guaranteed by the head being *one person* rather than a council (i.e. a corporate or "moral person") [4] is quite clear, but, that this one person should be "hereditary", Hegel admits is difficult for "purely analytical understanding" to see. In PP28An., he says that it can only be grasped from the "speculative" perspective of the philosophy of logic. Again, a monarch best *displays* and *secures* a single subjectivity for a state. These are not unconnected. Hereditary succession best displays the sort of single subjectivity which a head of a model state should exercise in the following way. His constitutional subjectivity should not be more than a formal "I will" which he adds to the formulations of "advice" given to him by the representative assembly and the government of the day. The model says that this should be the case *unless* such majoritarian mediations are absent. In this absence, however, the monarch is required to rule at his own "unconfined discretion" in the context of the 'state prerogative council'. In this case, his personal subjectivity must speak for the divided or ambivalent whole of his subjects. The relatively unmediated or natural subjectivity of the monarch should rule only when majoritarian mediation has failed to achieve its own single subjectivity.

When an hereditary head rules directly as caretaker, this graphically points out to his subjects their own failure to achieve a mediated, collective unity. This lack is most strikingly brought home by the rule of the one person who by his hereditary succession best personifies "inner and outer unmediatedness",[5] "unmediated singularity",[6] and "unmediated naturalness",[7] i.e. by "the organ of naturalness".[8] As hereditary, his or her rule, most transparently suggests that his or her single subjectivity is only like that natural subjectivity granted to all adults by their birth. Thus, when

---

(1) Both Hegel's and the model's constitution "requires ... only a human being", PP28Oz. (2) PP279.
(3) In PP280 and An., PP281 and An. and Z, PP286 and An., and PP320. (4) PP279An.
(5) PP281. (6) PP280An. (7) PP280. (8) PP280.

*his* or *her* personality has "come to the fore",[1] it broadcasts the inescapable fact that in the absence of majoritarian mediation within a state, either unmediated (or less mediated) rule or the disintegration of this state must follow. Rule by a natural or unmediated, single subjectivity is, therefore, a necessary part of the best fail-safe, constitutional arrangement. This is to say, that, while majoritarian, mediated, uniting subjectivity is better because it involves *more* rational living, the unmediated, single subjectivity of the monarch is better than anarchy because it tends most both to preserve and to create the public conditions which foster either the initial or subsequent re-development of majoritarian unity. Hereditary rule is the clearest demonstration and personification of the non-rational threats to democracy. In this way, the caretaking role of the monarch has the best chance of assisting a majoritarian recovery. Hereditary rule will best engender another chance that the requisite changes in the attitudes of the citizenry and its representatives will take place. This role challenges the other two organs constitutionally to build or to reconstruct majority rule in which the hereditary head will again be confined simply to saying "yes"[2] to whatever mediated and majoritarian singularity which may be "advised" by the representative assembly and its government.

The monarch's hereditary character also best *displays* that the state's singularity is purely human. The rational state does not depend on "oracles" or on any other sources "outside the circle of human freedom".[3] Equally, monarchy fosters best the public understanding that the subjectivity given to all normal adults by their *birth* enables all to will their own unity, individual or collective. They can do this well or badly and with or without yet having philosophically experienced their own "self-relating negativity and ... self-determining generality",[4] and thus, with or without yet discovering their own subjectivity as a capacity "groundlessly" to will their own unity, either ignorantly, evilly or rationally. Hegel's phrase, the monarch's "inner unmediatedness", is taken to express this natural subjectivity or "finalising, groundless self" of every person, which is institutionalized in the person of the monarchy. In contrast, the monarch's "outer unmediatedness" or his "groundless existence" refers to the hereditary position of the monarch within the rational constitution. The fact that he at least has natural subjectivity or inner unmediatedness, like an elected head of state, makes it possible for the monarch to give his finalising "I will" to state decisions.

Hegel says that the monarch's "inner and outer unmediatedness" constitutes the two sides of the monarch's "majesty",[4] i.e. the ability to inspire a sense of *awe* and *security* in others. According to his definition, an elected head of state could not have as much majesty because he or she does not have the "outer unmediatedness" or "groundless existence" of monarchy which "originates out of itself".[6] Instead, he or she only displays 'outer mediatedness' or a purely 'constitutional groundedness'. This mediatedness has two flaws. Firstly, it tends to *obscure* rather than to display the last resort character of his or her "I will" as the head of state. Secondly, his or her mediated selection tends more to encourage a constitutionally elected head to compete with or to replace the single, mediated subjectivity which best issues through the working majority's prime minister and is best guaranteed in the first instance, if the 'working majority' breaks down, by the 'governor general' previously elected by a 2/3rds majority. This obscuring of the best structuring arrangement for securing collective singularity, which sees the head's will only to be purely formal unless majoritarian mediation fails, when added to such built-in conflicts within a presidential republic, makes it less possible for an elected head to inspire the same sense of awe and security as does the majesty of the monarch.

The monarch's "inner and outer unmediatedness" means that both the monarch's *inner,* personal subjectivity and his *outer,* hereditary position are "groundless" in the sense that each "originates out of itself". The unity or singularity issuing from a person's subjectivity need not rest on any externally given assumptions or presuppositions. Similarly, monarchy originally arose as an objective institution out of itself, i.e. out of the will and action of an outstanding progenitor.[7] The hereditary succession of his heirs enshrines this truth that monarchy arose and can arise again without needing the prior intellectual, political or constitutional mediations of others. This is what the "outer unmediatedness" and the "groundless existence of the monarchical organ"[8] signifies. The phrase, "inner unmediatedness" also suggests that a monarch might arise and reign in spite of his own lack of intellectual mediation. He might easily rule without philosophical theorizing or even without consciously making deductive calculations from defined presuppositions. His birth, rise and reign might issue purely from one or a combination of the following: instincts,

(1) PP280Z. (2) PP28Oz. (3) PP279An. (4) PP278An. (5) PP281. (6) PP279An. (7) PP322An. (8) PP281.

impulses, pride, or unreflected traditions or customs. Historically and biographically, the intellectually unmediated always comes before and provides the soil in which intellectual mediation can grow.

Constitutional monarchy tends to give a people a greater sense of *security* than does any other set of political arrangements. It fosters best the public awareness that there will always tend to be both,
1) a clear and public statement of what the operative law is and how it applies to the particular circumstances which may be in the minds of those concerned, and
2) a clear public knowledge of the persons who are officially and actually responsible for the formulation and particularization of such laws.

Also, constitutional monarchy has the advantage over republics in that the state's power to decide and to act does not depend to the same extent on the contingent achievement of a working majority. In the absence of this majority and even in the possible absence of a majority to elect a president, the monarch may be able, both legally and effectively, to speak and act for the whole state. In a monarchy, it is more likely that there will always be a nameable person who can be held "responsible" for any decision currently operative, e.g. the leader of the working majority, or one of the monarch's counsellors (e.g. a minister or the prime minister), or the monarch himself. In a republic, no law might have been formulated, no executive action taken, or no responsible official elected because of the failure to achieve the requisite majorities. Thus, Hegel's argument for a constitutional monarch is that he or she best symbolizes the relation between humankind and nature. His or her natural unmediatedness displays and, in the last resort helps to secure, a collective *unity* or *singularity*. This is a condition for the maximization of the quality and quantity of free, rational living.

This chapter has compared democratic monarchy with Hegel's constitutional monarchy as outlined in some of his most difficult paragraphs. It has been discovered that, while the model requires the rejection of two of Hegel's own phrases, the rest of his formulations are either plain enough or ambiguous enough to allow them to be read as elaborations of my own prescriptive ideal.

Summary

'Democratic monarchy' was seen,
1) to be superior to republican arrangements of either the 'parliamentary' or 'congressional' type;
2) to repair the flaw in Plato's political theory left by his unwarranted assumptions about the expected reliability and numbers of philosopher rulers; largely
3) to be present in a 'lenient interpretation' of Kant's republicanism and wider philosophy;
4) to provide the best contingency plan for Marx's classless society; and
5) to formulate the model which would seem to be more firmly rooted in Hegel's wider system than his own constitutional monarchy.

However, in contrast to Hegel's own political philosophy, the model openly affirms rather than denies its own prescriptive import. In spite of Hegel's claim that the essence of his monarchy is its "rationality", democratic monarchy claims to be *more* rational. It claims more clearly and completely to guarantee the deliberative unity which Hegel himself can be leniently read to value most. The broad three *function* and three *organ* structure of the model follows Hegel's lead, but his two phrases which denied *ultimate* sovereignty to the 'working majority' in the elected chamber were rejected.

In order to complete the reconstruction of Hegel's state, the model *added* ten provisions which explicitly *go beyond* his own formulations:
1) A.P.R.
2) the procedure for constitutional change,
3) universal adult suffrage,
4) the procedure for recalling deputies,
5) no legislative veto for the non-elected chamber,
6) the 'figurehead' and 'caretaking' roles,
7) the 'state prerogative council',
8) some 'life peers' in the non-elected chamber,
9) the 'constructive vote of no confidence', and
10) the procedure for impeaching and replacing a monarch.

The *first six* of these were argued in varying degrees to have followed from 'lenient interpretations' of Hegel's brief or equivocal words but in some case required some 'lenient additions' to be made. Provisions *seven, eight,* and *nine* were simply 'lenient additions', while *ten* was logically demanded by the 'improving changes' which were made to the two phrases in which Hegel gave his monarch "unconfined discretion" in the appointment of ministers and "exclusive" control" over foreign affairs.

The *Introduction* reported some of the charges which commentators have made against Hegel's monarchy. They suggested that it was unnecessary, "smuggled in", "obscure and implausible", "irrational" and "nauseating". While it is understandable how some of Hegel's equivocal, and abstruse passages invited such readings, it has been shown that these harsh yet plausible observations can be avoided. In any case, none of these criticisms could be sustained against the monarchy in the model.

The most rational constitution was sought and 'democratic monarchy' was found. This model's claim to be an integral element of a *comprehensive* theory was sketched and it was not found to be faulted by any of the *experiential, logical,* or *comparative* tests examined. No empirical evidence about constitutions, no contradictions in its formulation, and no competing political theories were found to require us to retain any 'specific doubts' about this ideal. In short, no obstacles were discovered which would prevent us from granting to it the status of having 'philosophical necessity'.

# Selective Bibliography

Only the sources cited are listed. The works of Hegel are listed in the alphabetical order of their abbreviated titles. Hegel's German texts, the *Werke*, are from,
> Georg Wilhelm Friedrich Hegel, *Werke in 20 Banden,* Auf der Grundlage der Werke von 1832-1845, neu edierte Ausgabe Redaktion Eva Modenhauer und Karl Markus Michel, Suhrkamp Verlag, Frankfurt am Main 1970

## A) WORKS OF HEGEL CITED

*Eng.:* "About the English Reform Bill" (1831) or "The English Reform Bill", p.295 in *Hegel's Political Writings,* tr. by T.M. Knox with an introductory essay by Z.A. Pelczynski, Oxford 1964 (Über die englische Reform bill, S.83, Werke II: Berliner Schriften 1818-1831).

*Enz.* I: "The Science of Logic" or "The Logic of Hegel", tr. by W. Wallace from the first part of *The Encyclopaedia of the Philosophical Sciences,* Oxford 1873 (Werke 8 : Die Wissenschaft der Logik, Enzyklopadie der philosophischen Wissenschaften im Grundrisse (1830)).

*Enz.* III: "The Philosophy of Spirit" or *Hegel's Philosophy of Mind,* tr. by W. Wallace and A.V. Miller from the third part of the *Encyclopaedia,* Oxford 1971 (Werke 10. Die Philosophie des Geistes).

*Domestic Affairs:* "On the Recent Domestic Affairs of Wurtemberg, especially on the Inadequacy of the Municipal Constitution", p. 234, in *Hegel's Political Writings,* op. cit. (Dass die Magistrate von den Bürgern gewahlt werden mussen [Über die neusten inneren Vehältnisse Württembergs, besonders über die Gebrechen der Magistratsverfassung] (1978), S.268, Werke 1: Fruhe Schriften).

*G. Cons.:* "The German Constitution", P. 143 in *Hegel's Political Writings,* op. cit., (Die Verfassung Duetschlands, S. 461, Werke 1).

*Geschichte:* *The Philosophy of History,* tr. by J.Sibree, Dover, New York 1956. (Vorlesungen über die Philosophie der Geschichte, Werke 12).

*Logik* I, II: *Hegel's Science of Logic,* tr. by A.V. Miller, George Allen and Unwin, London 1969 (Wissenschaft der Logik, Werke 5 und 6).

*Philosophie* I, II, III: *Hegel's Lectures on the History of Philosophy,* tr. by E.S. Haldane and F.H. Simson, Routledge and Kegan Paul, London 1896 (Vorlesungen über die Geschichte der Philosophie, Werke 18, 19 and 20).

*Rechts:* *Hegel's Philosophy of Right,* tr. by T.M. Knox, Oxford 1965 (Grundlinien der Philosophie des Rechts, Werke 7).

*Wurt.:* "Evaluating the Proceedings within the Assembly of the Country's Representative Chamber of the Kingdom of Wurtemberg in The Year 1815-1816", page 246 in *Hegel's Political Writings,* op. cit. ("[Beurteilung der] Verhandlungen in der Versammlungen der Landstande des Königreichs Württemberg im Jahr 1815-1816", S.462 in Werke 4: Nürnberger und Heidelberger Scriften 1808-1817).

## (B) WORKS OF OTHERS CITED

Arblaster, Anthony — "Taking Monarchy Seriously", *New Left Review,* 1989, Issue 74, pp.97-110.

Aristotle — *Metaphysics,* ed. and trans. by John Warrington, Introduction by Sir David Ross, Dent, London 1966.

Avineri, Shlomo — *Hegel's Theory of the Modern State,* Cambridge University Press, 1972.

Brehier, Emile — *The Hellenistic and Roman Age,* (vol. 2 of The History of Philosophy) Chicago U.P., Chicago 1965.

Brudner, Alan — "Constitutional Monarch as the Divine Regime: Hegel's theory of the Just State", *History of Political Thought,* Vol. II No. 1, Spring, January 1981.

Cristi, F.R. "The Hegelsche Mitte and Hegel's Monarchy", *Political Theory,* 1983, 11:4, pp.601-622;
Engels, F. *Anti-During* (1878), Lawrence and Wishart, London 1969.
Finer, S.E., ed. *Five Constitutions,* The Harvester Press, Brighton 1979, pp.219&220.
Findlay, J.N. *Hegel: A Re-examination,* George Allen & Unwin, London 1959.
Goldman, Alvin *A Theory of Human Action,* Princeton University Press, 1980.
Habermas, Jürgen *Theory and Practice,* Heinemann, London 1974.
Hobbes, T. *Leviathan,* ed. by M. Oakeshott, Basil Blackwell, Oxford n.d.
Ilting, Karl-Heinz "Hegel's Concept of the State and Marx's Early Critique", trans. by H. Tudor and J.M. Tudor, *The state and Civil Society: Studies in Hegel's Political Philosophy,* Z.A.Pelczynski, ed., Cambridge University Press, Cambridge 1984.
Kant, I. *Critique of Practical Reason,* tr. by Lewis White Beck, Boobs-Merrill, Indianapolis 1956.
" " *Critique of Pure Reason,* tr. by Norman Kemp Smith, St. Martin's Press, New York 1965.
" " *Grounding for the Metaphysics of Morals,* tr. by J.W. Ellington, Hackett, Indianapolis 1981.
" " *The Metaphysical Elements of Justice,* tr. by John Ladd, Bobbs-Merrill, Indianapolis 1965. (see "Nisbet").
Kaufmann, Walter (ed.) *Hegel's Political Philosophy,* Atherton, New York 1970.
Kiernan, Victor, "Meditation on a Theme by Tom Nairn", *New Left Review,* 1989, Issue 174, pp.111-120.
Kosok, Michael "The Formalization of Hegel's Dialectical Logic", in MacIntyre, Alasdair (ed.) *Hegel: A Collection of Critical Essays,* Anchor Books, 1972.
Ladd, John (tr.) *The Metaphysical Elements of Justice,* by I. Kant, Boobs-Merrill, Indianapolis 1965.
Lee, Taik-Ho *In Rehabilitation of Hegelianism,* Ph.D. thesis, The University of North Carolina at Chapel Hill, 1987.
Lenin, V.I. *State and Revolution,* Foreign Languages Publishing House, Moscow, n.d.
MacIntyre, Alasdair, ed. *Hegel: A Collection of Critical Essays,* Anchor Book, 1972.
Maker, William, ed. *Hegel on Economics and Freedom,* Mercer University Press, Macon, Georgia 1987;
Marcuse, H. *Reason and Revolution: Hegel and the Rise of Social Theory,* Routledge and Kegan Paul, London 1941.
Marx, Karl *Capital,* Vol. I,. Penguin, Harmondsworth 1976.
" " *Critique of Hegel's 'Philosophy of Right',* ed. J.O'Malley = tr. with Annette Jolin, Cambridge University Press, 1970.
" " *Early Writings,* Penguin, Harmondsworth 1975.
" " *The German Ideology,* Collected Works, Vol. 5, Lawrence & Wishart, London 1976.
" " *Grundrisse,* Penguin, Harmondsworth 1973.
" " *Surveys from Exile,* Penguin, Harmondsworth 1973.
" " *The First International & After,* Penguin, Harmondsworth 1974.
" " *The Revolutions of 1848,* Penguin, Harmondsworth 1973.
Marx, Karl & Engels, F. *Selected Works,* Vol. II, Lawrence & Wishart, London 1962.
Mill, J. S. *Utilitarianism, Liberty, Representative Government,* Dent, London, 1962.
Montesquieu *The Spirit of the Laws,* Hafner, New York, 1949.
Nairn, Tom *The Enchanted Glass: Britain and its Monarchy,* Radius, London 1988.
Nisbet, H. B. (tr.) *Kant's Political Writings,* ed. Hans Reiss, Cambridge University Press, 1971.
Pelczynski, Z.A. (ed.) *Hegel's Political Philosophy: Problems and Perspectives,* Cambridge University Press, 1971.
Plant, Raymond *Hegel,* Allen & Unwin, London 1973. "Economic & Social Integration in Hegel's Political Philosophy", *Social & Political Thought: The Philosophy of Objective Spirit,* D. P. Verene (ed.), Humanities Press, 1980.
Plato *The Republic,* by Desmond Lee (tr.) Penguin, Harmondsworth 1974; also translated by Allan Bloom, Basic Books Inc., New York 1968; by F. M. Cornford Oxford University Press, 1960; and by G. M. A. Grube, Hackett, Indianapolis 1974.
Popper, K. *Conjectures and Refutations,* Routledge and Kegan Paul, London 1963.

| | |
|---|---|
| Reiss | see "Nisbet" |
| Reyburn, H. A. | *The Ethical Theory of Hegel,* Oxford University Press, 1921. |
| Rousseau, J. J. | *The Social Contract and Discourses,* Dent, 1966. |
| Saint Augustine | *The City of God,* tr. by John Healey and ed. by R.V.G. Tasker, Dent, London 1945. |
| Smith, Steven B. | "What is 'Right' in Hegel's Philosophy of Right", *American Political Science Review,* 1989, Vol.83, No.1; |
| Stace, W. T. | *The Philosophy of Hegel,* Dover, New York 1955. |
| Taylor, Charles | *Hegel,* Cambridge University Press, 1975. |
| Taylor, Paul W. | *Problems of Moral Philosophy,* Wandsworth, 1978. |
| Weber, Marx | *The Methodology of the Social Sciences,* trans. and ed. by Edward A. Shils and Henry A. Finch, The Free Press, New York 1949. |
| Williams, Howard and Levin, Michael, | "Inherited Power and Popular Representation: a Tension in Hegel's Political Theory" *Political Studies,* 1987, Vol.35, pp.105-115. |
| Wilson, Edgar | *The Myth of British Monarchy,* Journeyman Press and Republic, London 1989. |
| Winfield, Richard Dien | *Reason and Justice,* State University of New York Press, Albany 1988. |

**Appendix:**
**Literal Translations**

This list of literal translations for each text is arranged in page or paragraph number order. The texts are arranged in page and in alphabetical order according to the abbreviations used for each work listed in the *Bibliography*. In these translations, I have written my own interpretive additions between single 'inverted commas', while the explanatory additions which quite easily follow directly from Hegel's own wider context are written between [square brackets].

*Eng.*, S.86:

Now when also the aristocratic element in England when compared with the democratic element is the most significant force (macht),...[and when] it finds its security and stability in the submerging of the people it rules in their collective sensuality and in their ethical depravity, ... it is to be recognized as a **good sign of the reawakening of the moral sense** within the English people, that there is a feeling of the need for **reform** which involves the repugnance with regard to that depravity (Verderbheit). One (Mann) comes at the same time to recognize that the **correct way should** have become established that **the seeking of the improvement** is no more merely by the moral means of notions (Vorstellungen), [by] admonishions, or [by] a uniting of isolated individuals in order not to be beholden to and in order to work against the system of corruption, but is by the alteration (Veränderung) of institutions [.] The usual prejudice of laziness always to cling to the old faith in the goodness of an institution even when it hangs upon a wholly depraved circumstance, has in this manner finally given way. A thoroughgoing reform has thus become all the more demanded ...

*Eng.* S.89:

In England the features (die Momente) have been **lacking** (mangelten) hitherto which have an important share in those [above mentioned] so **glorious and fortunate advances**. Under these features stands highest the scientific codification (Bearbeitung) of the law (Rechts) ...

*Enz.* **I, PP6:**

... it is equally important to understand that the content (Inhalt) of philosophy is none other than the domain of the living spirit (Geist) which originally has been brought forth and which continues to bring itself forth to the world, i.e. its content is **actuality** (Wirklichkeit). The initial consciousness of this content we call **experience** (Erfahrung). Even a sensuous study (sinninge Betrachtung) of the world distinguishes, from within the wide realm of outer and inner definite existence (Dasein), between what is only appearance (Ersheinung), transitory and insignificant, and what inherently (in sich) and genuinely deserves the name, **actuality**. In this respect (Indem), philosophy is distinguished from the other modes of coming to be conscious (anderem Bewusstwerden) only in form, [i.e. they have] one and the same contents (Gehalt). Therefore (so), [a] philosophy's (ihr) compatibility (Übereinstimmung) with actuality and experience is necessary (notwendig). Indeed, this compatibility can become seen to be at least one external test (äusseren Prüfstein) of the truth of a philosophy. Similarly (so wie), it is seen to be the highest and ultimate aim (hochsten Endzweck) of science to bring forth to us (hervorzubringen) the reconciling of the self-conscious reason (selbstbewussten Vernunft) with the Reason which has **being** (seienden Vernunft), with the actuality, through the knowledge (Erkenntnis) of this compatibility.

*Enz.* **I, PP6An.:**

In the Preface to my *Philosophy of Right* can be found the propositions: 'Some of' what is rational, that is actual; and 'all of' what is actual, that is rational. These simple propositions have conspicuously occasioned much and suffered hostility, and indeed, this same (selbst) from such one is not allowed to speak of being without the possession of philosophy and especially (wohl) without religion. It is unnecessary (unnötig) to cite religion in this connection, there its doctrines about the divine world government too specifically express these propositions. However, what is the concern with regard to [the] philosophical meaning [of these expressions] is that [we] presuppose so much of the cultural foundation (Bildung), that one (man) knows not only that God is actual, that He is the most actual, that He alone is true actuality, but also, in the sight of the formal [questions], that, broadly speaking (überhaupt) the definite existence (Dasein) is in part appearance and only in part actuality.

In common life we perhaps call every incident an actuality, even a mistake (Irrtum), an evil and whatever belongs to this side [of things]. Thus (sowie), each existence (Existenz), however stunted (noch so verkummerte) and transitory, gets called an actuality in a casual way. Nevertheless, a fortuitous existence (Existenz) has not come to merit the emphatic name of an **actual** entity (eines Wirklichen) even within customary sensibility (gewöhnlichen Gefuhl). The fortuitous [entity] is an existence (Existenz) which has no greater value (Wert) than an 'imaginable' possibility, 'i.e. its existence is a matter of indifference to Reason'. However, when I spoke of actuality, so would it be by itself [appropriate] to think upon it, in which sense I used this expression, [i.e.] that [sense (da)] in which actuality in a full-length **logic** is treated, not only [as distinct] from contingent [definite being] which also has existence, but [which also offers] a closer [treatment] of definite being (Dasein), [i.e.] existence and other specifications also being precisely distinguished.

The actuality of the rational [definite being] itself indeed stands opposed to the notion (Vorstellung), equally either that the 'specific' Ideas '(i.e. specific elements of Reason)' or ideals are nothing more than chimeras and philosophy is a system of such fancies, or conversely, that the 'specific' Ideas and ideals are something much too superior (Vortreffliches) to have actuality, or equally something too important as to procure itself. However, the separation of actuality from the Idea is particularly loved by the 'abstractive' understanding, that which holds for something genuine both the illusions of its abstractions and [with regard to (auf)] the **ought**, the [ought] which the 'abstractive' understanding (er) happily and proudly prescribes, especially within the political fields, as if the world has waited for such understanding (auf ihn), in order to hear (um zu erfahren) what it ought to be but is not [.] Were the world (sie) as it ought to be, what would become of (wo bliebe) the precociousness of its ought? When 'abstractive' [understanding] turns the ought (Sollen) against the trivial, external (äusserliche) and transitory objects (Gegenstände), arrangements (Einrichtungen), circumstances (Zustände), etc., which also, perhaps, have a great relative importance for a certain time or for a particular (besondere) circle, then understanding (er) may indeed rightly find in such cases, much which does not accord with generally correct specifications (Bestimmungen). Who is not acute enough to see much of his 'social and political' environment (Umbegung) which, in fact, is not as it ought to be? But this acuteness has mistakenly (unrecht) imagined that such objects (Gegenstände) and that which they ought to be (deren Sollen) are themselves to be found within the interests of a philosophical science. Philosophy (Diese) has only to do with the Idea and therefore with an actuality. The Idea (welche) is not so impotent that it only ought to be but is not actual. [Thus philosophy is concerned with] an actuality, in relation to which, those objects (Gegenstände), arrangements, circumstances, etc., are only the superficial exterior.

*Enz.* I, PP7:

... *philosophy* ... is concerned with (beschäftigt) the knowledge (Erkenntnis) of the permanent measure and the **general** within the sea of empirical details (Einzelheiten) and of the **necessary** [aspect, i.e.], the **laws** (Gesetze), within the seeming disordered, endless mass of contingent [details] and with that at the same time, philosophy's (seinen) content has been taken from our own considering and observing (eigenen Anschauen und Wahrnehmen) of the external and inner [world] (des Ausseren und Inneren), [i.e.] out of the presented (präsenten) nature as out of the presented spirit and presented breast of humankind.

*Enz.* I, PP7An.:

The principle of experience (Erfahrung) contains the infinitely important condition (Bestimmung), that in order for the accepting and for the holding to be true of a content, humankind **must** itself **be** in contact with it (dass für Annehmen und Fürwahrhalten eines Inhalts der Mensch selbst dabei sein müsse), more specifically we (er) [must] find such a content united in agreement (in Einigkeit) with the certainty of our own selves ... We call those sciences which have been named philosophy, empirical sciences, because of the starting point which they take. However, the essential [goals] which they ring for and at which they aim (Aber das Wesentliche, das sei bezwecken und herforschaffen), are laws (Gesetze), general propositions, a theory; [i.e.]

the thoughts of what is present-to-hand (die Gedenken des Vorhandenen).

*Enz.* I, PP13:

The most recent (Die der Zeit nach letzte) philosophy [provided it is philosophy] is the result of all previous philosophies and must, therefore, contain the principles of all [these philosophies]. The most recent philosophy (sie), provided it is philosophy, consequently, is the most developed (entfalteste), the most rich, and the most concrete.

*Enz.* I, PP209Z:

Reason is as cunning as it is strong (mächtig). In the main, cunning resides in the mediating activity in which the objects (Objekte), '(e.g. individual men and women)' influence (einwirken) and wear each other down (sich aneinander abarbeiten). The objects '(e.g. people)' are left to follow their own natures. [Reason, which is the "power of these processes" (PP 209)] does not directly interfere with this process (ohne sich unmittelbar ... einzumischen). Nevertheless, only Reason's aim (nur ihren Zweck) is brought forth (zur Ausführung bringt). One can in this sense say, that divine Providence, as absolute cunning, retains itself behind (gegenüber) the world and its process. God [or Reason] has left human beings (menschen) with their particular passions and interests to continue (lässt ... gewähren) [to shape events] and what thereby comes to pass (was dadurch zustande kommt), is the fulfilment of His intentions. [What comes to pass] is other than that which was at first (zunächst zu tun war) [intended by the people involved].

*Enz.* I, PP234Z, S.387

... dass der Endzweck der Welt ebenso vollbracht ist als er sich ewig vollbringt ...

*Enz.* III, PP536:

The state is a) at first (zunächst) its inner formation (Gestaltung) as the state's self-relating development (als sich auf sich beziehende Entwicklung), i.e. the *internal state law or the constitution [.]* The state (er) is b) a particular individual and so is within the relation to other particular individuals [i.e. states.] 'This requires Reason-as-the-state to include' **interstate law.** c) However, these particular 'national' spirits are only 'inessential' moments within the developing of the general Idea-as-the 'objective'-spirit within spirit's (seiner) actuality[. This development is] **world history.**

*Enz.* III, PP544:

Broadly speaking, the representative assembly is concerned to take part in all that belongs to civil society and ... in the particularizing function (an der Regierungsgewalt), and especially in the giving of laws, i.e. (nämlich) in the **generalness** (Allgemeinen) of interests which do not concern the conduct and business (das Auftreten und Handeln) of the state as an individual (i.e. war and peace) and therefore not exclusively of the character (Natur) of belonging to the monarchical **organ.**

*Enz.* III, PP552:

The spirit of the nation (Volksgeist) includes natural 'or external' necessity (Naturnotwendigkeit) and [thus] stands within external definite existence (in aüsserlichen Dasein). The inherently (in sich) infinite ethical substance [of a nation] considered by itself (für sich) is a particular (Besondere) and limited [substance]. Infected with contingency, this substance's (ihre) subjective side, [which is partially] unconscious ethical practice (bewusstloss Sitte), and [partially] a consciousness of its content (Inhalt) as a temporarily present entity (eines zeitlich Vorhandenen), [finds itself in] a juxtaposed relation (im Vehältnisse gegen) to an external nature and [to the] world. However, [because the essentiality of the spirit is to rise toward a knowing of itself], it is the thinking spirit (denkende Geist) within ethical life (Sittlichkeit) which immanently overcomes (in sich aufhebt) [these limits] by rising toward a knowing (sich zum Wissen) of its essentiality within its essentiality.¹ [Spirit can do this in spite of] its finitude as the spirit of a nation. [This finitude is marked by the spirit (er) being the] spirit of a [particular nation and] state which has temporary interest within [its particular] system of statutes and ethical practices. [Thus finitude marks this spirit's knowing of its essentiality. This knowing still has [the] restrictedness of the spirit of a nation (Volksgeist). In contrast, the thinking spirit (denkende Geist) of world history, at the same time 'philosophically' stripes off every restrictedness of the particular spirits of nations (der besonderen Volksgeister) and the spirit's own worldliness (seine eigene Weltlichkeit), 'i.e. philosophy's empirical foundation and focus', to grasp its own concrete generality and 'thus'

(1) The phrase, "knowing of its essentiality within its essentiality", I take to be an alternative way of noting that "the concept of Reason" is within "Reason", i.e. it is at 12 o'clock on the circle in FIGURE 1.

raises itself toward [a] knowing of 'Reason-as-'the-absolute-spirit (Geist). [This knowing sees the absolute spirit (Geist)] as the eternal actual truth in which knowing Reason is free for itself (frei für sich), 'i.e. self-consciously free'. [This same knowing sees] nature and [human] history, [i.e. the realms which include natural or external] necessity, as subordinate (dienend) to the absolute spirit's (seiner) revelation 'within the conception of Reason' and to be vessels of [this spirit's] splendour (Ehre).

*Geschichte*, S.49:
It is not the universal Idea 'or Reason' which is exposed to danger in the opposition and struggle [in history]. The Idea (sie) holds itself in the background, untouched and undamaged. This may be called the **cunning of Reason**. Reason (sie) lets [human] passions work for it. [They are what through the Idea (sie) has been set into existence (Existenz) [and it is they] which suffer loss and injury. Because [this struggle takes place (ist) in the world of our empirical experience (die Erscheinung)], one part is transitory (nichtig) and one part is affirmative, 'i.e. has greater durability because it positively contributes to the rational progress of Reason'. The particular (Partikuläre) [people and passions involved] are for the most part (meistens) negligible when compared with the general [interests which are also present]. Individuals (Individuen) are 'frequently' sacrificed and abandoned.

*Geschichte*, S.49:
While we may allow that [most] individualities (Individualitäten) and their aims and their satisfaction are sacrificed because their happiness in the main, 'unavoidably' belongs to the realm of chance; [a view which accepts that] individuals (Individuen) in the main (überhaupt) are to be seen as abandoned [by Reason] and to be considered under the category of means (Mittel) [or tools of Reason]; yet there is one side 'or one possible implication' of this viewpoint that we [must] oppose (Anstand nehmen). [That is to say, that] this viewpoint [must not] be taken (in diesem Gesichts punkte zu fassen) to separate [individuals in every respect] from the Highest (gegen das Höchste) 'or from Reason'. Immanent within individuals (in ihnen), there is an eternal [or] divine quality which is in no way subordinate [to Reason] (ein schlechthin nicht Untergeordnetes). This [quality] is found for example, in people's *moral, ethical and religious lives* (moralität, Sittlichkeit, Religiosität) ...(50) When we speak of a means (Mittel) [to an aim] we at first (zunächst) imagine stellen ... vor) that it stands outside the aim (Zweck), [or] has no share in that aim. In fact, even natural things speaking broadly must have a characteristic (Beschaffenheit) within them which accords (entsprechen) with the [rational] aim (Zweck), something which is common between them and it. Humans behave less [than other creatures] according to that wholly external meaning (jenem ganz äusserlichen Sinne) [of means] ... Humans are not satisfied with this (diesem) [merely external relation] even though it provides them with the opportunity to satisfy personal aims which [may] be different from the aim of Reason (von ihm). Humans have a share in that aim of Reason (Vernunftzweck) and for that every reason (eben dadurch) they are aims in themselves (Selbstzwecke). Humans are not [purely] formal [aims in themselves] as are [other] living things (das Lebendige), broadly speaking ... whose properties (Gehalte) are indeed correctly (mit Recht) subordinated to human life and used as means (mittel). In contrast, humans are aims in themselves (Selbstzweck) [in the sense that they form] the content of the [rational] aim (Zweck). In this context (In dies Bestimmung) [we must say that the contents of our moral, ethical, and religious living (Moralität, Sittlichkeit, Religiosität) require us to remove humans from the category of sheer [bloss)] means (Mittel). It is only because divinity is in humans (Mensch) that they can be an aim in themselves (Zweck in ihm selbst). [This property] from the outset is 'self-conscious' reason and in so far as it is active and self-determining, it is called Freedom (Freiheit) ... 'This property partially' raises humans above the [realm of] external necessity and chance (äussere Notwendigkeit und Zufälligkeit). However, it must 'also' be said that to the extent that individuals (Individuen) appropriately (anheimgegeben sind) can claim freedom, [to that same extent] they are responsible (Schuld) for ethical and religious corruption and for the weakening of ethical practices and of religion (Sittlichkeit und Religion). This is the mark of the absolute and high specific characteristic of human kind (das Siegel der absoluten hohen Bestimmung des Menschen). A human being [can] know what is good and what is evil (er wisse, was gut und was böse ist), [51] and this specific characteristic (sie) is 'logically' the very willing of either good or evil. In one word, humans can have the responsibility for ... all ... the good and evil [in the world]. Only animals are genuinely without responsibility ...

What makes people, 'e.g. the utopian idealists', morally unsatisfied is that they find the aims which they hold to be right and good (especially, nowadays, ideals of political arrangements (Ideale von Staatseinrichtungen), do not accord with the present [state of affairs]. They set their **ought** (Sollen) over against the law of the events (das Recht der Sache) within present definite existence (Dasein) ... [52] In order to assess such a feeling and such views we would have [to take note of] their displayed demands and of their highly assertive opinions within our investigation. At no time previous to our own, have more general propositions and thoughts with greater pretension been laid down. If history has indeed seemed to present itself as a struggle of passions, in our time, while passions are not absent, the struggle between thoughts with authoritative [pretensions] have been predominant. Some of these high authorities are essentially titles under which passions and subjective interests contend. These [propositions] which pretend to be derivations (Bestimmungen) of reason pass for justified demands (Rechtsforderungen), even as absolute aims, equal to [the demands of] religion, ethical life, morality.

Nothing is more common now ... than the complaint that **ideals** (Ideale), which phantasy (Phantasie) has produced, are not realized - that these glorious dreams are destroyed by cold actuality. These ideals which have been stepped to the ground in the journey of life upon the rocks of hard actuality, could initially belong only to the subjective [imagination] of a most lofty and most clever idiosyncratic individual (Individualität des Einzelnen). These qualities, however, are not pertinent (Die gehören eigentlich nicht hierher), because what the individual (Individuum) spins out for himself in his isolation (Einzelheit) cannot be 'expected to be' the law (Gesetz) for general actuality. Equally, the world's law (Weltgesetz) is not for isolated individuals alone (einzelnen Individuen allein).

Thus the dreams of individuals can fall too short, (die dabei sehr zu kurz kommen können), [i.e.] an ideal (Ideal) of reason, of the good, [or] of the truth as commonly understood (Man versteht) [falls too short]. Poets like Schiller have thus written very touchingly and with great sensitivity, in feeling and deep sorrow, that it is not possible to find the actualization of such ideals. In contrast, we say that general Reason is accomplishing itself ... [53] In the above ways (So ware denn), many faults are found within the isolated details (Einzelheiten) of 'the empirical world of' appearance (Erscheinung). [To offer] these subjective criticisms, which only have the singular case and its deficiency before its gaze (nur das Einzelne und seinen Mangel vorsich hat), without knowing (erkennen) the general Reason within [these cases], is easy ...

*Geschichte*, S.53 (page 76):

It is easier to see the deficiencies within individuals (Individuen), within states, and within the progress of the world (Weltleitung) than it is to discover (einzusehen) their genuine value (wahrhaften Gehalt). [While engaged] in this negative fault finding, with a noticeable countenance, one (man) stands over events without grasping that these events themselves are shot through and through (in sei eingedrungen zu sein), with a [predominantly] positive [aspect] (ihr Positives) ...

Now, in contrast to those simple (blosse) ideals, the insight to which philosophy should lead (führen soll), is that the actual world (wirkliche Welt) is as it should be, i.e. that the genuine Good, the universal and divine Reason also is the power to bring itself to completion (auch die Macht ist, sich selbst zu vollbringen). The most concrete image notion (Vorstellung), 'i.e. not the fully rational theory which is the conception' of this Good or of this Reason is God. God governs the world. The content of His governing, [i.e.] His plan, is world history. Philosophy wishes to grasp this plan because only that which is carried out according to this plan is actuality (Wirklichkeit). What is not in accordance with this plan (was ihm nicht gemäss) is only foul existence (faule Existenz). [Those who have those simple ideals seem to view] the world as if it were [only] an appearance of mad or foolish happenings. This appearance fades before the pure light of 'Reason or before' this divine Idea (and the Idea is no mere ideal (die kein blosses Idea ist)). Philosophy wishes to know (erkennen) the content [of these happenings, i.e. to know] the actuality of the divine Idea. [Thus,] philosophy wishes to justify the actuality which is despised [by the above mentioned utopians]. In this way, 'self-conscious' reason 'or philosophy' is the comprehension (das Vornehmen) of the divine work ...

...[54] Broadly speaking, this can be held firmly, that, there is also a higher claim than what is authorized in the world as honourable and glorious. The claim (Recht) of the world Spirit (Weltgeist), '(i.e. of Reason), which can be known philosophically', takes precedence over (geht über) all particular (besonderen) [or transitory (verganglichen)] authorities ...

This may be enough about the means (Mittel) which the world Spirit (Weltgeist) 'or Reason' uses in realizing its 'own' conception (seines Begriffes). Put simply and abstractly, [this realization results from] the activity of subjects (Subjekt) in which Reason is present as their immanent and substantial essence. At first, Reason (ihr) is still obscure (zunächst noch dunkler), [though it is] their hidden foundation (Grund). [55] .... When we take individuals (Individuen) ... with their specific religious and ethical contents (mit bestimmteren Inhalt ihrer Religion und Sittlichkeit), characteristics (Bestimmungen) which share in Reason and by which they also have their absolute justification (Berechtigung) ... the relation of [human kind as being] sheer means (blossen Mittels) to the [rational] aim (Zweck) falls away ...

*Logik* II, S.75:
The common experience (Erfahrung) 'of physical motion' itself enunciates that at least there exists 'in the empirical world' a multitude of contrary things, contrary arrangements, etc. [This experience demonstrates that this contrariety] is not outside such motion [or occurring purely] within the reflexions of the observer ... [This contrariety] is the negative in its essential specification, [i.e. it is] the principle of all self-movement which in [sensuous motion] has established itself no further than to display itself 'empirically'. [This is to say, that] the external, sensuous motion is its unmediated, definite existence. [Definite existence] moves itself in this way only (etwas nur), not in the sense (nicht indem) that it is here in this instant (Jetzt) and in another instant there, but in the sense that it is at one and the same instant here and not here, or in the sense, that in this here it is and is not at the same time ... Movement is itself the definite existence of contrariety.

Similarly, is not the distinctively inner self-movement of the impulse ... [e.g. the impulse to eat], nothing other than something which contains within itself a deficiency? [This is to say, that any positive impulse (Etwas) is at one and the same time (in einer und derselben Rucksicht)] the negative of itself. An impulse depends on something which is not this impulse, 'e.g. hunger would be impossible without food'. 'The abstract identity of A = A by itself has as yet no life', [but a definitely existing something which has negativity immanent within itself must go out of itself 'into the world which alters it, (e.g. hunger drives an animal to move, to shape, and to be shaped by the other beings in the world)' [Therefore, something is living only in so far as it can embrace negativity within itself, i.e. in so far as it has the strength to sieze and to sustain contrariety within itself ... Without this strength, it perishes rather than lives because of its contrariety.] Speculative thinking 'or philosophy' resides solely by thinking this contrariety and holding it fast within thought ...

*Logik* II, S.273:
[Each of these three] moments is as much the whole 'specific' conception 'of which it is a moment' as a specific conception 'itself' and as one specification of the conception 'of Reason'.

*Logik* II, S.295:
The specifications 'of generality, particularity and singularity' are specific conceptions [which] are themselves essentially the totality of all specification.

*Logik* II, S.298:
Because it is only [a] general [conception, a] **particular** [conception] is on the same basis (Das Besondere ist aus demselben Grunde) also a **singular** [conception.] And conversely, because [a] singular [conception] is [a specific [and] general [conception] it is as much a particular [conception].

*Philosophie* I, S.13-14:
The courage (mut) [to search for] the truth, [i.e.] the belief (Glaube) in the power (Macht) of the [human] spirit (Geist), is the first condition for [the pursuit of] philosophy. Humankind (Mensch), because it is spirit (Geist), can and should respect itself (darf und soll sich selbst) as worthy of the highest. [We humans] cannot think too highly (nicht gross genug) of the greatness and power of our spirit (Geist). With this conviction (Glauben), nothing will be so coy or difficult that it will not reveal (eröffnete) itself to us. The essence of the universe which at first is hidden and locked away has no strength to resist the courage of 'our attempting' to know [it] (dem Mute des Erkennens). This essence must (es muss) lay out its wealth and depth before the eyes of the searcher (ihm) for his enjoyment.

*Philosophie* I, S.46:
This movement is concrete as one sequence of developments (Entwicklungen) which must not be represented as a straight line [extending] into the abstract infinity (Unendliche hinaus) but as

a circle, as a [line] turning back into itself. This circle has at [its] periphery a great crowd of circles; the whole is one great, within itself bending back series of elucidations (Entwicklungen).

*Philosophie* I, S.55:
... the length of time which the world Spirit (Geist) 'or Reason' requires to achieve (zu erarbeiten) philosophy ... can ... surely [strike our] ... first reflection ... [as something as astonishing (etwas Auffallendes) as] the immensity of the space of which astronomy has come to speak ... [We must recognize, however (so ist zu bedenken)], that the world Spirit (Weltgeist) is not in a hurry ... It has time enough ... just because it is itself outside of time, 'i.e. not confined to anyone time span' because it is eternal. Exhausted, ephemeral beings (Die übernachtigen Ephemeren) ... do not have enough time. Who does not die before he has finished with [many (viel) of] his aims. [However,] it is not time alone which is used for the acquisition of a conception (Begriff), it costs much else. Accordingly, it does not matter, that 'Reason or' the world Spirit (er) has spent many races and generations in its labour to come to be conscious (an diese Arbeiten seines Bewusstwerdens wendet), [i.e.] that the world Spirit (er) has made a huge display (Aufwand) of rising up and passing away. The world Spirit (er) is rich enough for such a display. It has produced (triebt) its work (Werk) on a large scale (im Grossen). It has nations and individuals enough to exempt [some from having to contribute to this achievement] (er hat Nationen und Individuen genug zu dispensieren).[1] It is a trivial proposition, that nature comes by the shortest path to its goal. This is correct, but the path of the 'human' spirit (Geist) 'in history' is [one of] mediation, [and therefore appears to be] indirect (Umweg). Considerations [relating to] finite living such as time, inconvenience (muhe) and expense, do not belong here.

*Philosophie* I, S.96:
The essence of my spirit (Geist) is my essential being (wesentliches Sein), my very substance (mine Substanz selbst) without which I would not be actual (mine Substanz (sonst bin ich wesenlos)). This essence is, so to speak, the combustible material which can become kindled and illuminated by the universal Essence as such, [which is the object of philosophical study (als gegenständlichem)]. Only in so far as this phosphorus is in humankind (im Menschen) is the comprehending (das Erfassen), the kindling and the illuminating possible. Only thus is the feeling (Gefuhl), intuiting (Ahnung), and knowing (Wissen) of God in humankind [at all]. Also, without this essence (dies), the divine Spirit could not be the in-and-for-itself universal 'Reason'.

*Philosophie* I, S.74:
This is the position of philosophy under the 'historical, spiritual or social' formations (Gestaltungen [of its time]. One implication of this relation (davon) is that philosophy is wholly (ganz) identical with its time. Philosophy does not stand above its time. Philosophy (sie) is the knowing (Wissen) of the substantial 'or actual aspect' of its time. Even less does an individual (Individuum), as a son of his time, stand above his time. The substantial 'or actual aspect' of his time is his own essence. A son (er) is only a manifestation [of the time] in individual form (seiner Form). No one can genuinely stand beyond (Über ... hinaus) his time any more (sowenig) than out of his skin. Yet, on the other hand, philosophy does stand above its time in (nach) form. In this respect, philosophy, as thinking about the time (indem sie als das Denken dessen). [i.e. thinking about] what the substantial 'or actual' spirit (Geist) of the time is, makes itself an object (Gegenstand). In so far as philosophy (sie) is within the 'cultural' spirit (Geist) of its time, that spirit (er) 'as human life' is philosophy's (ihr) specific worldly content (bestimmter weltlicher Inhalt). At the same time, philosophy, as knowing (Wissen), is also above and beyond [the social formations which are manifestations of the human life of the time, i.e. in this respect] Spirit (sich)-'as-philosophical-consciousness' stands opposite itself (stellt ihn sich gegenüber) [i.e.opposite the human actualities of which it is a party]. However, this is only formal because philosophy (sie) has no genuine content other [than that provided by its time]. This knowing (Wissen) is itself, indeed, the actuality of the spirit (Geist) [of the time], the self-knowing of 'Reason-as-'the-spirit (Geist).

Therefore the formal distinction is also a real and actual distinction (so ist der formell Untershied auch ein realer, wirklicher Untershied). This knowing (Wissen) is what a new form of development [or a new formation] has brought forth. New forms 'or new social and political formations' are only an indication [for the] knowing [process] (nur Weisen des Wissens). Through

(1) Reading *depensieren* (sic) as *dispensieren*.

the knowing [process], Spirit 'as human philosophical consciousness' has established (setzt) a distinction between the knowing [process] and what is. The knowing process again contains [at least] one new distinction and so a new philosophy comes forward (kommt ... vor). Also, philosophy is yet a more advanced character [of the time] (ein weitere Charakter des Geistes). Philosophy sie is the inner birth place (Geburtstätte) of the Spirit (Geist)-'as-human-history', of the Spirit (der) 'as social, political and cultural structures which' will come later to actual formation (der spater zu wirklicher Gestaltung). That [process of becoming] concrete will be expanded for us [below] (Das Konkret heirvon werden wir weiter haben). Accordingly, we will see, that what Greek philosophy had become, entered into the actuality of the Christian world.

*Philosophie* II, S.19:

However, [subjective] theorizing (das Theoretische) does not meet (reicht ... nicht hin) [the requirements] of a constitution (Verfassung). It is not [isolated] individuals (Individuen) which make a constitution. It is [something] divine and human (ein Gottliches, Geistiges) which makes itself through history. This something (es) is so strong that the thought of one individual (Individuum) when compared with (gegen) this power of 'Reason-as-'the-world-spirit (diese Macht des Weltgeistes) is not significant. When these thoughts have some significance, [i.e.] can become realized, they are 'themselves' none other than the product of this power of the universal Spirit (Geist).

*Philosophie* II, S.112-113:

It can, therefore, certainly not be said that a true constitution (eine wahrhafte Konstitution) suites any and every people (Volk) ... This is because each nation falls within the historical process (Denn das Volk fallt in die Geschichte). Just as individual people (einzelne Mensch) are raised by their education within [their] states from having a perspective of singularity (Einzelheit) [their] states from having a perspective of singularity (Einzelheit) to [one of] generality (Allgemeinheit), so each people is 'or tends to be' educated [over time]. Each nation as a child, i.e. in its barbarian stage (Zustand), 'tends to' move over to a 'more' rational situation (einen vernünftigen Zustand). Peoples do not remain where they are but alter (Veränderungen) over time. The same is true of a people's constitution, and it is in this context that we can ask the question of what is the true [constitution] towards which each people (das Volk) must (muss) move. This true constitution [once discovered could be said to stand] in front of each historical nation as that towards which it moves. With the passage of time, each nation must (muss) alter its existing (vorhanden) constitution so that it is continually brought nearer to the true [constitution] ... The constitution of a nation [should truly] express a people's consciousness of its own spirit (Geist), what it is implicitly (was er ansich ist). It [should] give these immanent structures the form of truth, i.e. a people's constitution should enshrine that people's knowledge of itself (des Wissens vonsich). If a people can no longer accept as implicitly true what its [existing] constitution expresses to it as true, i.e. if its consciousness or theory of itself (Begriff) and its reality are different, this, by definition, marks a division in the very body (Zerrissengeteiltes Wesen) and living spirit of that people (Volksgeist). [In this case], two things may occur. First, the nation may either by a violent internal eruption smash that law (Recht) which still has [a degree of] acceptance (das noch gelten soll) or it may alter the 'relevant' law quietly and gradually, which no longer expresses that truth of its ethical practice (Sitte). A people may do this when its spirit (Geist) has moved beyond [some of the existing elements of its constitution]. Second, a people may not have the understanding (Verstand) or strength (Kraft) either quickly or slowly to remove these elements. In this case, the people will either retain its inferior law (dem niedigeren Gesetze) or it will become subordinated (unterliegen) to a superior people (ein vortreff licheres Volk) which has reached a higher constitution. In this context, we can see why it is essential to know (zu wissen) what the true constitution is. What may stand against it cannot endure because such an element has no truth. Such an appearance (es) has a temporary existence which it can not sustain. It has been valued but this valuing (gelten) will not be perpetual. That it must (muss) be repealed or abolished lies in the very Idea 'or is Reason-as'- the-constitution. This insight can only be reached by philosophy. A non-violent political revolution can occur when the insight is general (allgemeinen) ... A government **should** (muss) recognize (wissen) when the time for [such change] has come. If it does not (unwissend), it [may be because it] is tied (Knupft) to these temporary and inessential institutions, taking them to be its defence. In this case, in fact, it sets its inessential against the truly essential [institutions] i.e. against that which is contained within the Idea 'or within Reason'. The pressure of this spirit (Geist) 'of Reason' may overthrow this government and with the dissolution of the government comes the dissolution of the people. [As a result], a new government [may become established. On the other hand, the [existing] government and the inessential[institutions] may retain the upper hand.

*Rechts,* S.15 Zusatz:
There are two kinds of laws (Gesetze), laws of nature and [human] laws [accepted by people as] right (Recht). The laws of nature simply are and are thus accepted (sind schlechthin und gelten so). They are not subject to curtailment although man can violate them (sich) in isolated cases (in einzelnen Fallen). Concerning the process of our coming to know (um zu wissen) what the law of nature is, we must familiarize ourselves with nature (müssen wir dieselbe kennenlernen) because these laws are correct, only our views of them may be false. The measure of these laws is outside us, and our knowing (Erkennen) them neither affects nor adds to their operation (tut nichts zu ihnen hinzu, befordert sie nicht). Only our knowledge (Erkenntnis) about these laws can be extended ... Being acquainted (Kenntnis) with right is in one way the same and in another not (einseits ebenso, andersetis nicht). We become acquainted with [both sorts of] laws as simply those which are there. Thus the citizen (Bürger) more or less, and the positive [law] jurist stand and remains no less 'than the natural scientist' by what is given. However, the difference is that the 'human' spirit of [critical] study is aroused by the laws [which are widely accepted as] right (Rechtsgesetze), and indeed, the variety of [such] laws 'as between peoples and times' calls our attention [to the fact] that these laws are not absolute. The laws [accepted to be] right are man made a (von Menschen Herkommendes). Necessarily with these laws, there enters [the possibility either of] a clash [between] one of these laws (Mit diesem) and [our] inner voice or of their agreement. Humankind does not remain [satisfied] with what [only] has definite existence (Dasein), but it claims to have the standard of what is right within itself. [While] humankind (er) can [have a sense of] being subjected to the 'external' necessity and external authority 'say, of the oppressive government under which one may be living', in no case (aber niemals) can we feel the same way (wie) in relation to the necessity of nature because an inner [voice] says what the [human laws] should be and within itself humankind finds the proof or the disproof (Bewahrung oder Nichtsbewahrung) of what is to be accepted ... Here, therefore (also) is the possibility of a conflict between what is and what ought to be. [That is to say, there is a possible conflict between] the right which has being in and for itself (an und für sich seienden Rechts) which remains unaltered, and a human law (dessen) which [has been] determined arbitrarily (Willkürlichkeit der Bestimmung) over what should be accepted as right ... (S.17). Humankind must meet its [own] reason within [the laws it accepts as] right. Humankind must, therefore, consider the rationality of the [laws which pass for] right, and this is the subject matter (die Sache) of our science [of the state, i.e. the philosophy of right] in contrast to the simple study of positive law (im Gegensatz der positiven Jurisprudenz) which often only has to do with contradiction. The present world ... has a pressing need [for this science, because the dominant) culture (Bildung) of the time ... has placed thought (Gedanke) at the summit of all which should be valued. Theories have placed themselves over against the definitely existing [human laws] (Daseienden) and [each wishes] to appear as in-and-for-itself correct and necessary ...

*Rechts,* S.26:
This book, in so far as it contains a science of the state (Staatswissenshaft), seeks nothing else but to **conceive and present** (zu begreifen und darzustellen) **the state as an inherently rational** [entity] (ein in sich Vernünftiges). As a philosophical work, it must be as far as possible from the attempt to construct a state as it ought to be. The teaching (Belehrung) which may be within this book (in ihr) cannot extend to instructing the state about what it ought to be. Far more, it [teaches] how the state (wie er), the ethical universe, should become [philosophically] known (erkannt) ... Because 'some of' what is, is Reason (denn das was ist, ist die Vernunft), the task of philosophy is to conceive what is (Das was ist begreifen). As for the individual, every one is a son of his time anyway and therefore philosophy also is its time grasped (erfasst) in thoughts (Gedanken). It is ... foolish to imagine that anyone philosophy could go over and beyond its contemporary world ... If, in fact, a theory goes over there and behind [the world as it is] to build a world as it ought to be, then that world exists (existiert), indeed, but only in an individual's (seinem) intentions - a fluid area (einem weichen Element) in which an individual (sich) is left (lass) to build anything (alles) [that he might] fancy (Beliebige).

*Rechts*, S.27:
>One word more remains to be said about the teaching of how the world ought to be. Philosophy **always** (immer) comes too late to give it anyway (kommt dazu ohnehin). As the thought of the world, philosophy (sie) **first** appears in time **after** actuality's structuring process has been completed and has made itself ready (Bildungsprozess vollendet und sich fertig gemacht hat) 'to be conceived in thought by philosophy'. The ideal [world] 'or the *actual* model discovered by philosophy' as distinct from the real, 'empirically concrete, existent world' (das Ideale dem Realen gegenüber ersheint) first (erst) appears within the ripeness of the 'relevant' actuality. The above (Dies) is a teaching of the conception (Begriff), 'i.e. a teaching of philosophy' and history equally shows it to be necessary. This ideal itself grasps this same world (jenes sich dieselbe Welt ... erfasst) in its substance. This ideal builds up this world into the shape (in Gestalt) of an intellectual realm. [Thus], when philosophy paints its grey in grey, then has a shape of living become old, and with [this] grey in grey, that shape (sie) is not able to rejuvenate itself (lasst sie sich nicht verjüngen), but **only** (nur) to know (erkennen) itself: The owl of Minerva first begins its flight with the falling of the dusk (beginnt erst mit der einbrechenden Dämmerung).

*Rechts*, **PP258An.**:
>[Speaking broadly, the question of] what is or was the **historical** origin of the state or much more [the question of the origin] of each particular state, 'e.g. the Prussian or French state of 1820', [the question] of its laws [which it accepts as right (Rechte)] and [of its] institutions (Bestimmungen); [the question of] whether the state (er) at first arose (hervorgegangen) out of patriarchical relationships, [or] out of fear or trust, [or] out of corporations, etc.; and [the question of] how and upon what have such laws (Rechts), being grounded (gründen) within [the] consciousness 'of a state's citizens' as divine [or] positive law (Recht), or [as] contract, custom, etc., been apprehended (gefasst) and fortified (befestigt) 'by statesmen or political theorists' [all these questions are] not the [special] concern of [our study of] the Idea 'or of Reason-'as-the-state[.] On the contrary (sondern), with regard to (im Rucksicht) the scientific knowing [of the state] which is here the only [concern of our] discourse, [all the above questions are seen only to relate to the mere] appearance [of things, an appearance which provides] the subject matter for historical [rather than philosophical discourse] (als die Ersheinung eine historische Sache)[. Such historical study] to the extent that it includes a concern with the grounds of authority in one actual (wirklichen) state, 'only' extracts (genommen) these grounds (diese) from the forms of accepted law (des ... gultigen Rechts) within that state (in ihm).
>
>The philosophical consideration [of the state] only has to do with the inwardness (dem Inwendigen) of all this [law, i.e. it only has to do with its] **theorized conception** (dem gedachten Begriffe), 'i.e. with the conception of the law which is immanent within all historically existing bodies of law'.

*Rechts*, **PP259**:
>The Idea 'or Reason-as-'the-state has:
>a) unmediated actuality and is the individual state as the state's self-relating (sich auf sich beziehender) organism, i.e. it has a **constitution** or an **internal state law**;
>b) [as] going over into the **relation** of the single state to other states, it [has] **interstate law**;
>c) [as] the general Idea as genus and [as] an absolute power (macht) over (gegen) the individual states, it is the Spirit which gives itself its actuality within the process of world history.

*Rechts*, **PP259Z**:
>The state as actual is essentially [a] an individual state and still beyond [that] a particular state, 'i.e. it is a state which also must include an indefinite multiplicity of inessential particulars'. This (Die) individuality is to be distinguished from this (von der) particularity [.] This individuality (sie) is a moment of the Idea 'or of Reason-'as-the-state itself, while 'inessential' particularity belongs to history. The [particular] states as such are independent from each other, and the relation [between them] can thus only be an external [one] so that there must be a third uniting 'principle' of these states (so dass ein drittes Verbindendes über ihnen sein muss). This third 'principle' is thus 'Reason-as-the-objective-human-'spirit (Geist), [i.e.] that which gives itself actuality in world history and that which constitutes the absolute arbiter (Richter) over these states (sie). It is indeed possible that several states as a confederation (Bund) can form (bilden) a jurisdiction over others [.] It is possible that combinations of states (Staatsverbindungen) can arise (können ... eintreten), as for example, the Holy Alliance, but these are always (immer) only relative and limited, like the 'so called' perpetual peace (wie der ewige Frieden). The only absolute arbiter which always and against the

'inessential', particular [states] makes itself good is the in-and-for-itself Spirit (Geist) which has being, 'i.e. Reason-as-the-objective-human-spirit' [or] that which establishes itself there within world history as the general 'principle' and as the effective genus.

*Rechts*, PP272An.:
How the conception 'of a specific element of Reason' and thus [how] in a more concrete way, the 'specific elements or' Ideas themselves immanently (an ihnen) define (bestimmen) themselves, and therewith [how] their moments of generality, particularity and singularity are abstractly established (abstrakt ... setzen) is discovered in 'the philosophy of' logic (auf der Logik ... zu erkennen).

*Rechts*, PP273:
The political state, 'i.e. Reason-as-the-constitution', accordingly articulates itself (dirimiert sich somit) into the [following three] substantial functions (Unterschiede):
a) The function to specify and firmly to fix the **general** (die Gewalt, das Allgemeine zu bestimmen und festzusetzen) 'i.e. to specify the standards of behaviour to be required of **all** citizens and institutions within the state' [i.e. the statute or] **law-giving** function (die gesetzgebende Gewalt),
b) the [function of] subsuming the particular spheres, 'e.g. the associations within civil society' and singular cases under [these] general laws (die Subsumtion der besonderen Sphären und einzelnen Fälle unter das Allgemeine), [i.e.] the governing function, 'i.e. the particularizing function',
c) [the functions of] subjectivity as 'the human ability' willingly to finalise decisions (die Subjectivität als die letzte Willensentscheidung) [,i.e.] **the monarchical function** (die fürstliche Gewalt) 'i.e. the finalising function'. Within this finalising function (in der), the [three] distinguishable organs are held together within an individual unity [.] The finalising function (die) is accordingly the pinnacle and the beginning of the whole of **constitutional monarchy**.

*Rechts*, PP273An. (S.439):
If the question presupposes an already present constitution, then the making only signifies a modification (Veränderung) [.] Also, the presupposing of a constitution itself directly (unmittlebare) entails (enthalt) that the modification can occur only in a constitutional way. For the most part (Überhaupt), however, it is completely (schlechthin) essential that the constitution, although it has arisen within time, to be looked upon **not as a made** [structure]. This is because (denn) it is far more the completely in-and-for-it self being (Seiende) which is therefore to be considered as the divine and solid 'structure' and as above the sphere which becomes made.

*Rechts*, PP275:
The monarchical organ includes within itself the three functions (momente) of the totality (PP272), 'i.e.the totality which is Reason-as-the-constitution'. [The three moments are 1)] the generality of the constitution and laws], 'i.e. the law-giving function', [2) the deliberating which connects 'each' **particular** [case] to the general constitution and laws,'i.e. particularizing' (die Beratung als Beziehung des Besonderen auf das Allgemeine), and 3)] the moment of finally deciding, 'i.e. the finalising function' (und das Moment der letzten Entscheidung als ... )]. This last moment is the function which most has the character of being (als)] self-determining (als der Selbstdbestimmung) [.] It is into the exercise of this function (... in welche ...) that all else (alles Übrige) '(e.g. the other two functions)' returns[. It is also] from the exercise of this function (wovon) that all else takes the beginning of its actuality. This [function of the state,] absolutely to determine itself (Dieses absolute Selbstbestimmen) '(i.e. the finalising function)', constitutes the distinctive principle of the monarchical organ as such[. It is this principle] which is to be developed first (... welches zuerst zu entwickeln ist).

*Rechts*, PP275Z:
We begin with the monarchical organ, that is to say, the moment of singularity, because it holds within itself the three moments of 'Reason-as-'the-state's constitution. That is to say (nämlich), [that a living human self, i.e. an] "I", is at the same time the most singular and the most general [being]. At first sight (zunächst), a singular [being] also stands within nature, but reality, [i.e.] that which has no ideality (die Nicht-Idealität), [i.e.] the one-outside-another [singularity] (das Äussereinander), is not the existing-with-itself (dan Beisichseiende) 'singularity which characterizes human life', but the various singularities 'in nature just' stand next to one another. In contrast [to these singularities,] human (Im Geistes) 'singularities tend to live' only 'within Reason or' within the Idea 'and thus' as one 'self-knowing' unity (... alles

Verschiedene nur als Ideelles und als eine Einheit). 'Reason-as-'the-state, as 'an element of Reason-as-the-human-'spirit (als Geistiges) is therefore an exhibition of all its moments, but at the same time, singularity is [its] very soul and [its] animating principle, [i.e.] sovereignty [is the principle which] contains all the differentiations within 'Reason-as-'the state (die Seelenhaftigkeit and das belebende Prinzip, die Souveränität, die alle Unterschiede in sich enthalt)

*Rechts,* **PP276:**
The basic characteristic (Grundbestimmung) of 'the constitution or of Reason-as'-the-political-state is [its] substantial unity as the ideality of its moments, 'i.e. its organs and functions'. [Within this ideality] the particular organs and functions (Gewalten und Geschäfte) are as much peeled off (aufgelöst) 'from this unity' as retained (erhalten) 'within this unity'. They are retained only in such a way that they have no independence, excepting only the sort of 'constitutional' authority [which] goes as far as is specified within 'Reason or' the Idea-[as]-the-whole-'constitution'. From the whole's strength (von seiner Macht) [they] emanate (ausgehen) and are [its] ready organs (flüssige Glieder) in such a way (als) that it is their single (einfachen) self ...

*Rechts,* **PP278:**
These two provisions (Bestimmungen) 'of Reason-as-the-constitution' that neither the particular functions and organs (die besonderen Geschäfte und Gewalten) of the state are [firmly] to be isolated (für sich) nor are the wills of state officials (Individuen, see PP277) firmly to be standing by themselves (weder ... noch ... selbständig und fest sind), make up the [internal] sovereignty of the state. This is to say that the provisions which require the functions, organs and officials to have their finalising (letzte) root, [i.e.] their single self within the unity of the state, [these provisions] make up the [internal] sovereignty of the state 'i.e. the individual state as a self-relating organism'.

*Rechts,* **PP278An.:**
This system of provisions (Dies) 'tends' to make up (ist) the sovereignty with regard to [the] internal (nach innen) [concerns and operations of the state (See PP277: "Die ... Geschäfte und Wirksamkeiten des Staats ...")]. However, sovereignty (sie) has another side, [i.e.] the sovereignty with regard to the external [concerns and operations of the state (die nach aussen)].

Within the former feudal monarchy, the state was indeed [sovereign] in relation to external [affairs.] However, in relation to internal [affairs,] not only was the monarch usually (etwa) not [sovereign] but the state [was] not sovereign. 'This absence of internal sovereignty resulted' partly 'from the fact that' the particular functions and powers (die besonderen Geschäfte und Gewalten) of the state and of civil society were arranged into independent corporations and communities (Gemeinden), the whole was accordingly more an aggregate than an organism [.] 'This lack of internal sovereignty also resulted' partly 'from the fact that' the functions and powers (sie) were the private property of individuals and with that it followed (damit) that what those same individuals were obliged to do (getan werden sollte) in regard to the whole [state] rested within their opinion and option (in deren Meinung und Belieben gestellt).

The idealism [or ideality] which constitutes sovereignty is that same characteristic according to which, in relation to an animal organism, the so called **parts** (Teile) are not parts, but organs (Glieder), i.e. organic moments, whose isolation and resting by themselves constitute disease (deren Isolieren und Für-sich-Bestehen die Krankheit ist) (see *Enz.* II, PP371)[. This is the] same principle which within the abstract conception of the will (see *Rechts,* PP279An.) came before [us earlier] (*Rechts,* PP7 as the will's self-relating negativity (sich auf sich beziehende Negativität) and with that the [will's] **self-determining generality** moving towards a singularity, [i.e. a singularity] in which all 'fixed' particularity and determinateness (Bestimmtheit) is transformed (aufgehobene)[.] 'The will's capacity for self-relating negativity and thus its capacity to transform both its essential and inessential characteristics (Bestimmungen) into one integrated whole, i.e. this capacity to will singularity, is the' absolute self-determining ground of the will [.] In order to grasp this singularity (um sie zu fassen), one must possess more widely (Überhaupt ... innehaben) the conception of 'Reason-as-'the-will' (dessen)[.] 'Reason-as-the-will' is the substance and the genuine subjectivity of 'Reason-as-the-conception 'of Reason'.

Because sovereignty is 'defined to be' the ideality of all particular authority (aller besonderen Berechtigung), so the misunderstanding lies nearby (so liegt der Missverstand nahe) which is also very common, that sovereignty (sie) is to be taken for mere force and bare arbitrariness [i.e. that] sovereignty is taken to have the same meaning as despotism

(Souveränität für gleichbedeutend mit Despotismus zu nehmen). However, [the term] despotism designates the condition of lawlessness, where the particular will as such, whether it be [the particular will] of a monarch or of a people (ochlocracy), stands as if it were by law (als Gesetz) or more exactly (vielmehr) takes the place of law [.] On the contrary, it is precisely within legal, constitutional conditions that sovereignty constitutes the moment of ideality [for] the particular spheres and concerns (Geschäfte), 'e.g. for the associations within civil society'. That is to say, that [when sovereignty is an active presence, it makes] each (eine) such sphere [so that it is] not independent in its aims and ways of working, [standing] by itself and absorbed only within itself (dass nämlich eine solche Sphäre nicht ein Unabhängiges, in ihren Zwecken und Wirkungsweisen Selbständiges und sich nur in sich Vertiefendes)[.] On the contrary, [the operation of sovereignty tends to make] these aims and ways of working to be shaped (bestimmt) by and dependent upon the aim of the whole (upon that which some people have called the welfare of the state, a broad and imprecise expression) den man im allgemeinen mit einem unbestimmten Ausdrucke des Wohl des Staats genannt hat). This ideality makes its appearance in a two fold manner [i.e. both in times of peace and in times of emergency].

In peaceful circumstances, the particular spheres and concerns (die besonderen Sphären und Geschäfte) 'within civil society usually' continue along the path of satisfying their particular concerns (Geschäfte) and aims, and it is only partly by (nach) means of the unconscious necessity of the case, 'i.e. by the force of the market' [that] self]-seeking is 'objectively' turned into (umschlagt) mutual support and [into] the support of the whole (see PP183)[.] Partly, however, it is by the direct influence from above (see governing organ, PP289) that they are as much continually lead back to the aim of the whole and accordingly limited[. By this influence from above, they are (als)] constrained to support this [aim of the whole] by making direct payments, 'e.g. the payment of taxes'.

In a situation of emergency (im Zustande der Not), however, whether it be internal or external, it is sovereignty, within whose simple conception the organism, [which in peaceful circumstances (dort)] exists in its particularities, 'i.e. exists as separate spheres and concerns', [which] comes together and [it] is to sovereignty [that] the saving of the state is entrusted (welcher ... anvertraut ist) [requiring as this does (mit) the sacrifice 'or the subordination' (Aufopferung) of the organism's otherwise authorized [particular spheres and concerns] (dieses sonst Berechtigten)[. For it is in the situation of danger that] that idealism [or that ideality] comes to its characteristic actuality (see below, PP321).

*Rechts*, PP279:

Sovereignty, to begin with (zunächst) 'has been discussed in PP276 to PP278' only [as] the general thought (der allgemeine Gedanke) of this ideality, but [it] exists only as the of-itself-certain subjectivity 'i..e. as the actual subjectivity of the whole organism as maximally guaranteed by the subjectivity of the monarch'.

*Rechts*, PP279:

[This subjectivity is] the abstract, and to that extent, the groundless self-determining 'capacity' of the will[. It is within this abstract and groundless capacity for self-determination (in welcher)] that the finality of deciding lies. This finality (Es) is thus the individual [moment] of the state as such, 'i.e. of Reason-as-the-constitution'. The state (der) is itself one only in that [finality of deciding]. However, subjectivity is only as [a] subject in its truth, 'i.e. subjectivity is only actual as a subject', personality 'is actual' only as [a] person, and within a constitution which is growing towards real (reellen) rationality 'i.e. towards actuality', each of the three moments of the conception has singled out its 'own' self-consciously actual formation (Gestaltung) 'or organ'. This absolute deciding moment of the whole for that reason is not broadly speaking (überhaupt) 'just' the individuality 'of the people' but is maximally guaranteed by the 'singularity of' one individual, the monarch.

*Rechts*, PP279An.:

The immanent development of a science, the derivation (Ableitung) of its whole content out from the single (einfachen) conception 'of that science's specific element of Reason' (a science otherwise [derived] would surely not deserve (verdient ... wenigstens nicht) the name of a philosophical science) displays, however, the peculiarity that the one and the same conception, here [the conception of] the will which at first is abstract because it is the beginning, itself supports (sich erhalt) its derivations (Bestimmungen). Also, a specific conception indeed equally through itself alone and in this manner concentrates and obtains a concrete content (und zwar ebenso nur durch sich selbst, verdichtet und auf diese Weise einen konkreten Inhalt gewinnt). Accordingly for example (so), it is the fundamental moment (Grundmoment) of personality which at first [was studied] within unmediated right, 'i.e. within Abstract Right' [and] which has been progressively studied through its various forms of subjectivity and [which is] now 'seen' within absolute right, 'i.e. right defined from' within the state, 'i.e. from' within the completely concrete objectivity of 'Reason-as-the-human-will' [i.e.] this finalising [capacity] which transforms (aufhebt) all particularity within its single (einfachen) self, 'can' break off the weighing of the arguments for and against some proposal, 'e.g. the sort of' arguments which allow for perpetual oscillation between over there and over here (das Abwägen der Gründe and Gegengründe, zwischen denen sich immer herüber und hinüber schwanken lässt, abbricht) [.] 'The personality of Reason-as-the-state through the monarch' [can break off such oscillation (sie)] and by the "I will" **decide** (beschliesst) 'the question at issue' and start all activity and actuality.

*Rechts,* **PP279An.**:
Furthermore, broadly speaking, however, personality and subjectivity plainly only have **truth** 'i.e. have actuality', as a 'genuinely' infinite [being] relating itself to itself[. This being] indeed has its best approximate unmediated truth, 'i.e. actuality', as a person, [i.e. as] a discretely existing subject, 'i.e. as the monarch'. Just so plainly is the discretely existing [subject] one [being] (Die Persönlichkeit und die Subjectivität überhaupt hat aber ferner, als unendliches sich auf sich Besiehendes, schlechtin nur Wahrheit, und zwar seine nächste unmittelbare Wahrheit als Person, für sich seiendes Subjekt,und das fur sich Seiende ist ebenso schlechthin Eines .

The personality of the state is only actual as one **person**, [or as] the monarch, 'i.e. is only maximally guaranteed with the monarch'. Personality is an expression of the conception as such, 'i.e. of the conception of Reason-as-the-state'. At the same time, the the person [of the monarch] contains the actuality of the same [conception], and the conception is only with this organ (Bestimmung) [the conception] 'of **Reason** or' of the **Idea**-'as-the-state', [i.e.] the truth.

A so-called 'purely' **moral** person; [e.g.] a society, an association, a family; however concrete it might be within itself, 'i.e. however precisely defined its decision making procedures might be', only has personality as a moment [which is] abstract with it[.] In such a **moral** person, personality (sie) has not come to the truth of its existence 'i.e. has not yet attained its full actuality'. In contrast, the 'rational' state is precisely (eben) this totality in which the moments of the conception 'of Reason-as-the-constitution' have reached the actuality appropriate to their own truth (nach ihrer eigentumlichen Wahrheit gelangen).

All these organs (Bestimmungen) 'i.e. the monarch, the government and the representative assembly, are indeed expounded (sind schon ... erörtert) within the whole course of this treatise [both] separately, 'i.e. theoretically', and in their formations, 'i.e. concretely' (für sich und in ihren Gestaltungen) [.] But [this exposition is] repeated here because, while, to be sure, most people (man) easily concede these organs in their 'historically' particular formations 'organs', [they] certainly do not in turn know and grasp these formations philosophically (aber das sie gerade nicht wieder erkennt und auffasst) in their true position 'within the conception of Reason'. It should not be conceded that these formations 'or organs' are isolated (nicht vereinzelt)[.] On the contrary, in accord with (sondern nach their truth, [they] are found to be (als) **moments** of 'Reason or of' the **Idea**.

That is why the conception of the monarch is the most difficult conception for ratiocination, i.e. for [one] considering 'the issue, merely by purely analytical or' reflective understanding (für das Räsonnement, d.h. für die reflektierende Verstandesbetrachtung)[.] [The conception of the monarch is the most difficult for ratiocination] because it remains standing within those isolated definitions (Bestimmungen) and with that therefore [it remains standing] also only [with] grounds, [i.e.] with finite points of view and it is [therefore only] acquainted with **deduction**. Accordingly, therefore, ratiocination (es), 'if at all', presents the office (Würde) of the monarch as something deduced (Abgeleitetes), not only its form but its character (Bestimmung) [. On the contrary (vielmehr), the monarch's (sein) conception is not [to be presented as] something **deduced** but [as] that which **simply originates out of itself** (nicht ein Abgeleites, sondern das schlechthin aus sich Anfangende). [These claims hold true when applied, therefore, to the similar notion (Am nächsten trifft daher hiermit die Vorstellung zu)] that the right of the monarch is to be treated as grounded (gegründet) in (auf divine authority, [believing that] that notion, therefore, contains the unconditionality of that same right (denn darin ist das Unbedingte desselben enthalten). However, it is acknowledged, what misunderstandings have been connected with that notion (sich hieran geknüpft haben), and the task of the philosophical mediation (betrachtung) is 'to remove these misunderstandings and' exactly to conceive this divinity (eben dies Göttliche zu begreifen).

[We] can [appropriately] come to speak of the **sovereignty of the people** (Volkssouveränität) in the sense that a people is broadly a self-dependent [entity] (ein Selbständiges sei) **towards other states** (nach aussen) and makes up its own state like the people of Great Britain [.] The people of England or Scotland, [or] Ireland, or of Venice, Genoa, Ceylon, etc. are no longer (kein ... mehr sei) sovereign peoples ever since they ceased to have their own discrete (eigene ... für sich) monarchs or supreme governments (Fürsten oder oberste Regierungen).

One can also [appropriately] speak of **sovereignty towards** internal [affairs. Broadly, one can say] that sovereignty (dass sie) resides within a **people** only when one speaks of the 'constitutional' whole, which has already been shown (PP277, PP278[.] That sovereignty belongs to 'Reason-as-'the-state. On the other hand (Aber), the usual sense in which the sovereignty of the people is taken is as in **opposition to the sovereignty existing in a monarch**[.] Recently, some people (man in neureren Zeiten) have begun to speak 'of the sovereignty of the people which opposes constitutional monarchy'. In this opposition, the sovereignty of the people belongs to the tangled thoughts whose ground is laid (zugrunde liegt) [by] an **uncultivated** notion of the people. The people taken without their monarch and plainly thus necessarily and immediately [taken without] the 'constitutional' articulation (Gliederung) of 'Reason-as-'the-whole-'state' which hangs together [with the monarch], is the formless mass which is no longer (kein ... mehr) 'Reason-as-' the state [. Moreover, to this absence of the state belongs an **absence** (und der keine ... mehr zukommt)] of the institutions (der Bestimmungen) which are present only with the **within-itself-formed** 'constitutional' whole, [e.g.] sovereignty, government, courts, authorities, associations (Stände) and [the other organs of the whole (und was es sei)]. That such [institutions] step forth into (auf) one organization, [into] the state's life [as] self-relating moments within one people, with that, this indefinite (unbestimmte) abstraction ceases (hört es auf) which the **people** signifies within the merely broad 'or vague' notion (in der bloss allgemeinen Vorstellung heisst).

If by sovereignty of the people is understood the 'constitutional' form of the republic (Wird unter der Volkssouveränität die Form der **Republik**) and indeed more specifically the the [constitutional form] of democracy (because under republic one commonly includes various other (begreift man sonstige) empirical mixtures which do not belong within a philosophical treatise), then what must 'be said in criticism of such sovereignty and of democracy already' has been said in part above (PP273) (so teils oben ... das Nötige gesagt). In part, 'however, it is now clear that' in opposition to 'Reason-as-'the-developed 'constitution, i.e. as constitutional monarchy, any' speaking 'in favour' of such an [indefinite] notion [of the people] is no longer 'possible' (nicht mehr von solcher Vorstellung die Rede sein).

Within a people, which is presented neither as a patriarchical clan nor [as] within the undeveloped condition in which the form of democracy or aristocracy is possible, nor [as] in another capricious and unorganized condition but [which] has become thought [to be] a within-itself-developed, genuinely organized totality, [within that people] sovereignty is as the personality of the whole 'constitution' and this personality [is] within the reality which is appropriate to personality's conception (diese in der ihrem Begriffe gemässen Realität) as the **person of the monarch** 'i.e. constitutional monarchy is the reality which is appropriate to the conception of singularity'.

At the before mentioned state [PP273An.], at which the classification of constitutions is made into democracy, aristocracy and monarchy, [i.e.] at the standpoint 'on the part of the members of such constitutions which naively assumes the security' of the as yet, within-itself-remaining [and] substantial unity 'of a people so organised', [i.e. at the stage which] has not yet come to its 'genuinely' infinite differentiation and deepening within itself (die noch nicht zu ihrer unendlichen Unterscheidung und Vertiefung in sich gekommen ist), [at this stage] the moment of the self, finally, itself determining voluntary decisions as an immanent organic moment of the state, 'i.e. of Reason-as-the-state's constitution' has not yet stepped out into its own discrete **actuality** (tritt das Moment der letzten sich selbst bestimmenden Willensentscheidung nicht als immanentes organisches Moment des Staates für sich in eigentümliche Wirklichkeit heraus). It is always true that 'within every historicly existing constitution if it is to endure', there must be a singularizing pinnacle (Immer muss zwar ... individuelle Spitze) even within those uncultivated formations of the state[. This is] present either [as a pinnacle so recognized (für sich)] as within the above harkened monarchies or as with aristocracies, but especially with in democracies [this pinnacle] raises itself within statesmen [or] generals according to chance and to the **particular** requirements of the **circumstances**[.] 'There is this tendency' because all action and actuality have their beginning and their completion within the deciding (entschiedenen) unity of a leader (eines Anführers). However, closed into the simple enduring union of the functions (Aber eingeschlossen in die gediegen bleibende Vereinung der Gewalten), such subjectivity of 'collective' decision must partly (teils) [and] accordingly originate and emerge contingently[.] In some cases (teils), 'this singularity is' for the most part (Überhaupt) subordinated 'to indecision and to relative disunity'. In such cases,] therefore, the unambiguous [and] pure decision making (das unvermischte, reine Entscheiden) can only lie nowhere else than on the other side of, 'i.e. beyond the decisions of' such limited pinnacles [i.e. leaders] (nicht anders wo daher als jenseits solcher bedingten Spitzen konnte ... liegen), [i.e.] a determining fate comes from outside (ein von aussen her bestimmendes Fatum). As a moment of the Idea 'or Reason-as-the-state', unambiguous decision taking (es) had to step (musste ... treten) into existence although rooted outside of human freedom and [outside] freedom's (ihres) circle, the circle (den) with which 'Reason-as-'the-state is occupied (befasst).

Here lies the source of the need to seek the **finalising decision** on the great affairs and for the important moments of state from **oracles**, [from] a **supernatural being** (dem Dämon) (for **Socrates**), out [from] the entrails of animals, [from] the feeding and flight of birds, etc.[.] Such a [finalising] decision (eine Entscheidung) [was sought because] humans had not yet laid hold of the depth of self-consciousness, 'i.e. of "the will's infinite negativity","its relating itself to itself", the experience of the "I = I"'. Humans had not yet come out of the stability (Gediegenheit) of substantial unity to this being-for-itself (Fürsichsein) 'found in "the depth of self-consciousness"'. Humans had not yet seen the strength inside of the human being.

Within the **supernatural being** of Socrates (compare above, PP138) we can see the beginning of the will which had only before transposed itself to **the beyond** (jenseits) shifting itself into itself, [into (und)] its will knowing its inward self, [i.e.] the beginning of **self-knowing** and with that [the beginning of] genuine freedom (dass der sich vorher nur jenseits seiner selbst versetzende Wille sich in sich verlegte und sich innerhalb seiner erkannte - der Anfang der sich wissenden und damit wahrhaften Freiheit). This real (reelle) freedom of 'Reason or' the Idea is precisely there [when] each of the moments of Rationality-'as-the-state' has been given its own, now present (gegenwärtige) **self-conscious** actuality[.] Accordingly, it is [the freedom] which itself makes up the finally determining certainty of itself, [the freedom] which makes up the [deciding] pinnacle within the conception of the will, [the freedom] supplied [within] the functioning of a consciousness (der Funktion eines Bewusstseins zuteilt). However, this final self-determining can fall into the sphere of human freedom only in so far as it has the location of having been raised to a **discrete** (für sich) pinnacle [which has been] **separated** and raised **over all particularizing** and [over all] **conditions** (als sie die Stellung der für sich abgesonderten, über alle Besonderung und Bedingung erhebenen Spitze hat).

*Rechts,* **PP279Z:**

With respect (Bei) to the organization of the state, that means with respect to constitutional monarchy, we must have nothing before us other than the within-itself necessity of the Idea 'or of Reason-as-the-constitution': all other points of view must vanish. The state must be treated as a great architectonic structure (Gebäude) as a hieroglyph of Reason which places itself there within actuality. Consequently, all that relates itself to sheer expediency (Nützlichkeit) [or to sheer] externality, etc. is excluded from the philosophical treatment. Now, [merely analytical and deductive thinking (die Vorstellung)] easily conceives of the state to be the self-determining and [self] completing will, [i.e.] to be 'the capacity for' final self-resolution (das letzte Sich-Entschliessen ist). The greater difficulty 'for such abstractive thinking' is that this "I will" must become grasped as [a] person. This (Hiermit) should not be [taken] to say that the monarch is permitted to act capriciously[.] It is far truer (vielmehr) [to say that] he is bound to the concrete content of the items of advice (der Beratungen) 'as offered by the representative assembly and by the government of the day'. [As a result (und)], when the constitution (Konstitution) is secure (fest), the monarch (er) often has nothing more to do than to sign his name 'to the law-making and particularizing initiatives coming from the assembly and government of the day'. However, this name is important: it is the pinnacle beyond which 'collective decision making' cannot go. one might say that an organic 'constitutional' structure (Gliederung) was already definitely present within the beautiful democracy of Athens, but we see at the same time that the Greeks had to extract [their] final decision from wholly external appearances, [i.e.from the oracles, [from] the entrails of sacrificial animals, [and] from the flight of birds[. We see] that the Greeks [took their relation] to nature [to be that] as to a force which acts (und dass sie sich zur Natur als zu einer Macht verhalten haben) [through these appearances (da)] to promulgate (verkündet) and express what is good for humankind (dan Menschen). Self-consciousness within that time had not yet come to the abstraction of subjectivity 'i.e. the intellectual isolation of human subjectivity, e.g. the experience of its "self-relating negativity and ... universality"', nor had it yet come (noch nicht dazu) beyond that self-consciousness (Über das) to 'the attainment of' decisiveness (zu Entscheidende), 'i.e. to the attainment of the human finality of decision', [i.e. to the attainment of] an "I will" which must become proclaimed by humankind itself. This "I will" constitutes the great difference [between] the ancient and modern world and so it must have its own distinctive (eigentümliche) existence within the great structure (Gebäude) of the [modern] state. Unfortunately, however, this 'finalising' function (Bestimmung) has become seen only as irrelevant or optional (als äussere und beliebige).

*Rechts,* **PP280:**
This final self of 'Reason-as'-the-state's willing (Dieses letzte Selbst des Staatswillens) is simple (einfach) within this its abstraction and is therefore **unmediated singularity**[.] Therefore, within the conception of the state's willing itself (in seinem Begriffe selbst) lies the organ (Bestimmung) of natur**alness**[.] Accordingly, the monarch is essentially appointed (bestimmt) as **this** individual, abstracted from all other content, 'i.e. this or that individual is designated as monarch irrespective of his personal characteristics other than that given by his very birth'. This individual is designated for the office of monarch in an 'intellectually' unmediated way, [i.e.] through natural **birth.**

*Rechts,* **PP280An.:**
This going-over (Übergang) from the conception of the pure self-determining (der reinen Selbstbestimmung) 'capacity of the will' into the 'intellectually' unmediatedness of being and with that into naturalness is of a purely 'philosophical or' speculative character (Natur), [i.e.] its knowledge (Erkenntnis) therefore belongs to logical philosophy 'i.e. to the conception of Reason-as-logic'. Moreover, on the whole it is the same familiar going-over disposition (natur) of the will more widely (überhaupt) which is the process of translating a content out of subjectivity (e.g. an envisaged aim (als vorgestellten Zweck) into definite existence (in das Dasein) (PP8). However, the peculiar (eigentümliche) form of the Idea 'or of Reason' and [of] the going-over which is being considered here is the 'intellectually' **unmediated conversion** (Umschlagen) of the pure self-determining 'capacity' of the will into one 'specific being (Dieses), i.e. into the monarch'. This conversion into a definite and natural existent (und natürliches Dasein) [does not require (ohne)] the 'intellectual' mediation of a particular 'conscious' content, [e.g.] of a 'conscious' aim within 'the history of' behaviour (einen Zweck im Handeln)

Within the so-called **ontological proof** of the definite being (Dasein) of God it is the same conversion of the absolute conception, 'i.e. of the conception of Reason', into being (Sein)[. This conversion (was] has come to constitute the 'intellectual' depth within modern times (in der neureren Zeit), but within more recent times [this conversion] has become posed as the **inconceivable** (was aber in der neuesten Zeit für das Unbegreifliche ausgegenben worden ist)[.] In consequence of that, men (wodurch man denn) have carried out a resignation (Verzicht geleistet hat) from the knowledge (Erkennen) of the **truth** because the truth is only the unity of the conception 'of Reason' and of definite existence (des Daseins) (PP23). Within that resignation (Indem), the consciousness of the 'purely abstractive ratiocination or of sheer' understanding does not have this unity within itself [. This consciousness (und)] remains standing by the **separation** of both moments of the truth [.] With regard to this subject-matter, 'i.e. with regard to this definite existence, this consciousness' may still allow for a **faith** in that unity 'between this subject-matter and itself' (gibt es etwa bei diesem Gegenstande noch einen Glauben an jene Einheit zu). However, within this consciousness (indem), the notion of the monarch becomes seen as falling entirely within ordinary consciousness (als dem gewöhnlichen Bewusstsein) [.] Therefore, 'sheer' understanding 'tends to' remain standing so much the more (um so mehre) by its (seiner) separation 'of itself from definite existence, i.e. by its belief in the separation of the two moments of the truth'. It also [remains standing] by the conclusions which flow out from its ratiocinative cleverness (und den daraus fliessenden Ergebnissen seiner räsonierenden Gescheitheit) and [which] then deny that the moment of finalising decision within the state **in and for itself** (i.e. within the conception of Reason (d.i. im Vernunftbegriff)) must be connected (verbunden sei) with the unmediated naturalness 'of the monarch'. Out of this denial (woraus), the **contingency** of this combination immediately follows next (zunächst die Zufälligkeit dieser Verbindung) and further, [because] within 'the sheer abstractive understanding' the absolute discrepancy [between both] those moments [of the truth] becomes claimed to be the rational view (indem die absolute Verschiedenheit jener Momente als das Vernünftige behauptet wird), the irrationality of such a combination [follows next.] It is in this way that the other unhinging conclusions tie themselves to the 'ordinary notions about the state', notions which tend to conceal the Idea 'or Reason-'as-the-state (so dass hieran sich die anderen, die Idee des Staats zerrüttenden Konsequenzen knüpfen).

*Rechts,* **PP280Z:**
Men often affirm against the monarch, that it is through him that dependency on contingency within the state is approached (dass es durch ihn von der Zufälligkeit abhänge, wie as im Staate zugehe)[. It may be alleged that (da)] the monarch could be improperly (übel) educated, [or that] perhaps he will not be worthy to stand at the pinnacle itself, and that it is indeed against sense (widersinnig sei) that such a situation rather than a rational [situation] should exist[. If such are affirmed against the monarch (Wenn ..., so)], clearly the assumption here is nugatory that the particularity of the [monarch's] character matters. Within a completed organisation [of the state] it only has to do with (Es ist ... nur um ... zu tun) the pinnacle of formal decision, and one (man) requires in a monarch only a human being (einen Menschen) 'with quite ordinary subjectivity' to say "yes" and to place the dot on the "i", for the pinnacle should be such (so) that the particularity of the [monarch's] character is not the significant [matter].¹ What the monarch has over and above (noch über) this 'capacity' finally to decide (diese letzte Entscheidung) is something which falls to the 'monarch's personal' particularity (Partikularität) which must not be regarded as important (auf die es nicht ankommen darf). Indeed there can be given circumstances in which this particularity alone comes forward, but then the state is not yet fully formed (ausgebildeter) or not well designed (konstruierter). In a well-ordered monarchy, only the objective side 'of human life' comes to the law, 'i.e.formulates and applies the law (i.e. within such a monarchy all law-giving and particularizing decisions are effectively taken by the representative assembly and by the government in accordance with constitutional procedures)' (kommt dem Gesetz allein die objektive Seite zu)[.] The monarch only has the subjective "I will" to add to the law (welchem).

*Rechts,* **PP281:**
Both moments within their undivided unity, [i.e. 1] the finalising, groundless self 'to be associated with the finalising function', and with that, [2] the equally groundless existence [of the monarchical organ] constitute the **majesty** of the monarch. This groundless existence] is the organ left to **nature** (als der Natur anheimgestellte Bestimmung)[.] [Both moments constitute] this Reason (Idee)-as-the-majesty of the monarch,'i.e. Reason-as-'the not-to-be-moved (des ... Unbewegten). 'The monarch is less likely to be moved' by the arbitrariness (von der Willkür) 'which may be associated with one or all of the contending factions within a political system'. Within this unity lies the actual unity of 'Reason-as-'the state, 'i.e. the monarch's unity helps maximally to guarantee the unity of the state'. [This is to say, that] the unity of the state (welche) 'is maximally' removed from (entnommen ist) the possibility of becoming pulled down into the sphere of **particularity** only through the monarch's inner and outer unmediatedness (durch diese ihre innere und äussere Unmittelbarkeit) [.] 'This is to say, that the monarch helps maximally to remove the unity of the state from being pulled down into the sphere associated with' arbitrary actions (deren Willkür), aims and opinions, [with] the struggle of factions against factions around the throne, and [with] the weakening and splitting (Zertrümerung) of the state's power (Staatsgewalt).

*Rechts,* **PP281An.:**
Birth and the right of descent constitute the ground of the 'monarch's' **legitimacy**[. This ground is not (als Grund nicht) purely one of positive law but [is] at the same time within the Idea-[Reason]-'as-the-state'. That through the fixed specification of the throne's continuation

(1) The second edition reads: "Within a completed organization of the state, it only has to do with the pinnacle of formal decision and with a natural solidity against the 'possibly destructive' passion 'of a people'. Wrongly, therefore (daher mit Unrecht) do men (man) demand objective qualities of the monarch: he only has "yes" to say and to place the dot on the "i". thus the pinnacle should be such that the particularity of the [monarch's] character is not the significant [matter]. This specification (Bestimmung) for the monarch is rational for it is in accordance with the conception 'of Reason-as-the-constitution'. However, because this specification (sie) is difficult to grasp, it often happens that the rationality of the monarch, 'i.e.of the monarchical organ' is not perceived. The monarch must be secure within himself, and what the monarch ..."

(festbestimmte Thronfolge), i.e. [through] the natural succession, the winding up of the throne by the factions is prevented, is one side which with right has long been urged in support of the hereditary character of the throne. This side is nevertheless only a result and to make it into a **foundation** (zum Grunde) is to pull the majesty 'of the monarch' down into the sphere of ratiocination[. This side] gives majesty's (ihr) [character], whose (deren) character is this groundless unmediatedness and [is] this final within-itself-being 'of Reason-as-the-state', not its [character of being] the immanent the Idee-[Reason]-as-the-state[.] Rather, [this side gives majesty's character to be] something **outside** majesty's [character] (sondern etwas ausser ihr), [i.e.] a [character] of majesty [which has] miscellaneous notions (einen von ihr verschiedenen Gedanken) at its foundation, e.g. the welfare **of the state or of the people** (etwa das Wohl des Staates oder Volkes zu ihrer Begründung). Indeed, the hereditary character [of the throne] can become traced out from such a notion through **secondary premises** (Aus solcher Bestimmung kann wohl die Erblichkeit durch medios terminos)[.] However, [such a] notion (sie) also allows other **secondary premises** and with that other conclusions beside (andere Konsequenzen zu), and it is only too familiar which conclusions have been drawn out of this welfare of the people (salut du peuple). That is why only philosophy may thoughtfully consider this majesty, for every other method of investigating than the speculative [method] of the 'genuinely' infinite, within itself grounding (begründeten) Reason (Idee) suspends (hebt ... auf) the in-and-for-itself character (natur) of the 'monarch's' majesty.

The election 'by the whole' realm (Das Wahlreich) 'or the selection of the monarch by a general election' easily seems to be the most natural notion, i.e. this notion (sie) lies closest to the superficiality of though[. Such thought may say that] because it is the concern and the interest of the people which the monarch has to attend to, so must it also remain left to the election of the people [to decide] who the people(es) desire to commission (beauftragen wolle) with the attending to (mit der Besorgung) of its welfare, and only out of this commissioning arises the right to the governing [official] (und nur aus dieser Beauftragung entstehe das Recht zur Regierung). This view, like the notions of the monarch as the highest state official (als oberstem Staatsbeamten) [or like the notions] of a contractual relation between the monarch (demselben) and the people, etc., comes from 'the notion of the will of the people which assumes that this will is indistinguishable from' the will as [the] **pleasure**, [the] **opinion** and [the] **arbitrary action** of the many[.] In relation to this disposition (einer Bestimmung), which (die) was considered long ago 'within this book' as prevailing (als erste gilt) within civil society, or rather wishes only to put itself forward [within civil society, this disposition] is neither the principle of the family nor [even] less [is it the principle] of 'Reason-as-'the state, but broadly stands opposed to the Idea-[Reason]-as-ethical practice (Sittlichkeit).

That the election 'of the head of state by the whole' realm is the worst (schlechtste) of institutions shows itself already for ratiocination [to see] from the results[.] However, these results (die) appear to ratiocination (für dasselbe) only as something **possible** and **probable**, but in fact [they] lie essentially within this institution. That is to say, that through the relation [between the elected head of state and the people] within an electoral system (in einem Wahlreich) which makes the particular (partikulare) will, 'i.e. the factional or minority will' into the finally deciding [will of the state] (zum letzten Entscheidenden), the constitution becomes an elective capitulation (einer Wahlkapitulation), i.e. becomes (zu) a surrendering of the state's power (Staatsgewalt) to the destruction of the particular will, 'i.e. the minority factional will'[.] Out of this comes forth the transformation of the particular state functions (der besonderen Staatsgewalten) into private property, 'i.e. into minority, factional property'[. Out of this comes forth] the weakening and the loss of the sovereignty of the state and with that [comes] the inner disintegration and the external destruction (Zertümmerung) [of the state].

*Rechts*, PP281Z:

If we (man) wish to grasp Reason the Idea-[Reason]-as-the-monarch, then we cannot be content with saying that God has instituted the kings, for God has made everything, also the worst [of institutions]. Nor (Auch ... nicht) can we get far by the viewpoint of utility, because it [also] permits us again and again (und es lassen immer wieder) to point out disadvantages 'to any existing or proposed constitutional arrangement'. It is even of less help if we look upon (betrachtet) the monarchs as like (als) a positive right. That I [should] have property is 'philosophically' necessary, but [that I have] this particular possession is contingent[.] Accordingly, the right that one 'specific human being' must stand at the pinnacle 'of an existent constitution' [appears to be contingent] if we look at (betrachtet) it as abstract and positive. However, this right is [both] as a felt requirement (Bedürfniss) and as a requirement of the case, [i.e. it is] in-and-for-itself present. Monarchs frankly do not distinguish themselves through bodily strength or through intellect (Geist), and yet millions [of people] allow themselves to be ruled over by them. If one (man) now says, [that] human beings allow themselves (liessen sich) to be governed against their interests, aims, [and] intentions, then this is absurd (ungereimt) for human beings are not so stupid[.] It is their requirement[.] It is the inner force (macht) of the Idee-'Reason-as-the-monarch working within them'. [This] force (die) urges (nötigt) [millions of] human beings (sie) to [be ruled over by monarchs (dazu)] and maintains [them] within this relation 'even when it is' against their own apparent consciousness. If in this way (Wenn so) the monarch steps forward as pinnacle and organ (Teil) of the constitution, then we must say that a conquered people is not 'in the same way' identical with the monarch (mit dem Fürsten). In war, if within a conquered province an insurrection (Aufstand) occurs, accordingly, this [insurrection] is something other than a rebellion (Empörung) within a well organized state. The conquered [people] are not in revolt (im Aufstande) against *their* monarch (Fürsten), they commit no treason (Staatsverbrechen), for they are not with the commander (mit dem Herrn) in the 'same' community (im Zusammenhang) of the Idea-'Reason-as-the-state'. 'That is to say, that they do not yet consciously or intuitively live within the same state and are thus' not within the inner necessity of the 'same' constitution. 'At most', it is only a contract, not a political union (Staatsverband) [which is here] present. Napoleon replied to the Erfurt envoys, "I am not your prince. I am your master".

*Rechts,* **PP282:**
Out of the sovereignty of the monarch flows the **right to pardon** (das Begnadigungsrecht) criminals, for only to sovereignty (ihr) comes the actualization of the strength (Macht) of the 'human' spirit (des Geists) to make undone what happens (das Geschehene ungeschehen zu machen) and to annual the crime by (im) the 'human' forgiving and forgetting.

*Rechts,* **PP282An.:**
The right to pardon is one of the highest recognitions of the majesty of the 'human' spirit (Geist). By the way, this right belongs to, 'i.e. is an example of one of' the applications or reflections of specifications of the higher sphere 'of the state, i.e. of sovereignty in this case', onto a previous [sphere, i.e. onto a sphere outlined earlier within this book (in this case, crime, which was expounded within the sphere of abstract right).] However, such applications belong to [each] particular science which has to treat its subject-matter (Gegenstand) within that subject-matter's (seinem) empirical compass (Umgange) (cf. PP270An.Fn.).

The injuries of the state in general or of the sovereignty [of the state, or of the] majesty and personality of the monarch (des Fürsten) [are examples of such applications and are thus] (Zu solche Anwendungen gehört auch, dass ...) subsumed under the conception of crime which came before [us] earlier (PP95 - PP102)[. These injuries] indeed become defined (bestimmt werden) as the **highest** crimes, [requiring] procedures of a particular sort (die besondere Verfahrungsart), etc.

*Rechts,* **PP282Z:**
Pardoning is the reducing of the punishment which does not repeal (aufhebt) the rightful law (das Recht). Rather, this [law] remains, and the pardonee (der Begnadigte) is after as before a criminal[.] Clemency does not express that the pardonee (er) had committed no crime. This removal of punishment can itself proceed through religion, for the event of the 'human' spirit can become undone by (im) the Spirit. To the extent that this [undoing] is to be performed within the world, it has its place only within the majesty 'of the monarch' and can only be fit the groundless deciding 'capacity of the monarch'.

*Rechts,* **PP283:**
The **second** inclusion (Enthaltene) '(i.e. function)' within the monarchical organ is the moment of **particularity**, i.e. (oder) [the moment] of 'empirically' exact content (des bestimmten Inhalt) and the subsumption of this exact content (desselben) under the general 'constitutional and rational statutory law'. In so far as the moment (es) [of particularity] maintains a 'separate' particular existence, 'the cabinet or' the highest counselling positions (oberste beratende Stellen) and individuals are it[.] They (die) bring before the monarch for 'final' decision [either] the content of the ongoing affairs of state (den Inhalt der vorkommenden Staatsangelegenheiten) or [the content of] the changing statutory provisions required by the needs at hand (oder der aus vorhandenen Bedürfnissen nötig werdenden gesetzlichen Bestimmungen)[. These affairs and these provisions are appropriately brought before the monarch] with their **objective** side, 'i.e. with a statement of the relevant empirical facts, with a statement of' the grounds for deciding (den Entscheidungsgründen), (i.e. daraus sich) the covering statutes, circumstances, etc.). The choice

of the **individuals** to [perform] this function (Die Erwählung der Individuen zu diesem Geschäfte) like their (deren) removal falls within the monarch's unconfined discretion (seine unbeschrankte Willkür) because they have dealings with the unmediated person of the monarch (da sie es mit der unmittelbaren Person des Monarchen zu tun haben) 'i.e. because they do not deal with the monarch through others but directly'.

*Rechts,* **PP284:**
[Not the monarch but these counselling positions and individuals alone are subject to accountability.] To the extent that the **objective** [side] of deciding, [i.e.] the acquaintance with the 'empirical' content and with the [relevant] circumstances, i.e. the statutory and other determining grounds, these advisory officials alone are **accountable**[. This] objectivity is capable of proof, and therefore [in so far as it is] advice which can be distinguished from the 'purely' personal will of the monarch as such, [to that extent] these positions or individuals alone are subject to accountability (Insofern das Objektive der Entscheidung, die Kenntnis des Inhalts und der Umstände, die gesetzlichen und andere Bestimmungsgründe, allein der Verantwortung, d.i. des Beweises der Objektivität fähig ist und daher einer von dem persönlichen Willen des Monarchen als solchem unterschiedenen Beratung zukommen kann, sind diese beratenden Stellen oder Individuen allein der Verantwortung unterworfen) [.] However, the distinctive (eigentümliche) majesty of the monarch as the finally deciding subjectivity is raised above all accountability for the governmental actions.

*Rechts,* **PP285:**
The **third** moment, '(i.e. the third constitutional function)' of the monarchical organ (der fürstlichen Gewalt) pertains to the in-and-for-itself generality 'of Reason-as-the-constitution' (das an und für sich Allgemeine)[.] This generality (welches) subsists in a subjective way (Rücksicht) within the **conscience** of the **monarch**, [and] in an objective way within the **whole** of the **constitution** and within the laws (Gesetzen)[.] Accordingly, the monarchical organ (die fürstliche Gewalt) presupposes the other organs (Moments) [just] as each of them presupposes it.

*Recht,* **PP286:**
The **objective guarantee** of the monarchical organ, [i.e.] the justified (rechtlichen) succession according to the hereditary character of the throne, etc., lies within [the above mentioned mutually presupposing organs (liegt darin).] According to that presupposing, just as (dass, wie ... ebenso) this sphere '(i.e. the monarchical organ)' has a separated out (ausgeschiedene) actuality, [i.e. separated out] from the other specific organs (Momenten) [which are also] 'consciously or unconsciously' [separated out] through Reason, so do the other [organs] taken separately (für sich) have the characteristic (eigentümlichen) rights and obligations of their organ (Bestimmung)[.] Each organ (Glied) 'both' maintains itself separately (für sich) within itself (indem) [and] is maintained within [the] rational organism, 'i.e. within Reason-as-the-constitution'. Equally, therefore, the other [organs are maintained] in their 'constitutional' characteristicness (Eigentümlichkeit).

*Rechts,* **PP286An.:**
According to primogeniture, the monarchical constitution has been hewn out (herausgearbeitet zu haben) with an hereditary, firmly determined succession to the throne[.] Thus, [the monarchical constitution has been hewn out] in such a way that it (so dass sie hiermit) has been led back to the patriarchical principle, the principle from which (von dem) it historically emanated[.] However, [within constitutional monarchy, the patriarchical principle is] in the higher specification as the absolute '(i.e. as the finalising)' pinnacle of an organically developed state[. This monarchical constitution] is one of the later results of history, a result which (das) is of the greatest importance for public freedom and [for the] rational constitution[.] As remarked before, [this is so in spite of the fact that] although this result (es) is already respected, [it] still has become [one result which] is frequently conceived '(i.e. theorized)' least 'adequately' (obgleich es, sie vorhin bemerkt, wenn schon respektiert, doch häufig am wenigsten begriffen wird). That is why the former merely feudal monarchies as well as the despotisms in history show that alternation of rebellion, violent acts of monarchs (Gewaltentaten der Fürsten), internal wars, the fall of individual princes (fürstlicher Individuen) and dynasties[.] Out of that alternation (daraus) [history shows] the resulting (hervorgehende) internal and external general devastation and decay [. History shows these resulted] in such circumstances because of the segmentation (teilung) of state business (des Staatsgeschäfts) in such a way that (indem) its segments were delegated (übertragen sind) to vassals, pashas, etc.[.] This is only a mechanical [differentiation], not a differentiation of function (Bestimmung) and form but only a differentiation of greater or less power (Gewalt). So within this circumstance (So ... indem),

each segment is supported and made[.] Each segment (er) supports itself [but] **only itself and therefore** (darin) does not at the same time [bear] forth the other [segments. Each segment] has become independently self-dependent, every moment 'or segment has become' complete in itself (und hat zur unabhängigen Selbständigkeit alle Moments vollständig an ihm selbst). Within an organic situation (Verhältnisse) organs (Glieder), not segments, hold themselves in relation to one another (sich zueinander verhalten), each organ maintains the other while it fulfils its own sphere[.] Within each is a substantial aim and product of maintaining its own self [and equally of] maintaining the **other** organs (jedem ist für die eigens Selbsterhaltung ebenso die Erhaltung der anderen Glieder substantieller Zweck und Produkt). The guarantees about which [we] ask, be they for the stability (es sei für die Festigkeit) of the succession to the throne, broadly of the monarchical organ (der fürstlichen Gewalt überhaupt), for justice, public freedom, etc., are protections (Sicherungen) through **institutions**. As **subjective** guarantees, affection of the people, [the] 'personal' character 'of the monarch, of the monarch, of the public functionaries, or of the people', oaths 'of allegiance', force (Gewalt), etc., can be looked at, but as soon as [we] speak about a **constitution**, the discussion (Rede) is about **objective** guarantees alone ([i.e. about] the institutions), i.e. [about] the organically interlaced and self-limiting moments 'or organs'. These institutions are such that (So sind sich) public freedom in general and the hereditary character of the throne are mutual guarantees and stand in complete interrelation (im absoluten Zusammenhang)[. This is because public freedom is the rational constitution and [because,] as demonstrated 'already', the hereditary character of the monarchical organ [is] a moment lying within the rational constitution's conception (und die Erblicheit der fürstlichen Gewalt das, wie gezeigt, in ihrem Begriffe liegende Moment).

*Rechts,* **PP290Z (S.460):**
... The lower [part of society], the multitude (das Massenhafte) of the whole, has clearly (leicht) been left more or less unorganized and yet it is of the highest importance that it become organized for only so is it mighty (Macht), is it powerful (Gewalt), otherwise it is only a crowd, a multitude (Menge) split into atoms.

*Rechts,* **PP292:**
[The appointment of civil servants from the longer lists of equally qualified individuals appropriately] belongs to the monarchical [organ] as the deciding and sovereign organ of the state's power (Staatsgewalt).

*Rechts,* **PP293:**
The particular state functions (Staatsgeschäfte) which the monarchy gives over to the ministries (Behörden) constitute a part of the **objective** side of the sovereignty living within the monarch
...

*Rechts,* **PP298::**
The law-giving 'or representative assembly' organ concerns the statutes (die Gesetze) as such, insofar as they require further [and] continuous specification[.] Also, [it is] accordingly [concerned] with their content, [i.e.] the wholly general internal affairs 'of the state'. This organ is itself one part (Teil) of the constitution, [and] the constitution (welche) is presupposed by this organ (ihr) and to that extend in-and-for-itself lies beyond (ausser) this organ's (deren) direct 'or unmediated' specification[.] However, the constitution's (ihre) further development is fostered (erhalt) within the progressive elaboration of the statutes and within the ongoing character of the 'comprehensive or' general 'character of' governmental affairs.

*Rechts,* **PP298Z:**
The constitution must in-and-for-itself be the secure valued ground (Boden), upon which the law-giving or 'representative assembly' organ stands and, therefore, the constitution (sie) must not first become made. The constitution accordingly is[.] However, it equally essentially **becomes**. This is to say that it progresses within 'its own' structure (Bildung). The progressing is a modifying (Veränderung) which is imperceptible (unscheinbar) and [which does] not have the form of modification ... Thus, the progressive elaboration of a condition (eines Zustandes) is an apparently tranquil and unnoticed [elaboration]. After a long time, in this way, a constitution comes to a wholly other condition than before.

*Rechts,* **PP300:**
Within the law-giving function (Gewalt) as a totality are active, to begin with, the two other organs (momente) [i.e. the two organs other than the organ most prominently associated with the execution of the law-giving function], 'i.e. the representative assembly' [. These two organs are 1),] the **monarchical** [organ] as the organ (dem) to which the highest 'or the finalising' decision belongs, [and 2,] the governing organ (die Regierungsgewalt) as that [organ] with the concrete

acquaintance [with] and over sight of the whole 'state' in its many sidedness[. The governing organ oversees this whole according to] the fundamental principles 'as formulated in the established rational constitution and laws which' have firmly become actual (und den darin festgewordenen wirklichen Grundsätzen)[.] As well as [this, the governing organ oversees this whole] with the acquaintance of the requirements of the state's power (Staatsgewalt)[. This acquaintance] especially [characterizes] the advising moment [of the governing organ, i.e. "the cabinet" (PP329Z).] Finally (endlich) [3], the third organ which is active within the law-giving function is] the **representative** assembly organ (das ständische Element).

*Rechts,* PP300Z:
... The unity of the state ... is that which is to be sought before all else (vor allem zu verlangen).

*Rechts,* PP301:
[In] the representative assembly, ... the public consciousness as an **empirical generality** of views and thoughts of the many therefore comes into existence.

*Rechts,* PP301An.:
... it is far more the case that the people, insofar as with this word [it is] one part of the members of a state which is signified, it expresses the part which does not know what it wills. To know (wissen) what one (man) wills, and even more, [to know] what is the in-and-for-itself Will which has being (seiende Wille), [i.e.] the will [of] Reason, is the fruit of a deeper knowing (Erkenntnis) and insight which is plainly not the subject-matter (die Sache) [possessed by] the people.

*Rechts,* PP308:
The fluctuating side of civil society falls within the 'elected chamber' of the representative assembly (In den andern Teil des ständischen Elements), which side, externally because of the great number (menge) of its members, but essentially because of the character (natur) of its specificity (Bestimmung) and structure (Beschäftigung), can only enter [the assembly] through representatives (Abgeordnete).

*Rechts,* PP309:
... 'Reason-as-'the-assembly (Zusammenkunft) has the character (Bestimmung) to be a living, mutually teaching, convincing and collectively advising 'representative' assembly (Versammlung).

*Rechts,* PP314:
Above all ... public acquaintance (der allgemeinen Kenntnis) provides its extensions through the publication of the representative assembly's proceedings.

*Rechts,* PP315:
The opening of this opportunity for 'such public' acquaintance has the general side 'or character' that in this way (so) public opinion first approaches (erst zu ... kommt) true thoughts and insight into the condition (Zustand) and [the] conception of the state[.] With that 'acquaintance', public opinion first approaches an **ability to judge more rationally about state affairs** (dessen Angelegenheiten und damit erst zu einer Fähigkeit, darüber vernünftiger zu urteilen)[.] Then also [in this way, public opinion] becomes acquainted with and learns to respect the operations (Geschäfte), the talents, [the] virtues and [the] skills of the state authorities and servants. Equally, by such publication, these talents are provided an opportunity for developing and [for providing] a show-place of higher distinction[.] In this way (so) again, 'this' publicity (sie) is the antidote to the self-conceit of isolated individuals (Einzelnen) and of the multitude and [is] a means of education for these and, indeed, one of the greatest [means].

*Rechts,* PP315Z:
The publicity of the representative assemblies is supremely (vorzüglich) a great cultivating drama for the citizens[.] Thereby, for the most part, the people learn to become acquainted with the genuine [character] of its interest. As a rule, the notion (Vorstellung) prevails that all which is good for the state is already known (wissen) and that it only comes to be spoken within the representative assembly[.] However, in fact, [we] find the talents and the skills develop themselves which come to serve as a model [for the citizens (die zu Mustern zu dienen haben)]. Of course, such assemblies are troublesome for the ministers who must put on wit and eloquence in order to meet the criticisms which here become directed against them[.] Nevertheless, broadly speaking this publicity is the greatest means of education concerning (für) state interests. Within a people where this takes place, they display a wholly other liveliness in connection with the state than where the representative assembly is absent or is not public. Only through this familiarity do the 'representative' chambers hang together at each and every

step (eines jeden ihrer Schritte hängen) with the changes (mit dem Weiteren) in **public opinion**[.] Also [thereby,] it displays itself, that it is one thing what every man imagines at home with his wife or his friends and quite another thing what happens in a great assembly where one intelligent [position] (Gescheitheit) devours another.

*Rechts*, **PP316Z**:
At all times public opinion is a great force (Macht) and it is particularly in our time where the principle of subjective freedom has this importance. What now is valued should no more be made good through force (Gewalt) [nor even] less through habit and custom but indeed through 'intellectual' insight and grounds.

*Rechts*, **PP317**:
Therefore, public opinion holds within itself the eternal substantial principles of justice, [i.e.] broadly speaking, holds the genuine content and the result of the whole constitution, [of] law-giving and of the general situation (Zustandes) in the form of common sense (des gesunden Menschenverstandes), [i.e.] the wholesome human understanding which (der) in the shape of prejudices through all 'people' penetrates ethical principles as much as the genuine needs and correct tendencies of 'social' actuality ...

*Rechts*, **PP317Z**:
The principle of the modern world demands that what everyone (jeder) should acknowledge [must] display itself as justified (als ein Berechtigtes zeige), 'i.e. must display itself to be rational'. However, still apart from that, everyone wishes to have a share in discussing and advising ... freedom of speech ...

*Rechts*, **PP320**:
'The subjectivity of isolated individuals and groups within civil society, i.e.' the **subjectivity** which has its **most external** appearance within the wanted and equally self-destructive believing and ratiocinating [which] fosters state life's haphazardness, [i.e. subjectivity] as a disintegrator of the established state life,[1] this subjectivity] has its genuine actuality within its opposite [. This is to say, that this subjectivity] 'is objectively guaranteed' within the subjectivity which is (als) identical with the substantial will '(i.e. with the singular will of Reason-as-the-state)' which constitutes the conception of the monarchical organ and which as an **ideality** of the whole [constitution] has not yet come to its right and definite existence (Dasein) within the foregoing (in dem Bisherigen).

*Rechts*, **PP320Z**:
Once already we have treated subjectivity as the pinnacle [feature] within the monarch. The other side of subjectivity (sie) is its arbitrary display within public opinion as the most external appearance. The subjectivity of the monarch is by itself abstract but it should be a concrete [subjectivity] and as such [it should be] the ideality which spreads itself over the whole. The state of peace is the state (der) where all branches (Zweige) of civil life become established (bestehen) but this establishing (Bestehen) of the [branches] next to and outside of one another has arisen (hervorgehend) out of the Idea-[Reason]-as-the-whole-[state]. 'The dependence of' this arising 'from within the whole' must also come to 'its' appearance [i.e. (als)] the ideality 'or united, self-knowing structure' of the whole 'should become actual'.

*Rechts*, **PP321**:
II. *The sovereignty towards external [states]* [2]
**The sovereignty with regard to internal** [affairs] (PP278) is this 'very' ideality 'of the whole constitution (PP320)' in so far as the moments of the 'human' spirit (des Geistes) and its actuality, [i.e.] the [state's] 'constitution', are **unfurled** in their 'inner' necessity and **exist** (bestehen) as organs (Glieder) of [the state's constitution (desselben)]. However, the 'human' spirit [or the state] as an **infinitely negative** relating to **itself** within the freedom 'of Reason' is essentially thus a discretely existent being which **has taken up** the existing differentiations '(e.g. the organs)' **within itself** and with that separates 'itself from other states'.[3] The-[rational]-state within this specification has an **individuality** 'or a *singularity*' which as an

(1) Die Subjektivität, welche als Anflösung des bestehenden Staatslebens in dem seine Zufälligkeit geltend machen woollenden und sich ebenso zerstörenden Meinen und Räsonieren ihre äusserlichste Erscheinung hat ...
(2) **Die Souveränität gegen aussen.** Aussen could just as easily be read to refer to "external" [sovereignties], [states], [affairs] or operations and concerns *Rechts*, PP277 and PP278An.)].
(3) Aber der Geist, als in der Freiheit unendlich negativ Beziehung auf sich, ist ebenso wesentlich Für-sich-sein, das den bestehenden Untershied in sich aufgenommen hat und damit ausschliessend ist.

individual [state among other states] and [which] within the sovereign 'or monarch' is as an actual, unmediated individual (PP279).[1]

*Rechts*, PP322:
The individuality 'of Reason-as-the-state', as a separate discrete being appears as a relation to other states. Each of these states is self-dependent vis-as-vis the others (Die Individualität, als ausschliessendes Für-sich-sein, ersheint als Verhältnis zu anderen Staate, deren jeder selbständig gegen die anderen ist). Within this self-dependence, the discretely existent being of the actual 'human' spirit (Geist) 'or of Reason-as-the-state' has its **definite existence** (Dasein), because this self-dependence (sie) is the prime freedom and the highest distinction (Ehre) of a people.

*Rechts*, PP322An.:
Those people (Diejenigen), who speak of aspirations of a collectivity (einer Gesamtheit) which makes up a more or less self-dependent state and [which] has its own centre (Zentrum), [i.e. those who speak] of aspirations to give up this central point (Mittelpunkt) and this point's (seine) self-dependence in order to (um) make up a whole with another central point, know little of the character (Natur) of a collectivity and the sense of self (Selbstgefühl) which a people has in its independence.

For that reason, broadly speaking, the first force (Gewalt) with (in) which states historically come forward is this self-dependence even if the self-dependence (sie) is wholly abstract '(e.g. is a collective aim rather than an achievement)' and [even if the self-dependence] has no further internal development '(i.e. does not have a rational constitution)'. That is why it belongs to this original appearance [of the state], that an individual stands at its pinnacle, a patriarch, a chief, etc.

*Rechts*, PP329:
The state has its orientation (Seine Richtung) towards external [states] because of this 'truth' that (darin, dass) the state (er) is an individual subject. Its relation to other [states], for that reason, falls to the monarchical organ[. This is to say,] therefore, that [its relation to other states (es)] directly and solely accrues to the monarchical organ (der), [e.g.] to command the armed might, to maintain the relations with the other states through envoys, etc., to conclude war and peace and other treaties.

*Rechts*, PP329Z:
In nearly all European countries the individual pinnacle is the monarchical organ (die fürstliche Gewalt) which has to attend to the relations toward external [countries]. Where there are representative assembly (ständische) constitutions, the question may arise whether war and peace should not come to be concluded by the representative assembly (von der Ständen), and in any case, the assembly (sie) retains its influence particularly in respect to financial means. For example, in England no unpopular war can be conducted. However, if some people (man) believe that monarchs and cabinets (Fürsten und Kabinette) are more subject to passion than 'are representative' chambers, and for that reason, [a role to play must be put (zu spielen sucht)] in the hands of the chambers in the deciding over war and peace, then it must be said, that often whole nations may become still more enthused than their monarchs and [more] steeped (gesetzt) in passion. Several times in England, the whole people have pressed for war and, to a certain degree, [have] compelled the ministers to conduct it. The popularity of Pitt came for this reason, that he knew [how] to fall in with what the nation wanted at that time. Here, only later did the cooling [of the enthusiasm] bring [it] to (hervorgebracht) consciousness, that the war was neither requisite nor profitable (unnütz und unnötig) and [that the war] had been started without [the] calculation of the means (ohne Berechnung der Mittel). Beyond this, the Idea-[Reason]-as'-the-states not only in the relation with one other [state] but with many, and the intricacies of the relations become so delicate, that they can only be handled from out of the pinnacle (nur von der Spitze aus behandelt werden können).

---

(1) Der Staat hat in dieser Bestimmung Individualität, welche wesentlich als Individuum Souverän als wirkliches, unmittelbares Individuum ist.

*Wurt.*, S.492:
> It is an infinitely important step forward of the culture (der Bildung) 'of a state' that it has forged ahead to the knowledge (Erkenntnis) of the simple fundamental principles (Grundlagen) of state arrangements and has grasped them in simple propositions as an elementary catechism ... hung on placards in the churches, made a standing article of school and church teaching ... such principles (Grundsätze) being publicly acknowledged by the government and [being] 'items' [of] public acquaintance (der allgemeinen Kenntnis) ...

*Wurt.*, S.530:
> Just as it is given by experience, so it is equally easily perceived also according to the 'very' nature of the case, that no one can have less skill to make a constitution than that which we (man) may call the people, or than an assembly [representing] the people's (seine) sections, even if we wish not to consider 'the fact', that the 'very' existence of a people and a representative assembly already presupposes 'the existence of' a constitution, an organic condition, an ordered life of the people.

# Glossary

This glossary and index lists my special terms in 'single inverted commas', Hegel's in "double inverted commas" and some key German terms in round brackets, e.g. (Allgemeinheit).

"absolute"

'absolute theory'

"abstractive understanding"
(Verstand *Enz.* I, PP356Z, PP80 and Z). i.e. "analytical understanding" or "understanding".
"accountability"
(Verantwortung, *Rechts,* PP284).
'actual ideal',
see *Philosophie* II, S.110, for a similar use of "actual" and "ideal".
"actualities",
see 'human actualities' and 'natural actualities'.
"actuality"
(Wirklichkeit, *Enz.* I, PP6 and An., PP147). "Actuality" is the "rational" aspect of the sort of "definite being" which Hegel calls "existence", "reality" or "the present-to-hand". Thus, "actuality" is not to be confused with the "present-to-hand",i.e. with that which is simply "grasped with the hand and immediately observed" (...mit dem Handgreiflichen und unmittelbar Wahrnehmbaren ..., *Enz.* I, PP142Z). The following is another textual confirmation that Hegel's "actuality" is not to be simply equated with empirical reality: "The eternal world ... is actuality (Wirklichkeit), not over there, not on the other side, but the present actual (gegenwärtige wirkliche) world considered in its truth, not as it appears to the hearer, the seer, etc., or as it falls into the sense." *(Philosophie,* II, S.III (p.96)). This explains why Hegel sometimes calls "actuality", "true reality" (wahrhafte Realität, *Rechts,* PP270Z (S.429)). Contrast with "inessential appearance".
"actuality's structuring process",
*(Rechts,* S.27).
(Allgemeine, das),
usually translated as "the general", but see "Universal" *(Philosophie* I, S. 96) and "universal" *Geschichte,* S.52).
(Allgemeinheit),
"generality".
"analytical understanding",
i.e. "abstractive understanding".
"appearance"
(Erscheinung). See "experience".
'arc',
i.e. the pictorial representation of a "specific element of Reason" or of a "specific conception".
Aristotle,
See "inner necessity".
'association',
i.e. a formal organization of one of the interests listed under "sections(s)".

"associations",
>(Genossenschaften, *Rechts*, PP308; *Wurt.*, S.483 (p. 263)). *Rechts*, PP290Z, says that "the distinctive strength of the rational state lies within the associations". See "section(s)". In *Rechts*, PP288, Hegel suggests that the appointment of elected association officials would appropriately be subject to "higher confirmation and appointment", presumably, by the government acting in the name of the monarch. In fact, Hegel might be read to have the equally objectionable proposal in mind, that not only would elected association officials be subject to such "confirmation and appointment", but that the candidates for representing each association within the elected chamber should be similarly screened. His discussion of "boards of examiners" in *Eng.*, S.104 (p. 311), perhaps implies this.

"augment",
>*Rechts*, PP301An. (S.470) and PP314.

'axiom of non-contradiction',
>i.e. "the law of contradiction".

(Begriff)
>i.e. "conception", not "notion" nor "Notion".

"cabinet"
>(Kabinett, *Rechts*, PP329Z, *Eng.*, S.117 (p.321) and S.125 (p.328). Possible equivalents: "the council of ministers" *Eng.* S.124 (p. 3272)), "state council" (Staatsrat, *Wurt.*, S.473 (p. 256)), "the supreme governing organ" (*Rechts*, PP290), "the organized governmental organ" (*Rechts*, PP302), and "...the representatives (Abgeordnete) of the governing organ '(i.e. the members both of the elected chamber and of the government)' ... i.e. the higher counselling [representatives flow together (zusammenlaufen)] ... within the supreme, [i.e.] within the monarch touching pinnacles, 'i.e. within the councils of ministers which have personal contact with the monarch in a well ordered states'" (in den obersten, den Monarchen berührenden Spitzen," *Rechts*, PP289. This paragraph is explicitly referred to by Hegel in PP278An., as concerned with the "governing organ").

"child of his times",
>(*Rechts*, S.26) Also see *Philosophie* II, S. 111 (p.96): "... no man can spring over his time, the spirit of his time is also his spirit".

"citizen",
>Hegel's usual term for citizen is *der Burger,* i.e. "townsman", "commoner", "freeman" or "civilian" *Rechts*, PP261An. (S.409, PP271Z); but the following are some of the other related terms he uses: "state citizen" (der Staatsbürger, *Wurt.*, S.484 (p. 264)), "fellow citizen" (der Mitbürger, *Wurt.*, S.485 (p. 265)), "the citizenry" (der Bürgerstand, *Wurt.*, S.480 (p.261)), "subjects" (die Untertanen, *Wurt.*, S.468 (p.251), *Rechts*, PP261An. S.409) and die Subjekten, *Rechts*, PP274), "the governed" (die Regierten, *Rechts*, PP295, *Enz.* III, PP539An. (S. 332)), "the members of the state" (die Mitglieder des Staats, *Rechts*, PP258), "those who belong to the state" (die Staatsangehörigen, *Enz. III* PP486An. (S. 305), "the electors" (die Abordnenden, *Rechts*, PP309), "the voters" (die Wahlmänner, *Wurt.*, S.476 (p. 258); die Wählenden (*Rechts*, PP309Z and PP310An. (S. 479)), and "the electorate" or "the electoral assemblies" (die Wahlversammlungen, *Wurt.*, S. 482 (p. 262)).

"conception",
>(Begriff, *Enz.* I, PP156Z). Translated by Knox as "concept" and by most others as "Notion". I take the following to be interchangeable expressions: "reason" (*Enz.* I, PP6, *Geschichte*, S.53), "specific knowing" (bestimmten Wissen, *Rechts,* PP318), "rational consideration" (Die vernünftige Betrachtung, *Rechts*, PP308An.). See "conception of Reason" and "specific conception".

"conception of Reason, the"
>(der Begriff der Idea, *Enz.* I, PP162, PP236). I take the following terms and phrases to be equivalents in Hegel's usage for "the concept of Reason" but to be either to vague, misleading, or superfluous: "the conception" when unqualified *Logik* II, S.252 (p.582), S. 271 (p.597) *Rechts,* PP278An.; "a speculative, genuinely infinite conception" (*Logik* II, S.261 (p. 590)); "the whole conception" (*Logik* II, S.299 (p.621)); "the conception itself" (der Begriff selbst, *Enz.* I, PP17); "the conception of the conception" (der Begriff selbst des Begriffes, *Logik* II, S.290 (p. 596)); "the adequate conception" (*Logik* II, S.271 (p. 597)); "the true and rational conception" (der wahre und vernünftige Begriff, *Enz.* I, PP182Z); "the broad conception" (der Begriff überhaupt, *Enz.* I, PP193An.); "the general conception" (*Logik* II, S. 273 (p. 600)); "the absolute conception" (der absolute Begriff, *Rechts*, PP30), "the real (reelle) conception" (*Logik* II, S. 271 (p. 597)); "the realized conception" (der realisierte Begriff, *Enz.* I, PP242); "the pure conception which itself as conception has come into existence" (... Dasein, *Logik* II, S.253 (p. 583)); "the

established concept" (der gezetste Begriff, *Enz.* I, PP172An.); "the philosophical Idea" (die philosophische Idee, *Rechts,* S.27); "Reason as philosophy" (die Idee der Philosophie, *Enz.* III, PP577); "Reason (Idee) ... as ... absolute spirit" *(Enz.* III, PP577); "the consciousness of Reason (das Bewusstsein der Idee, *Rechts,* PP308An.); "the speculative or absolute Idee (die spekulative oder absolute Idee, *Enz.* I, PP235 "the in-and-for-itself General" (das an und für sich Allgemeine, *Philosophie,* I, S.96)) "the in-and-for-itself Generality which has being" (an und für sich seinde Allgemeinheit, Rechts, PP341), "the genuinely infinite General *(Logik* II, S. 279 (p. 605); "the in-and-for-itself, rational Will" (der an und für sich allgemeine vernünftige Wille, *Enz.* III, PP513); "the in-and-for-itself-free Will" (der an und für sich freie Wille, *Rechts,* PP33), "the in-and-for-itself Will which has being" *Rechts,* PP301An. , "the truth (die Wahrheit, *Enz.*I, PP213An.), "the absolute truth" (die absolute Wahrheit, *Enz,*. I, PP24Z3, PP162, PP244), "exact knowledge" (die exakte Erkenntnis, *Enz.* I, PP99Z), "rational knowledge (die vernünftige Erkenntnis, *Enz.*, I, PP234Z); "reason" *Logik* II, S.271 (p. 597); "thinking knowledge" (das denkende Erkenntnis, *Enz.* I, PP213Z) "conceptual knowing" (das begreifende Erkennen, *Enz.* I, PP160Z), "philosophical knowing" (das philosophische Erkennen, *Enz.* I, PP231An.).

"conception of the state"
*(Rechts,* PP3165), i.e. the "science of the state".

'congressional'

"constitution",
(die Verfassung, der Konstitution). See "rational constitutional". I take the following to be equivalent terms: "the political state" *(Rechts* PP273; "internal state law" *(Rechts,* PP272); "the organism of the state, the genuinely political state" (... eigentlich politische Staat, *Rechts,* PP267); and 'model constitution'.

"constitutional change",
(Veränderung). See *Eng.* S.86 (p. 297); *Philosophie* II, S.19 (p. 8); *Rechts,* PP273An. (S.439), PP298 and Z, PP301An. (S.469); *Wurt.,* S.530.

"constitutional monarchy",
*(Rechts,* PP273, PP297Z).

"contradiction",
(Widerspruch, *Logik* II, S.45). Also see "contrariety".

"contrariety",
(Widerspruch, *Logik* II, S. 75). Also "contradiction".

"contrary",
(widersprechend, *Logik* II, S.74).

"cunning of Reason, the"
*(Geschichte,* S.49 (p.70) and *(Enz.* I, PP209 and Z (p. 78)), i.e. "the cunning of the conception" *(Logik* I, S.398 (p.336).

"definite being"
(das Dasein, *Enz.* I, PP88An.). See "definite existence" and "actuality".

"definite existence",
(das Dasein). Referring to "definite beings" which exist, i.e. are bound by space and time.

"deliberating",
(die Beratung, *Rechts,* PP275).

'deliberative reason'.

'democracy',
majority rule within a "rational constitution".

"democracy".
See "sovereignty of the people" and the following for derogatory comments about "democracy": "democratic formlessness" *(Wurt.,* S.485 (p. 265)); "democratic abstractions" *(Wurt.,* S.472 (p.254)); "democratic element" *(Rechts,* PP308An. (S.477)); "democratic or even anarchic" *(Wurt.,* S. 482 (p.263)). Also see *Eng.,* S.84 (p. 296).

'determinism',
i.e. 'total, external determinism'. See "cunning of Reason" and the following references: *Philosophie* II, S.19 (p.8); "God governs the world" *((Geschichte),* S.53); "ultimate aim ... completed" *(Enz.* I, 234Z).

"development",
(Entwicklung), *(Philosophie* I, S.46). Also see "elucidation".

"differentiations",
(die Unterschiede, *Rechts,* PP275Z).
'dialogue'

"dialectical",
*(Enz.* I, PP161Z, PP239 and An.). Referring,
1) to the pursuit of the "true" by a question and answer discussion by examining competing "definitions", "theories", etc. (Plato);
2) to the dynamic "totality" of somewhat opposing elements which are seen as essentially characterising all reality, e.g. the empirically existent world (Plato, Hegel and Marx);
3) to the scientific and philosophical processes of discovery (Plato, Hegel and Marx); or
4) to the structure of all such theories once achieved (Hegel and Marx).

"elected chamber",
see "representative assembly organ".

"electorate",
see "citizen".

"elucidation".
(Entwicklung), *Philosophie* I, S.46). Also see "development".

"empirical generality",
see "generality".

'epistemology'.

'essential particularity',
contrast with 'inessential particularity'.

"ethical practice",
(Sittlichkeit), i.e. 'Reason as ethical practice'.

"existence",
(Existenz). See "definite existence" and "actuality".

"experience",
(Erfahrung, *Enz.* I, PP6). Assumed to be interchangeable with "appearance" (Erscheinung). My distinction between 'sensuous' and 'non-sensuous experience' might also be read into the following quotation: "an absolute specification of the Essence must find itself in all experience, in all aspects of actuality (in allem Wirklichen) as in every conception" *(Logik* II, S.75 (p.440).

"External",
referring to realities which are both beyond our control and not yet reconciled with our "self-conscious reason" (Enz.I. PP6). Also see *Rechts,* PP320.

external necessity",
(äusserliche (or "aussere") Notwendigkeit, *Enz.* I, PP232; *Geschichte,* S.50; *Logik* II, S.283 (p.608), S.284, *Rechts,* PP261, PP301An.). I read the context of Hegel's following uses of "necessity" to suggest that he is referring to "external necessity": *Enz.* I, PP12; PP147An.; PP147Z: "... fate (Schicksal) ... [i.e.] the unrevealed necessity ... as thoroughly impersonal [and] ... blind ...", PP147Z: "... [external necessity as immanently the concept 'of Reason', PP149,PP150, PP151, PP152: "... the first form of necessity ... the relation of causality (Kausalitätsverhältnis), PP153, PP153Z: "... the relation of causality [is] ...only one side within the process of necessity ...", PP157: "... necessity as such ...", PP158Z: "... the unmediated or abstract necessity ... We have seen how the process of necessity [is] of the sort to overcome the rigid externality which was present-to-hand at first (dass durch denselben die zunächst vorhandene starre Äusserlichkeit Überwunden), *Enz.* I, PP159 An.; *Enz.*III, PP484, "conceptionless necessity"; paradoxically, "merely an inner necessity" [i.e. still locked within external nature] *(Logik* II, S.251 (p.581), S.397 (p.700), S.270 (p.596)); *Rechts,* PP29Z (S.381), PP236 (S.385), PP265, PP266, PP267, PP267, PP267Z, PP278An. (S.444): "unconscious necessity", PP301Z and PP306Z. Contrast with "inner necessity".

"finalising function",
"the princely function" (die fürstliche Gewalt, *Rechts,* PP273).

'formally',
contrast with 'primarily' and 'ultimately'.

"freedom",
(Freiheit). See "rational freedom".

# Glossary

"function",
: Usually a translation of *Gewalt* (i.e. contrasted with "organ"): *Enz.* III, PP542 and An., PP543, PP544An. (S.343); *Rechts,* PP272, PP300, PP303. However, "function" occasionally seems also to be the best translation of the following German terms: *die Funktion (Enz.* I, PP80Z (S.171), *Enz.* III, PP538, *Rechts,* PP278, PP279An. (S.449), PP303An.), *die Geschäfte* ("concern", *Enz.* III, PP543, *Rechts,* PP276, PP277), *die Staatsgeschäfte* ("the state functions", *Rechts,* PP277, PP286An.), *der Macht* ("power" - *Eng.,* S.125), *der Moment (Enz.* III, PP542An., *Rechts,* PP275), *die Seite* ("side", *Rechts,* PP269), *der Teil* ("part", *Rechts,* PP298), *der Unterschied* ("differentiation" or "distinction", *Enz.* III, PP541An., *Rechts,* PP271, PP275Z), and *die Wirksamkeit* ("operation" or "activity", *Rechts,* PP270, PP272Z, PP277). See *Gewalt.*

(Geist),
: i.e. "human spirit". Neither "spirit" nor "mind" offer a fully satisfactory translation of *Geist.* "Spirit" seems to be almost exclusively associated with ghosts or merely religious matters, while "mind" seems merely to suggest the internal brain states of an individual. This is why such translations as "the *mind* of a nation" (Volksgeist) seem strange to English ears. In this example, "the *spirit* of a nation" would be better, but "spirit" does not always convey the import of *Geist* which seems to refer us to that distinctively human ability to strive, both collectively and individually, to attain full scientific or philosophical knowledge of ourselves and of our world. In addition to this human striving for knowledge, *Geist* seems also to include all those *internal* (i.e. subjective) human qualities and relations which consciously or unconsciously provide some of the conditions for the eventual development of this striving and this knowledge. This *internal* area is what Hegel calls Reason-as-"the-subjective-'human'-spirit". The *external* (i.e. objective) and non-human conditions for this development constitute "Reason-as-nature" while the external human conditions (e.g. historical, social, political conditions) for this development are called Reason-as-"the-objective-'human'-spirit". The relatively higher level of human productions and beliefs which, according to Hegel, have directly fostered the successful achievement of this philosophical knowledge together constitute Reason-as-"art", Reason-as-"religion", and Reason-as-"philosophy", the last being capable of achieving 'Reason-as-the-conception of Reason'.

: I have interpreted *Geist* to refer to the wide area covered by "spirit" and "mind" when taken together, i.e. to refer to all the individual and collective human experiences; which directly or indirectly contribute to our eventual achievement of the conception of Reason. It refers, for example, to the following wide range of human qualities, practices and structures: psychic, social, political, aesthetic, religious and philosophical. In short, I take the "object" (Gegenstand) of "the philosophy of the human spirit" to be human history and life in its widest sense.

: It would seem that this human history and life is seen by Hegel to be distinguished from "Reason-as-nature" by the feature that only humans have demonstrated an ability to be *geistig.* Thus, Hegel divides Reason-as-the-world into the two 'arcs': Reason-as-nature (all the beings and relations which provide all the non-human conditions for the evolution and development of humankind); and Reason-as-the-human-"spirit" (the life and history of the species which has the demonstrated ability to be *geistig).*

: It is because "spirit" is not and entirely satisfactory translation, though it is usually the best, that we have followed the practice of freely translating *Geist* as 'human spirit'. However, to have translated *geistig* as "spiritual" would have been too misleading. Therefore, I have rendered *geistig* as "human", "intellectual", "conscious" or "mental". Sometimes, one would be tempted to translate *Geist* as 'humankind', as 'humanity', as 'mankind' or as 'human living'.

"generality",
: (Allgemeinheit, *Enz.* I, PP163), e.g. "abstract generality" *(Enz.* I, PP171An.), "relative generality" *(Enz.* I, PP173), and "empirical generality" *(Rechts,* PP301).

"genuine Infinity",
: (die wahrhafte Unendlichkeit, *Enz.* I, PP95).

(Gewalt)
: Usually translated either as "organ" or as "function" depending on the context. However, at the following points, *Gewalt* seems equally capable of being translated either by "organ" or by "function": *Enz.* III, PP542An.,PP544An. (S.344); *Rechts,* PP270Z, PP272An., PP275, PP276Z, PP277, PP300Z. Also, at some places, *Gewalt* seems to mean "power" not in the sense of a constitutional "function" or of a constitutional "organ" but in the sense of "a governmental department" or "ministry", or of an associational or a corporate "authority" within civil society *(Enz.* III,

PP541An., PP543; *Rechts,* PP271Z, PP276 and Z, PP287, PP295); in the sense of constitutional "authority" or "institution" *(Enz.* III, PP541An.; *Rechts,* PP295, PP301An.); or in the sense of unconstitutional "force" *(Enz.* III, PP544An., PP545, *Rechts,* PP286An., PP322An. This ambiguity seems to correspond to that of the English word which is its most ready equivalent, i.e. "power". For example, an institution's constitutional power can mean for us the *roles* which the constitution gives to that institution, i.e. that institution's constitutional *function(s).* Also, I frequently refer to an institution so described as itself being a constitutional power, as being one of the powers of the constitution, i.e. as being one of the *organs* of the constitution. These multiple uses of *Gewalt* tend to obscure the clear distinction which should nevertheless be made between the tree "organs" of the constitution (i.e. the representative assembly, the government, and the monarch) on the one hand, and the three constitutional "functions" which they jointly exercise on the other hand (i.e. the law-giving function, the particularizing function, and the finalising function). My translations correspond exactly to Hegel's own use in *Enz.* I, PP80Z (S. 171): "... und wenn die dem Begriffe nach verschiedenen politischen und obrigkeitlichen *Funktionen* noch nicht in derselben Weise zu besonderen *Organen* herausgebildet sind ...". One way of distinguishing the organs from the functions is to note that the organs are made up of nameable persons and are more empirically encounterable while the functions are first appreciated only by intellectual abstraction. This is not to deny that the natures of the organs are *fully* appreciated only by intellectual abstraction, i.e. within the conception of Reason-as-the-constitution. It is hoped that my consistent translation of *Gewalt* and all the other relevant terms either as "function" or as "organ" makes Hegel's position clearer than does his own German.

"governing organ",
(die Regierungsgewalt, die Regierung), i.e. the "government".

"government",
(Regierung). See "cabinet". Occasionally, Hegel uses other terms for "the government": "state government" (Staatsregierung, *Wurt.,* S.489 (p. 268)), "the executive organ" *(Rechts,* PP272An. (S.434)), and "the practical organ" (ausübende Gewalt) which also here is said to include both the "governing or administrative organ" (Regierungs-oder administrative Gewalt) and "the judicial organ" (richterliche Gewalt, *Enz.* III, PP541An. (S.337)). See "governing organ", "cabinet", "ministers", and "prime minister".

"ground",
or "foundation" (Grund *Enz.* I, PP238, *Rechts,* PP268An. (S.414) and Z, PP270Z (S.431), PP278An., PP281An. (S,452), PP283, PP284 and PP316Z).

"grounding".
*Rechts,* PP281An.

"groundless",
(grundlose, *Rechts,* PP279, PP281 and An., PP282Z).

"head of state",
Staatsoberhaupt, *Wurt.,* S. 478 (p. 251)).

'historical necessity',
i.e. one sort or "external necessity" resulting from my interpretations of such texts as the following: *Enz.* III, PP544An., *Rechts,* S.24 (p. 9), PP269, PP270 and PP279Z.

'human actualities',
See "specific elements of Reason".

"human spirit",
(Geist, *Enz.* I, PP187Z), i.e. "human life or living", "humankind", "human history" or 'Reason-as-the-human-spirit'.

"Idea, the",
(die Idee, *Enz.* I, PP162). See "Reason" and "conception of Reason, the".

"idealism",
see "idealism" and "reality".

"ideality",
i.e. "idealism" (Idealität, Idealismus), *Rechts,* 275Z, i.e. 'a united, self-knowing structure'.

*(Idee, die),*
"the Idea" *(Enz.* I, PP162), i.e. "Reason"

"individuality",
(Individualität), see "singularity".

"inessential appearance",
    (wesenlos Erscheinung, *Rechts,* PP1An.). Broadly speaking, I take the following to be interchangeable terms: "transitory definite being, external contingency, untruth, illusion" (vorübergehendes Dasein; äusserliche Zufälligkeit ... Unwahrheit und Täuschung, *Rechts,* PP1An.); "trivial, alien (äusserliche) and transitory objects (Gegenstände), and transitory and insignificant appearance" *(Enz.* I,PP6An.). I see the following as examples of various sorts of "inessential appearances": "mere concepts (blosse Begriffe), i.e. "notions" or "image thoughts" (Vorstellungen) and "opinion" *(Meinung, Rechts,* PP1An.); "a mistake, an evil ... stunted ... existence" *(Enz.* I, PP6An.) and "foul existence" *(Geschichte,* S.53). Compare with "spurious infinity" and 'inessential particularity'. Contrast with "actuality".

'inessential particularity',
    Compare "inessential appearance" and "spurious infinity". Contrast with 'essential particularity'.

"inner necessity",
    (die innere Notwendigkeit, *Rechts,* PP268Z, PP281Z, PP301An.), i.e. 'philosophical necessity'. Contrast with "external necessity". While Aristotle lists five meanings for "necessity" *(Metaphysics,* Chapter V, p. 10), all five can be seen as suitably modified and integrated into Hegel's "inner necessity". Hegel lists three of Aristotle's five meanings in *Philosophie,* II, S.162. I read the contexts of the following uses of "necessity" to be examples of his references to "inner necessity": "inherent necessity" (in sich Notwendigkeit, *Philosophie* I, S.55 (p. 36), *Rechts,* 270Z (S.429); "actual necessity" *(Rechts,* PP261An. (S.408)); "immanent necessity" *(Logik* II, S.249 (p. 580)), "ethical necessity" *(Rechts,* PP148An.); *Enz.* I, PP1: "Philosophy can thus indeed ... advance toward a thinking, knowing and conceiving (zum denkenden Erkennen und Begreifen) [of its objects (Gegenstände)]. However, within this very thinking consideration (Betrachten), the demand that it show that it has locked within itself the *necessity* [i.e. PP9: "broad necessity" (die Notwendigkeit überhaupt) (PP1)] of its content (Inhalt), 'i.e. the system of specific elements of Reason', is soon recognized (gibt's sich bald kund)"; *Enz.* I, PP10: "The claim needs to become justified that this thinking of philosophical knowledge (Erkenntnis) is both to be seized in its necessity and is capable of knowing (zu erkennen) the absolute objects (Gegenstände), 'i.e. the specific elements of Reason'; *Enz.* I, PP12: "... free in the sense of fundamental thinking only according to the necessity of the case itself" (des ürsprunglichen Denkens nur nach der Notwendigkeit der Sache selbst); *Enz.* I, PP42An., PP88An. 1: "... when generally the whole course of philosophizing is methodical, [i.e.] necessary ..."; *Enz.* I, PP99Z, *Enz.* I, PP162An., PP176Z: "judgement (Urteil) of necessity" PP158Z: "The ethical human being (Mensch) is himself conscious of his conduct as a necessary [practice, i.e.] in-and-for-itself binding"; *Enz.* I, PP191: "conclusion (Schluss) of necessity"; *Enz.* I, PP229Z, PP231An.: "... the necessity of the conception's specifications (Begriffsbestimmungen)"; *Enz.* I, PP232Z: "The necessity to which knowing (Erkennen) has reached through proof is contrary to that [external] *necessity* (dasselbe) which formed its starting point. In its starting point, knowing has a given and contingent content: however, at the conclusion of its movement, 'i.e. in Reason-as-the-conception of Reason', it knows (weiss) the content as a necessary [content], and this necessity is mediated through the subjective activity 'of reason in people and more especially through the subjective activity of philosophers'"; *Enz.* III, PP549An.: "... that Reason generally is in history, must become settled (ausmachen werden) by philosophy alone (für sich selbst philosophisch) and thus as in-and-for-itself-necessary (an und für sich notwendig)"; *Rechts,* S.17 *Zusatz:* "... [theory] to appear correct and necessary in-and-for-itself"; *Philosophie* I, S.55 (p. 36): "... the whole within itself necessary history of philosophy ... Just as the development of the conception of Reason within philosophy is necessary, so also is its development in history"; *Logik* II, S. 255 (p.585), S.271 (p. 597), S.285 (p. 610).

'intersubjective',

"intuited or unmediated Reason",
    *(Enz.* I, PP244).

"knowing and willing",
    *(Geschichte* S.49).

Knox:
    In summary, my 'free translations' are consistently different from Knox's translation of *The Philosophy of Right* in the following respects:
    1) he refers to my "law-giving function" and "representative assembly" as the "Legislature";
    2) he refers to my "particularizing function" and "government" as the "Executive";

3) he refers to my "finalising function" and "monarch" as the "Crown";
4) he renders *Gewalt* as "power" rather than making my distinction between "function" and "organ"; and
5) he translates,
    a) *die Idee* as "the Idea" rather than as "Reason",
    b) *Vorstellung* as "idea" rather than as "notion",
    c) *Einzelheit* as "individuality" rather than as "singularity",
    d) *Allgemeinheit* as "universality" rather than as "generality",
    e) *Begriff* as "concept" rather than as "conception",
    f) *Geist* as "mind" rather than as "human spirit",
    g) *Selbstständigkeit* as "independency" or "autonomy" rather than as "self-dependence", and
    h) *Verstand* as the "Understanding" rather than as "abstractive" or "analytical understanding".

"law",
    (Satz, *Logik* II, S.45).

"law-giving function, the",
    *(die gesetzgebende Gewalt, Rechts,* PP273), i.e. 'Reason-as-the-law-giving-fuction'.

"liveliness",
    (Leblichkeit, *Rechts,* PP314). See "rational living".

"logical categories",
    see "specific elements of Reason".

"logical Idea",
    *(Enz.* I, PP187Z) or 'Reason-as-logic'.

"majority",
    (Majorität, *Rechts,* PP309Z, *Enz.* III, PP542, *Eng,*. S.83 (p.295) and S.124 (p.327)), and (die Mehrzahl der Stimmen, *Wurt.,* S.476 (p.258)). *G.Cons.,* S.579 (p.240), comes the closest to offering us explicit textual support for 'majority rule' by possibly recommending a change in the existing Imperial constitution. Hegel might be read to suggest here, that "a majority" (Mehrheit) of "the Cities Bench", some of whose members were to be elected in proportion to the populations which they represented, could bind the other two benches of "the Imperial Representative Assembly" (Reichstag), especially, or at least, when levying taxes for the support of the Empire's armed forces.

"methodical",
    *(Enz.* I, PP24Z, PP42An., PP88An.)
'methodological'.

"ministers",
    i.e. members of the "cabinet" (Minister, *Rechts,* PP300Z and PP315Z, *Wurt.,* S.468 (p.251) and S.470 (p.253)). Possible equivalents: "highest counselling positions and individuals" *(Rechts,* PP283), "representatives of the governing organ" *(Rechts,* PP289), "state councillors" (Staatsräten, *Wurt,* S.473 (p.256)), "principal state officials" (Staatsvorstehen, *Eng.,* S.85 (p.297)), "members of the government" *(Rechts,* PP297 and PP300Z), "the higher state positions" (die höheren Staatsstellen, *Rechts,* PP302, "state authorities" (Staatsbehörden, *Rechts,* PP315, and *Wurt.,* s.471 (p.253), "governmental authorities" (Regierungsbehörden, *Enz.* III, PP544An. (S.343)), and "authorities" (Behörden, *Rechts,* PP295 and PP319An. (S.488)). See "government" and "prime minister".

'model',
    'a general prescriptive goal', a "rational ideal" *(Rechts,* S.27, page 72), "... an intellectual realm" *(Rechts,* Preface, S.27).

'model constitution'.
    "rational constitution".

"model",
    (... zu Mustern zu dienen, *Rechts,* PP315Z).

"moment",
    (Moment, *Enz.* I, PP163). See "function", "organ" and "specific element of Reason".

"monarch",
    i.e. the "monarchical organ".

"monarchical organ",
    (die fürstliche Gewalt, *Enz.* III, PP544An., *Rechts,* PP286An.), i.e. 'Reason as the monarchical organ'. Contrast with the "finalising function" (die fürstliche Gewalt, *Rechts,* PP273).

## Glossary

"moral consciousness",
   (Moralität).
'natural actualities'.
   See "specific elements of Reason".
'natural necessity',
   cf. "external necessity" and 'human necessity'.
"necessity",
   (Notwendigkeit). See "inner necessity" and "external necessity". Compare 'historical necessity' and 'natural necessity'. Also see "the relatively necessary connection" *(Rechts,* PP306Z).
'non-sensuous experience',
   "Experience" which is not reducible to our five senses, e.g. some dreams, emotions, thoughts and "conceptions".
"notion",
   (Vorstellung, *Geschichte,* S.53 (p. 36). An 'image' or 'vague thought' as opposed to a philosophically exact thought or "conception". See "inessential appearance".
"object",
   (Objekt, Gegenstand).
"objective guarantee",
   *(Rechts,* PP286 and An.).
"organ",
   (Organ, *Enz.* I, PP80Z (S.171), *Rechts,* PP302). Usually one translation of *Gewalt* (compare "function"), *Enz.* III, PP544An. (S.344), *Rechts,* PP269, PP270, PP272An. and Z, PP276, PP277 and PP300Z. The following terms are also translated as "organ": "element" (Element, *Rechts,* PP300, PP301, PP302An., PP304, PP313), "differentiation" (Unterschied, *Rechts,* PP269Z, PP270An. (S.418), PP321), "branch" or "organ" or "member" (Glied, *Enz.* III, PP539, *Rechts,* PP69Z, PP276, PP286 and An., PP321; Zweig, *Enz,* III, pp539, PP544An. (S.343), *Eng.* S.124 (p. 328)), "body" (Körper, *Rechts,* PP300Z), "the state institutions" (die Staats institutionen, *Rechts,* PP301An. (S.470), "institutions" (Institutionen, *Rechts,* PP286; Staatseinrichtungen, *Rechts,* PP270An. (S.420); Bestimmungen, *Enz.* III, PP539, *Rechts,* PP260Z, PP270Z (S.430), PP279An., PP280, PP281, PP286, PP286An.), "formations" or "structures" (Gestaltungen, *Enz.* III, PP544, *Rechts,* PP261An., PP279 (S.444) and An. (S,446)), "moment" (Moment, *Enz.* III, PP542, *Rechts,* PP261An. (S.470)) and "sides" (Seiten, *Rechts,* PP269 and Z.
"ought",
   (Sollen), i.e. "should".
"owl of Minerva" paragraph,
   *(Rechts,* S.27).
'parliamentary'.

'participation',
   See *Rechts,* PP314. See "sovereignty of the people" and "democracy".
"particularity",
   (Besonderheit, *Enz.* I, PP163). See 'essential' v. 'inessential particularity'.
"parties",
   i.e. political parties within the elected chamber are occasionally mentioned approvingly (e.g. *Wurt.,* S.476 (p. 258)), and *Eng.* S.123 (p. 326). They are also mentioned in *Enz.* III, PP544An. (S.344 and S.345) and in *Rechts,* PP302An.
"particularizing function",
   "the governing function", (die Regierungsgewalt, *Rechts,* PP273), i.e. 'Reason-as-the-particularizing-function'.
'philosophical necessity',
   The status which I would grant a theory which seemed both to be 'comprehensive' and to have passed all of our 'experiential', 'logical' and 'comparative' tests.
"positive aspect",
   *Geschichte,* S.53.
"prescribe",
   (war an geordnet, *Eng.,* S.113 (p. 319), vorschreiben, *Enz.* I, PP6An.
'prescription',
   *Chapter Eight* quotes and discusses the "owl of Minerva" paragraph's clearly implied denial that philosophy can offer 'prescriptions' as well as discussing many other ambiguous denials. It also

'prescription', (continued):
quotes and discusses many of the passages which reveal Hegel as clearly or implicitly offering prescriptions. This section of the *Glossary* seeks further to support the argument for making some modifications to Hegel's position on the question of prescription,
1) by alphabetically listing Hegel's *evaluative* terms and phrases which provide a basis for making general prescriptions, and
2) by alphabetically listing terms and phrases in which Hegel is more clearly *prescribing* actions.

**EVALUATIVE:**
"*Actuality* is not an irrational being" *(Rechts,* PP270Z (S.429)),
"*argument*",
"*appropriately*" *(Rechts,* PP309),
"this happens *best* through philosophical insight" *(Rechts,* PP270Z S.430)),
"*complete* (vollendeten) state" *(Rechts,* PP270Z),
"in-and-for-itself *correct* and necessary" *(Rechts,* S.15),
"a *cultured* state" *(Enz.* III, PP544An.),
"an organically *developed* state" *(Rechts,* PP286An.),
"only *deserve* the name 'constitution' if ... what *should* happen, happens" *(Wurt.,* S.486),
"*education* (Rechts,* PP315),
"has an *equal right*" *(Rechts,* PP311An.),
"it is *essential*" *(Philosophie* II, S.112-113),
"An *Evaluation* (Beurteilung) of the proceedings ..." *(Wurt.,* S.462),
"a *false* notion (Vorstellung) of the state" *(Rechts,* PP300Z),
"*foul* existence" *(Geschichte,* S.53),
"*freedom*" *(Rechts,* PP270An.),
"*genuine* Infinity",
"*glorious* and fortunate advances" *(Eng.,* S.89),
"*good* ... moral sense" *(Eng.,* S.86),
"a *high* political right" *(Wurt.,* S.482),
"*inessential* appearance",
"*inferior* ... a *superior* people ... *higher* constitution" *(Philosophie* II, S.112-113),
"*inner necessity*",
"an infinitely *important* step *forward* of *culture*" *(Wurt.,* S.492 (p. 270)),
"*irrational* ... and *wrong*" *(Enz.III.* PP529An.),
"*is* concerned" *(Enz.* III, PP544),
"all other constitutions belong to *lower* stages of the development and realization of Reason", *(Enz.* III, PP542 (S.339)),
"Germany ... *must* organize itself anew into a state" *(G.Cons.,* S.577 (p. 238)),
"the constitution ... *progresses* ..." *(Rechts,* PP298Z),
"*rational*",
"*rational* constitution",
"*rational* state",
"to judge more *rationally*" *(Rechts,* PP315),
"*Reason*",
"*responsible*" *(Geschichte,* S.49),
"*right*",
"a *rotten* (schlechter) state" *(Rechts,* PP270An. (S.429)),
"a *superior* people" *(Philosophie* I, S.112-113),
"*true* constitution" *(Philosophie* II, S.112-113),
"*true* significance" *(Rechts,* PP301Z (S.471)),
"*truth*" (Wahrheit, *Philosophie* II, S.112-113),
"*undeveloped* ... institutions" *(Rechts,* PP295An.),
"*unfortunate*" *(Rechts,* PP301Z (S.471)),
"the genuine *value* ... a positive aspect" *(Geschichte,* S.53), and
"a *well* organized state" *(Rechts,* PP281Z).

**PRESCRIPTIVE**
"must recognize and accept with the highest *approval*" *(Wurt.,* S471),
"is *best* guaranteed" (Rechts, PP279),
"*cannot* be" *(Rechts,* PP277),

*Glossary*

"the *correct* way to seek improvement is ... by the alteration of institutions ... scientific remodelling" *(Eng.,* S.86, S91),
"*desirable*" *(Rechts,* PP306Z),
"is ... its greatest *justification*" *(Wurt.,* S.476),
"required and *justified*" *(Rechts,* PP295An.),
"*justify*" *(Wurt.,* S.473 (p. 255)),
"It is against all sense and against *honour* ..." *(Domestic Affairs,* S.270 (p. 244)),
"multitude ... highest *importance* that it become organized" *(Rechts,* PP290Z),
"the unity of the state is ... before all else to be *longed for* (zu verlangen, *Rechts,* PP300Z),
"*must* (muss), *Philosophie* II, S.112-113; *Eng.,* p. 313; *Enz.* I, PP99An.),
"Humankind *must* find its own reason within the human law" *(Rechts,* S.15),
"Religion *must not* be the governing principle" *(Enz.* III, PP468Z),
"*ought*" *(Rechts,* S.15, S.27),
"*rightly* subordinated to human life" *(Geschichte,* S.50),
"*should* *(Rechts,* PP280Z and PP320Z, PP300Z, PP306Z, and PP316Z),
"what everyone *should* acknowledge must prove itself to be justified" *(Rechts,* PP317Z),
"all the greatest interests *should* be represented ... but it is a *defect* (Mangel) of a constitution that it leaves to chance what is necessary" *(Eng.* S.107 (p. 313)),
"the state ... *should* [both] rest on and arise out of Reason" *(Rechts,i PP270Z),*
"*should* be equal before the law" *(Enz.* III, PP539An. (S.333)),
"conditions for freedom ... *should*" *(Enz.* III, PP486),
"*should* be consulted" *(Eng.* S.107 (p. 314)),
"the gradual abolition of slavery is more *suitable*" *(Geschichte,* S.129 (p. 99)),
"the *necessity* ... *to support* the poor ... so strongly *demanded* by *justice*" *(Eng.,* S.93 (p. 303)),
"...with right urged in *support* of the hereditary character of the throne" *(Rechts,* PP381An., and
"the courage which *wills* ... *justice* ... *the honesty* to will it and not merely to pretend" *(Domestic*
*Affairs,* S.270).
"present-to-hand",
(das Vorhanden, *Enz.* I, PP7An.). See "actuality".
'primarily',
Contrast with 'ultimately' and 'formally'.
"prime minister",
(Premierminister, *Rechts,* PP290Z). Equivalents: "president of the council of ministers" *(Eng.,* S.117 (p. 321)), and "state chancellor" (Staatskanzler, *Rechts,* PP290Z).
'proportionality',
"proposition",
(Satz)
"quantity",
(Quantität). E.g."quantity must also come into its right in the objective world, as much in the natural as in the human world", *(Enz.* I, PP99An.)Also, see 'to maximize the quality and quantity of free, rational living'.
"rational",
(vernünftig, *Enz.* I, PP6An., *Rechts,* 270An. (S.419 and S.422)).
"rational constitution",
*(Rechts,* PP274An., PP286An.) i.e. "Reason-as-the-constitution" (die Idee der Konstitution, *Philosophie* II, S.113 (p.97)). We take the following to be equivalents: "constitutional monarchy" *(Rechts,* PP273), "rational organism" *(Rechts,* PP286), "true constitution" *(Philosophie* II, S.112), "rational state law" *(Wurt.,* S.470 (p. 254)), "the rational definite existence of political arrangements" (Staatseinrichtungen, *Rechts,* 270An. (S.419)), "the fundamental rational principles of a constitutional (Staatsrechtlichen) condition" *(Wurt.,* S.491 (p. 270)).
"rational freedom",
*(Rechts,* PP301An.).
"rational institutions",
*(Enz.* III, PP539 (S.332)).
"rational living",
(vernünftige Leben, *Rechts,* PP270An. (S.422)).

"rational state",
  i.e. "an organically developed state" (Rechts, PP286An.), "a well organized state" (Rechts, 281Z), "a cultured state" (Enz. III, PP544An. (S.343), "completed (vollendeten) state" (Rechts, PP270Z).
"rationality",
  (Vernünftigkeit, Enz. III, PP539 (S.332) and An. (S.333); Rechts, PP270An. (S.419), PP273Z (S.440), PP274An. and Z, and PP360; Wurt., S.472 (p. 254)).
"rationally",
  (Rechts, PP315).
"reality",
  (Realität). See "actuality".
"reason",
  i.e. "self-conscious reason" or "conception".
"Reason",
  (Vernunft, Enz. III, PP542 (S.339), PP549An.; Eng. S.89; Rechts, PP270An. (S.419), PP273Z (S.440), PP286, and PP301An.). For the drawing of this circle in FIGURE 9, see Enz. I, PP18, PP24Z2 (S.84) and PP187Z (also see the reference for the second largest circle in FIGURE 9, i.e. 'Reason-as-the-human-spirit'. I take "Reason" to be central organizing principle of Hegel's philosophy. Also, given the superfluity of his exposition, the following are examples of the other terms which are replaceable by "Reason" (Of course, the references which follow each term do not begin to offer a complete list of the texts in which the relevant term is used in this way, let alone of the instances in which the term seems not to be replaceable by "Reason".): "the Reason which has being" (die seiende Vernunft, Enz. I, PP6); "the Idea" (Idee, Rechts, PP308An.); "the conception in its objectivity" (Logik II, S.271 (p. 597); "God" (Gott, Enz. I, PP12, Geschichte, S.52 (p. 36)); "the Absolute" (das Absolut, Logik II, S.80 (p.443); Enz. I, PP12, PP86Z2); "the genuine Good" (das wahrhafte Gute, Geschichte, S.52 (p. 36); "the Rational" (Rechts, PP274Z (S.440)); Rationality (Rechts, PP270An.), Substance, the Eternal (die Vernünftigkeit, die Substanz. das Ewige, Rechts, S.25 (p. 10)); sometimes, "the Spirit" (der Geist, Rechts, PP259); "the world Spirit" (der Weltgeist, Rechts, PP30An.); "the Spirit of the world" (der Geist der Welt, Rechts, 273An.); "the universal Spirit" (der allgemeine Geist, Rechts, PP340); "the General" (das Allgemeine, Rechts, PP259Z); "the universal Essence as such" (das allgemeines Wesen als solches, Philosophie, I, S.96 (p. 75)); "the Idea of the universal Essence" of appearance (in der Idee des allgemeines Wesens dieser Erscheinungen, Enz. I, PP12); "the absolute Contrariety within itself" (der absolute Widerspruch in sich, Logik II, S.78 (p. 442).
'Reason as civil society',
  i.e. "civil society" (die bürgerliche Gesellschaft).
'Reason as the conception of Reason',
  i.e. "the conception of Reason".
"Reason as ethical practice",
  (Sittlichkeit). I take my drawing of the fourth largest circle in FIGURE 9 to be based on Enz. III PP517.
'Reason as family living',
  (die Familie).
'Reason as interstate relations',
  (das Verhältnis des einzelnen Staates zu anderen Staaten, Rechts, PP259).
"Reason as logic",
  (die logische Idee, Enz. I, PP187Z, PP236).
'Reason as moral consciousness',
  (Moralität).
"Reason as nature",
  (die ... Idee ... als Nature, Enz. I, PP187Z, PP244).
'Reason as the absolute human spirit',
  (der absolute Geist).
"Reason as the constitution",
  See "constitution".
'Reason as the finalising function',
  i.e. "the finalising function".
"Reason as the governing organ",
  i.e. "government" or "governing organ" (die Regierungsgewalt, Rechts, PP273An.).

*Glossary*

'Reason as the human spirit',
See the following reference for this circle in FIGURE 9: *Enz.* I, PP187Z, *Enz.* III, PP474An. (S.297), PP385 and Z, PP483, and PP486; i.e. "spirit", "human spirit", "world spirit"; or 'humanity', 'humankind' or 'human history and life'.

'Reason as the law-giving function',
i.e. the "law-giving function".

"Reason as the monarch",
i.e. 'Reason as the monarchical organ'.

'Reason as the monarchical organ',
i.e. "monarchical organ".

'Reason as the objective human spirit',
i.e. "objective human spirit" (objektiven Geist, *Enz.* III 539 (S.333)). Sometimes expounded under the following fully equivalent names: Reason as "free will" *(Enz.*III, PP483 and PP487), Reason as "rational will" *(Enz.* III, PP485), and Reason as "right" (see the last part of *Enz.* III, PP487, which is not translated by A.V. Miller). These are the tree replacement names which dominate the exposition in *The Philosophy of Right*. In a different connection, Hegel calls Reason as "objective spirit" (Geist), "the empirical generality" of Reason-as-the-human-spirit. I take the above references to warrant my drawing of the third largest circle in FIGURE 9.

'Reason as right',
i.e. "right" or 'Reason as the objective human spirit'.

'Reason as the particularizing function',
i.e. the "particularizing function".

'Reason as the representative assembly organ',
i.e. the "representative assembly".

"Reason as the state",
(die Idee des Staates, *Rechts,* PP258An.).

"Reason as willing",
(die Idee des Wollens, *Enz.*I, PP232).

'Reason as world history',
i.e. "world history" (Weltgeschichte).

"Reason which has being, the",
(die seiende Vernunft, *Enz.* I, PP6) i.e. "Reason".

"reconciliation",
*(Enz.*I, PP6).

'reduction'

"reduction",
(Reduktion, *Logik* II, 259 (p. 588)), "lead back to the simple thought determinations" (Gedankenbestimmungen, *Enz.* I, PP25An., *Logik* II, 263 (p. 591)).

'reflexive'.

(Regierung, die,)
Usually means "government" but at the following points it seems to refer to the whole organization of "state power" (Staatsmacht, *Enz.* III, PP539), i.e. where "government" has its common American meaning; "... the government as the organized totality which contains 1) ... the *monarchical* governing organ" *(Enz.* III, PP542), i.e. 'the monarchical organ', "2) ... the *particular* governmental organ" (PP543), i.e. 'the governing organ', and "3) the representative assembly" (PP544). Also see PP539An., and PP541.

"representation",
(Repräsentation, *Rechts,* PP309Z).

"representative assembly",
i.e 'Reason as the representative assembly organ' (die gesetzgebende Gewalt, *Rechts,* PP272Z, PP273An.). See *Gewalt.* To simplify, I have translated the following terms and phrases by the single phrase, "the representative assembly": "the sectional element" (das ständische Element, *Rechts,* PP300, PP301, PP302An., PP313) of the law-giving function, "the politically [organized] sectional element" (des politisch-ständische Element, *Rechts,* PP304), "the sectional assembly(s)" (Ständeversammlung(en), *Wurt.,* S.472 (p. 255), *Enz.* III, PP544An., *Rechts,* PP315Z), "the sectional authority" (die ständische Behörde, *Enz.* III, PP544), "the assembly(s)" (Versammlung(en), *Rechts,* PP315Z), "the gathering or convention" (Zusammenkunft, *Rechts,* PP309), "the country's estates"

(Landstände, *Wurt.*, S.462 (p. 246)), "the country's legislature" (der Landtag, *Wurt.*, S.477 (p. 258)), "the national assembly" (die Nationalversammlung, *Eng.*, S.113 (p.319), "the nation in its great council" (der Nation in ihrem grossen Rate, *Eng.*, S.106 (p. 313) and S.119 (p.323)), "the law-giving assembly" (die gesetzgebende Versammlung, *Eng.*, S.108 (p.314)), "the law-giving body" (der gesetzgebenden Körpern, *Rechts*, PP300Z "the chambers" (Kammern, *Wurt.*, S.472 (p.255), *Rechts*, PP312, PP315Z, PP329Z). Hegel mentions or discusses several historically existent "representative assemblies" by name, e.g. "the feudal German Imperial Die" (Reichstag, *G.Cons.* S.578 (p. 239), *Eng.*, S.106 (p.313)), the French "Chamber of Deputies" *Wurt.*, S.476 (p. 258) and *Eng.*, S.118 (p.323)), "the English Parliament" (das englische Parlament, *Eng.*, S.83 (p.295)), and "the Congress of the U.S.A" (der nordamerikanische Kongress, *Rechts*, PP270An. (S.421)). While "the representative assembly" within Hegel's Reason-as-the-constitution is most easily read to be divided into two chambers, he did occasionally speak with a degree of approval for unicameral assemblies, e.g. 1) the feudal German Imperial Diet with its three "benches" ("the Cities Bench" (die Städtebank, *G.Cons.*, S.578 (p.239)), or with its "three Colleges ... [i.e.] the Electors [College] ... the Princes College ... and the Cities College" (drei Kollegien ... das Kurfürsten und das Fürstenkollegium ... und das Städtekollegium, *G.Cons.*, S.579 (p. 240)), and 2) the unicameral assembly which was proposed by the King of Wurtemberg in 1815 in which 73 elected deputies and 50 non-elected members were to vote *(Wurt.*, S.472 (p.254)). In his article, *About the English Reform Bill*, Hegel spoke both of the "upper house" and of the "lower house" *(Eng.*, S.108 (p.314)). *The Philosophy of Right* speaks of "the representative assembly accordingly dividing itself into *two chambers* (die ständische Versammlung wir sich somit in zwei Kammern teilen, PP312). While *The Philosophy of Right's* constitution requires "two chambers", the argument there does not necessarily exclude the appropriateness of "the two parts" being organized into two "benches", into two "colleges", or into two "houses" in different circumstances. In contrast, what is essential is that while one part must be elected, the other part must be hereditary and tied to a number of legally defined landed estates. I have referred to the first part as the "non-elected" or the "hereditary chamber" (i.e. "the substantial section" *(Rechts*, PP307), "the first part" (PP310) and "the mediating Moment" (PP313)), and to the second part as the "elected chamber" (i.e. "the moving side" (die bewegliche Seite, *Rechts*, PP308), "the second part" (PP310) and "the second section" (PP313)) of the "representative assembly". Hegel sees both these chambers and their members as representative of the various "sections" of civil society.

"**representative assembly organ**",
i.e. "representative assembly".

"**representatives**",
For simplicity, I have translated all of the various terms which Hegel uses for the members of his "representative assembly" as "representatives": "members" (die Mitglieder der Stände, *Rechts*, PP301An.), "the elected representatives ... the elected deputies" (die gewählten Repräsentanten ... gewählten Deputierten, *Wurt.*, S.470 (p. 253), and "the delegates" (der Abgeordneten, *Rechts*, PP301An.). I agree with Hegel's view, as expressed in *Rechts*, PP309Z, that the position of a "representative" should be such that he can become a mediator and a voice of the interest of the whole community and not only a spokesperson for his own association.

"**responsible**",
See 'prescription'.

"**right**",
(Rechts). "Right is ... the definite being of all the conditions of freedom" *(Enz.* III, PP486), i.e. all the sorts of human relations and activities which have the approval of 'philosophical necessity' or "inner necessity". Especially see the following confirming passages: *Rechts*, S.15 (p.24), *Enz.* III, PP486, and see "Reason as the objective human spirit".

(Satz),
i.e. "law", "theory", or "proposition".

"**science**",
(Wissenschaft).

"**science of the state**",
*(Rechts*, S.26), i.e. "the conception of the state".

"**section(s)**",
(Stände, *Rechts*, PP311An. (S.480)) of civil society, i.e. those varied groupings which may become organized "associations" of common interests. The following "sections" could become the bases for the "associations" to be represented within the "elected chamber": "classes" (Klassen, *Wurt.*, S.468 (p.251), S.576 (p.293), S.489 (p.268), *Eng.*, S.83 (p.295)), "orders" or "ranks" (Stände, *Eng.*,

S.107 (p. 314), *Rechts,* PP276Z, PP288, PP308), "districts" (Bezirken, *Wurt.,* S.473 (p. 255), "counties" a (Grafschaften, *Eng.,* S.84 (p.297)), "municipalities" or "communities" (Gemeinden oder Gemeinschaften, *Wurt.,* S.400 (p.261), S.481 (p.261) *Eng.,* S.84 (p.296), *Rechts,* PP270An., PP288, PP290Z, PP308), Gemeinwesen, *Wurt.,* S.483 (p.263), *Rechts,* PP303An.). "communes" (Kommunen, *Rechts,* PP290Z), "corporations" (Korporationen, *Wurt.,* S.483 (p.263), *Rechts,* PP229 and Z, PP251, PP263, PP270An., PP276Z, PP288, PP308), "interests" *(Rechts,* PP309An., PP311An., *Eng.,* S.106 (p.313)), "circles" (Kreise, *G. Cons.,* S.578 (p.239), *Rechts,* PP290Z, PP297Z, PP303An.), "cities" (Städte, *G.Cons.,* S.578, (p.239), "fractions" (Fraktionen, *Eng.,* S.83 (p.265)), "parties" (Parteien, *Enz.* III, PP544An. (S.344 and S.345). *Wurt.,* S.476 (p.258), *Eng.,* S.123, "guilds" (Zunft, *Wurt.,* S.483 (p.263), S.485 (p.264), "branch" (Zweig, *Rechts,* PP311An., PP320Z), "the particular spheres" (die besondere Sphären, *Rechts,* PP288, PP290Z, PP302), "trades", "crafts" and "professions" (Gewerbe, *Rechts,* PP288), "associations" (Genossenschaften, *Wurt.,* S.483 (p.263), *Rechts,* PP308). See "associations".

Selbständigkeit,
"self-dependence".

"self-conscious reason",
*(Enz.* I, PP6), i.e. "reason".

"self-dependence",
(Selbstständigkeit, *Enz.* I, PP157, *Rechts,* PP322).

"self-determining",
*(Rechts,* PP278An.).

"self-relating negativity and ... self-determining generality",
*(Rechts,* PP278An.).

'sensuous experience',
The "experience of the five senses", cf. 'non-sensuous experience'.

"should",
(Sollen), i.e. "ought".

"singularity",
(Einzelheit, *Enz.* I, PP163).

"Some of what is rational is actual, and all of what is actual (or only part of what exists) is rational",
*(Enz.* I, PP6An., *Rechts,* S.24. See the references and modifications of the more literal translation under "What is rational ...".

'Some of what is philosophically necessary is rational living, and all of what is rational living is philosophically necessary'.

"sovereignty of the people",
(Volkssouveränität). See relevant discussions in *Rechts,* PP279An. (S.447), and see "the principle of the many and of the multitude" *(Enz.* III, PP544An. (S.343)), "the citizens ... and the electoral assemblies" *(Wurt.,* S.482 (p. 262), "the public voice (die öffentliche Stimme) ... not infrequently ... has proven ... to be impractical or ... fatal ... and [changeable]" *(Eng.,* S.84 (p. 295)), and "the ignorance of the multitude" *(Eng.,* S.90 (p.300)). Also see *Rechts,* PP310An. (S.479), and *Eng.,* S.103 (p.310).

"specific conception",
(bestimmter Begriff, *Logik* II, S.253 (p.583), S.264, 270, 282, 288, 292, 299; *Enz.* I, PP162An., PP171An., PP213An., PP214An.). Terms taken to have the same meaning: "a specification of the conception" or 'of Reason', or "a particular conception" (besonder), *(Logik* II, S.273-274 (p.600-607)); "each conception" *(Logik* II, S.282 "particularizing of the conception" *(Enz.* I, PP166Z). I take the following terms usually to be equivalent: "categories", "differentiations" or "distinctions", "specifications", "moments", and "the general types" (der allgemeine Typus, *Enz.* I, PP230Z) and "relations" (Verhältnissen).

"specifications",
(Bestimmungen).

"specific elements of Reason",
i.e. "specific Ideas" (bestimmten Ideen, *Enz.* I, PP213An.), "Ideas" (Ideen), or "a specification of Reason" (eine Vernunftbestimmung, *Enz.* III, PP539An. (s.333)). I take this phrase to name the "logical categories", the 'natural actualities' and 'human actualities' as possible "objects" of knowledge.

"spirit",
(Geist, *Enz.*I, PP187Z). See "human spirit".

"Spirit",
   i.e. "Reason".
"spurious infinity",
   (die schlechte Unendlichkeit, *Enz.* I, PP94, PP111Z). The boring or diverting endless, or indefinite multiplicity. See "inessential appearance".
"structuring process",
   (*Rechts,* S.27).
"subject",
   (das Subjekt, *Enz.* I, PP163An.).
"subjectivist moralizing",

"subjectivity",
   (Subjectivität, *Enz.* I, PP147Z).
"teleological aim",
   (Zweckbezieung ... teleologische Verhältnis, *Enz.* I, PP194Z).
"theory of the state",
   (*Enz.* I, PP163Z), i.e. "conception of the state".
'to maximize both the quality and quantity of free, rational living',

'total, external determinism',
   The claim that all empirical effects result either from unknowable (e.g. spontaneous or divine) causes, i.e. fatalism or predestination; or from a humanly knowable chain of causes and effects. Both versions deny that we can have any genuinely 'free will', i.e. a will which is in any measure free of external determining forces. See "determinism".
"totality",
   (Totalität, *Enz.* I, PP214An.).
"true constitution",
   see "constitution".
(überhaupt),
   "broadly", "broadly speaking", "in the main", "by and large", "largely", "on the whole", or "for the most part".
'ultimately'.
   Contrast with 'formally' and 'primarily'.
"unconfined discretion",
   (*Rechts,* PP283).
"understanding",
   i.e. "abstractive understanding".
"universal",
   (allgemeine (*Geschichte,* S.52)).
"Universal",
   (Allgemeine, *Philosophie* I, S.96).
'universal adult suffrage',

"voter",
   see "citizen".
"voting qualifications",

"What is rational, that is what is actual; and what is actual, that is what is rational",
   (Was vernünftig ist, das ist wirklich; und was wirklich ist, das ist vernünftig, *Rechts,* S.24 (p.10)). This conclusion is repeated and more fully discussed in *Enz.* I, PP6An., and it reappears in various forms elsewhere, e.g. *Philosophie,* II, S.110 (II p. 95); II, S.111; (III, p. 23); *Rechts,* S.26. See "Some of what ...".
'What is rational must embrace what is contrary within itself, all what is contrary but not contradictory is rational'.
"world Spirit",
   (Weltgeist), i.e. "Reason". "World Spirit" has "nations and individuals enough to exempt some", (*Philosophie* I, S.55).
"world spirit",
   i.e. 'Reason as the world spirit'.

For Product Safety Concerns and Information please contact our EU representative GPSR@taylorandfrancis.com
Taylor & Francis Verlag GmbH, Kaufingerstraße 24, 80331 München, Germany

www.ingramcontent.com/pod-product-compliance
Lightning Source LLC
Chambersburg PA
CBHW081817300426
44116CB00014B/2397